R UND-UP 6
CONTENTS

D1665163

Introduction

Round-up Grammar Practice 6 combines games and fun with serious, systematic grammar practice. It is ideal for upper-intermediate students of English.

Students see grammar points clearly presented in colourful boxes and tables. They practice grammar through lively, highly illustrated games and activities.

Round-up is especially designed for different students studying English in different ways.

It can be used:
● In class with a coursebook. Students do both oral work - in pairs and in groups - and written work in Round-up.
● after class. The 'write-in' activities are ideal for homework. Students can practise what they have learned in the classroom.
● in the holidays for revision. Round-up has clear instructions and simple grammar boxes, so students can study at home without a teacher.

The Round-up Teacher's Guide includes a full answer key and four progress tests plus answer keys.

Pearson Education Limited
Edinburgh Gate, Harlow
Essex CM20 2JE, England
and Associated Companies thoughout the world
www.longman-elt.com

First published 1995 by E. Vlachou - "Express Publications".
This edition first published by Addison Wesley Longman Limited 1998.
Fifth impression 2000

Printed in Spain by Mateu Cromo, S.A. Pinto (Madrid)

Illustrated by Philip Vazakas

ISBN 0-582-33788 7

1 Tense Forms

Speech bubbles:
Mum, come quickly, I've knocked over the ladder in the garden.

I'm making lunch now, dear. Go and tell your father.

He knows. He's been hanging from the roof for the past five minutes.

Present Forms

1 **Identify the tenses, then match them with the correct description.**

1 He **runs** a large travel agency.
2 The thief **enters** the room and **opens** the safe.
3 Skill **comes** with practice.
4 She**'s been practising** that song for hours.
5 He**'s working** hard **these days.**
6 He**'s gained** a lot of weight **recently.**
7 Tom**'s picking** me **up** at 7 o'clock **tonight**.
8 She**'s staying** with a friend in London **at present.**
9 The ferry **arrives** at 10.00 am.
10 They**'ve been talking** on the phone **since** 9 o'clock this morning.

a actions taking place at or around the moment of speaking; temporary situations
b emphasis on duration of an action which began in the past and continues up to the present
c reviews/sports commentaries/dramatic narratives
d actions started at a stated time in the past and continuing up to the present
e fixed arrangements in the near future
f timetables/programmes (future meaning)
g permanent situations or states
h permanent truths or laws of nature
i personal experiences or changes which have happened

1....*g*..... 2.......... 3............ 4............ 5.......... 6 .... 7............ 8.............. 9 .... 10 ....

2 **Put the verbs in brackets into the correct present forms.**

Dear Sir/Madam,

I 1) ...*am writing*... (write) on behalf of Midfield School. Every year, our students 2) .... (choose) a project on an environmental problem. Then, they 3) .... (work) to raise money to help solve this problem. We 4) .... (recently/**see**) your advertisements about protecting dolphins, so, for the last few weeks, we 5) .... (try) to learn about the dolphins that 6) .... (live) in the sea near here. We 7) .... (already/**be**) on two boat trips and 8) .... (persuade) local fishermen to change their fishing nets because the ones they 9) .... (use) at the moment can trap dolphins. Could you please send the children some World Wildlife Fund posters to add to the work that they 10) .... (do) so far?

Yours faithfully,
J. Hopkins (Teacher)

3 **Ask your partner questions using the following time expressions:**

eg. every morning   A: *What time do you get up every morning?*
                    B: *I get up at 7.30 every morning.*

1	for the past ten minutes	4	usually	7	tonight	10	already
2	right now	5	every Sunday	8	yet	11	ever
3	since 11 o'clock	6	twice this week	9	still	12	for four years

4 **Identify the tenses, then match them with the correct description.**

1 Oh no! Someone**'s been reading** my diary again.
2 You feel dizzy because you**'ve been lying** in the sun **for** too long!
3 He **has just cleared out** the garage.
4 He's such a boring man, who**'s always making** a fuss about nothing.
5 With the help of a good teacher, Gary**'s becoming** a very good pianist.
6 We**'ve been** out **four times** this week.
7 He **has** lunch at the Plaza Hotel **every day**.
8 They **have sold** their house and **gone** on a tour of the world.
9 Here **comes** the train!

a actions which happened at an unstated past time and are connected to the present
b changing or developing situations
c expressing anger, irritation, annoyance or criticism
d recently completed actions
e repeated/habitual actions
f past actions of certain duration having visible results/effects in the present
g exclamatory sentences
h emphasis on number; frequency
i frequently repeated actions with "always" expressing the speaker's annoyance or criticism

1 ....*c*..... 2 .... 3 .... 4 .... 5 .... 6 .... 7 .... 8 .... 9 ....

5 **Put the verbs in brackets into the correct present forms.**

Dear Sal,

    You'll never guess where I 1) ...*am writing*... (write) from. I 2) .... (sit) on a bench on the shore of Lake Windermere! The air 3) .... (smell) wonderful - so clean and fresh. I 4) .... (stay) here for nearly a week now and I 5) .... (expect) I'll stay for one more, as I 6) .... (begin) to fall in love with the place. Every morning I 7) .... (get up) at 7 o'clock and 8) .... (go) for a swim in the lake before breakfast. The owner of the hotel 9) .... (just/tell) me that I can borrow his boat for the afternoon. This holiday 10) .... (become) better and better as the days go by. Well, I think I 11) .... (write) enough. I 12) .... (sit) here for half an hour and now it's time for my boat trip.

                            See you,
                            Mary

6 **Which of the present forms in the letter above are used to express:**

1 actions happening at or around the time of speaking/writing   *1, 2*

2 repeated/habitual actions

3 actions started in the past and continuing up to the present

4 recently completed actions

5 permanent states (stative verbs)

6 changing or developing situations

Stative Verbs

Stative verbs express a permanent state rather than an action and do not have continuous forms.
These are: **verbs of the senses** (to express involuntary actions): feel, hear, see, smell, taste etc.
(**Can** or **could** are often used with these verbs. *Turn the radio down, please. I can't hear you.*) **Look,
watch** and **listen** express deliberate actions and can be used in continuous forms. *John is watching a
football game on TV. He can't see or hear you.* **Feel** and **hurt** can be used in either continuous or
simple forms. *John feels/is feeling worse today.*
verbs of feelings and emotions: adore, appreciate (= value), detest, dislike, enjoy, forgive, hate, like,
loathe etc. *He hates the show they are watching on TV now. (not: He is hating)*
verbs of opinion: agree, believe, expect (= think), see (= understand), suppose, understand etc.
I believe he is innocent. (not: I am believing)
other verbs: appear (= seem), belong, concern, contain, depend, fit (= be the right shape and size
for sth), have (= possess), know, mean, owe, own, possess, need, prefer, require, want, weigh,
wish, keep (= continue), seem etc. *He wants some more biscuits. (not: He is wanting)*

Some stative verbs (be, love, see, smell, taste, think etc) have continuous forms but there is a
difference in meaning.

STATE	ACTION
• He **thinks** he's really clever. (= he believes)	• I'm **thinking** about his offer. (= I'm considering)
• What **does it taste** like? (= What is its flavour?)	• He's **tasting** the food to see if it's good. (= he's testing the flavour)
• He **has** two houses. (= he owns; he possesses)	• She's **having** lunch. (= she's eating)
• The silk shirt **feels** soft. (= it has a soft texture)	• Ann **is feeling** the cat's fur. (= she's touching)
• **Do you see** what I mean? (= Do you understand?)	• I'm **seeing** Paula tonight. (= I'm meeting)
• Your perfume **smells** of apples. (= it has the smell)	• She **is smelling** the roses. (= she's trying the smell of)
• I **love/enjoy** good films. (= I like in general)	• I'm **loving/enjoying** this film. (= I like specifically)
• It **looks** as if it's going to rain. (= it appears)	• He **is looking** at the painting. (= he's viewing it)
• He **appears** to be working. (= he seems to be)	• The opera singer **is appearing** on stage tonight. (= he will make an appearance)
• The box is heavy. It **weighs** a lot. (= its weight is)	• He **is weighing** the potatoes on the scales. (= he is finding out the weight of)
• Luciano **is** naughty. (= His character is bad.)	• Suzy **is being** very naughty. (= she is misbehaving)
• These shoes **fit** me perfectly. (= They are the right size).	• We **are fitting** a new carpet in the hall. (= laying)

Certain adjectives can be used with "be" in the continuous form to express a temporary
characteristic. These are: careful, foolish, kind, lazy, nice, patient, (im)polite, rude, silly etc. *John is
usually careful but today he's being careless. You're being very foolish.* (normally used as a warning)

7   Fill in with Present Simple or Continuous.

1   A: I **1)** ....*am thinking*........... (think) about visiting Jane this afternoon.
         B: I wouldn't bother. I **2)** .... (think) she's away on holiday.

2   A: Mr Jones **3)** .... (have) a telephone message from his wife.
         B: Can it wait? He **4)** .... (have) a business meeting and I don't want to disturb him.

3   A: The police **5)** .... (still/look) for fingerprints left in the room.
         B: It **6)** .... (look) as if they won't find the criminal.

4   A: I **7)** .... (love) breathing in clean, country air!
         B: So do I. I **8)** .... (love) every minute of this walking trip.

5   A: I **9)** .... (see) my boss about a pay rise this afternoon.
         B: I **10)** .... (see). That's why you're wearing a suit and tie.

6
  A: Why **11)** .... (you/taste) the soup? Is there anything wrong with it?
     B: Yes - it **12)** .... (taste) too sweet. I think I've used sugar instead of salt.

7
  A: Why **13)** .... (you/feel) the baby's forehead, Mum?
     B: I think she's got a temperature. She **14)** .... (feel) rather hot.

8
  A: John **15)** .... (be) a very rude person, you know.
     B: I know. Sheila **16)** .... (be) very rude these days too, although she's usually polite.

9
  A: It **17)** .... (look) as if it's going to rain this afternoon.
     B: I know. I **18)** .... (look) for my umbrella to take out with me.

10
  A: Why **19)** .... (you/smell) the inside of your car?
     B: Because it **20)** .... (smell) of petrol and I want to check for leaks.

11
  A: How much **21)** .... (your new baby/weigh)?
     B: I don't know yet. The nurse **22)** .... (weigh) him at the moment.

8   Underline the correct item.

1 John **is / is being** usually rude, but today he **is / is being** polite to his colleagues.

2 Ann **is / is being** usually patient, but today she **is / is being** impatient.

3 Sam **is / is being** rude to his mother now, but he **is / is being** normally pleasant to her.

4 John **is / is being** a kind man, but at the moment he **is / is being** selfish.

5 Julie **is / is being** silly at the moment, although I know she **is / is being** really very sensible.

9   Put the verbs in brackets into the Present Simple or Present Continuous.

Ted: Hello Dad, I am in Birmingham. It **1)** ....*'s*....... *pouring*... (pour) with rain, and I **2)** .... (not/have got) any money.

Bob: What **3)** .... (you/want) me to do about it?

Ted: Could you come and pick me up?

Bob: Ted, you **4)** .... (always/ask) me to do this! I **5)** .... (get) tired of it.

Ted: Please, Dad. I am tired and hungry. My evening classes **6)** .... (start) at 7.00 and I have to be there on time. Can't Mum come and get me?

Bob: The Smiths **7)** .... (visit) us tonight and she is busy in the kitchen. She **8)** .... (bake) a cake at the moment.

Ted: Please Dad. I **9)** .... (ask) you to do this for me one last time. The success of my presentation tonight **10)** ....(depend) on you.

Bob: OK. I'll be there in half an hour. But this is the last time. I **11)** .... (mean) it!

10   Which of the present forms in the dialogue above are used to express:

1 changing or developing situations	*5*	**4** actions happening at the moment of speaking		
2 states (stative verbs)		**5** timetables/programmes (future meaning)		
3 frequently repeated actions with "always" expressing annoyance		**6** fixed arrangements in the near future		

11 Fill in: yet, already, since, for, usually, tonight, how long, ever, at the moment or still.

1   I don't think Frank has ...*ever*... been to a live concert. Why don't we take him to one for his birthday?
2   I haven't seen Louise .... Jeff's wedding. I wonder what's happened to her.
3   I don't know .... Jack's been working on that project, but it seems like weeks.
4   Mr Louis hasn't rung me back about the contract ....
5   We're meeting some friends for a meal .... Would you like to come along?
6   Pam has .... finished her test and I've only done half of mine.
7   Patrick .... gets to school at eight o'clock sharp, but it's half past and he hasn't arrived yet.
8   Are you .... reading that book, or have you started another one?
9   I'm trying to finish clearing up .... Can you ring back later?
10 My neighbour has lived in that house .... nearly 60 years.

12 Fill in: since or for.

David Jones has been working for the same company **1)** ...*for*... 20 years. He has been a supervisor **2)** ....
1991 and he quite likes the work, but he has been thinking about changing jobs **3)** .... he discovered that
he has a real talent for garden design. He has been studying garden design part-time **4)** .... two years and
5) .... last month he has been preparing for his final examination. David has been interested in gardening
6) .... he was a child and he has known **7)** .... years that his present job was not the best one for
him. He has been much happier **8)** .... he started the course and **9)** .... weeks he has been
looking forward to the tour that his college has organised. **10)** .... David started the course, his wife has
become interested as well and now they are talking about setting up a business together.

Have gone to / Have been to / Have been in

She **has gone to** Madrid. (= She's on her way to Madrid or she's there. She hasn't come back yet.)
She **has been to** Paris once. (= She has visited Paris; she is not there now. She has come back.)
She **has been in** Berlin for two years. (= She lives in Berlin now.)

13 Fill in: "has / have been in/to", "has / have gone to" in the correct form.

1   I ...*have been to*... New York several times, but I ...*haven't been to*... Atlanta.
2   My boss .... Lisbon for a week, so I'm doing some of his work for him.
3   We .... Milan for very long, so we don't know it very well yet.
4   Martin isn't here. He .... the library to get some books.
5   Martha .... the school to pick up the kids. She should be back by 4.00.
6   I ....that gallery twice but I haven't seen the painting you mentioned.

14 Fill in with Present Perfect or Present Perfect Continuous.

Dear Sir,

I am writing to you to apply for the position of Sports Editor at your newspaper. I 1) ...*have been working*... (work) as a reporter on "The Morning Globe" for eight years, and 2) .... (write) about every major sporting event in England in that time. I 3) .... (also/make) several important contacts within the sporting world such as football managers and race-horse trainers, who 4) .... (be) of great help to me in my career. The editor of "The World" 5) .... (recently/offer) me the post of Senior Sports Reporter, but as I 6) .... (never/really/like) the newspaper I think I will turn it down. However, I 7) .... (read) your newspaper since I was a young boy and I 8) .... (always/admire) it. I 9) .... (wait) for an opportunity like this to turn up all my working life. My editor 10) .... (agree) to give me time off to attend an interview should you wish to meet me.

Yours faithfully,
Gordon Bennett

Past Forms

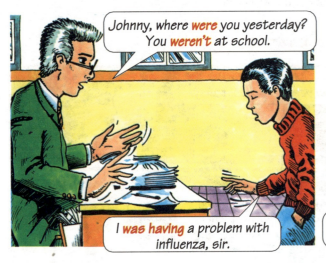

*Johnny, where **were** you yesterday? You **weren't** at school.*

*I **was having** a problem with influenza, sir.*

*Oh! I **didn't know** you **had been** ill.*

*Oh, no! I **had been trying** to spell it for so long that I **was** too tired to come to school.*

15 Identify the past forms then underline the correct time expression.

1 I **still/yet/just** hadn't done my homework when Mum came home. .....*(Past Perfect - Past Simple)*.....
2 Meg was lying in the sun **before/while/as soon as** the children were playing in the pool. ....
3 **How long ago/How long/While** did you pass your driving test? ....
4 He continued his journey **before/after/ago** he had changed the tyre. ....
5 I was walking down the street **when/as soon as/while** a car stopped next to me. ....
6 She had been singing for years **since/for/before** she finally became a star. ....,..........
7 I went on an excursion to the Lake District **last week/since/just**. ....
8 He hadn't eaten turkey **since/ever/for** the previous Christmas. ....
9 Our team had scored three goals **by the time/until/while** we got to the match. ....
10 The professor didn't start speaking **how long/until/yet** everyone was quiet. ....
11 Do you know **how long/when/while** he had lived in Portugal before he moved to Turkey? ....
12 They had been sailing **for/since/while** a month before they reached a port. ....
13 She took off her coat **just/as soon as/already** she entered the house. ....

16 **Identify the tenses, then match them with the correct description.**

1 She **opened** the cupboard, **took out** a dress and **put** it **on**.
2 They **received** the telegram **at 10 o'clock that evening.**
3 She was upset because she **had been waiting** to hear from her son **for** days.
4 They **were still discussing** the plan at midnight.
5 They **were flying** over the Andes when the plane crashed.
6 James Dean **made** one film with Natalie Wood.
7 Tom **was reading out** the data **while** Sara **was writing** it **down.**
8 She **had finished** most of the work **by the time** her boss arrived.
9 She missed the end of the film because she **had fallen** asleep.
10 He **always went** to work by train.
11 She was pleased because she **had been given** the job.
12 We **had been living** in the same house **for twelve years before** we decided to move.
13 He left his job because **he had been feeling** dissatisfied **for** months.

a past action in progress interrupted by another past action
b past action which occurred before another action or before a stated past time
c two or more simultaneous past actions
d action continuing over a period up to a specific time in the past
e complete past action which had visible results in the past
f past actions which happened immediately one after the other
g past action of certain duration which had visible results in the past
h past habit or state
i Past Perfect as the past equivalent of the Present Perfect
j action in the middle of happening at a stated past time
k Past Perfect Continuous as the past equivalent of the Present Perfect Continuous
l action not connected to the present which happened at a definite past time not mentioned
m complete action or event which happened at a stated past time

1 ...*f*.... 2 .... 3 .... 4 .... 5 .... 6 .... 7 .... 8 .... 9 .... 10 .... 11 .... 12 .... 13 ....

17 **Fill in with an appropriate past form.**

In 1894 a steamship 1) ...*was sailing*... (sail) across the Atlantic Ocean from England to America. The sun 2) .... (shine) and a gentle breeze 3) .... (blow). The ship 4) .... (sail) for three weeks and was halfway to its destination - New York. The passengers 5) .... (relax) on deck when suddenly they 6) .... (hear) a loud bang. They all 7) .... (jump) up, 8) .... (run) to the edge of the boat and 9) .... (look) over the side. To their horror they saw that they 10) .... (hit) some hard object which 11) .... (tear) a hole in the side of the ship. Water 12) .... (pour) into the steamship at an alarming speed. Fortunately another ship arrived half an hour later, just in time to save everyone on board.

18 **Which of the past forms in the text above are used to express:**

1 past action of certain duration continuing up to a specific past time | *4*
2 background description to events or longer actions in the story
3 shorter actions which interrupt longer actions

4 longer actions which are interrupted by shorter actions
5 past action which occurred before another past action
6 past actions which happened one immediately after the other

19   **Fill in with Past Simple or Continuous.**

Simon **1)** ...*was walking*... (walk) home from work the other day when he **2)** .... (notice) something shining on the pavement on the other side of the road. A car **3)** .... (come) down the street, so he waited until it had driven past, then he **4)** .... (cross) over. When he **5)** .... (get) to the other side he saw that it was a shiny gold coin! He **6)** .... (look) around to make sure no one **7)** .... (look), then he **8)** .... (bend) down to pick it up. Imagine his surprise when he **9)** .... (not/can) move it! He **10)** .... (be) just about to give up when he **11)** .... (hear) a strange sound behind him. Someone **12)** .... (laugh) at him, but he couldn't see who it **13)** .... (be). Two little boys **14)** .... (hide) behind a hedge, laughing at anyone who tried to pick up the coin they had stuck to the pavement with glue!

Present Perfect	Past Simple
● **complete past actions connected to the present with a stated or unstated time reference** She **has gone** to Madrid. *(unstated time; we don't know when she went - she's still there now)* Jim **has seen** her in a café **this morning**. *(stated time; it's still morning - action connected to the present)* I**'ve spoken** to Prince. *(He's still alive - action connected to the present)* He **has lived** in Spain for two years. *(It implies that he is in Spain now. - action connected to the present)*	● **complete past actions not connected to the present with a stated or implied time reference** She **went** to Madrid **last year**. *(stated time - "When?" "Last year.")* Jim **saw** her in a café there. *(implied time - "When?" "When Jim was there.")* I **spoke** to James Dean. *(action not connected to the present - James Dean is dead.)* She **lived** in France for three years. *(It implies that she doesn't live in France now - action not connected to the present)*
● **to announce news or give new information** The Prime Minister **has decided** to call a general election.	● **to give details of the news** He **announced** the decision to Parliament this morning.

20   **Fill in with Present Perfect or Past Simple.**

1   A: ...*Did you see*... (you/see) the Bruce Lee film on TV last night?
     B: No. But I .... (see) all of his films on video already this year.

2   A: I .... (live) in Germany for five years now. I .... (move) here in 1989.
     B: I .... (live) in Portugal for a time, but I live in Rome now.

3   A: My Uncle Tom .... (meet) Winston Churchill.
     B: That's nothing! My mum .... (meet) Prince Charles.

4   A: Where's Jane?
     B: She .... (go) to America. She .... (leave) last week.
     A: Really? Why .... (she/go) there?

5   A: My father .... (work) in that shop for twelve years. Then he ....
        (get) a job in a bank.
     B: He .... (work) at the bank for quite a few years now, hasn't he?

6   A: How long .... (you/learn) Italian?
     B: I .... (start) learning the language when I .... (be) twelve.

21 Fill in with Past Simple or Past Perfect.

The biggest event in Tom's life **1)** ...*happened*... (happen) by chance. He **2)** .... (be) 22 and he **3)** .... (just/leave) college. He **4)** .... (get) his degree and he was looking for a job. He **5)** .... (want) to be a journalist but he **6)** .... (know) he **7)** .... (not/have) enough experience. You see, as a student, he **8)** .... (spend) most of his time in the university theatre. He **9)** .... (write) to all the newspapers but he **10)** .... (not/receive) any replies. Then one day, the phone **11)** .... (ring). It was a woman who **12)** .... (offer) him a job as an actor. She **13)** .... (see) him in a play at the university and **14)** .... (enjoy) the performance. He **15)** .... (take) the job and since then he's been very successful. Last night he **16)** .... (discover) he **17)** .... (win) an award for his performance in the play.

22 Complete the sentences using any appropriate past forms.

1 She ...*went to the market*... and bought some vegetables.
2 What .... when the fire started?
3 I could tell she .... because her eyes were red.
4 She .... when she slipped and landed on the ice.
5 My arm .... for two weeks, before I went to the doctor.
6 She got on the motorbike and .... away.
7 He .... the road when a flower pot fell on his head.
8 While Sally .... dinner Steve was laying the table.
9 The patient .... in hospital for five weeks before he fully recovered.
10 He was upset because he .... the exam.
11 Nobody knew where Jane .... the front door key.
12 Tom .... tennis every day for months before entering his first tournament.

Used to-Be used to +ing form / noun / pronoun -Would-Was going to

- **Used to** expresses past habits, regularly repeated actions in the past or past states. (Stative verbs are not used with "would.")

  She **used to tell** me stories. (also: **would** tell me ...)
  He **used to live** in the country. (not: ~~would~~ - state)
  He **used to have** a beard. (not: ~~would~~ - state)

- **Would** expresses regularly repeated actions and routines in the past. It isn't used for states.

  Mum **would** always make me a big breakfast. (also: Mum **used to make** ...)

- **Be used to** means "be accustomed to", "be in the habit of".

  She **isn't used to living** in tropical climates. (= she isn't accustomed to living ...)

- **Was going to** expresses actions one intended to do but didn't do.

  She **was going to move** to London but then she decided to stay in York.

23 Look at the notes below, then write sentences as in the example:

TEN YEARS AGO

He was fat.
He had long hair.
He didn't wear glasses.
He rode a bicycle.
He didn't wear suits.

NOW

He is thin.
He has got short hair.
He wears glasses.
He drives a car.
He wears suits.

He used to be fat but he is thin now. ....
....
....

24   **Fill in: used to, be used to, would or was going to.**

Although my friend Tom has lived in the city for three years he still **1)** ...*isn't used to*... it. He **2)** ....
live in the country so he **3)** .... living in a more peaceful environment. His first few days
in the city were so unpleasant that he **4)** .... move straight back home, but he found a
job and decided to stay. That's when I met him. He **5)** .... come into my office with the
coffee every morning and he **6)** .... often stop and talk for a while about what his life
7) .... be like in the country. His family **8)** .... have their own vegetable garden
and his mother **9)** .... prepare wonderful meals. In autumn they **10)** ....
.... go for long walks and they **11)** .... collect wild mushrooms and fruit. Tom
made it sound so wonderful that, at one point last year, I **12)** .... quit my job and leave town
forever. But I didn't. I **13)** .... too .... the noise and excitement of the city to ever feel at
home in the country.

Future Forms

25   **Identify the tenses, then match them with the correct description.**

1 I think **I'll go** home now.	**a** action which may (not) happen in the future
2 The bus for Brighton **departs** in an hour.	**b** action in progress at a stated future time
3 We**'ll be sailing** around the islands this time next month.	**c** fixed arrangement in the near future
4 By May he **will have been living** abroad for six years.	**d** action which will be finished before a stated future time
5 The men **are delivering** the furniture tomorrow.	**e** timetable/programme
6 Look at the baby! He**'s going to eat** that worm!	**f** decision taken at the moment of speaking
7 Perhaps we**'ll see** Nicky at school today.	**g** action which is the result of a routine
8 He**'s going to** take a few days off next week.	**h** duration of an action up to a certain time in the future
9 I'm sure you**'ll have** a wonderful holiday.	**i** prediction about the future
10 **Will** Jo **be staying** with you this Easter?	**j** action intended to be performed in the near future
11 I**'ll be having** lunch with Sam tomorrow as usual.	**k** asking politely about people's arrangements
12 They **will have made** a decision by Friday.	**l** evidence that sth will definitely happen

1 ...*f*....   **2** ....   **3** ....   **4** ....   **5** ....   **6** ....   **7** ....   **8** ....   **9** ....   **10** ....   **11** ....   **12** ....

26 **Look at Appendix 1 then fill in: will, won't or shall.**

Fred: I hope you **1)** ...*will*... be able to come to my party this weekend, Emma.
Emma: Of course I **2)** ...., Fred. But I'm afraid Sue **3)** .... be able to.
Fred: Oh dear! I know a certain boy who **4)** .... be very disappointed about that!
Emma: **5)** .... I phone her and try to persuade her to come? It probably **6)** ....
          do any good, but it's worth a try.
Fred: Yes, **7)** .... you do that? Gary **8)** .... enjoy himself if she doesn't come.

27 **Fill in the correct present or future forms.**

Dear Mum,

   By the time you receive this letter I **1)** ...*will have finished*... (finish) my final exams and, whether they
went well or not, I **2)** .... (celebrate). I **3)** .... (start) looking for a job
at the end of the summer because I **4)** .... (go) on holiday around Europe for a month,
starting next week. Sue **5)** .... (probably/come) with me, although she's not sure yet. If
she does, I'm sure we **6)** .... (have) a great time. I **7)** .... (see) her
this evening, as usual, so I expect she **8)** .... (tell) me her decision then. Anyway,
my first exam **9)** .... (start) at 9 o'clock tomorrow so I **10)** .... (drive)
down to the library to do some last-minute revision. Even though I **11)** .... (study)
Russian for four years by the time these exams are over, I feel I've still got a lot to learn about the
language. Give my love to Sam and Rover.

                                                                                          Yours,
                                                                                          Jason

- **We never use future forms after: as soon as, as long as, after, before, by the time, if** (conditional),
  unless, in case, until/till, when (time conjunction), **whenever, while, once, suppose/supposing, on
  condition that etc.** *The manager will see you **as soon as** he **comes** out of the meeting.*
  *I'll buy a new sofa **when I get** paid. (not: I'll buy a new sofa ~~when I'll get paid.~~)*
- **When** used as a question word and **if** meaning "whether" particularly after the expressions, I don't
  know, I doubt, I wonder etc can both be used with future forms.
  ***When will** John go to Paris?*
  *I don't know **if** the teacher **will** punish Tim for that. (= whether)*

28 **Fill in the correct present or future forms.**

If you **1)** ...*want*... (want) to travel long distances on your
bicycle, you must learn how to mend a puncture. As soon
as your tyre **2)** .... (become) flat, get off
the bike or you **3)** .... (damage) the wheel.
Then turn the bicycle upside down. Once it **4)** ....
.... (be) in position, remove the tyre using tyre-
levers or, if you **5)** .... (have) nothing
else, use spoons. When the tyre **6)** .... (be)
off, pump up the inner-tube. Put it in some water and turn
it until you **7)** .... (see) bubbles coming from
it. This is your puncture. Before you **8)** ....

(apply) the patch, you must clean and dry the area around the hole. After this you **9)** ....
(put) glue around the hole and wait until it **10)** .... (dry) a little. Then select a suitably
sized patch. Stick the patch over the hole and don't forget to put some chalk over it. Unless you do this, the
inner-tube **11)** ....: (stick) to the inside of the tyre. Replace the tube, pump up the tyre
and ride away. I don't know if you **12)** .... (be able to) remember all this, but it's worth
trying because you never know when it **13)** .... (be) useful to you.

29 **Underline the correct item.**

1 "I really need a drink." "OK, I'**ll buy** / '**m buying** you one. What would you like?"
2 "You look dreadful." "I know, I'**m seeing** / '**ll see** the doctor tomorrow at 4 o'clock."
3 "Did you remember to water the plants today?" "Oh no, I forgot; I'**ll water** / **water** them now."
4 I've already told you why I can't see you tonight. I'**m having** / '**ll have** guests.
5 I'm sorry. I promise I'**ll stay** / '**ll be staying** out of trouble in the future.
6 I'm sure he'**ll understand** / '**s going to understand** if you explain it to him clearly.
7 I **will have finished** / **will finish** my exams by the end of August.
8 "I've burnt the dinner". "Never mind, I'**ll go** / '**m going** to the restaurant and get a takeaway pizza."
9 I'**ll have been working** / '**ll work** here for forty years by the time I retire next week.
10 "I forgot to invite Fergus to the party." "That's OK. I **see** / **will be seeing** him this afternoon."
11 If I **have** / **will have** enough money, I'll buy a new bicycle.
12 I don't think I'**ll have finished** / '**ll finish** these exercises by 3 o'clock.
13 Excuse me, Colin. **Will you be going** / **Will you go** to the library this morning?
14 I'm not sure when I **go** / '**ll go** on holiday this year.
15 If we **go** / **will go** to Greece in the summer, we will visit the islands.
16 We can't get into the office until Jane **arrives** / **will arrive** with the key.
17 I doubt if they **are** / **will be** on time.

30 **Look at Appendix 1, then fill in: will or be going to.**

1 A: Have you decided where to go for your holidays?
   B: Yes, I...**'m going to**... tour Spain.
2 A: We've almost run out of petrol.
   B: Don't worry. We .... get some on the way home.
3 A: Does your tooth really hurt?
   B: Yes, I .... see the dentist tomorrow.
4 A: Did you buy any stamps?
   B: I forgot to, but I .... get some now if you like.
5 A: Have you heard about Sharon?
   B: Yes. She .... have a baby.
6 A: When did you last speak to Susan?
   B: Oh weeks ago, but I .... meet her tonight.
7 A: Your car is very dirty.
   B: I know. My son .... wash it this afternoon.
8 A: Have you found your bracelet yet?
   B: No, but I'm sure I .... find it when I tidy my room.
9 A: Do you know what the weather forecast is for tomorrow?
   B: No, but I expect it .... be warmer than today.
10 A: Shall we go out tonight?
   B: Sorry! I .... eat at the Chinese restaurant with Paul.
11 A: What do you want to eat?
   B: I .... have a hamburger and some chips, please.
12 A: Are you watching TV tonight?
   B: Yes, I .... watch the interview with the Queen.

31 **Look at Appendix 1, then fill in the correct present or future forms.**

We 1) ...**'re going**... (go) on holiday next Friday. The plane 2) .... (leave) at 5.00 am, so we 3) ....
.... (sunbathe) in Bermuda by lunchtime! We've got a lot of luggage and neither of us wants to
drive so we 4) .... (get) a taxi to the airport. My sister has never flown before so she 5) ....
.... (probably/be) quite nervous. I 6) .... (have to) sit by her and hold her hand all the
time. By the time we get there, we 7) .... (fly) for quite a long time and so we 8) .... (be)
quite tired. However, I hope we 9) .... (recover) by 8 o'clock, in time to go to the welcoming party!

Time Words

- **Ago:** back in time from now (used with Past Simple). *Jane **moved** to Canada two weeks **ago**. (two weeks back in time from now)*
- **Before:** back in time from then. *Last week I met Paul and he told me that Jane had moved to Canada two weeks **before**. (two weeks back in time from last week).* **It can also be used with present or past forms to show that one action preceded another.** *I'll leave **before** he comes. (not: ~~before he will come~~). He (had) finished his homework **before** he had dinner.*
- **Since** is usually used with Perfect tenses to express a starting point. The Perfect tense is used in the main clause. *He **has been** here **since** July. I've **known** him **since** we were at school.*
- **For** is used to express the duration of an action. *She has been in Lisbon **for** ten days. She had been working there **for** two years before she applied for a new post.*
- **Already** is used with Perfect tenses in mid or end position in statements or questions. *She had **already** dressed when Tim arrived. Has she cooked dinner **already**?*
- **Yet** is used with Perfect tenses in negative sentences after a contracted auxiliary or at the end of the sentence. *She **hasn't yet** passed her exams. She hasn't passed her exams **yet**.* In questions **yet** comes only at the end. *Has he come **yet**?*
- **Still** is used in statements and questions after the auxiliary or before the main verb. *I **can still** walk long distances. **Can she still** play the piano well? Are you **still** doing your exercises? He **still plays** in the same band.* In negative sentences, **still** comes before the auxiliary. *She **still can't** walk very well. She **still hasn't** got married.*

32 **Underline the correct item.**

1 Brad has been studying Japanese <u>**for**</u> / **since** three months.
2 I'm afraid I haven't posted your application form **still** / **yet**.
3 She met her husband ten years **ago** / **since**.
4 They have lived in the same house **for** / **since** they came here.
5 I'm sure I've **yet** / **already** seen this film.
6 She has been to Belgium once **before** / **ago**.
7 I **still** / **yet** haven't read this book.
8 He hasn't driven a car **for** / **since** he had the accident.
9 He can **still** / **already** dance quite well even though he's 90.
10 Have you **already** / **yet** done the cleaning?

In Other Words

- He's never driven a Porsche before.
  It's the first time he's ever driven a Porsche.
- They have never heard such a funny joke.
  It's the funniest joke they've ever heard.
- She hasn't phoned yet. She still hasn't phoned.
- It's a week since she visited me.
  She hasn't visited me for a week.

- The last time I called her was two days ago.
  I haven't called her for two days.
- When did you last meet him?
  When was the last time you met him?
- When did she buy the car?
  How long ago did she buy the car?
  How long is it since she bought the car?

33 **Complete the second sentence so that it has a similar meaning to the first sentence. Use the word given and other words to complete each sentence. You can use between two and five words. Don't change the word given.**

1 The last time I went to Brussels was two years ago.
   been   I ...*haven't been to Brussels*... for two years.
2 I've never heard such a silly story.
   silliest   It's .... ever heard.
3 He hasn't been to work for a week.
   since   It's a .... to work.

4 How long ago did they move into their house?
   moved   How long .... into their house?
5 She's the cleverest person I've ever met.
   never   I've .... person.
6 It's a month since I saw him.
   for   I .... a month.
7 When did you buy that suit?
   bought   How long .... that suit?
8 I haven't written to them for a month.
   is   It .... I wrote to them.
9 How long is it since you tidied your room?
   ago   How long .... your room?
10 When did you last go to London?
   time   When .... went to London?
11 I haven't finished my homework yet.
   still   I .... homework.

Oral Activity 1

Look at the four prisoners below. Work in pairs and make up each prisoner's story. Say what they usually do in prison, what they're doing now, what they had been doing before going to prison, why they're in prison, what they were doing when the police caught them, how many years they will stay in prison, and what they will do when they come out of prison.

  Bob: thief   **John: robber**   **Ben: kidnapper**   **Tom: murderer**

eg. Bob is a thief. He is reading a book at the moment. Before he went to prison he ...

Writing Activity 1

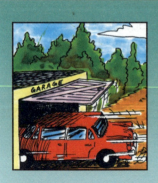

It's 10 o'clock on Sunday night. The Miltons are at home making a statement to the police. Look at the pictures and write their statement about the burglary. Use a variety of tenses.
eg. "Well, my wife and I had been to the cinema ...

34 ▶ **Choose the item which best explains the idioms, then make sentences using them.**

1	**a big hand**	A	friendly slap on the back	(B)	enthusiastic round of applause
2	**a big mouth**	A	over-talkative person	B	a liar
3	**a big noise**	A	powerful and influential person	B	insignificant and ineffectual person
4	**a big head**	A	knowledgeable person	B	over-confident and conceited person
5	**a bitter pill**	A	upsetting fact difficult to accept	B	harmful fact difficult to accept
6	**a blessing in disguise**	A	sth advantageous initially but later unpleasant	B	sth unpleasant initially but later advantageous
7	**a bright spark**	A	clever and lively person	B	devious and unfriendly person
8	**a close shave**	A	unforeseen disaster	B	narrow escape

35 ▶ **Complete the sentences using the words in bold as in the example:**

1 I started working there two years ago.
   have   I ...*have been working there for*... two years.
2 Kate hasn't been to the dentist's for six years.
   last   The .... to the dentist's was six years ago.
3 I can't tolerate his bad behaviour any more.
   put   I can't ....behaviour any more.
4 Terry and June haven't sent out invitations to their wedding yet.
   still   Terry and June .... invitations to their wedding.
5 I can't remember when I last laughed so much.
   time   I can't remember .... so much.
6 When did you hear from him?
   since   How long .... from him?
7 It's been over a month since she phoned me.
   for   She .... over a month.
8 She's never seen such a terrifying film.
   ever   It's the most .... seen.
9 We've never been on an aeroplane before.
   first   It's the .... on an aeroplane.
10 They haven't won a competition for years.
   since   It's .... a competition.

36 ▶ **Look at Appendix 2, then fill in the correct particle(s).**

Phrasal Verbs

1 If you are seen stealing that car the police will **be** ...*after*... you.
2 What **are** the children ....? They are very quiet.
3 We **are** .... bad weather this week.
4 I hope nobody disturbs me; my favourite television programme will **be** .... in five minutes.
5 I have broken my leg skiing, so I will **be** .... work for two months.
6 If they are late for the meeting again, I will **be** .... with them.
7 If you press the wrong buttons, the machine will **break** ....
8 School **breaks** .... for Easter on 2nd April.
9 The robbers used iron bars to **break** .... the bank.
10 When she was told her mum was in hospital she **broke** ....
11 The troops managed to **break** .... the enemy lines.
12 Sheila **broke** .... her engagement last week.

1 after, back, for, through
2 up, up to, up against, over
3 away, on at, in for, over
4 out, off, after, on

5 over, at, back, off
6 over, through, out of, off
7 down, in, off, through
8 out, up, down, off
9 in, into, through, away
10 down, off, through, in
11 off, down, through, over
12 in, up, out, off

37 Look at Appendix 3, then fill in the correct preposition.

1 The president **was accompanied** ...by... his wife on his recent tour.
2 He could not **account** .... £5,000 missing from the company's books.
3 You must be **acquainted** .... all the facts before stating your opinion.
4 The police will **advise** you .... how to discourage burglars.
5 Jane did not **agree** .... John's interpretation of the situation.
6 She'll never **agree** .... marry you.
7 He **aimed** .... the target and fired his gun.
8 The money that the children collected **amounted** .... £590.
9 The government **appealed** .... the public to stay calm during the crisis.
10 My parents do not **approve** .... my new hairstyle.
11 Henry is very **ashamed** .... his behaviour at last night's party.
12 She's extremely **attached** .... her parents.
13 Thomas is always **aware** .... his mother's over-protective attitude.
14 There has been another military **attack** .... the bases in southern Spain.

Prepositions

1 of, by, with
2 of, for, in
3 in, with, at
4 of, on, to
5 to, of, with
6 to, with, in
7 to, in, at
8 in, on, to
9 at, to, in
10 of, for, on
11 for, of, with
12 to, on, with
13 on, at, of
14 in, for, on

38 Think of the word which best fits each space. Write only one word in each space.

BIN YOUR RUBBISH

When was the **(0)** ...last... time you walked down a litter-free street? Although millions of pounds **(1)** ....
year are spent **(2)** .... clearing rubbish, this alone cannot solve the problem. The solution lies
(3) .... our hands.
Dropping litter is, in **(4)** ...., against the law in Britain. You can be fined up **(5)** .... £1,000.
Not **(6)** .... is litter ugly, but it can also be dangerous. Litter encourages vermin **(7)** .... as rats.
Why is there so **(8)** .... litter? Most consumer products are over-packaged; a single item **(9)**
.... be wrapped in plastic, put in a box, wrapped in cellophane and then put in a plastic carrier bag.
What can we do about this growing problem? If every citizen **(10)** .... his or her job, together we can
clean up the streets. Try recycling paper and plastic bottles. Never drop litter; **(11)** .... the smallest
piece of paper contributes **(12)** .... the problem. Avoid buying over-packaged items from supermarkets,
and take your **(13)** .... carrier bags. You could also organise day-trips to the local countryside and
beaches in **(14)** .... to pick up rubbish. If everyone makes **(15)** .... responsible for
maintaining high standards of cleanliness in their area, the problem may be solved.

39 Use the words in capitals to form a word that fits in the space in the same line.

STRESS

In today's world people seem to be very **(0)** ....
and suffer from stress. This stress is often **(1)** .... and
some people need to seek medical **(2)**.... in order to
recover. However, a more **(3)**.... solution is for people to learn
to relax. This can be achieved through a **(4)** ....of leisure
(5) ... such as sport, reading, music or even gardening.
(6)... is placed on people spending time doing things
that they enjoy, the ultimate aim being **(7)** .... .
Unfortunately, some people find this **(8)** .... and
therefore need to take drugs prescribed by their doctor.
These drugs are called **(9)** .... . They calm people down, but
can be dangerous if taken for long periods of time. Alternative
methods are much **(10)** .... and have no side effects.

ANXIETY	0	*anxious*	0
HARM	1		1
TREAT	2		2
EFFECT	3		3
VARY	4		4
ACTIVE	5		5
EMPHASISE	6		6
RELAX	7		7
POSSIBLE	8		8
TRANQUIL	9		9
SAFETY	10		10

The Infinitive/-ing form/Participles

We believe **in making** our guests feel welcome. The best **way to do** this is **to call** them by their names. You **can find out** their names **by reading** their luggage labels.

Very well, sir. I'll remember **to do** that.

Ah, good afternoon Mr & Mrs Cow's Leather.

Forms of the Infinitive

	Active Voice	Passive Voice
Present	(to) repair	(to) be repaired
Pres. Cont.	(to) be repairing	
Perfect	(to) have repaired	(to) have been repaired
Perf. Cont.	(to) have been repairing	

Forms of the -ing form

Active Voice	Passive Voice
repairing	being repaired
—	—
having repaired	having been repaired
—	—

* Passive Present Continuous and Perfect Continuous infinitives are rarely used.

40 Write the appropriate form of the infinitive.

1 I went   ...*to have gone*..
2 she has been playing   ....
3 he had worked   ....
4 it was read   ....
5 they have been informed ....

6   he is writing   ....
7   it is fixed   ....
8   he will type   ....
9   he was cleaning   ....
10 she will be sleeping ....

● The **Present Infinitive** refers to the present or future. *I hope* **to meet** *her tonight.* **The Present Continuous Infinitive** expresses an action happening now. *He must* **be sleeping** *now.* **The Perfect Infinitive** is used to show that the action of the infinitive happened before the action of the verb. *He claims* **to have worked** *here before. (First he worked here, then he claimed he had worked here.)* **The Perfect Continuous Infinitive** is used to emphasise the duration of the action of the infinitive, which happened before the action of the main verb. *He looks tired. He seems* **to have been studying** *for the test all night.* **The Present Cont., the Perfect and the Perfect Cont. Infinitives are used with the verbs: appear, claim, happen, pretend, seem etc and with modal verbs. (see p. 40)**

● The **Present Gerund** (-ing form) refers to the present or future. *Ann enjoys* **walking** *in the woods.* **The Perfect Gerund** (-ing form) shows that the action of the -ing form has happened before the action of the main verb. We can use the Present Gerund instead of the Perfect Gerund without a difference in meaning. *He denied* **having killed** *James.* **OR** *He denied* **killing** *James.*

2 The Infinitive / - ing form / Participles

41 Fill in the correct form of the infinitives.

1 My boss expects me ...*to work*... (work) overtime.
2 The suspect claimed .... (watch) TV at the time of the robbery.
3 Jill's teacher is worried about her as she seems .... (have) difficulty coping with her studies.
4 Young children often ask .... (take) to the zoo.
5 The burglars must have come in through the window as the lock seems .... (force).
6 "I happen .... (pass) my driving test two years ago, you know," he said.
7 Robert is expecting .... (inherit) a large house when his grandfather dies.
8 "Mark appears .... (overtake) John on the last lap. Yes, he's passed him!"
9 Leslie seems .... (enjoy) her new job.
10 I'd like .... (book) a return ticket to Denver, please.
11 Stop pretending .... (eat) your food - just finish it up, please.
12 The manager seems .... (get) impatient with the interviewee.

42 Fill in with the appropriate preposition or particle and -ing forms.

Dear Sir/Madam,

   As I dine out regularly in good quality restaurants I am accustomed
1) ... *to receiving*... (receive) service of the highest standard. The staff at
your establishment could certainly not be accused 2) ....
(provide) this! In addition 3) .... (be) extremely
rude, the waitress who served us was also guilty 4) ....
(get) our order wrong twice. My wife was also very upset 5) .... (be) told that she
shouldn't be so impatient. The chef too, seemed incapable 6) .... (do) anything right. As
well 7) .... (forget) to heat up our soup, he burnt my steak and overcooked my wife's
vegetables. All I can say is that he is obviously used 8) .... (cook) for very
uncritical diners. To make matters worse, the waitress tried to prevent us 9) ....
(leave) the restaurant because we hadn't left a tip! I'm not interested 10) .... (get) my
money back but I am looking forward 11) .... (hear) from you in the near future with a
full apology to my wife and myself 12) .... (spoil) our 25th wedding anniversary.

Yours faithfully,
Michael Crawford

Subject of the Infinitive /-ing form

**When the subject of the infinitive or of the -ing form is different from the subject of the verb, then
an object pronoun (me, you, him, her, it, us, you, them) or a noun is placed before the infinitive
or the -ing form.** *I want **him**/**John** to help me. (= He should help me.) but: **I** want to help. (= **I** should
help.)* **The subject of the -ing form can also be a possessive adjective (my, your etc) or the
possessive form of the noun.** *I remember **his**/**him**/**Tim's**/**Tim** talking about that island.*

43 Rephrase the following using the infinitive or the - ing form as in the example:

1 You have to eat your carrots.   I want ...*you to eat your carrots.*...............................
2 I must exercise more often.   I want ....
3 She has to take her medicine every day. The doctor wants ....
4 I saw him give you the letter.   I remember ....
5 He has to talk to me politely.   I want ....
6 They mustn't go to bed late.   I don't want ....
7 We visited Sue before Christmas.   I remember ....

The to-infinitive is used

- to express purpose. *He went to university to become a lawyer. (in order to become)*

- after certain verbs (agree, appear, decide, expect, hope, plan, promise, refuse etc). *He refused to pay the bill.*

- after certain adjectives (happy, glad, sorry etc). *She was happy to win the prize.*

- after I would like/would love/would prefer to express specific preference. *I'd like to see the manager.*

- after certain nouns. *What a surprise to see him there!*

- after too/enough constructions. *He's too young to have his own car. He's clever enough to do the crossword. He's got enough money to live on.*

- with: it + be + adjective (+ of + noun/pronoun). *It was generous of him to offer £1,000.*

- with: so + adjective + as. *Would you be so kind as to help me move the sofa?*

- with "only" to express an unsatisfactory result. *She came in only to find Bob had left.*

- after: be + the first/second etc/next /last/best etc. *He was the last to come to work.*

- in the expression: for + noun/pronoun + to -inf. *For him to be so rude was unforgivable.*

- in expressions such as: to tell you the truth, to begin with, to be honest etc. *To be honest, I don't like him.*

Note: If two infinitives are joined by "and" or "or", the "to" of the second infinitive can be omitted. *I want to call Mr Jones and fax or post him a letter.*

The -ing form is used

- as a noun. *Walking is good exercise.*

- after certain verbs (admit, anticipate, appreciate, avoid, consider, continue, delay, deny, discuss, enjoy, escape, excuse, fancy, finish, forgive, go (physical activities), imagine, involve, keep (= continue), mention, mind, miss, object to, postpone, practise, prevent, quit, recall, recollect, report, resent, resist, risk, save, stand, suggest, tolerate, understand etc). *They discussed selling the company. "Let's go jogging!" "No, I'd rather go sailing."*

- after: dislike, enjoy, hate, like, love, prefer to express general preference. *She likes painting. (in general)*
  * Note: like + to-inf = it's a good idea *I like to wash my hair every day.*

- after: I'm busy, it's no use, it's (no) good, it's (not) worth, what's the use of, can't help, there's no point (in), can't stand, have difficulty (in), in addition to, as well as, have trouble, have a hard/difficult time. *He can't stand being treated like a slave. He had difficulty finding his way back.*

- after: spend/waste (time, money etc). *He spends his free time (in) digging the garden.*

- after prepositions. *He left the shop without paying so he was accused of stealing.*

- after: look forward to, be/get used to, be/get accustomed to, object to, admit (to) etc *I'm looking forward to hearing from you soon.*

- after: hear, listen, notice, see, watch to express an incomplete action, an action in progress or a long action. *I saw Tim doing his homework. (I saw part of the action in progress. I didn't wait until he had finished.)*

BUT: hear, listen, see, watch + infinitive without "to" express a complete action, something that one saw or heard from beginning to end. *I saw Tim do his homework. It took him an hour. (I saw the whole action from beginning to end.)*

The infinitive without to is used

- **after: most modal verbs (can, must, will etc).** *You* **can** *leave now if you want.*
- **after: had better / would rather.** *I'd* **rather not go** *out tonight. I'd* **better stay at** *home.*
- **after: make / let / see / hear / feel+ object.** *They* **made** *him* **pay** *for the damage.* but: **in the passive: be made / be heard / be seen + to -infinitive.** *He* **was made to pay** *for the damage.*
- **"know" and "help" are followed by a to-infinitive or an infinitive without to.** *I've never* **known** *him* **(to) be** *so mean. Could you* **help** *me* **(to) fix** *the car?* but: **in the passive: be known, be helped + to-infinitive.** *She* **was known to have worked** *as a teacher.*

44 **Write what each word is followed by: F.I. (full inf.), B.I. (bare inf.) or -ing form.**

1 enjoy +.*ing form*.	5 it's no use + ...	9 resist + ...	13 would + ...
2 promise + ...	6 can't stand + ...	10 agree + ...	14 refuse + ...
3 be made + ...	7 can't help + ...	11 can + ...	15 spend time + ...
4 object to + ...	8 had better + ...	12 would like + ...	16 avoid + ...

45 **Put the verbs in brackets into the -ing form or the infinitive.**

The Jackal is known 1) ...*to be*... (be) one of the most dangerous criminals in the world. 2) .... (rob) banks is his speciality, although he also enjoys 3) .... (kidnap) every now and again. So far, the police have failed 4) .... (catch) him, and they would be very happy 5) .... (receive) any information that could lead to his arrest. The public have been warned

6) .... (not/ approach) the Jackal if they see him, as he has a gun and he doesn't mind 7) .... (use) it. The last person 8) .... (try) to arrest him was shot in the foot. Fortunately, we are unlikely 9) .... (come across) the Jackal in this country in the near future. He was last seen 10) .... (sunbathe) on a beach in Brazil.

46 **Complete the sentences using an infinitive or an -ing form.**

1 City life is too busy for me; I really miss ...*living*... in the country.
2 We had to postpone .... tennis because of the bad weather.
3 She goes .... at the pool every weekend.
4 If you will keep .... so much, you're bound to get fat.
5 She's been training so hard recently that she deserves .... the race.
6 He couldn't sleep, so I suggested his .... some warm milk.
7 Because of his fear of jellyfish, he doesn't like .... in the sea.
8 I'd really like .... my uncle in Chicago one day.
9 That man seems to be having trouble .... his car. Why don't you give him a push?
10 Mr Roberts is much too old .... climbing like he used to.
11 Before the interview, I was required .... an application form.
12 The dog seems .... hungry - you'd better feed him.
13 Becoming an Olympic athlete involves .... for years.
14 Would you ever consider .... married to someone twice your age?
15 I much prefer .... letters to .... on the telephone.
16 Let me be the first .... you on your remarkable success.
17 I'm sorry .... that I'll be unable to attend the meeting tomorrow.
18 He said he would prefer .... the train to London rather than .... his mother's old car.
19 It's no use .... to university if you don't intend to study.
20 I think you should give up .... because you have a very poor voice.

47 **Complete the sentences by using an infinitive or an -ing form.**

1 He heard the phone ...*ringing*... but it stopped before he could answer it.
2 When I entered his room I saw him .... his homework.
3 Then I saw him .... the house, ... into his car and .... away.
4 As they were walking past the house, they saw it .... into flames.
5 I saw Gary Lineker .... the winning goal in the FA Cup Final.

48 **Put the verbs in brackets into the -ing form or the infinitive.**

The best way **1)** ...*to explore*... (explore) China is by land. Anyone who has been there, will **2)** .... (tell) you what a great experience it is. **3)** .... (travel) round China involves **4)** .... (cover) great distances as the country is enormous. As a result, some tourists would rather **5)** .... (fly), as it is quicker and they consider **6)** .... (sit) on a bus or train a waste of time. For those who don't mind **7)** .... (take) a bit longer, there is so much **8)** .... (see) which is not visible from a plane. From a bus you can **9)** .... (see) women **10)** ....:..................... (work) in the rice fields. You can even spend some time **11)** .... (learn) a few Chinese phrases. Few can resist **12)** .... (taste) the local delicacy - bird's nest soup, though you may **13)** .... (have) difficulty in **14)** .... (acquire) a taste for one-hundred-year-old eggs!!

49 **Fill in "too" or "enough" with the adjectives from the list. Add an object where necessary.**

small, tall, warm, early, busy, strong, difficult, tired

1 The exercise is ....*too difficult for me*.. to do.
2 The shoes are .... (wear).
3 We didn't go to the beach last weekend because it wasn't .... (swim).
4 She isn't .... (lift) the weights.
5 I'm .... (do) the ironing now.
6 We weren't .... (get) good seats for the concert.
7 She can't make dinner tonight. She's .... with office work .... (make) dinner tonight.
8 He isn't .... (be) in the basketball team.

Verbs taking to-infinitive or -ing form without a change in meaning

● begin, continue, intend, start + to-inf or -ing form. However, we don't normally have two -ing forms together. *She began **crying** / **to cry**. The days are beginning **to get** shorter.*
not: *The days are beginning getting shorter.*
● advise, allow, encourage, permit, recommend, require when followed by an object or in passive forms take a to-infinitive. They take the -ing form when they are not followed by an object. *The teacher **doesn't allow us to eat** in class. We **aren't allowed to eat** in class. They **don't allow eating** in class.*
● need, require, want are followed by to-inf, the -ing form or the passive infinitive. *You **need to polish** your shoes. Your shoes **need polishing**. Your shoes **need to be polished**.*

50 **Put the verbs in brackets into the -ing form or the infinitive.**

There has been a bomb scare in central London. The police advise everybody **1)** ...*to stay*... (stay) clear of the area. You are recommended not **2)** .... (travel) by tube as the service has been suspended. We'd recommend **3)** .... (take) the bus, but only if your journey is essential. The police require any members of the public with any information relating to this incident **4)** .... (come forward).

Verbs taking to-infinitive or -ing form with a change in meaning

1 forget + to-inf (= forget to do sth)
*I'm sorry, I **forgot to lock** the car.*
forget + -ing form (= forget a past event)
*We'll never **forget visiting** Paris.*

7 try + to-inf (= do one's best; attempt)
*She **tried** hard **to cope** with her new job.*
try + -ing form (= do sth as an experiment)
***Try adding** some more sauce to your pasta.*

2 remember + to-inf (= remember to do sth)
***Remember to read** the instructions.*
remember + -ing form (= recall a past event)
*I don't **remember meeting** Al before.*

8 want + to-inf (= wish)
*I **want to find** a better job.*
want + -ing form (= sth needs to be done)
*Your dress **wants cleaning**.*

3 mean + to-inf (= intend to)
*He **means to move** to Newcastle.*
mean + -ing form (= involve)
*Working harder **means getting** more money.*

9 stop + to-inf (= pause temporarily)
*He **stopped to buy** some milk on his way home.*
stop + -ing form (= finish; cease)
***Stop talking** to each other, please!*

4 go on + to-inf (= finish doing sth and start
doing sth else) *After finishing her BA, she
went on to get a master's degree.*
go on + -ing form (= continue)
*She **went on watching** TV.*

10 be sorry + to-inf (= regret)
*I'm **sorry to hear** he has been injured.*
be sorry for + -ing form (= apologise)
*I'm **sorry for misunderstanding**/**having
misunderstood** what you said.*

5 regret + to-inf (= be sorry to)
*I **regret to tell** you that you have failed.*
regret + -ing form (= have second thoughts
about sth already done) *I **regret telling** lies.*

11 hate + to-inf (= hate what one is about to do)
*I **hate to interrupt**, but I must talk to you.*
hate + -ing form (= feel sorry for what one is
doing) *I **hate making** you feel uncomfortable.*

6 would prefer + to-inf (specific preference)
*I'd **prefer to have** an early night tonight.*
prefer + -ing form (in general)
*I **prefer reading** a book **to watching** TV.*
prefer + to-inf + (rather) than + inf without to
*I **prefer to read** a book **(rather) than watch** TV.*

12 be afraid + to-inf (= be too frightened to do
sth) *I'm **afraid to drive over** the old bridge.*
be afraid of + -ing form (= be afraid that what
is referred to by the -ing form may happen)
*She **is afraid of breaking** her leg if she jumps
over the wall.*

51 Put the verbs in brackets into the -ing form or the infinitive.

1 Tom stopped ...*to pick up*... (pick up) his washing on the way home.
2 If you don't stop .... (smoke), you'll make yourself ill.
3 Try .... (phone) John at the office if he's not at home.
4 I tried my best .... (finish), but there just wasn't enough time.
5 He was promoted in 1990 and went on .... (become) a company director.
6 The band went on .... (play) even after the lights had gone out.
7 "Why is the baby crying?" "I think he wants .... (feed)."
8 Sharon wants .... (talk) to you.
9 Jane was afraid .... (show) her school report to her parents.
10 I'm afraid of .... (lose) my way in the forest.
11 What do you mean .... (do) with all that money?
12 Playing a musical instrument well means .... (practise) for years.
13 I regret .... (inform) you that your husband has been arrested.
14 She regrets .... (spend) so much money on her new dress.
15 Do you remember .... (ride) a bicycle for the first time?
16 Remember .... (post) the letters on your way home.
17 I'd prefer .... (pretend) I didn't hear what you just said.
18 I prefer .... (borrow) books from the library to .... (buy) them.
19 Don't forget .... (bring) some cash in case they don't accept credit cards.

20 I was sorry .... (hear) about you failing the exam.
21 He said he was sorry for .... (speak) to you so rudely.
22 Oh no! I totally forgot .... (turn off) the cooker.
23 I'll never forget .... (sail) through that storm in the Atlantic.

52 Put the verbs in brackets into the -ing form or the infinitive.

Kim: I'll never forget **1)** ...*going*... (go) to America for the first time. I was incredibly excited although I was trying **2)** .... (act) cool and casual.
Tom: I know. I remember **3)** .... (be) quite envious because I wanted **4)** .... (go) there too.
Kim: Yes, I know. I was a bit over the top, wasn't I? I'm sorry for **5)** .... (behave) so badly.
Tom: Yes, you were! You just went on **6)** .... (talk) about America constantly. It was quite funny though when I think back. You hardly let me **7)** .... (say) a word.
Kim: I'm sorry, but you know that in my excitement I nearly left a lot of things behind like my camera and my money.
Tom: I didn't know you had such a bad memory.
Kim: I'm not usually so forgetful. I had a lot on my mind. Anyway, I don't remember actually **8)** .... (leave) anything behind in the end.
Tom: How did you feel when you first arrived there?
Kim: I remember **9)** .... (worry) about what to do and where to go. I wanted **10)** .... (see) everything but I didn't know where **11)** .... (begin).
Tom: So where did you go first?
Kim: Well, we started in New York. At first, the traffic was so bad that I was afraid **12)** .... (cross) the road. But it got easier. I saw the Empire State Building and the Statue of Liberty and lots of other things. It was incredible! I love New York!

53 Put the verbs in brackets into the infinitive or the -ing form.

I hate **1)** ..*sitting*... (sit) in this awful cell day after day. I must admit that I regret **2)** .... (rob) that bank but I regret **3)** .... (be) caught even more! I tried so hard **4)** .... (become) a successful criminal because I've never really wanted **5)** .... (work). My mother meant **6)** .... (bring me up) properly, but she failed. I remember **7)** .... (lie) and **8)** .... (steal) when I was a teenager and I stopped **9)** .... (go) to school when I was 15. I'll never forget the police **10)** .... (arrest) me for the first time. I still went on **11)** .... (break) the law when I got out of prison. Being a criminal means **12)** .... (spend) most of your life in prison. When I get out of here, I'm going to try very hard **13)** .... (stay) out of trouble.

54 Put the verbs in brackets into the correct passive infinitive or -ing form.

1 We are waiting for his first novel ...*to be published*... (publish) in English.
2 His music seems .... (influence) by the rock culture of the seventies.
3 .... (hurt) badly in the past, she found it very difficult to trust anyone again.
4 Don't tease him any more. He doesn't enjoy .... (laugh at).
5 Many film stars now hire bodyguards because they want .... (protect).
6 .... (award) an Oscar was the most memorable event in the actor's life.
7 Ann claimed .... (invite) to Tom Cruise's wedding while she was in America.
8 I was very upset when I failed the audition, so you can imagine how delighted I was .... (give) a second chance.
9 I'm not used to .... (approach) by complete strangers asking for my autograph.
10 Listen carefully because I don't want .... (misunderstand).

11 I wouldn't phone her after midnight. She won't like .... (wake up).
12 I don't remember .... (tell) the news before. Are you sure you mentioned it yesterday?
13 Ten more people have asked .... (include) in the conference.
14 He always wears such outrageous clothes because he wants .... (notice).
15 I see that .... (send) to prison for five years has taught you nothing.
16 Actors consider .... (see) on television as the first step to fame.

Participles

Present participles (verb + ing) describe what somebody or something is.	Past participles (verb + ed) describe how someone feels.
The exhibition was **fascinating.**	The students were **fascinated** by the exhibition. (How did the students feel about the exhibition? Fascinated.)
(What was the exhibition like? Fascinating.)	

55 **Underline the correct participle.**

A: I didn't know you were **1) interesting / interested** in gardening.
B: I'm not. I think it's really **2) boring / bored** but my mum's hurt her back and she was **3) concerning / concerned** that the garden would become a mess.
A: Oh, I understand now. I was reallly **4) surprising / surprised** to see you with a spade in your hand!
B: Don't laugh! This is really **5) tiring / tired**, I feel **6) exhausted / exhausting** already.

56 **Fill in the blanks with the appropriate participle.**

Carla has been **1)** ...*interested*... (interest) in dancing since she was a little girl. When she put on her own "performances" at home for her relatives, they were all **2)** .... (entertain) by the sight of the young girl twirling around in her home-made costumes. No one guessed, however, that by the age of eighteen she would be an **3)** .... (entertain) spectacle for a much larger audience. Carla's family were **4)** .... (thrill) to attend a Royal Performance and to witness their little girl's **5)** .... (excite) debut. Carla herself was more **6)** .... (excite) and **7)** .... (frighten) than she'd ever been in her life. Her climb to fame had been extremely **8)** .... (reward). And now, here she was, dancing for the Queen. How **9)** .... (please) she felt! But the **10)** .... (amaze) reviews she received the next day were even more **11)** .... (thrill).

57 **Put the verbs in brackets in the -ing form or the to-infinitive.**

I've been trying **1)** ...*to get*... (get) fit for years but it has been impossible **2)** .... (find) a method that has not ended in disaster. Two years ago I started **3)** .... (go) to karate classes. On the second day I broke my arm. When I had recovered from that, I took up **4)** .... (swim). At first I really enjoyed **5)** .... (race) my friend up and down the pool. But I regret **6)** .... (say) that it wasn't long before I slipped over on the pool side and cracked my head on the tiles. I needed **7)** .... (go) to hospital to make my head stop **8)** .... (bleed). A few months later a friend advised me **9)** .... (try) aerobics. That didn't last long either, because I hate **10)** .... (listen) to loud disco music. Then last month I bought a bicycle. I had always loved **11)** .... (cycle) ever since I was a child. I really regret **12)** .... (buy) that bike, though. At this very moment, I am lying in hospital with two broken legs. I have decided **13)** .... (give up) trying **14)** .... (get) fit. From now on, I'm going to concentrate on **15)** .... (stay) alive.

In Other Words

- Driving fast is dangerous.
  It is dangerous to drive fast.
- They made him admit (to) his guilt.
  He was made to admit (to) his guilt.
- I prefer driving to flying.
  I prefer to drive (rather) than fly.
- She was too inexperienced to get the job.
  She wasn't experienced enough to get the job.
- It was difficult for him to do the crossword.
  He had difficulty (in) doing the crossword.
  He found it difficult to do the crossword.
  He could hardly do the crossword.

- He's too ill to go to work.
  He isn't well enough to go to work.
- We were interested in the lecture.
  The lecture was interesting to us.
- They allowed him to enter the building.
  They let him enter the building.
- Could you clean up the room?
  Do/Would you mind cleaning up the room?
  Would you be so kind as to clean up the room?
- It took her an hour to prepare the meal.
  She took an hour to prepare the meal.
  Preparing the meal took her an hour.
  She spent an hour preparing the meal.

58 ▶ **Complete the second sentence so that it has a similar meaning to the first sentence. Use the word given and other words to complete each sentence. You must use between two and five words. Do not change the word given.**

1 He wasn't tall enough to be a policeman.
   short   He was ...*too short* ... to be a policeman.
2 They made her scrub the bathroom floor.
   was   She ....the bathroom floor.
3 We were shocked by the news.
   shocking   The news ....to us.
4 Would you mind moving over a little?
   kind   Would you be..over a little?
5 She was so tired she couldn't keep her eyes open.
   too   She was...her eyes open.
6 The horror film was terrifying.
   were   We.. the horror film.
7 It was difficult for her to cope with city life.
   found   She..with city life.
8 He spent hours wallpapering the sitting room.
   took   It...the sitting room.
9 Sarah prefers skiing to ice-skating.
   ski   Sarah...ice-skate.
10 Dad didn't allow me to drive his car.
   let   Dad...his car.

Oral Activity 2

Make sentences using the following verb combinations:
be used to/discuss, encourage me/buy, remind me/wear, avoid/answer, enjoy/sail, suggest/visit, warn me/not go, allow me/leave, offer/lend, look forward to/go, continue/talk, hope/recover

Writing Activity 2

Write a letter to a friend about a frightening experience you had using words followed by the -ing form or the infinitive.
Dear Al,
   I had the most frightening experience of my life yesterday. Ann had suggested going out ...

59 **Complete the second sentence so that it has a similar meaning to the first sentence.**
Use the word given and other words to complete each sentence.
You must use between two and five words. Don't change the word given.

1 They thought the way he jumped the fence was amazing.
   amazed   They ...*were amazed at the way*... he jumped the fence.
2 It's not my decision - it's yours.
   up   It's...decide.
3 These tests have to be corrected.
   need   These ....corrected.
4 He complained about his noisy neighbours.
   complaint   He ....his noisy neighbours.
5 Mr Smith is the owner of this house.
   belongs   This ....Mr Smith.
6 He was too scared to enter the haunted house.
   bold   He .... to enter the haunted house.
7 They made him admit to his guilt.
   was   He ....his guilt.
8 She paid £5,000 for her new car.
   cost   Her...her £5,000.
9 He finds it difficult to address large audiences.
   has   He .... large audiences.
10 The station clock showed midnight.
   according   It .... the station clock.
11 The Whites arrived here two hours ago.
   been   The Whites .... two hours.
12 Barry finished his homework before the film started.
   had   By the time the film .... his homework.
13 She hadn't expected to get so many presents.
   such   She hadn't expected to get .... presents.
14 His decision to marry did not meet with his father's approval.
   approve   His father .... his decision to marry.
15 It's too cold for us to go swimming.
   warm   It .... for us to go swimming.

60 **Look at Appendix 2, then fill in the correct particle.**

Phrasal Verbs

1 By stealing, Mark **brought** ...*about*... his dismissal from work.
2 This music **brings** .... happy memories.
3 The author will **bring** .... his new novel soon.
4 We managed to **bring** him .... by splashing his face with water.
5 The meeting has been **brought** .... to tomorrow evening.
6 She was eventually **brought** .... to my point of view.
7 They had to **call** .... the football match because of the weather.
8 My boss is **calling** .... us tonight at 8 o'clock.
9 All men over 18 will be **called** .... to fight in the war.
10 This situation **calls** .... immediate action.

1 down, about, off, over
2 to, back, out, along
3 in, about, to, out
4 about, round, together, on

5 in, forward, out, to
6 round, off, on, back
7 back, in, off, out

8 on, to, back, up
9 in, back, up, over
10 over, for, out, in

61 **Look at Appendix 3, then fill in the correct preposition.**

Prepositions

1 to, in, at
2 at, to, on
3 in, with, on
4 on, over, in
5 with, of, for
6 in, on, to
7 for, with, of
8 in, with, for
9 of, in, about
10 of, for, with
11 about, with, of
12 at, in, with
13 at, of, for
14 with, to, of
15 about, to, for
16 of, on, in

1 Dave was very **bad** ...*at*... maths and always failed the tests.
2 Sally was very **bad** .... her brother.
3 Mum can't come to the phone. She's **busy** .... the cooking.
4 This film is **based** .... a true story.
5 You can't **blame** me .... the accident; I wasn't even there.
6 She always puts the **blame** .... me for things that I haven't done.
7 There will be an extra **charge** .... delivering the goods to your home.
8 The suspect has been arrested and **charged** .... robbery.
9 It's very important nowadays to **care** .... our environment.
10 Sarah was fond of Peter and **cared** .... him very much.
11 You should take **care** .... your teeth.
12 Jane was **clever** .... history and always received the highest marks.
13 It was very **clever** .... you to find the answer.
14 The patient was **complaining** .... a pain in his chest.
15 The secretary was always **complaining** .... having too much work.
16 I would like to **congratulate** you .... passing your exams.

62 **For questions 1 - 15, read the text below and choose the word which best fits each space. There is an example at the beginning (0).**

THE LATE, LATE FLIGHT TO LONDON

Passengers **(0)** ...*travelling*... **(travelling / going / waiting / wanting)** on a flight from Washington to London were in **1)** .... **(for / at / on / with)** a very long wait. They had **2)** .... **(still / already / however / yet)** been waiting eight uncomfortable hours for takeoff, only to be **3)** .... **(said / told / mentioned / announced)** that the flight was **4)** .... **(late / retarded / delayed / behind)** even further. The cabin crew advised passengers to take pillows and blankets from the overhead lockers in **5)** .... **(case / order / time / turn)** to sleep inside the airport terminal. Many passengers **6)** .... **(mislaid / wasted / missed / lost)** their tempers and fights broke **7)** .... **(up / off / out / down)**. People shouted and **8)** .... **(asked / applied / demanded / took)** information. A member of the staff panicked and called airport security guards. A **9)** .... **(few / number / couple / little)** lucky passengers were put on alternative flights, **10)** ....

.... **(although / even / in spite / despite)** about 100 others spent the next day in the airport. Many people missed connecting flights and **11)** .... **(should / would / could / had)** be delayed for several days. First-class passengers were **12)** .... **(still / many / more / much)** fortunate. They were put **13)** .... **(up / off / out / about)** in luxury hotels and provided with food and drink. Other passengers had to be content with vouchers for Burger King, as the airline staff were not able to find hotels with **14)** .... **(much / enough / too / a lot)** free rooms to accommodate them. One woman carried a silver horseshoe for **15)** .... **(fortune / chance / luck / probability)**. As she said, "It didn't work this time!"

63 Use the words in capitals to form a word that fits in the space in the same line.

LONDON BOMB BLAST

An **(0)** ... bomb attack in west London has injured 18 people. The victims were mostly **(1)** ... to the area's popular market which was **(2)** ... as usual. The police expressed their **(3)** ... about the bombing because they had received a **(4)** .... call earlier, but the caller had suggested that the bomb was in a **(5)** ....different place. The **(6)** .... shocked the residents of the area and several shops had **(7)** ....windows. Only three people suffered serious **(8)** ..... . The bombing was probably a **(9)** .... to the arrest of three men suspected of **(10)** ..... in the bombing of a premises in Sheffield.

EXPECTED	0	unexpected
VISIT	1	
CROWD	2	
ANGRY	3	
WARN	4	
COMPLETE	5	
EXPLODE	6	
BREAK	7	
INJURE	8	
REACT	9	
INVOLVE	10	

64 Read the text carefully. Some of the lines are correct and some have a word which should not be there. If a line is correct, put a tick (✓) in the space provided. If a line has a word which should not be there, write it in the space provided.

LEARNING A FOREIGN LANGUAGE

0	When one learning a foreign languge, the selection of a system	one
00	of teaching becomes a calculation of time, money and need.	✓
1	French learnt at school may be very enough to book a hotel room or	
2	shop in a supermarket but will not must be enough to	
3	understand and contribute on to a social conversation.	
4	Even the ability to mix socially leaves one far away from having a	
5	full understanding of a language and its usage. What	
6	are the more best ways of learning a language? A book	
7	alone gives a limited guide to pronunciation, which it is	
8	essential to understanding and being understood. Students	
9	keen on to learn should read newspapers, listen to the radio	
10	and to watch programmes in the target language. Of course, this is	
11	easier in the case of a European language than an obscure	
12	language such as the Thai or Armenian. Ideally, students should	
13	attend a class. Needless is to say, the establishment must	
14	be chosen carefully - language teaching attracts some	
15	dishonest people who they want to get rich quick.	

65 Choose the item which best explains the idioms, then make sentences using them.

1	a hair's breadth	**A** very short distance	**B** short person
2	a dead end	**A** sth leading to death	**B** sth leading nowhere
3	a drop in the ocean	**A** hint	**B** insignificant amount
4	a false alarm	**A** unnecessary warning	**B** incomplete message
5	a feather in one's cap	**A** achievement one is proud of	**B** burden one is fed up with
6	a matter of opinion	**A** one-sided argument	**B** issue for discussion
7	a night owl	**A** sb who stays up late	**B** sb who looks tired
8	a hard nut to crack	**A** sb/sth difficult to deal with	**B** sb/sth annoying and silly

PART 1

For questions 1 - 15, read the text below and decide which word A, B, C or D best fits each space. Mark your answers in the answer boxes provided.

THE BAT

The bat may **(0)** .... an ordinary creature, but in fact it is an amazing animal. The bat has wings and is the only mammal **(1)** .... of true flight. There are many **(2)** .... species of bat; in Britain **(3)** .... there are fourteen types of bat, which range in size from a few inches to **(4)** .... feet in wingspan.

Bats are nocturnal animals **(5)** .... become active only at dusk. Many species **(6)** .... on a "radar" system to find their way around. The bat emits squeaks and then measures the echoes to "see" how far away any **(7)** .... is.

The **(8)** .... of bats survive on a diet of insects while others eat fruit. There are two species which eat fish and there are **(9)** .... some bats which eat meat! Some vampire bats take blood **(10)** .... their sleeping victims. These bats may **(11)** .... the deadly disease rabies.

Bats are sociable creatures and **(12)** .... large colonies. Most bats hibernate **(13)** .... the winter months. Many people are **(14)** .... of bats without ever having seen one. Perhaps if we learn **(15)** .... about these wonderful creatures, we will no longer fear them.

0	A represent	B seem	C declare	D present		0
1	A possible	B able	C capable	D probable		1
2	A different	B contrasting	C differing	D conflicting		2
3	A all	B lonely	C alone	D lonesome		3
4	A various	B several	C little	D few		4
5	A which	B who	C whose	D they		5
6	A put	B confide	C stand	D rely		6
7	A hindrance	B obstacle	C barrier	D blockage		7
8	A amount	B population	C majority	D number		8
9	A even	B too	C ever	D so		9
10	A out	B off	C of	D from		10
11	A hold	B grasp	C carry	D send		11
12	A connect	B relate	C structure	D form		12
13	A at	B whole	C throughout	D among		13
14	A fearless	B afraid	C scary	D frightful		14
15	A many	B little	C some	D more		15

Answer boxes (A B C D) are provided for questions 0–15; question 0 has B marked.

PART 2

For questions 16 - 30, read the text below and think of the word which best fits each space. Use only one word in each space. Write your answers in the answer boxes provided.

HOTELS

A stay in a hotel is **(0)** .... always a pleasant experience. There are many things **(16)** .... can ruin an otherwise enjoyable visit. Many problems occur in the bathroom. Instructions for using the shower are not only complicated, **(17)** .... are often written in an obscure language as **(18)** ....

Many travellers have **(19)** .... scalded, frozen or soaked while still dressed. Over-enthusiastic staff **(20)** .... another source of irritation. Maids appear at inconvenient times, ignoring the "Do Not Disturb" sign, in **(21)** .... to check the linen. Bellboys surround guests and grab their luggage, hoping **(22)** .... a tip.

"Free" samples of soap and shampoo **(23)** .... rise to mixed reactions. **(24)** .... some visitors love these "gifts" and eagerly take them home, **(25)** .... consider such things a waste **(26)** .... money and resent paying high room prices to cover the cost of these useless items.

What **(27)** .... a hotel guest happy? **(28)** .... people agree that large, comfortable beds are an important factor. Business travellers value facilities such **(29)** .... fax machines and direct-dial telephones. However, courteous, efficient service comes at the **(30)** .... of everyone's list.

0	*not*	0 ▭ ▬
16		16 ▭ ▭
17		17 ▭ ▭
18		18 ▭ ▭
19		19 ▭ ▭
20		20 ▭ ▭
21		21 ▭ ▭
22		22 ▭ ▭
23		23 ▭ ▭
24		24 ▭ ▭
25		25 ▭ ▭
26		26 ▭ ▭
27		27 ▭ ▭
28		28 ▭ ▭
29		29 ▭ ▭
30		30 ▭ ▭

PART 3

For questions 31 - 40, complete the second sentence so that it has a similar meaning to the first sentence. Use the word given and other words to complete each sentence. You must use between two and five words. Do not change the word given. Write your answers in the answer boxes provided.

0 I finished the book in two days.
took
It .... to finish the book.

| 0 | *took me two days* | 0 ▭ ▬ |

31 Someone stole my car last night.
had
I.. last night.

| 31 | | 31 ▭ ▭ |

32 I thought that woman was your mother.
mistook
I.. your mother.

| 32 | | 32 ▭ ▭ |

33 He locked the doors in case burglars broke in.
fear
He locked the doors .... break in.

| 33 | | 33 ▭ ▭ |

34 It's possible she hasn't received your message yet.
might
She .... message yet.

| 34 | | 34 ▭ ▭ |

35 The doctors won't allow him to leave the hospital.
let
The doctors.. the hospital.

| 35 | | 35 ▭ ▭ |

36 It's very difficult to raise a child nowadays.
bring
It's .... a child nowadays.

| 36 | | 36 ▭ ▭ |

37 I don't feel like going out tonight.
mood
I'm not.. out tonight.

| 37 | | 37 ▭ ▭ |

38 I have never met such a kind person.
kindest
He is .... ever met.

| 38 | | 38 ▭ ▭ |

39 Shall I carry your luggage?
want
Do .... your luggage?

| 39 | | 39 ▭ ▭ |

40 It took him all afternoon to clear out the attic.
spent
He.. out the attic.

| 40 | | 40 ▭ ▭ |

PART 4

For questions 41 - 55, read the text below and look carefully at each line. Some of the lines are correct and some have a word which should not be there. If a line is correct, put a tick (✓) by the number in the answer boxes provided. If a line has a word which should not be there, write the word in the answer boxes provided.

BEING AN AIR-HOSTESS

0	Ever since I was at school, I've wanted to be	0	✓
00	an air-hostess. It sounded so many glamorous and	00	many
41	exciting, flying all over in the world to exotic places	41	
42	and meeting the interesting people from different	42	
43	countries. At school I studied French and Italian in order	43	
44	that to achieve my ambition. Finally, when I was 18, I	44	
45	have had an interview with Air France, who accepted me.	45	
46	I had to attend a three-month training course, which it	46	
47	included waitressing, swimming and first-aid. We also	47	
48	had to learn how to put on a make-up and do our hair	48	
49	so that as to be smart at all times. Learning mouth-to-mouth	49	
50	resuscitation it was the most difficult thing - we	50	
51	practised on plastic dolls and then on each other one.	51	
52	Eventually, the day I had been looking forward to for	52	
53	so much long arrived. Before the plane took off I showed	53	
54	the whole passengers the emergency exits. One hour later	54	
55	than we landed in Paris. A perfect start to my dream job!	55	

PART 5

For questions 56 - 65, read the text below. Use the word given in capitals at the end of each line to form a word that fits in the space in the same line. Write your word in the answer boxes provided.

LONDON

London is the capital city and main (0) .... centre of the United Kingdom. Its (56) .... began with the Roman invasion in 45 AD.
It is now popular with (57) ...., who visit the city in order to see many of its (58) .... buildings and tourist (59) ..... It is also popular for its shops in the (60) .... part of the city.
Apart from (61) .... and business, London is known for being the United Kingdom's (62) .... heart. It is also home to one of the country's most important (63) ...., the Queen.
Although London is a big city, it would be (64) .... to say that it's an unhealthy place to live, since attempts to reduce (65) .... levels have been quite successful.

INDUSTRY	0	industrial
DEVELOP	56	
	57	
FOREIGN		
FAME	58	
ATTRACT	59	
CENTRE	60	
TOUR		
POLITICS	61	
	62	
RESIDE	63	
CORRECT	64	
	65	
POLLUTE		

Modal Verbs

Mum, you **must** buy Grandma new glasses.

Why **should** I? She **can** see very well. Look! She's watching dad's boxer shorts in the washing machine.

Oh, Mum! I **ought to** have told you. Grandma thinks she's watching the wrestling on TV.

- The modal verbs are: **can, could, may, might, must, ought to, will, would, shall, should**. They take no -s in the third person singular. *He can* ride fast. They come before the subject in questions and are followed by "not" in negations. *"Could I* leave now?" *"I'm afraid you can't* leave." The modal verbs are followed by an infinitive without to except for "ought to". *She could leave* early but I really *ought to stay* till the end. Each modal verb normally has more than one use. *Shall* I help you with the dishes? (offer) *Shall* we go out tonight? (suggestion)

- Certain verbs or expressions have virtually the same meaning as some modals. These are: **need** (= must), **had better** (= should), **have to/have got to** (= must), **be able to** (= can), **used to** (= would) etc. *I have got to* hurry to catch the bus. (= I must hurry.)

- We use modal verbs to express: **ability, advice, criticism, logical assumptions, necessity, offers, obligation/duty, permission, possibility, probability, prohibition, requests** or **suggestions**.

66 Identify the use of the verbs in bold, then write a synonymous expression.

1 **Can** I park my car in your garage? ...permission... ...May I?/Could I?...
2 You **should** book a hotel room. ....
3 He **has got to** go and see the headmaster. ....
4 She **must** be home. ....
5 You **needn't** wear a tie to the interview. ....
6 **Shall** I cook spaghetti for dinner? ....
7 Gary **may** come round tonight. ....
8 You **should** go on a diet. ....
9 **Would you mind** moving your car, sir? ....
10 She **can't** still be at work; it's already 6 pm. ....
11 You **ought to** be more patient. ....
12 **Can** I give you a hand with that bag? ....
13 Children **must not** play football in the streets. ....
14 I **have to** see the dentist. ....
15 The car **needs** filling up with petrol. ....

Functions of Modal Verbs and Synonymous Expressions

USE	PRESENT/FUTURE	PAST
ability	He **can** read Arabic. She**'s able to** run a marathon.	He **could/was able to** read Arabic when he was four. (repeated action - ability in the past) He **was able to** escape. (single action)
possibility	He **can** win the race. (90% certain) They **could** still be at school. (50% certain; it's possible they are still at school.) Tom **may** be studying in his room. (perhaps; 50% certain; it's possible that he's studying.) He **might** want some more food. (40% certain; perhaps he wants some more food.) **It is likely that** he will arrive tonight. **He is likely to** arrive tonight.	—— She **could have** been killed in the car crash. (Luckily, she wasn't killed.) He **may have** spoken to Jenny yesterday. (Perhaps he spoke to Jenny.) He **might have** forgotten. (Perhaps he has forgotten.) **It was likely that** he had arrived the day before. **He was likely to** have arrived the day before.
probability	They **will** be home soon. (100% certain; prediction) Greg **should** win easily. (90% certain; future only; he'll win easily.) They **ought to** be home by now. (90% certain; they will probably be home.)	—— He **should have** received his prize by now. (He has probably received it by now.) They **ought to have** arrived an hour ago. (They have probably arrived.)
logical assumptions	She **must** be working. (90% certain - positive; I'm sure she's working.) She **can't** be over forty.(negative; I'm sure she isn't over forty.) He **couldn't** be at work (negative; I don't think **he's** at work.)	She **must have** been working. (positive; I'm sure she was working.) She **can't have** stolen the money. (negative; I'm sure she didn't steal the money.) He **couldn't have** been at work yesterday. (negative; I don't think he was at work yesterday.)
permission	You **can/can't** borrow my car. (giving or refusing permission; informal) **Could** I use your phone? (more polite; asking for permission) You **may** use the phone. (formal; giving permission) **Might** I speak to Mr Jones, please? (more formal; asking permission) I'm afraid you **can't/mustn't** see the patient. (informal; refusing permission) Children **may not** be left unaccompanied. (formal; refusing permission - written notice)	He **wasn't allowed to/couldn't** cross the border. He **was allowed to** enter the country. (not: ~~could~~) —— —— —— ——
necessity	I **must** buy a new jacket. (I say so.) He **has to** put some petrol in the car. (necessity coming from outside the speaker) I**'ve got to** go to the bank now. (informal) My car **needs** repairing. or My car **needs to** be repaired. (it's necessary) They **don't have to/don't need to/needn't** come if they don't want to. (it isn't necessary - absence of necessity) I **ought to** get my hair cut. (it's necessary)	I **had to** buy a new jacket. (I was obliged to.) Since his car was being repaired he **had to** go to York by train. I **had to** go to the bank yesterday. My car **needed** repairing. or My car **needed to** be repaired. (it was necessary) She **didn't have to** go. (it wasn't necessary - absence of necessity) He **needn't have** worn such heavy clothes. (It wasn't necessary for him to wear such heavy clothes but he did.) She **didn't need to/didn't have to** buy any apples. (It wasn't necessary for her to buy any apples and she didn't.)

Functions of Modal Verbs and Synonymous Expressions

USE	PRESENT/FUTURE	PAST
advice	You **should** drink more water. (general advice; I advise you) You **ought to** respect the elderly. (I advise you; most people believe this) You **had better** finish it. (it's a good idea; advice on a specific situation) **Shall I** buy that car? (asking for advice)	You **should have** gone to bed earlier last night. (but you didn't) He **ought to have** seen a doctor earlier. (but he didn't) It **would have been better** if you had finished it yesterday. (but you didn't) ——
criticism	You **could** at least help me. —— ——	You **could have** at least helped me last night. They **should have** tried harder. (but they didn't) You **ought to have** behaved yourself yesterday. (It was the right thing to do but you didn't do it.)
obligation	I **must** go on a diet. (I'm obliged to; I say so.) I **have to** go on a diet.(I'm obliged to; the doctor says so.) We **ought to** help the poor. (It's the right thing to do, but people don't always do it.)	I **had to** go on a diet a month ago. I **had to** go on a diet a month ago. ——
requests	**Can I** borrow your book? (informal) **Could I** borrow your book? (polite) **May I** have a cup of coffee, please? (formal) **Might I** use your phone? (very formal) **Will you** phone Jane tonight? (very friendly) **Would you mind** sending this fax? (polite)	—— —— —— —— —— ——
offers	**Can I/we** do anything for you? (informal) **Shall I/we** do it for you? (informal) **Would you like me** to help you?	—— —— ——
suggestions	**Shall we** dance? **I/We can** go now if you like. **We could** leave if you want.	—— —— He **could have** consulted a lawyer.
prohibition	You **can't** smoke there. (you aren't allowed to) You **mustn't** smoke there. (it's forbidden) You **may not** smoke there. (formal)	They **couldn't** smoke there. (they weren't allowed) —— ——
duty	Everyone **must** obey the law. People **ought to** be more tolerant. (**It's** the right thing to do but they do not always do it.)	All the villagers **had to** obey the law. He **ought to** have been more tolerant. (**It was** the right thing to do but he didn't do it.)

67 Rephrase the following in as many ways as possible.

1. She may be late. **2.** It's likely that he'll approve our plan. **3.** I'm sure they're planning to come. **4.** I don't think he'll remember me. **5.** They may have told him already. **6.** You ought to return that book.

68 Fill in: May I ...? (= Will you allow it?) or Am I allowed to ...? (= What is the rule?).

1 *...May I...* ask you the time?
2 .... feed the animals in the zoo?
3 .... keep pets in my apartment?
4 .... see what you're reading?
5 .... help you with that suitcase?
6 .... make personal phonecalls?

Can · Could · Was able to (ability)

- **Can** expresses ability in the present and future. **Could** expresses ability in the past. The verb **can** is used only in the present or future and **could** in the past. **Can** borrows the rest of its tenses from **be able to**. *could climb up mountains before he had an accident. He **can't** climb mountains now but he **had been able to** do so before his accident.*
- **Was able to** (= managed to) is used to express ability in the past for either **single** or **repeated** actions. *He **was able to** reach Brighton before midnight. (single action) (not: ~~could~~)*
- **Could** is used in **statements** to express general ability in the past for **repeated** actions. *She **could/was able to** read when she was four. (could/was able to are both correct)*
  However with "feel", "hear", "see", "smell", "understand" etc we normally use **could** for single actions. *I **could hear** a noise coming from the dining room. (single action) (not: ~~was able to~~)*
- **Could/Was able to** are both used in **negations** and **questions** for either **single** or **repeated** actions. *They **weren't able to/couldn't** win the race. (single action) **Could you/Were you able to** drive a car when you were fifteen? (repeated action - general ability in the past)*

69 Fill in: was/were able to, could(n't), had been able to, should be able to or can.

1 You ...*could/were able to*... run much faster when you were younger.
2 On entering the house I .... smell something burning in the kitchen.
3 If you work quickly, you .... finish on time.
4 Ann .... read by now; she's already six.
5 When we lived on the coast, we .... swim in the sea every day.
6 If Gordon .... find his way out of the jungle, he would have survived.
7 Last week he .... arrange a meeting with the Prime Minister.
8 I'm not usually very good at tennis, but yesterday I .... beat my brother.
9 Tom .... finish this today, shouldn't he?
10 He .... fix the tap so he called a plumber.

Must · Have to · Have got to

- **Must** is used when the speaker decides what it is necessary to do. *I **must** buy some new clothes. (I say so. I decide what to do.)*
- **Have to** is used when the necessity comes from outside the speaker or when others decide for the speaker what it is necessary to do. *He **has to** be at work at 9.00. (The boss says so.)*
- **Have got to** has the same meaning as **have to** but it is used in spoken English. *"Mum, I've got to go to the library."*
- **Must** is stronger than **have to** and indicates urgency and importance. *I **must** meet Jane tonight. (It's very urgent that I meet her.) I **have to** meet Jane tonight. (I need to meet her.)*
- **Must** is used only in the present or future. *I **must** go to the meeting tomorrow.* It borrows the rest of its tenses from **have to**. *She **had to** be present at the lecture last Monday.*

70 Fill in: must or have to.

"Welcome on behalf of Newton Industries. I'd like to explain a few of the factory rules. Mr Newton has said we **1)**... *have to*.... wear overalls at all times. He wants us to arrive at 8 am and we **2)** .... clock in. There is a possibility of working overtime but you **3)** .... decide whether you want to work extra hours. Mr Newton insists that we **4)** .... have fifteen-minute breaks every three or four hours but we **5)** .... choose when we would like those breaks. There is a problem with parking. The city insists we **6)** .... use the public garage. They believe parking on the grass is too damaging to public property and I **7)** .... say I agree. Finally, as far as health insurance is concerned, you **8)** .... register as soon as possible. Are there any questions?"

Mustn't · Needn't

- **mustn't** (it's forbidden) *You **mustn't** get off the bus before it stops.*
- **needn't/don't have to** (it isn't necessary) *Today is a holiday - you **needn't**/**don't have to** go to work.*

71 Fill in: mustn't or needn't.

Tom,
    Thanks for offering to chair tomorrow's meeting for me. Apart from Sally and Dave, the sales staff 1)... *needn't* ... attend, but the Personnel people 2) .... miss it, as several matters concern them. You 3) .... mention the new offices - we can deal with that later and you 4) .... discuss the changes in the computer course timetables since they're not urgent. Don't forget that you 5) .... mention the visit by the inspectors - we don't want people panicking. You 6)............................. forget to bring up the matter of the Smithson contract, and you also 7) .... leave out the new manager's appointment. You 8) .... go into details unless people have questions. But remember you 9) .... give anyone the idea that their job is at risk because of this. Make it clear that employees 10) .... speak unless they want to. Last but not least, you 11) .... mention the staff party - Mr Jones wants to announce that himself. By the way, you 12) .... take notes, as my secretary will be there to do that.
                                                                                                                                    Thanks,
                                                                                                                                    Laura

Needn't · Didn't need to · Needn't have

- **don't have to/don't need to/needn't + present infinitive** (it is not necessary in the present or future) *You **don't have to**/**don't need to**/**needn't** worry about it any more. I'll take care of that. (It is not necessary to worry ...)*
- **didn't need to/didn't have to** (It was not necessary in the past and we may not know if the action happened or not.) *She **didn't need to**/**didn't have to** buy a dress for the party. (It wasn't necessary for her to buy a dress, and we don't know if she bought one.)*
- **needn't + bare perfect infinitive** (We know that something happened in the past although it was not necessary.) *You **needn't have** said that. She was very upset by your remarks. (You said it, although it was not necessary.)*

72 Fill in: needn't have or didn't need/have to, don't need/have to/needn't and the correct form of the verbs in brackets.

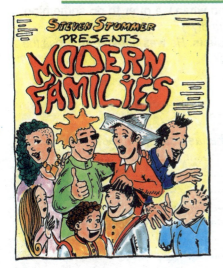

"Have you seen *Modern Families* yet?" Paul asked Mary as he was checking through the cinema listings. "I saw it last night," she replied. "I **1)**....*needn't have gone*... (go) though - I already knew what it would be like." "Didn't you like it?" "Not really. The director **2)** .... (spend) so much money presenting such a weak story. It's a good thing I **3)** .... (pay) to get in." "I low did you manage that?" asked Paul. "I went with Tom," she answered. "Critics **4)** .... (pay) to see films you know." "How was the acting?" "Well, the director **5)** .... (hire) such good actors for a film like that, " said Mary. "I mean you **6)** .... (have) much talent to sit around talking about nothing for hours." "Did Tom review it?" "He **7)** .... (write) about it. Somebody else had already done it for his paper. We just went out of curiosity, but really we **8)** .... (go).

Continuous and Simple Forms with Modal Verbs

- **Modal + be + -ing** expresses an action in progress now. *She **may be sleeping**.*
- **Modal + have been + -ing** expresses an action in progress in the past. *He **may have been sleeping** then.*
- **Modal + have + past participle** expresses a complete action in the past. *He **might have met** them before.*

*Waiter! You **shouldn't have served** my soup with a dead fly in it. Don't stare at me like that. Say something.*

How sad sir! That fly was too young to die.

73 Fill in: must, can't, should, may, might, could and the appropriate form of the verbs.

Fred: I've been trying to phone Rupert all day, but there's no answer. He **1)** ...*must be working*... (work).
Jill: No. He **2)** .... (work). He never works on Sunday.
Fred: Oh! Then I suppose he **3)** .... (go) away somewhere for the day.
Jill: Possibly. But I'll be upset with him if he has. He **4)** .... (tell) me, so that I **5)** .... (go) with him.
Fred: I hope he's OK. He **6)** .... (have) an accident, you know.
Jill: Don't worry. He **7)** .... (still/sleep). You know he has a lot of work on at the moment. He **8)** .... (work) until late last night.
Fred: I suppose so, or he **9)** .... (go) to Ted's party.
Jill: That's it! He **10)** .... (go) there and stayed out till really late.

Expressions similar to Modal Verbs

- **Be supposed to + infinitive** means "should" but it expresses the idea that someone else expects something to be done. *I'm supposed to attend the seminar. (The manager **expects** me to do so. I **should** attend the seminar. It's a good idea because I might get some useful information.)*
- **Be to + infinitive** means "must" but it expresses the idea that someone else demands something. *I **am to** be at the airport at 9.00. (My boss has told me to go there, so I can't avoid it.) I **must** be at the airport at 9.00. (If I don't go there, there will be no one to meet Mr Jones who is coming tonight.)* **Be supposed to** and **be to** are used to express what someone expects about a previously arranged event. *The conference **is supposed to**/**is to** start tomorrow. (It is scheduled.)*
- **Be likely to** means "may" (possibility). To express possibility in questions we don't use "may". We use: Is he likely to ...?, Is it likely that he ...?, Can he ...?, Could he ...?, Might he ...?. *Is he likely to win the race? Is it likely that he will win the race? Could he win the race? etc*
- **Would you mind** is used to express polite, formal requests. *Would you mind lending me a hand?*
- **Let's.../How about...?/Why don't we...?/What about...?** are used to make suggestions. *Let's go for a ride. How about going for a ride? Why don't we go for a ride? What about going for a ride?*
- **Would you like to/Would you like me to...?** (= Shall I...?) are used when we offer to do something. *Would you like me to pick up your laundry? (Shall I pick up your laundry?)*
- **Be allowed to** is used to express permission, to say what the rule is. *He **was allowed to** cross the border. (not: He could cross) **Was he allowed to** enter the building?*

74 How else can you express the following?

1 Can I have the last cake, please? ....*May/Could/Might I have the last cake, please?* ....
2 Let's go for a bike ride. ....
3 She might be on holiday. ....
4 Could you hold this for me, please? ....
5 She couldn't drive until last year. ....
6 You can't take photos in here. ....
7 I've been scheduled to take you to the airport. ....
8 Shall we go to the basketball match? ....

9 Is it possible that he will be offered the job soon? ....

10 I should go to the launderette today. ....

11 Would you mind moving your car, please? ....

12 Would you like me to make lunch? ....

13 You must post this before the end of the week. ....

14 He'll be sleeping now, I'm sure. ....

15 You are expected to be here on time. ....

16 I'm sure Paula's train left on time. ....

17 I'm sure Jim didn't mention the matter to anyone. ....

18 It's possible that Liverpool will win the match. ....

75 **Fill in a modal or a synonymous expression and the appropriate form of the verbs in brackets.**

1 I'm getting fat. I really... *have to try*... (try) to lose some weight, like the doctor said.

2 What a lovely day! .... (we/go) for a walk?

3 I'm not sure where Gary is. He .... (be) at the library.

4 That .... (not/be) Bill's car. He doesn't own one.

5 Tom .... (sleep) but I'm not sure. Why don't you go and see?

6 Don't worry. You .... (not/dress) formally for the party.

7 If you wanted to borrow my car, you .... (ask) me.

8 This dog .... (belong) to Harry. It's got his address on its collar.

9 Only authorised personnel .... (enter) this area.

10 You .... (not/smoke) in some public places.

11 I saw John in the town centre this morning. He .... (go) to Spain yet.

12 Fortunately he .... (convince) the police that he was innocent.

13 Tom drives really well now. He .... (pass) his driving test easily.

14 She .... (be) at the party last night. She was ill.

15 They .... (announce) the winners on March 16th. It's scheduled.

16 She .... (start) working on Monday. The manager has told her to.

17 I missed the film last night because I .... (work) late.

18 Everyone in the world .... (have) food and shelter.

19 You .... (comply) with the regulations. We expect you to do so.

20 People .... (treat) animals in a better way but they don't always do so.

76 **Fill in the blanks as in the example:**

MODAL	USE	SYNONYMOUS EXPRESSION
1 ...Shall... I help you?	...........offer...................	*Would you like me to help you?*
2 You .... have seen a doctor.	....	It would have been a better idea if you had seen a doctor.
3 You mustn't talk in class.	....	....
4 .... I use the phone, please?	..........polite request.......	....
5 You .... eat your lunch.	....	It's a good idea to eat your lunch.
6 We .... be formally dressed.	..........obligation............	We are expected to be formally dressed.
7 Tom .... be on holiday.	....	I'm sure Tom is on holiday.
8 You may ask questions now.	....permission (formal).....	
9 He .... call any minute.	....	Perhaps he'll call any minute.
10 .... working overtime?	.......polite request..........	....
11 I .... clean my bedroom.	....	It's necessary; my mother said so.
12 Shall we go to the cinema?	...........suggestion..........	....
13 She could read at the age of five.	....	....
14 I .... lose some weight.	..........obligation............	It's urgent that I lose some weight.
15 You .... work from 9 to 5.	..........obligation............	You're supposed to work from 9 to 5.

Oral Activity 3

Look at the pictures, then guess what the people are saying using modal verbs.

   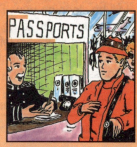

eg. Picture 1: May I speak to Mr Brown, please? Could you put me through to Mr Brown, please? etc

In Other Words

- Perhaps she moved to Rome.
  She may have moved to Rome.
- I'm sure she is sleeping.
  She must be sleeping.
- I'm sure he hasn't left.
  He can't have left.
- It's forbidden to smoke in hospitals.
  You mustn't smoke in hospitals.
- He is likely to win the race.
  It is likely that he'll win the race.
  He'll probably win the race.
- Let's go for a walk.
  Shall we go for a walk?

- It wasn't necessary for you to finish it today.
  You needn't have finished it today.
- Was it necessary for Ann to leave the party that early?
  Did Ann need to/have to leave the party that early?
- You'd better ask for some advice.
  You should ask for some advice.
- Shall I help you with the dishes?
  Would you like me to help you with the dishes?
- It isn't necessary to do the ironing today.
  You don't have to/don't need to/needn't do the ironing today.
- Would you mind if I used your phone?
  May/Might I use your phone?

77 **Complete the second sentence so that it has a similar meaning to the first sentence. Use the word given and other words to complete each sentence. You must use between two and five words. Do not change the word given.**

1 It wasn't necessary for you to bring me flowers as I already had a lot.
  needn't   You ....*needn't have brought me* ....flowers.
2 Perhaps he left the car unlocked.
  may   He .... the car unlocked.
3 I'll carry that bag for you.
  like   Would ....that bag for you?
4 I advise you to drive more slowly.
  should   You ....slowly.

5   It would be a good idea for you to leave early.
    better   You ....early.
6   Driving without headlights is forbidden.
    drive   You ....headlights.
7   Let's go shopping in town.
    about   What ....in town?
8   I'm sure he lied to you.
    have   He ....to you.
9   I don't think he has been feeling well lately.
    have   He ....well lately.
10 It's possible that Ann is looking for a new job.
    may   Ann ....a new job.
11 He will probably pass his driving test.
    likely   He ....his driving test.
12 It was not necessary for him to pay for the damage, although he did.
    needn't   He ....for the damage.
13 You are not allowed to leave until the exam has finished.
    mustn't   You ....the exam has finished.
14 I'd better start saving for my summer holiday.
    should   I ....for my summer holiday.
15 We'll probably stop and get something to eat on the way home.
    likely   It .... stop and get something to eat on the way home.
16 It's possible that you forgot to pick up your change.
    have   You ....up your change.
17 You mustn't take photos in the cathedral.
    allowed   You .... photos in the cathedral.
18 It wasn't necessary for them to pay for our meal, but they did.
    paid   They ....for our meal.
19 Is it possible that hats are coming back into fashion?
    be   Could .... back into fashion?
20 It wasn't necessary to get dressed up, so we didn't.
    need   We .... get dressed up.

78 **Write what each person would say in each situation using modals, then identify their use. Sometimes more than one answer is possible.**

1   A student has just come into the class and left the door open. It is noisy outside. You say to him:
    .... *Will/Would/Can/Could you close the door, please? (request)*............................
2   You have opened the kitchen window to let in some fresh air. Your sister, who is recovering from a bad cold, comes in. You say to her: ....
3   Your friend wants to pay for your dinner. You tell her it's not necessary.
    ....
4   Your mother wants to know where your sister is. You think she is helping your father in the garden. You say to her: ....
5   A friend from Portugal phones to tell you she will be coming to England for two weeks next summer. You want her to stay with you. You say to her: ....
6   You're going on holiday. Your sister wants to take so many pairs of shoes that her suitcase won't fasten. You ask if it is necessary. ....
7   Your friend is sure your father goes to a gym every morning before work as he always looks so healthy. He says to you: ....
8   Tom was driving fast when he accidentally went off the road. Fortunately no one was killed or injured. You say to him: ....
9   Your friend failed his exam. He hadn't revised at all. You say to him:
    ....
10 John is taking part in a horse race. You don't know if John will win. You ask your friends if it's possible.
    ....

3 Modal Verbs

79 **Write sentences with should (have) or ought to (have).**

1 Sophie didn't turn off the oven before she went to bed. ...*Sophie ought to/should have turned it off.*.
2 James smokes in the office. ....
3 The students left the light on in the classroom. ....
4 People don't keep the beaches clean. ....
5 My brother didn't send our grandmother a birthday card. ....
6 They destroyed parts of the rainforest. ....

80 **Answer the questions using may or might.**

1 What time does the plane leave? ...*It might/may leave at 7.00 pm.*..................
2 What time did the plane leave? ....
3 Where's Laura? ....
4 Where was Laura last week? ....
5 Where will Laura be next week? ....
6 What is he doing? ....
7 What did Sam do yesterday? ....
8 How much do you think that dress costs? ....

81 **Fill in: can, can't, couldn't, have to, haven't been able to, should, need to, must or must have.**

Dear Mum and Dad,

Here I am in my new flat. Sorry I 1) ...*haven't been able to/couldn't*... write earlier, but, of course, I was busy moving in and unpacking. Now, I just 2) .... buy curtains and a few rugs to make the flat really homely. When I unpacked, I 3) .... find my toaster anywhere. I 4) .... left it behind in the old flat! I'll come to see you on Sunday 14th. 5) .... I bring my flatmate? If we set off early, we 6) .... arrive in time for lunch. I 7) .... wait to eat your delicious apple pie! Anyway, I 8) .... go now. There's someone at the door. It 9) .... be the plumber; he is going to install the washing machine. See you on Sunday.

Love,
Judy

82 **Fill in: could, shall or would.**

Jill: It's such a beautiful day. **1)** ...*Shall*... we go to the beach?
Mike: Yes, let's go. We **2)** .... all do with a break from studying.
Sue: **3)** .... you mind if Simon came as well?
Mike: Of course not! We **4)** .... ask Patty too.
Sue: Good idea. **5)** .... you like to invite anyone Jill?
Jill: Well, I **6)** .... see if Rachael's free.
Sue: **7)** .... I phone them all up and ask?
Mike: Yes, that's a good idea.

83 **Rewrite the sentences using must, can't or may.**

1 I'm sure she is studying. ....*She must be studying.*.......................
2 I'm sure she studied. ....
3 I don't think she was studying. ....
4 I don't think she met him. ....
5 Perhaps she wants some help. ....
6 Perhaps he has been working in the garden. ....
7 Perhaps he is working in the garden. ....

Oral Activity 4

Make comments and speculations about each picture using modals.

eg. Pic. 1: **She should have been more careful. She must be in terrible pain. She'd better see a doctor. etc**

Writing Activity 3

Read the letter and fill in a correct modal verb or expression. Then look at Clare's notes and write what Clare wrote to Ann. Try to use as many different modals as possible.

Dear Clare,

I'm writing to ask if you 1) ..*could*... give me some advice. I'm a 20-year-old student who 2) .... survive on the money my parents send me. My parents live in a small village. When I succeeded in my exams, I 3) .... move to Leeds to attend university. My parents are over 60 and 4) .... no longer work. I feel like I 5) .... be giving them money to help them instead of getting money from them. On top of that, my sister leaves school next year and she 6) .... want to go to university, too. I feel I 7) .... do something for her as well. There 8) .... be a way. I think I 9) .... try to get a job but I 10) .... think of what I 11) .... do. It 12) .... be a good idea to work evenings so that I can study during the day. You see, I 13) .... attend all my lectures or I 14) .... fail my course. Of course I 15) ....leave university but I don't want to. I 16) .... do something soon but what? Please advise me. What 17) .... I do?

Regards,
Ann Wood

Clare's Notes: don't feel guilty about your situation/find a job as a waitress, baby-sitter etc/do not stop attending university/save money (eg cook your own meals, walk instead of using public transport etc)/apply for money from the Students' Support Fund/think of the future/be able to repay your parents when you've got a permanent job

Dear Ann,

I'm sorry to hear about your problem, but really there are so many things you can do to make your life better. ...

84 Fill in a correct modal verb.

"I simply **1)** ...*must*... have a holiday," said Jean. "I **2)** .... have taken one last year but we were too busy." "I thought you said you **3)** .... afford one this year," Robert said. "I **4)** .... have said that at the time, but I **5)** .... go on like this. I **6)** .... have a nervous breakdown," Jean said. "I agree. I **7)** .... work the hours that you do, no matter how interesting the job **8)** .... be. If I **9)** .... lend you some money, I **10)** ...., but you know I **11)** .... hardly manage on my salary myself. I **12)** .... ask for a rise."

85 Complete the sentences using the words in bold as in the example:

1 I'm sure Jenny didn't crash your car.
   have   Jenny ....*can't have crashed*........................ your car.
2 I'd rather stay in tonight.
   prefer   I'd ....tonight.
3 Tom does not play football as well as he used to.
   used   Tom ....than he does now.
4 It's ages since I last went abroad.
   been   I .... for ages.
5 "You stole my purse, Jill!" said Paula.
   accused   Paula .... her purse.
6 When do schools close for the Easter holidays?
   break   When .... for the Easter holidays?
7 It's your job to look after the cat.
   responsible   You .... after the cat.
8 Ann moved to Madrid after getting her diploma and she's still there.
   been   Ann .... she got her diploma.
9 He said he was sorry he was late.
   apologised   He .... late.
10 Anna's birthday is on 24th November.
   was   Anna .... 24th November.
11 He probably left early last night.
   have   He .... last night.

86 Look at Appendix 2, then fill in the correct particle(s).

Phrasal Verbs

1 I didn't mean to buy so much but I got **carried** ...*away*.....   1 off, on, away, out
2 The police are **carrying** .... an investigation into the   2 over, out, off, through
   cause of Andrew's death.
3 I don't feel well but I'**ll carry** .... working anyway.   3 on, off, away, over
4 Despite the difficulties, we managed to **carry** .... the project.   4 over, away, off, on
5 I **came** .... my old photo album while tidying up.   5 at, by, down, across
6 Good jobs are hard to **come** .... these days.   6 by, into, off, on
7 I feel terrible! I must be **coming** .... the flu.   7 up, down with, out, through
8 When Sally's uncle died, she **came** .... a small fortune.   8 by, up with, to, into
9 The details of the corruption scandal eventually **came** ....   9 in, off, out, round
10 He eventually managed to **come** .... a solution.   10 up to, through, in, up with

87 Look at Appendix 3, then fill in the correct preposition.

1 His **failure** ...*in*... the exam meant he couldn't apply for the job in London.
2 She looks **familiar** .... me. Maybe she's an actress.
3 As he was **familiar** .... Japanese culture, he wrote an article on it.
4 I'm so **fond** .... skiing that I go for a week every winter.
5 London is **famous** .... its black taxis and red buses.
6 He was very **fortunate** .... finding a publisher for his book.
7 Tony was **furious** .... Jane for spending their savings on clothes.
8 Kevin's not very **good** .... football. He'd rather play squash.
9 My grandfather was always **good** .... my grandmother.
10 Paul is a **genius** .... mathematics.
11 I haven't **heard** .... Sarah yet. I hope she will write soon.
12 Everybody has **heard** .... Coca-Cola. You can buy it everywhere.
13 The police say that there is no **hope** .... finding the stolen painting.
14 We're having a picnic on Sunday so we're all **hoping** .... fine weather.

Prepositions

1 at, to, in
2 with, to, for
3 with, to, for
4 at, of, for
5 of, from, for
6 about, in, at
7 to, with, by
8 in, to, at
9 to, at, of
10 at, with, on
11 of, from, by
12 from, for, of
13 in, of, for
14 for, to, at

88 Think of the word which best fits each space. Use only one word in each space.

TEACHING GOOD MANNERS

Today in Britain there is disagreement over how children **(0)** ...*should*... be taught to be polite. Should parents force their children to **(1)** .... "please" and "thank you", for instance? Or are there alternative methods they could use?

Most parents still **(2)** .... that teaching good manners to their children is essential. However, it does seem ironic that the methods **(3)** .... often include bullying, pleading and threats.

On the **(4)** .... hand, there are some schools which have a completely different attitude. Their philosophy is **(5)** .... on the idea that a small child will copy adults. In other **(6)** ...., adults should set a good **(7)** .... and the children will follow. In addition, adults should **(8)** .... more tolerant. Children should not be expected, for instance, to sit perfectly still **(9)** .... they are waiting for food in a restaurant.

The good manners of Britain today date **(10)** .... to the last century when children were considered to be animals **(11)** .... needed to be trained before they could be accepted into adult society. Yet in countries **(12)** .... as Brazil, children can be seen everywhere with adults and their behaviour is nothing to be ashamed **(13)** .... So, perhaps if children in Britain **(14)** .... allowed to be seen more in public, they would be **(15)** .... better behaved.

89 Use the word given in capitals to form a word that fits in the space provided.

WEATHER PREDICTION

Predicting the weather has always been **(0)** ..... to our lives since **(1)** ..... changes can seriously affect crops and therefore the **(2)** ..... of food. Today, forecasters use modern technology in order to increase their **(3)** ..... Knowing what the weather will be like is not only interesting to farmers, it is also relevant to sports enthusiasts such as **(4)** ..... and people who live in **(5)** ..... areas. Despite improvements in forecasting, the weather often remains **(6)** ..... and this has given forecasters a bad reputation. However, the climate is often so **(7)** ..... that even experts with the latest **(8)** ..... find it impossible to make accurate forecasts. Until further **(9)** .... are made in this field, it is likely that forecasters will be **(10)** ..... to be 100% certain of tomorrow's weather.

IMPORTANCE	0	*important*
CLIMATE	1	
PRODUCE	2	
ACCURATE	3	
	4	
SKI	5	
MOUNTAIN	6	
PREDICTABLE	7	
CHANGE	8	
EQUIP	9	
DEVELOP	10	
ABLE		

90 Read the text carefully. Some of the lines are correct and some have a word which should not be there. If a line is correct, put a tick (✔) in the space provided. If a line has a word which should not be there, write it in the space provided.

MY HOBBIES

0	I was never very good at knitting as a girl. It seemed the	0	✓	▭ 0 ▬
00	most boring thing in the world. Despite of my prejudices,	00	of	▭ 00 ▬
1	I went on to an evening class with my friend Ruby, who	1		▭ 1 ▭
2	she was looking for practical ways of expressing her creativity.	2		▭ 2 ▭
3	To having her for inspiration really helped me. Now I love	3		▭ 3 ▭
4	making clothes for my husband and grandchildren.	4		▭ 4 ▭
5	Sometimes I design my own patterns, but if I will see a good	5		▭ 5 ▭
6	one in a shop or magazine, I usually use it. Ruby, on the	6		▭ 6 ▭
7	other hand, always designs her own and has even had won	7		▭ 7 ▭
8	awards. She tells to me her success is thanks to me. Knitting	8		▭ 8 ▭
9	is great fun, but golf it is better. Many people seem to	9		▭ 9 ▭
10	think it is a sport for the rich, but the equipment	10		▭ 10 ▭
11	isn't really all that so expensive and the clubs can last a	11		▭ 11 ▭
12	lifetime. Golf combines with fresh air, skill, relaxation and walking	12		▭ 12 ▭
13	in beautiful countryside. Although it is traditionally a man's	13		▭ 13 ▭
14	hobby, I've become very much good at it. In fact, I'm as good as	14		▭ 14 ▭
15	the most best of the men at the country club.	15		▭ 15 ▭

91 Choose the item which best explains the idioms, then make sentences using them.

1	a storm in a teacup	Ⓐ	a lot of fuss about nothing	B	prediction that sth will happen
2	thick-skinned	A	not easily hurt physically	B	insensitive to criticism
3	a thorn in one's side	A	sth that helps back problems	B	sth that causes trouble/anxiety
4	a pet hate	A	sth one particularly hates	B	a pet one hates
5	all in all	A	extremely tired	B	considering everything
6	a wild goose chase	A	search for sth with no result	B	hunting wild animals
7	above one's head	A	too high to reach	B	too difficult to understand
8	all ears	A	listening eagerly	B	listening without hearing
9	all fingers and thumbs	A	working with one's hands	B	very clumsy
10	all in	A	exhausted	B	lively

92 Put the verbs in brackets into the correct tense.

A Oh no! I 1) ......'ve lost...... (lose) my wallet. 2) .... (you/see) it anywhere? I'm sure I 3) .... (have) it in my pocket when I 4) .... (leave) home today. I can't believe it. It's the third time I 5) .... (lose) my wallet this month.

B George asked me to go to a party with him on Saturday but I 1) .... (can/not) fit into the dress that I wanted to wear. So, I 2) .... (decide) to go on a diet. Tomorrow it 3) .... (be) three days since I 4) .... (start) and I 5) .... (starve). I 6) .... (not/be) on a diet for years and I 7) .... (forget) what a nightmare it is. Yesterday I 8) .... (have) two salads and a jacket potato with no butter. I don't think I 9) .... (last) until Saturday. I'd better go and get some chocolate now and start again tomorrow.

C I 1) .... (walk) down the street the other day when I 2) .... (bump) into an old friend of mine. We 3) .... (be) friends at university but we 4) .... (lose) touch. We 5) .... (talk) for a few minutes when he told me that he 6) .... (work) in computers for the past two years. I could hardly believe it; he 7) .... (do) a drama degree at university and 8) .... (act) in several films when he was younger. It 9) .... (be) funny how things turn out sometimes.

What's your new baby like?

Oh, he's the best baby in the world. He's as good as gold. He's better than any other baby I've seen. I'm a very lucky man.

It's amazing. He looks just like me!

Never mind! As long as he's healthy.

- **Adjectives describe nouns.** *They had a nasty experience. (What kind of experience? A nasty one.)* They can be **factual** *(big, square, red etc)* or **opinion** ones *(beautiful, nice etc).* **Adjectives are the same in singular and plural.** *the little girl/the little girls* **They normally precede nouns.** *He is a good boy.* **After linking verbs: appear, be, become, get, feel, look, seem, smell, sound, stay, taste we use adjectives, not adverbs.** *The soup tastes delicious.(not: deliciously)*

- **Many common adjectives** *(pretty, sad etc)* **do not have particular endings. There are some common endings, however, for adjectives formed from nouns and verbs. These are:**

-able	comfortable	**-ent**	dependent	**-ical**	historical	**-like**	businesslike
-al	accidental	**-esque**	picturesque	**-ious**	victorious	**-ly**	friendly
-ant	reluctant	**-ful**	careful	**-ish**	childish	**-ory**	compulsory
-ar	popular	**-ian**	Italian	**-ist**	racist	**-ous**	dangerous
-ary	imaginary	**-ible**	horrible	**-ive**	attractive	**-some**	wholesome
-ate	passionate	**-ic**	historic	**-less**	careless	**-y**	lucky

- **There are also compound adjectives which are formed with:**
  1 **present participles.** *a time-consuming task, a never-ending story*
  2 **past participles.** *worn-out shoes, a broken-down car*
  3 **cardinal numbers + nouns.** *a two-day seminar (not: a two-days seminar), a three-week holiday*
  4 **prefixes and suffixes.** *tax-free goods, a top secret file, an air-conditioned room*
  5 **well, badly, ill, poorly + past participle.** *a well-paid job, a poorly-paid worker, an ill-chosen remark*

- **Certain adjectives are used with the as nouns to talk about groups of people in general. These are: Age:** *the elderly, the middle aged, the old, the young etc,* **Physical/Health:** *the blind, the dead, the deaf, the disabled, the living, the sick etc,* **Social/Economic:** *the homeless, the hungry, the poor, the rich, the strong, the unemployed, the weak etc. Old people usually walk slowly. The old usually walk slowly. (= old people in general) but: The old people in the building are annoyed with the landlord.* **The old means a group of old people in general. The old people means a specific group of old people. When we talk about one person we say An/The old man, A/The blind man** *etc. The rich man pays a lot of income tax. The rich pay a lot of income tax. (rich people in general - all of them) The rich people of our town have a banquet every Christmas. (a specific group of rich people - not all of them)*

93 Fill in an appropriate adjective derived from the words in brackets.

Kingsley Manor is a **1)** ...*luxurious*... (luxury) residence, situated in the **2)** .... (picture) Kent countryside. It is also of **3)** .... (consider) **4)** .... (history) interest, as it was built in the 17th century. The **5)** .... (beauty) gardens and **6)** .... (style) interior make it a highly **7)** .... (desire) home for a **8)** .... (wealth) businessperson. The **9)** .... (finance) burden of running a place like this is **10)** .... (astronomy), so only those with an enormous bank balance should ask for further information.

94 Fill in: the + adjective or the + adjective + people.

1 The government is cutting back on benefits for ...*the unemployed* ... . (unemployed)
2 The minister's speech offended many of .... in the audience. (unemployed)
3 There are not enough hospital beds to accommodate .... (sick)
4 Some of .... in the hotel remember when it was bombed during the war. (old)
5 A new hostel is to be opened for .... (homeless)
6 .... (rich) threw a party for all .... in the town. (disabled)
7 Mother Theresa works to help .... of Bombay. (poor)
8 The survey showed that .... control 90% of the country's wealth. (rich)
9 There is a shortage of guide dogs for .... (blind)
10 Sign language is usually taught to .... to enable them to communicate. (deaf)

Order of Adjectives

- **Opinion** adjectives (*bad, pretty etc*) **go before** **fact** adjectives (*red, ancient etc*).
  *She's a **pretty Italian** girl.*
- **When there are two or more adjectives of the same category, the more general** adjective **goes before the more specific** one. *a **nice friendly** dog*
- We say **the first three months** (*not:* ~~the three first months~~), **the last two hours** etc.

- **When there are two or more fact adjectives, they normally go in the following order:**

Opinion		Fact Adjectives						
		size	age	shape	colour	origin	material	used for/ be about	noun
It's a	nice	small	old	square	white	Italian	wooden	dinner	table.

- The adjectives **afraid, alike, alive, alone, ashamed, asleep, content, glad, ill** etc are never followed by a noun. *The girl was left **alone**. (not:* ~~the alone girl~~*)*
- The adjectives **chief, elder, eldest, former, indoor, inner, main, only, outdoor, outer, principal, upper** can only be used before nouns. *This is the **main** entrance. (not:* ~~This entrance is main.~~*)*
- We can use **nouns as adjectives** before other nouns. In this case the nouns have no plural form. *I attend **evening classes**. I had a **three-week** holiday in Spain. (not:* ~~a three-weeks holiday~~*)*
- **Nouns** which express **purpose, material** or **substance** (*shopping, cotton, gold, silver, etc*) **can be used as adjectives** before other nouns. *He bought a new **cotton** shirt. I can't find my **shopping** bag. They're having a **stone** wall built.* **But we say: wooden table (not:** ~~wood table~~**), woollen scarf (not:** ~~wool scarf~~**). Note: golden hair (hair like gold) but gold watch (watch made of gold), silk dress (dress made of silk) but silky hair (hair which feels like silk), stone wall (wall made of stone) but stony look (cold look - like stone), feather pillow (pillow stuffed with feathers) but feathery leaves (leaves which look like feathers)**
- **Present** and **past participles** can be used **as adjectives**. Present participles describe what something is like. *The match was **exciting**.* Past participles describe how someone feels. *We felt **excited** at the match.*

95 **Underline the opinion adjectives, circle the fact ones, then put them in order.**

1 a(n) adventure / exciting / action-packed / book ....*an exciting action-packed adventure book*........
2 a(n) sweet / Italian / fresh fruit / dessert ....
3 a delicious / cheese / fresh / sandwich ....
4 a(n) Australian / thin / rugby / tall / player ....
5 a(n) fanatical / old / Liverpool / supporter ....
6 a(n) old-fashioned / lovely / marble / French / fireplace ....
7 a(n) pair of / grey / old / woollen / football / socks ....
8 a talented / jazz / black / musician ....
9 a colourful / cinema / huge / poster ....
10 a(n) old / well-designed / flower / English / garden ....

96 **Underline the correct item.**

When Laura got married she had a **1) silk** / **silky** dress made by one of the best designers and the **2) gold** / **golden** rings she and her fiancé had bought were extremely expensive. The church had beautifully-carved **3) wood** / **wooden** statues, and they had the **4) stone** / **stony** floors covered in expensive red **5) wool** / **woollen** carpets. On the big day she had her **6) silk** / **silky** blond hair styled and she wore a long **7) gold** / **golden** cape over her dress. She rode to the church in a fantastic old **8) metal** / **metallic** blue limousine. When she entered the church, her mother gave her a **9) stone** / **stony** look. Laura looked down and saw that she wasn't carrying her flowers, but a large white **10) feather** / **feathery** duster.

97 **Make compound adjectives to describe the following:**

1 An announcement which has been awaited for a long time. ....*a long-awaited announcement*.......
2 A book which is written badly. ....
3 A city that has no pollution. ....
4 A course that lasts three years. ....
5 A woman who works hard. ....
6 A bus journey that takes two hours. ....
7 A room that has good ventilation. ....
8 A hotel with five stars. ....

98 **Put the adjectives in the correct order.**

Dear Suzie,

   It's a shame you couldn't make it to the wedding, but thank you for the 1) ...*lovely crystal*... *dessert*.. (dessert/crystal/lovely) bowls which you sent us. The wedding was unforgettable and everyone looked beautiful, especially the bridesmaids in their 2) .... (silk/long/cream) dresses. At the reception we had a 3) .... (three-course/home-made/delicious) meal and the best man gave a(n) 4) .... (amusing/nice/short) speech. In the evening, more guests arrived and the hotel provided 5) .... (Irish/live/excellent) music. Before we left, we cut the 6) .... (wedding/white/iced) cake. Hope to see you soon.

Love,
Amanda & Tim

My Grandmother's 90 and she hasn't a grey hair in her head.

That's **extremely** rare.

Well, not **really**, she's as bald as a billiard ball.

- **Adverbs normally describe verbs, adjectives, other adverbs or whole sentences.**
  *She walks **slowly**. (How does she walk? Slowly.) **extremely good, incredibly quickly***
- **They say how (adverbs of manner - *carefully*), where (adverbs of place - *here*), when (adverbs of time - *yesterday*), how much/to what extent (adverbs of degree - *extremely*) or how often (adverbs of frequency - *usually*) something happens. There are also sentence adverbs** (*probably, surely etc*) **and relative adverbs** (*where, why, when*).

Formation of Adverbs from Adjectives

Adverbs are formed from adjectives + -ly. *careful ➡ carefully, serious ➡ seriously*
- **adjectives ending in consonant + -y ➡ -ily.** *cosy ➡ cosily, happy ➡ happily, angry ➡ angrily*
- **adjectives ending in -ic add -ally.** *drastic ➡ drastically, frantic ➡ frantically*
- **adjectives ending in -le drop -le and add -ly.** *horrible ➡ horribly, terrible ➡ terribly*
- **adjectives ending in -e add -ly.** *scarce ➡ scarcely but: whole ➡ wholly, true ➡ truly*
- **adjectives ending in -ly (elderly, fatherly, friendly, lively, lonely, lovely, motherly, silly, ugly etc) form their adverbs with in a(n) ... way/manner.** *in a silly manner, in a friendly way etc.*

Adjectives and Adverbs which have the same form

best, better, big, cheap*, clean*, clear*, close*, cold, daily, dead, dear*, deep, direct, dirty, early, easy, extra, far, fast, fine*, free, further, hard, high, hourly, inside, kindly, last, late, long, loud*, low, monthly, past, quick*, quiet*, right, slow*, straight, sure, thin*, thick, tight, weekly, well, wide, wrong, yearly etc
*Ann was our **last** guest. She came in **last**.* **Those adverbs with an asterisk (*) can be found with -ly ending without a difference in meaning, but then they are more formal.** *Walk slow! (informal) ALSO Walk slowly! (formal)*

Adverbs with two forms and differences in meaning

deep = a long way down	**full** = exactly, very	**late** = not early	**sure** = certainly
deeply = greatly	**fully** = completely	**lately** = recently	**surely** = without doubt
direct = by the shortest route	**hard** = intently; with effort	**near** = close	**wide** = fully; off target
directly = immediately	**hardly** = scarcely	**nearly** = almost	**widely** = to a large extent
easy = gently and slowly	**high** = at / to a high level	**pretty** = fairly	**wrong** = incorrectly
easily = without difficulty	**highly** = very much	**prettily** = in a pretty way	**wrongly** = incorrectly; unjustly
free = without cost	**last** = after all others	**short** = suddenly; off target	
freely = willingly	**lastly** = finally	**shortly** = soon	

- Most of the **-ly forms** can come before an adjective, a past participle or a verb. *I'm **highly aware** of the situation. (not: ~~high~~) He is **fully trained**. (not: ~~full~~) He **easily found** his way. (not: ~~easy~~)*
- **Hardly** means "almost not". *I could **hardly** see in the dark.* **Hardly** can be used with **any / anyone / anything / anywhere / ever**. *There was **hardly any** food left. (= almost no food left). She **hardly ever** goes out of the house. (= She almost never goes out of the house.)*
- **Wrongly** usually goes before verbs or past participles. *You **wrongly accused** him. He was **wrongly accused**. (not: ~~wrong~~)*
  Wrong goes after verbs but **wrongly** is also possible. *You have measured the room **wrong / wrongly**.*

99   Fill in: hard, hardly, hardly ever / anyone / anything.

All that day, I'd been thinking **1)** ...*hard*... to myself about whether or not to go to Jane's party. I **2)** .... go to parties, but this time I thought I'd make an effort. I worked **3)** .... all day so that I could leave early and get ready. When I got home, I looked for something nice to wear, and eventually decided on a red dress that I had **4)** .... worn and **5)** .... had seen me in before. Unfortunately, I got caught in the rain and when I eventually arrived there was **6)** .... left, just a couple of Jane's friends. I had **7)** .... talked to them before so making conversation was very **8)** .... As I had eaten **9)** .... all day, I spent the rest of the party in the kitchen alone!

100   Form adverbs from the following adjectives.

1 dreadful *dreadfully*...	5 wonderful	9 cowardly	13 scarce ....
2 easy	6 comfortable	10 rude	14 logical ....
3 dramatic	7 delicate	11 fantastic	15 happy ....
4 terrible	8 rare	12 free	16 lonely ....

How to form opposites

dis-, un-, in-, il- (before l), **im-** (before m or p), **ir-** (before r), **mal-** are negative prefixes which are used to make opposites of certain adjectives or adverbs. *attractive - **un**attractive*

101   Write the opposites of the following words.

1 honest .....*dishonest*.....	6 logically	11 true ....
2 legally	7 successful	12 capably ....
3 possible	8 polite	13 agreeable ....
4 tolerant	9 responsibly	14 moral ....
5 regularly	10 satisfied	15 gratefully ....

102   Underline the correct item, then explain the difference in meaning.

1 The soldier **near / nearly** died as a result of being hit **full / fully** in the chest by a bullet, which penetrated **deep / deeply** inside him.
2 Simon told everyone he would pass the exam **easy / easily**, so he was **deep / deeply** embarrassed when he came **last / lastly** in the class, with 20%.
3 "I **sure / surely** am happy to meet you," said the reporter to the **high / highly** respected singer. "You're **pretty / prettily** famous around here, you know."
4 When he was almost **full / fully** recovered from his illness the doctor told him to take it **easy / easily** and said that he would be able to return to work **short / shortly**.
5 As he was found **near / nearly** the scene of the murder with a knife in his hand, it is **hard / hardly** surprising that he was **wrong / wrongly** accused.
6 **Sure / Surely** you can't have answered every question **wrong / wrongly**.
7 Rob was a very poor archer. His first arrow fell **short / shortly** of the target, his second flew about 10 metres **wide / widely** and the third flew **high / highly** into the air and landed behind him.

8 Although he arrived an hour **late / lately**, he started work **direct / directly** and tried **hard / hardly** to make up for lost time.

9 **Lately / Late** she has been getting all her clothes **freely / free** from the fashion company, so I can't understand why she doesn't dress more **prettily / pretty**.

10 It is **wide / widely** believed that there is a bus that goes **direct / directly** from here to the airport, but it's not true.

11 **Last / Lastly**, I would like to say that I would **free / freely** give my life for the cause of world peace.

Word Order of Adverbs

● Adverbs can be used in front, mid or end position in a sentence. **Front position** is at the beginning of the sentence. **Mid position** is normally before the main verb or after the auxiliary. **End position** is at the end of the sentence.

Front	Mid	End
Obviously they will **never** see her **again.**		

● Adverbs of manner can come in front, mid or end position. *He answered the questions in the test **easily**. He **easily** answered the questions in the test. **Easily**, he answered the questions in the test. (only to give emphasis)*

● When there is more than one adverb in the sentence, their usual order is manner - place - time.

subject	verb	(object)	manner	place	time
He	*watched*	*TV*	***quietly***	***in his room***	***until 6.00.***

● When there is a verb of movement in the sentence the order is place - manner - time.

subject	verb	place	manner	time
Ann	*was rushed*	***to hospital***	***suddenly***	***an hour ago.***

● Time adverbs go in end position. They also go in front position to emphasise the time.

subject + verb	place	manner	time	time	subject + verb	place	manner
She goes	***to the gym***	***on foot***	***every day.***	***Every day***	*she goes*	***to the gym***	***on foot.***

● When there is more than one time adverb, we usually put the more specific before the more general ones (**time - day - date - year**). *He died at 22.15 on Tuesday March 17th, 1958.*

● **Adverbs of frequency** (**often, seldom, never, ever, usually, normally, scarcely, rarely, always** etc) come after the auxiliary verb but before the main verb. In short answers, we put them before the auxiliary, though. *"She **never** comes to work on time. She's **often** late." "Yes, she **always** is."*

● **Adverbs of degree** (**absolutely, completely, just, totally, extremely, quite, seriously, very** etc) go before the adjective or the adverb they describe. *He's **absolutely** hopeless at Maths.* **When these adverbs describe verbs, they go before a main verb or after an auxiliary verb.** *We **quite** enjoyed the film. I've **quite** finished.*

● **Absolutely, completely** and **totally** can go in mid or end position. *He **completely** forgot our appointment. or He forgot our appointment **completely**.* **A lot, much, a little, a bit, awfully, terribly** can go in mid position (before adjectives) or end position (when they describe verbs). *I'm **terribly** sorry. My tooth hurts **terribly**.*

● **Already, no longer, hardly, nearly, almost, still** go in mid position. *He **nearly** knocked the old lady down, as he could **hardly** see her in the dark.*

● **Sentence adverbs** (**probably, certainly, possibly, perhaps, maybe, clearly, luckily** etc) go in any position: front, mid or end; the front position is the most usual, though. ***Luckily**, he didn't crash into the tree. He **luckily** didn't crash into the tree. He didn't crash into the tree, **luckily**.* In negations **certainly, possibly** and **probably** usually go before the auxiliary or between two auxiliaries. *He **certainly** didn't do it. He **couldn't possibly** have done it.*

● We use **adverbs after action verbs** and **adjectives after linking verbs**: appear, be, become, get, feel, look, seem, smell, stay, taste. *It tastes **bad**. (not: badly). She looked **happy** at the party.* (**Looked** means "appeared" here and is a linking verb.) *She looked **happily** at the children.* (**Looked** is an action verb here, not a linking verb, and "happily" describes the action.)

103 **Put the adverbs in the right position.**

1 She has lived in England. (in a small village / luxuriously / all her life / in a large house)
   ...*She has lived luxuriously all her life in a large house in a small village in England.*......................

2 Train services have been affected. (already / by the heavy snow / seriously)
   ....

3 Susan can predict what will happen. (in the future / often / accurately)
   ....

4 John read my essay and changed everything I had written. (incorrectly / kindly / virtually / carefully / very)
   ....

5 The wind is blowing. (hard / still / today / extremely / outside)
   ....

6 We will be travelling. (around Australia / this summer / definitely)
   ....

7 Ted is polite, but he was rude to Jenny. (extremely / surprisingly / normally / last night)
   ....

8 I'm certain you'll be happy with the service. (in this hotel / very / absolutely)
   ....

9 Prices of produced vegetables have risen. (dramatically / freshly / recently)
   ....

10 The injured victims of the terrorist attack were taken to hospital. (quickly / seriously / fortunately)
   ....

104 **Rewrite the text putting the adverbs in brackets into their correct place in each sentence.**

When Paul opened his restaurant, he was inexperienced and found it was much more complicated than he had expected (two years ago/totally/soon). Although the restaurant was situated in a good area, he had forgotten an important thing: advertising (conveniently/completely/vitally). It was three months before he realised his mistake and he had run out of money by then (unfortunately/finally/nearly.) He sent a letter to his brother asking him to send some money (quickly/by first class post/as soon as possible). The money arrived and Paul put an advert in the local paper (the next day/immediately/on the front page). His restaurant became one of the most popular and he is planning to open another (within weeks/in town/in the near future).

105 **Make positive adjectives and adverbs from the following words:**

1	base	*..basic-basically...*	8	fun	....	15 fool ....
2	beauty	....	9	luck	....	16 day ....
3	accident	....	10	care	....	17 critic ....
4	brother	....	11	remark	....	18 society ....
5	hesitate	....	12	anger	....	19 progress ....
6	produce	....	13	romance	....	20 rely ....
7	curiosity	....	14	courage	....	21 forget ....

106 **Say what type of adverb each word in bold is.**

I will **1) never** forget my first job teaching at this university. The students were **2) very** noisy and they refused to listen to me. So, on the first day I shouted **3) angrily** at them. I could **4) hardly** believe that they were over 18 years old. I **5) soon** began to dread going into the class. I was **6) once** ill with fear. **7) Then** they **8) completely** changed. I couldn't believe it. They told me that they were **9) really** sorry for behaving **10) so 11) badly**. I began to enjoy teaching them and I will **12) certainly** be staying **13) here** for a few more years.

107 ▶ **Rewrite the text correcting the mistakes.**

Last June my friend and I were looking forward to a three-weeks holiday. We had chosen carefully our holiday and had spent hours looking through the travel brochures. Eventually we had decided on a modern luxurious four-stars hotel nearly a golden long beach. From the brochure it looked like a hotel for the rich people and famous. Then, before we knew it, it was time to leave. The journey went smooth, but as soon as we arrived at the hotel, I sensed that something was wrongly. The entrance looked dark and old-fashioned and there were hardly no other guests to be seen. High disappointed, we decided to go to the beach to relax. After a two-hours walk, we finally found a horrible small stone beach. There was not hardly anyone there - just an old man sitting on a rock. We were afraid to lie down because the beach was dirty extreme, so we went back to the hotel to prepare for dinner. Yet again, we were disappointed. The food tasted awfully, we were waited on by unsmiled, stone-faced waiters and we ate hardly nothing. For the next three weeks, all we could think about was going home. Well, we are back home now and still are waiting for an apology from the travel company. We yet haven't decided whether we will ever go abroad again, but one thing I can say for certain - we won't be visiting probably that place again.

108 ▶ **Put the word in brackets into its adjectival or adverbial form.**

Win the holiday of a lifetime with Skytours Travel! A two-month world tour of the most **1)** ...*expensive*... (expense), **2)** .... (luxury) hotels on earth could be yours. Relax in the **3)** .... (comfort) surroundings of the Paris Ritz, enjoy the glamour of the **4)** .... (style) furnished Sheraton of Bangkok and mix with the **5)** .... (fashion) guests of The Chelsea in New York. You will be flown from city to city, accommodated **6)** .... (space) in Executive Class and waited upon **7)** .... (elegance) by **8)** .... (help) flight attendants. How can you win this **9)** .... (thrill) prize? Simply complete the following sentence: *"Skytours is best because ..."*. The prize will be awarded for the most **10)** .... (origin) idea. Feeling **11)** .... (inspire)?

109 ▶ **Rewrite the letter and put the adverbs below in the correct position.**

for a long time, extremely, frequently, nowadays, too long, often, soon, very hard, at the office, probably, for three months, terribly, quickly, quite

Dear Kate,

I know I haven't written to you. I was sorry to hear about your accident. Accidents like that happen. I hope you won't have to stay in hospital and that your friends are able to visit you. I'm going to send you a present. I've been working lately. Paul will be working in France. I know I'll miss him. I hope you get better as I'd like to come and stay with you.

All my love,
Betty

Dear Kate,
I know I haven't written to you for a long time ...

Doctor, I have a **big** problem. I have three **expensive** cars. My children go to **the best** schools. My wife buys **the most expensive** clothes. Generally, we live **better than** royalty.

So what exactly is the problem?

I only earn £50 a week.

Regular Comparative and Superlative Forms

Adjectives	Positive	Comparative	Superlative
of one syllable add -(e)r/-(e)st to form their comparative and superlative forms	cold big safe	cold**er** (than) bigg**er** (than) safe**r** (than)	**the** cold**est** (of/in) **the** bigg**est** (of/in) **the** safe**st** (of/in)
of two syllables ending in -ly, -y, -w also add -er/-est	busy shallow	bus**ier** (than) shallow**er** (than)	**the** bus**iest** (of/in) **the** shallow**est** (of/in)
of two or more syllables take more/most	famous incredible	**more** famous (than) **more** incredible (than)	**the most** famous (of/in) **the most** incredible (of/in)

● We use the **comparative** to compare **one person** or **thing** with **another**. *Sally is **prettier than** Pam.This house is **more expensive than** the others. (We consider the others as a group.)*
● We use the **superlative** to compare **one person** or **thing** with **more than one** of the same group. *She's **the fastest** typist of all.*
● We often use **than** after a comparative. *He's shorter **than** you.* We normally use **the** before a superlative. We often use **of** or **in** after a superlative. We use **in** with places. *I'm **the tallest of** all. He's **the shortest in** his class.* Note: old - older - oldest. *He's **older** than me. (not: elder; elder isn't used with than)* **old - elder - eldest**. *My **eldest** sister is a lawyer. (We use elder - eldest to talk about relatives only.)*
● We can use **the** before a comparative when we compare only two things of the same kind. *Of the two cars this is **(the) faster**. (formal).* However, it is possible to use the superlative instead of the comparative when we compare two persons or things. *Which is **(the) fastest**, a Jaguar or a Fiat? (more usual)*
● Certain adjectives form their comparative and superlative in both ways, either by adding **-er/-est** to the positive form or by taking **more/most**. Some of these are: **clever, common, cruel, friendly, gentle, narrow, pleasant, polite, shallow, simple, stupid, quiet**. *simple - simpler - simplest* **ALSO** *simple - more simple - the most simple*

110 **Fill in the blanks as in the example:**

The **1)** *...most interesting of...* (interesting) all the cities I have ever visited was New York. It was **2)** .... (good) place I have ever been to. The buildings are **3)** .... (tall) those in any other city and the streets are **4)** .... (busy) streets .... the world, full of traffic and people all day. **5)** .... (exciting) thing .... all was the sightseeing. I saw some of **6)** .... (amazing) places. The only thing that spoilt my stay was the weather. While I was in New York, the city had one of **7)** .... (cold) winters on record and **8)** .... (bad) snowstorm in years.

Adverbs	Positive	Comparative	Superlative
adverbs having the same forms as their adjectives add **-er/-est**	long	long**er**	(the) long**est**
"early" drops **-y** and adds **-ier/-iest**	early	earl**ier**	(the) earl**iest**
two syllable or compound adverbs take **more/most** (Compound adverbs are adjectives + **-ly**. *careful - **carefully***)	often quietly patiently	**more** often **more** quietly **more** patiently	(the) **most** often (the) **most** quietly (the) **most** patiently

● **For further details on spelling rules see page 238.**

Irregular Forms

Positive	Comparative	Superlative
good / well	better	best
bad / badly	worse	worst
much	more	most
many / a lot of	more	most
little	less	least
far	farther	farthest
far	further	furthest

Well is the adverb of good. *She is a good cook. She cooks **well**.*

a) **further/farther (adv) = longer (in distance)**
   *His office is **further/farther** away than mine.*
   further (adj) = more
   *For **further** information contact Mr Smith.*
b) **very + positive degree** *It's **very** hot weather.*
c) **even/much/far/a bit + comparative degree**
   *He behaves **even worse** than before. Jenny is **much more patient** with children than Julie.*
d) **most + adj/adv of positive degree = very**
   *She was **most** obliging. (She was **very** obliging.)*
e) **any + comparative** (used in negatives and questions)
   *This essay wasn't **any better** than the previous one.*

---

111 Underline the correct item.

It is **very/far** more expensive to live in London than any other city in Britain. Rents are **much/very** higher and it is **most/far** difficult to find accommodation of any kind. Trying to find a flat in a convenient location is **even/very** more frustrating. You can live in the suburbs, but it will take you **much/any** longer to get to work and the fares are **very/far** high. Wages are normally **a bit/very** higher in London, but that doesn't mean you will have **many/much** more money to spend, since the cost of living there is **most/even** higher than you would expect.

112 Fill in with adverbs in their comparative or superlative forms.

When Mary arrived home that evening, two hours **1)** *...later than...* (late) usual, she found the children playing much **2)** .... (quiet) normally. She was used to her kids behaving much **3)** .... (noisy) this. Dennis, the youngest, and the one who usually acted **4)** .... (naughty), was behaving **5)** .... (good) she had ever seen him do before. Susan, the eldest, who usually stayed up **6)** .... (late) all her brothers and sisters, had gone to bed **7)** .... (early) usual and the rest of the children were peacefully watching the TV. It is true that her children are quite strange, but this was **8)** .... (odd) she had ever seen them acting. It was when she entered the kitchen that she realised why.

113 **Fill in the blanks as in the example:**

Two weeks ago, I went into town to buy a birthday present for my **1)** ...*eldest*... (old) sister. You couldn't meet a **2)** .... (wonderful) person .... her. She is one of **3)** .... (charming) and **4)** .... (funny) women I know. She is also **5)** .... (generous)-hearted person I've ever met. **6)** .... (bad) thing is that she has a **7)** .... (quick) temper .... me. Mother says she could also be a bit **8)** .... (tidy) .... she is. Anyway, the present I wanted to buy her had to be **9)** .... (good) I could afford. Eventually, I came across **10)** .... (beautiful) scarf I had ever seen. It was **11)** .... (long) .... the one she already had and much **12)** .... (colourful). Imagine my disappointment when I discovered the next day that Mother had bought her exactly the same scarf.

114 **Fill in the blanks as in the example:**

What was life like when I was a boy? Well, I think it was **1)** ...*better*.. (good) ..*than*... life now. It was **2)**............. .... (good) time .... my life. When I was **3)** .... (young), people were **4)**.......................... (happy) and **5)** .... (polite) .... they are now. Also, things were **6)** .... (cheap) and money lasted a lot **7)** .... (long) .... nowadays. Some say that life is **8)** .... (exciting) nowadays. It's true that you can travel **9)** .... (far) and **10)** .... (fast) .... when I was a boy and there is a lot **11)** .... (much) choice of entertainment. But, on the whole, I think life is much **12)** .... (bad) nowadays.

115 **Fill in the blanks as in the example:**

New Cross Memorial is **1)** ...*the busiest*... (busy) hospital ...*in*... New York. It has **2)** .... (new) medical equipment and **3)** .... (fast) ambulances .... the city. Its waiting lists are **4)** .... (short) .... other hospitals' and many people say the medical staff are **5)** .... (caring) .... America. Jane works in the children's ward. Her work is **6)** .... (hard) .... some of her colleagues' because she is **7)** .... (qualify) nurse on the ward. Despite this, she thinks she has **8)** .... (good) job .... the hospital. Her hours are **9)** .... (bad) .... her friends' but the rewards are **10)** .... (great) .... theirs.

116 **Put the comparative or superlative form of the adjectives in brackets.**

The sinking of the Titanic is one of **1)** ...*the most famous*... (famous) shipwreck stories ...*of*... all time. The Titanic was said to be **2)** .... (safe) ocean liner .... the world. When it set sail, all the cabins were full, from **3)** .... (expensive) to **4)** .... (cheap) ones on the lower deck. Some of **5)** .... (rich) people .... the world set sail for America on one of **6)** .... (long) and **7)** .... (dangerous) crossings attempted by such a liner. The captain was one of **8)** .... (good), but he made a big mistake which caused hundreds of deaths. As they sailed on, the going became **9)** .... (difficult). Suddenly the captain saw an iceberg ahead but, by then, it was too late to do anything. They sailed **10)**............................. (close) until finally they hit it. Everyone rushed to the lifeboats. Some survived but many died. The survivors said it was **11)** .... (frightening) experience .... their lives and they felt like **12)** .... (lucky) people on earth to have survived.

Quite · Fairly · Rather · Pretty

- **Quite** means "fairly", "to some degree". It is used in **favourable comments**. *He's **quite** clever.*
  Quite also means **completely**. It is used with adverbs, verbs and certain adjectives such as:
  alone, amazing, brilliant, certain, dead, dreadful, different, exhausted, extraordinary, false, good,
  horrible, impossible, perfect, ridiculous, right, sure, true, useless etc. *She's **quite** exhausted.*
  *(completely exhausted). She dances **quite** brilliantly. I don't **quite** agree with you.*
- **Rather** is used in **unfavourable comments**. *It's **rather** cold today.* It is also used in **favourable
  comments** when it means "to an unusual degree". *The film was **rather** interesting. (It was more
  interesting than we expected.)* **Rather** is also used with **comparative degree**. *It's **rather** warmer
  today than yesterday. (not: it's quite warmer ...)*
- **Fairly** and **pretty** are synonymous with **quite** and **rather**. **Quite** is used before **a/an**. *She's **quite** a
  good teacher.* **Rather** is used before or after **a/an**. *It was **a rather** hot day. It was **rather a** hot day.*
  Fairly and **pretty** are used after **a**. *She's **a fairly/pretty** good teacher.*

117 Fill in: quite or rather.

A: I found that book a **1)** ...*rather*... boring one.
B: Oh really? I thought it had **2)** .... a good plot.
A: Oh come on! The ending was **3)** .... improbable,
   don't you think?
B: No, not at all. In fact, I think the whole book was **4)** ....
   perfect.
A: Well, if you ask me, you've got **5)** .... strange
   taste in books.

118 Fill in: quite, rather, pretty or fairly.

I took my dog Spot for a walk even though it was
1) ...*rather*... cold outside. He's **2)** .... a
lively dog and he likes going for a run **3)** ....
often. The park was **4)** .... full considering
the bad weather, but it's a **5)** .... big park
and we had **6)** .... enough space.
Suddenly the dog ran off and I had to chase him for
7) .... a long time. I'm a **8)** ....
good runner, but he'd gone **9)** .... a long way
and, when I eventually caught him, I was **10)** ....
exhausted!

Adverbs of Degree

	very (+++)	rather (++)	a little (+)
with adjectives, adverbs or verbs	just, absolutely, totally, awfully, terribly, really, simply *I'm **terribly** sorry, sir.*	quite, rather *It's **quite/rather** late. We'd better go.*	a little, a bit *Can you wait **a little/ a bit**?*
with adjectives or adverbs	very, extremely *She's **very** rude and behaves **extremely** impolitely.*	pretty, fairly *I'm **pretty/fairly** sure he's lying.*	slightly *She's **slightly** fat.*
with verbs or comparative form	very much, a lot *I **very much** appreciate your help. I feel **a lot** better now.*	rather *It's **rather** warmer today.*	not ... much *He **isn't much** taller than me.*

119 Fill in one of the degree adverbs from the table on page 60.

I'm 1) ...*extremely*... (+++) sorry sir, but the manager is 2) .... (+++) busy at the moment.
He has 3) .... (+++) of customers to attend to. I would 4) .... (+++)
appreciate it if you could just sit here and wait 5) .... (+). I'm 6) .... (++)
sure he'll be available soon. Don't worry, you won't have to wait 7) .... (+) longer.

Types of Comparisons

• **as ... (positive degree) ... as** **not so/as ... (positive degree) ... as** **such a(n)/so ... as**	His hands were **as cold as** ice. It is **not so/as** cold **as** it was yesterday. This is **not such an** interesting book **as** his last one.
• **twice/three times etc/half as ... (positive degree) ... as**	Their house is **twice as big as** ours. His car cost **half as much as** mine.
• **the same as**	Your jacket is **the same as** the one I bought last month.
• **look, sound, smell, taste + like**	She **looks like** an angel.
• **less ... (positive degree) ... than** **the least ... (positive degree) ... of/in**	The green sofa is **less expensive than** the black one, but the blue one is **the least expensive of** all.
• **the + comparative ..., the + comparative**	**The sooner** you start, **the sooner** you'll finish. **The richer** you are, the **more** "friends" you have.
• **comparative + and + comparative**	Life is getting **harder and harder**.
• **prefer + -ing form or noun + to + -ing form or noun** (general preference)	I **prefer watching** TV **to going** out. I **prefer** lemonade **to** cola.
• **would prefer + to-inf + rather than + inf without to** (specific preference)	I **would prefer to eat** in **rather than go** to a restaurant. He **would prefer to leave rather than accept** a pay cut.
• **would rather/sooner + inf without to + than + inf without to**	I'**d rather** look for a new flat **than stay** in this house any longer.
• **clause + whereas/while + clause** (comparison by contrast)	Tom likes living in the country **whereas** his sister likes living in the city.

120 Fill in the blanks as in the example:

Three of my 1) ...*best*... (good) friends - Catherine, Beatrice and Anne - are triplets, although if you met them, you would not even think they were related. Beatrice, who is 2) .... (old) looks nothing 3) .... her sisters. She Is 4) .... (tall) 5) .... both Anne and Catherine and slightly 6) .... (thin). Her hair is 7) .... black .... coal whereas her sisters have much 8) .... (light) hair. They also have very different personalities. Catherine is probably 9) .... (loud) 10) .... the three and 11) .... (funny). Anne and Beatrice are 12) .... (quiet) and 13) .... (sensitive) 14) .... their sister, but they are all equally friendly. I think they are 15) .... (nice) triplets 16) .... the world.

121 Fill in: as, so...as, different from, whereas, more, than, like or same.

This year the Jones family decided not to go to the **1)** ...*same*... holiday destination **2)** .... last year. Their hotel, the Hotel Astoria, was **3)** .... expensive **4)** .... the last one, the Pueblo, but they didn't mind because the Astoria was exactly **5)** .... the brochure said; luxurious, with a breathtaking view. It was completely **6)** .... the Pueblo. It looked just **7)** .... a palace, **8)** .... the Pueblo resembled a prison. Furthermore, the owners of the Pueblo were not **9)** .... hospitable **10)** .... those of the Astoria.

122 Fill in: not as...as, the more...the more, would rather, prefer...to, as...as, the least...of, whereas, such...as, the same...as, more...than, the most...of, faster and faster or twice as much...as.

Dear Customer,

I'd like to tell you about three different cars: the BMW (£20,000), the Volvo (£15,000) and the Mini (£11,000). Cars today are gettting **1)** ...*faster and faster*... and the new BMW can reach speeds of up to 200 mph. The BMW is **2)** .... expensive .... the three, but as you know, **3)** .... you pay, ... you get. It comes with a fitted car stereo and air-conditioning. However, using almost twice **4)** .... petrol .... the Mini, it is **5)** .... economical .... the three. The Mini offers value for money, **6)** .... the BMW offers speed and comfort. If you are looking for a small, economical car, the Mini is **7)** .... good a bargain .... you will find anywhere. Because of its small size it is not **8)** .... a comfortable car .... the BMW, but it is the best car available for those who **9)** .... simplicity .... luxury. Finally, the Volvo is the best value for those who **10)** .... buy a family car. Seating up to six passengers comfortably, it is much **11)** .... spacious .... the other two cars and it is **12)** .... expensive .... the BMW. It is quite fast too, reaching speeds of up to 190 mph - nearly **13)** .... speed .... the BMW! Why don't you come down to the showroom and have a look for yourself?

Yours faithfully,
John Scarles

123 Fill in with: the sooner...the sooner, like, less...than, would prefer...rather than, three times as...as, such a.

When Trevor saw his neighbours' new car, he decided that he had to have one just **1)** ...*like*... theirs. He had never seen **2)** .... beautiful machine. "**3)** .... I get down to the car showroom, ... I'll have a car like theirs," he thought. But when he got there, it turned out the car was **4)** .... expensive .... he had expected. "Haven't you got anything a little **5)** .... expensive .... that?" he asked the salesman. "Perhaps sir, you **6)** .... to invest in a small motorcycle **7)** .... such an ... erm ... exclusive vehicle," he replied.

124 Fill in: further, furthest, better, best, worse and worst.

A: We've been driving for hours! The weather is getting **1)** ...*worse*... . How much **2)** .... is it?
B: I'm not sure, but according to the map, this is the **3)** .... route to take.
A: Give me the map, please. I'll find a **4)** .... way to get there. Why did Dave choose the **5)** .... restaurant out of town to go to on such a rainy night?
B: I don't know. I think it's also one of the **6)** .... places to eat.
A: Well, at this rate we're never going to get there!!

125 Fill in the blanks as in the example:

1 At the restaurant, the conversations got ...*louder and louder*... as the night went on. (loud)
2 Clothes seem to be getting .... all the time. (expensive)
3 The plane flew .... into the sky. (high)
4 Pets are very popular now and .... people enjoy looking after animals. (many)

126 Fill in the blanks as in the example:

1 ...*The longer*... (long) I had to queue at the bank, ...*the more impatient* ...(impatient) I became.
2 .... (much) the child cried, ... (angry) the mother became.
3 .... (small) a flat is, ... (low) the rent is.
4 .... (fast) you drive, ... (quick) we'll get there.

127 Fill in: more, most, less and least.

A: This new energy-saving washing machine is the **1)** ...*most*... economical model on the market.
B: Is that because it uses **2)** .... electricity than the others?
A: Yes. It uses the **3)** .... energy and saves you money.
B: That's great. It also seems to have **4)** .... functions than my old one. I'll take it!

128 Look at the pictures then make comparisons using the adjectives given.

 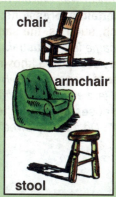  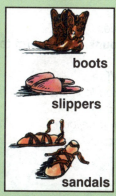 

| dangerous, dirty, well-paid, exciting, interesting | big, soft, hard, uncomfortable, expensive | economical, healthy, fast, clean, safe, spacious | comfortable, warm, heavy, light, expensive | fat, big, small, heavy, handsome, long, short |

eg. A miner's job is more dangerous than a fireman's job. etc

129 Read the following information about the two applicants, then make comparisons using: young, old, heavy, tall, short, well-qualified, experienced, few.

Ted Rogers	
Date of Birth:	23/11/67
Height:	187 cm
Weight:	75 kilos
Children:	3
Teaching experience:	4 years
Qualifications:	4 'A' levels, BA English, MA Computer Science

Simon Baker	
Date of Birth:	17/2/64
Height:	167 cm
Weight:	83 kilos
Children:	2
Teaching experience:	2 years
Qualifications:	2 'A' levels, BSc Computer Science

eg. Ted Rogers is younger than Simon Baker. Simon Baker isn't as old as Ted Rogers. **etc**

Tom's wife is just **like** the Mona Lisa.

No, I mean she ought to be in a museum.

Do you mean she's **as beautiful as** that?

Like is used

- **for similarities.** *She's just **like** a big baby.* *(She is not a baby though.)*
- **after: feel, look, smell, sound + noun.** *It sounds **like** jazz.* *He looks **like** Charles.*
- **with nouns, pronouns or -ing form to express similarity.** *This tastes **like** coffee.* *Is that your Dad? You look **like** him.* *(not: You look as him.)* *It was **like flying** in a balloon.*

As is used

- **to say what sb or sth really is (jobs or roles).** *She works **as** a pilot. (She's a pilot.)* *Liz Taylor was brilliant **as** Cleopatra.*
- **in certain expressions: as usual, as...as, as much, such as, the same as.** *He came late **as usual**.*
- **after: accept, be known, class, describe, refer to, regard, use.** *He's **regarded as** the best jazz singer of all time.*
- **in clauses of manner to mean "in the way that".** *Do it **as** I showed you.*

---

130 Fill in: as or like.

Mary: What do you want to do when you grow up, Fred?
Fred: I'd like to work **1)** ...*as*... a chef in a big hotel.
Mary: Oh no! I've worked in a kitchen before. It's **2)** .... working in an oven.
Fred: At least it wouldn't be **3)** .... boring **4)** .... working in a bank.
Mary: Don't you want to be something more interesting, such **5)** .... a lawyer, or a doctor?
Fred: No, I'd prefer to do something creative **6)** .... cooking. I could never see myself **7)** .... a lawyer or a doctor.
Mary: You're just **8)** .... my brother. He's always saying things **9)** .... that.

131 Fill in: as or like.

Mr Brown works **1)** ...*as*... a gardener. Although he regards his job **2)** .... interesting, he works **3)** .... a slave and gets so dirty that he looks more **4)** .... a miner at the end of the day. He doesn't earn **5)** .... much money **6)** .... his wife, because she works **7)** .... a teacher. Her job sounds **8)** .... fun, but, although she doesn't work **9)** .... hard **10)** .... her husband, she has just **11)** .... many problems. Sometimes she feels **12)** .... screaming because the children are naughty.

In Other Words

- I've never seen such a boring film.
  It's the most boring film I've ever seen.
- If you work more, you'll be paid more.
  The more you work, the more you'll be paid.
- She is taller than her brother.
  Her brother isn't as tall as her/she is.
- That table is similar to this one.
  That table and this table are alike.
- She's the quickest typist of all.
  No other typist is as quick as she is/her.
  She's quicker than any other typist.

- He's a terrible driver.
  He drives terribly.
- Tim has got the same number of books as Tom.
  Tom has as many books as Tim.
- This car is much more expensive than that one.
  This car is far/a lot more expensive than that one.
  That car is much/far less expensive than this one.
- Ann is very friendly to everyone.
  Ann behaves in a friendly way to everyone.
- He hasn't made as many mistakes as last time.
  He has made fewer mistakes than last time.

132 **Using the word given and other words complete the sentences so that the second sentence has a similar meaning to the first sentence. You must use between two and five words. Make sure you don't change the word given.**

1 No other gymnast is as graceful as she is.
 most She is ...*the most graceful*... gymnast of all.
2 I've never heard such a ridiculous statement.
 the That is .... I've ever heard.
3 "She cooks well," Ann said.
 good "She ....," Ann said.
4 If you try harder, you'll do better.
 the The .... you'll do.
5 She is always motherly towards her children.
 way She always .... towards her children.
6 Our house and theirs are alike.
 similar Our house .... theirs.
7 She is the best singer of all.
 good No other singer .... is.
8 Don't buy as much cheese as the last time.
 less Buy .... the last time.
9 He is noisier than his brothers.
 noisy His brothers are .... is.
10 This ring is much more valuable than that one.
 far That ring is .... this one.
11 He is the best teacher in the school.
 good No one else in the school is .... he is.
12 My car is not so fast as his.
 much His car .... mine.
13 Bob isn't such a nuisance as Ted.
 more Ted is .... Bob.
14 Ann is the best singer of all.
 better Ann .... else.
15 French isn't such a difficult language as Chinese.
 more Chinese is .... French.
16 Sue is more patient than Emily.
 as Emily isn't .... is.
17 Sally dresses more smartly than Pam.
 less Pam dresses .... Sally.
18 They arrived later than we expected.
 as They didn't arrive .... expected.

19 Paul thinks in a more profound way than Steve.

than Steve thinks .... Paul.

20 He is less aggressive than Jim.

as He is .... Jim.

Oral Activity 5

Bert Hard has fired his secretary Molly Bloomer and hired another one, Ann Stevens. Using the following adjectives and adverbs and their opposites say a) why he sacked Molly and b) why he hired Ann: patient/badly, lazy/carelessly, miserable/untidily, rude/too much, late/responsibly, bad-tempered/slowly

eg. *He fired Molly because she's impatient and behaves badly.* etc
He hired Ann because she's patient and behaves well. etc

Oral Activity 6

Look at the following advertisements and make comparisons using adjectives and adverbs from the list: few, effective, noisy, easy, durable, many, good, cheap, light, powerful, adaptable, big, heavy

Premium Super Vacuum

- £140 - best price on the market!
- can use it even when the baby is asleep
- small enough to store anywhere
- a set of six accessories
- tough metal casing
- weighs 15 kg
- 80 watts
- sweeps up everything, even broken glass

Conqueror 2000S

- £100 - unbeatable price!
- distinctive sound - warning you it's on
- can fit into most cupboards
- a set of ten accessories
- light-weight plastic casing
- weighs 12 kg
- 60 watts
- sweeps up dust and litter

Wonder - Vac GH

- £80 - can't miss out on this one!
- special noise-reduction button to minimize noise
- can be kept in your toolshed
- a set of eight accessories
- fibreglass casing
- weighs 14 kg
- 40 watts
- sweeps up dust in seconds

eg. **The Premium Super Vacuum has fewer accessories than the other two models.** etc

Writing Activity 4

Your friend Sarah wants to buy a vacuum cleaner. Look at the three advertisements above, then write a letter advising her which vacuum cleaner to buy using comparisons.

Dear Sarah,

I've just come back from the shops. I was able to find some brochures about vacuum cleaners and I have picked out three of them for you to choose from. To begin with, the Premium Super Vacuum is the most powerful model but it is also the most expensive of the three ......

English in use 4

133 **Complete the sentences using the words in bold.**

1 Can't you come up with a more original idea?
   most   Is ...*this the most original idea*... you can come up with?
2 It wasn't necessary for the watchman to leave all the lights on, but he did.
   left   The watchman .... all the lights on.
3 It is too cold for us to have an outdoor party.
   enough   It .... for us to have an outdoor party.
4 It's possible we'll stay another night.
   might   We .... another night.
5 He made a promise never to betray his friends.
   word   He .... to betray his friends.
6 It seems they have finished the report.
   have   They .... the report.
7 Fiona wishes she hadn't lent him all her savings.
   lending Fiona .... all her savings.
8 She attended a course which lasted three years.
   year   She attended .... course.
9 They began organising the advertising company six months ago.
   been   They .... advertising company for six months.
10 He is on friendly terms with his neighbours.
   gets   He .... his neighbours.

134 **Look at Appendix 3, then fill in the correct preposition.**

1 My grandmother takes great **delight** ...*in*... cooking.
2 David was **delighted** .... the tape he bought.
3 My grandfather **died** .... cancer.
4 Gary was driving too fast and **died** .... a car accident.
5 This holiday was **different** .... all the others.
6 There is a big **difference** .... English and Greek food.
7 Last night I **dreamt** .... my favourite pop star.
8 I can only **dream** .... owning a larger car.
9 He is an **expert** .... repairing cars and knows everything about them.
10 Mr Parrs is an **expert** .... physics and has written many books.
11 The teacher put **emphasis** .... completing the whole test.
12 Peter took **exception** .... having to smoke outside.
13 The children **exclaimed** .... the beauty of the scenery.
14 The school secretary was **experienced** .... first aid.

Prepositions

1 on, in, with
2 of, with, by
3 by, at, of
4 of, in, from
5 of, from, between
6 between, of, from
7 at, in, about
8 in, for, of
9 for, about, at
10 with, of, in
11 to, on, in
12 to, in, from
13 about, at, of
14 in, on, with

135 **Match column A with column B, then explain the similes.**

	A			B	
1	as black as	A	snow	1	....*E (very black)*....
2	as blind as	B	a post	2	....
3	as cool as	C	gold	3	....
4	as deaf as	D	a hatter	4	....
5	as white as	E	coal	5	....
6	as fit as	F	lead	6	....
7	as good as	G	a mouse	7	....
8	as heavy as	H	a cucumber	8	....
9	as mad as	I	a fiddle	9	....
10	as quiet as	J	a bat	10	....

136 **Look at Appendix 2, then fill in the correct particle(s).**

Phrasal Verbs	

1 If you don't pay your water bill, your water supply will be **cut** ...*off*... .
2 I'm not **cut** .... working in an office.
3 You must **cut** .... the amount of sugar you consume.
4 I wanted to overtake the lorry but a car from behind **cut** ....
   between us.
5 He **cut** .... the conversation to ask to go out.
6 The village was **cut** .... for days because of the snow.
7 The Prime Minister's decided to **cut** .... government spending.
8 Most countries have **done** .... the death penalty.
9 You shouldn't **do** your parents .... They care about you.
10 I'm really thirsty. I could **do** .... a drink.

Phrasal Verbs

1 across, off, back, in
2 out, out for, up, to
3 into, in, off, down on
4 to, through, up, in
5 across, into, up, down
6 off, out, up, to
7 off, through, back on, up
8 out, away with, with, up
9 out, with, down, up
10 up, with, out, in

137 **Use the words in capitals to form a word that fits in the space in the same line.**

TESTS

All students throughout the world sit for **(0)** .... at some
point in their lives. If students are **(1)** ..., they get a formal
(2) .... that enables them to get a job or continue
with further **(3)** ....
Most formal testing involves a **(4)** ... of techniques,
but the most common form requires students to show
that they have a detailed **(5)** ... of the subject area. Students
who do not pass, are not considered as **(6)** ...., they simply
need more time to study. Some of them are simply **(7)** ... .
The **(8)** .... who pass, do so because they have made a good
(9) .... on the examiner and have also succeeded in
showing their **(10)** .....

EXAMINE	0	*examinations*
SUCCESS	1	
QUALIFY	2	
EDUCATE	3	
MIX	4	
	5	
KNOW	6	
FAIL	7	
LUCKY	8	
MAJOR	9	
IMPRESS		
INTELLIGENT	10	

138 **Put the verbs in brackets into the correct tense.**

A If George **1)** ...*hadn't been caught*... (not/catch) driving through a red light, he **2)** ....
(not/be) in the trouble he is in now. The truth is, he **3)** .... (not/pay) much attention
when the policeman **4)** .... (step) into the middle of the road and **5)** ....
(stop) him. If George **6)** .... (not/notice) him in time, the policeman **7)** ....
(probably/kill). Anyway, he **8)** .... (arrest) and **9)** .... (take) to court,
where he **10)** .... (charge) with speeding, careless driving and failure to stop at a red
light. It **11)** .... (also/discover) that he had many parking fines which he **12)** ....
(not/pay). The judge told him that he **13)** .... (fine) £500 and his driving licence
14) .... (take) away for one year. "I know I **15)** .... (do) all these things,"
16) .... (say) George, "and I **17)** .... (pay) the fine. But you can't take
my driving licence away." "Why not?" **18)** .... (ask) the judge. "Because,"
he **19)** .... (reply), "I **20)** .... (never/have) one in my life."

B Sally **1)** ...*had missed*... (miss) the last bus home because she **2)** .... (work) late at the
office, so she **3)** .... (decide) to get a taxi. She got into the first one that came along, but
immediately regretted **4)** .... (do) so, because the driver **5)** .... (seem) a
bit crazy. After he **6)** .... (go) through the third red light at top speed Sally said, "You
7) .... (drive) a bit too fast. Please slow down. I **8)** .... (be) in two car
accidents already in my life." "That's nothing," **9)** .... (reply) the driver. "I **10)** ....
.... (be) in over a hundred!"

139 **Choose the word which best fits each space.**

GARDEN PARADISE

In the spring of 1976, the late George Rushton began **(0)** ....
...*creating*... (**doing / fixing / creating / inventing**) a flower
garden for his recently disabled wife, Mary. The area next to the
family home had been **(1)** .... (**overgrown /
overcrowded / overdone / overbooked**) for years. All the
trees and plants had grown **(2)** .... (**short /
straight / wild / green**) and the area had been used as a place
where people **(3)** .... (**bought / sold /picked /
threw**) their rubbish. When George started **(4)** ....
(**making / cleaning / washing / setting**) up the garden, he
found lots of things, including an old bicycle and several
kitchen sinks! Then, **(5)** .... (**while / before / after /
during**) the rubbish had been removed, he **(6)** ....
(**worked / hired / followed / recorded**) machinery to cut down
the unwanted plants and trees. This **(7)** ....
(**spent / was / gave / took**) five months. George spent a
(8) .... (**further / couple / little / few**) three months tidying up the garden and cutting the
grass, which had **(9)** .... (**arrived / been / found / reached**) an incredible height.
(10) .... (**Just / Only / After / Since**) then could he actually start moving plants around and
(11) .... (**making / planting / putting / fixing**) new ones. On the lawn, he dug a small pond,
and in the front garden he put down flower **(12)** .... (**beds / carpets / bottoms / tops**). A
year **(13)** .... (**after / while / then / later**), the whole place was **(14)** .... (**living /
lively / alive / lovely**) with colour. George also had concrete paths **(15)** .... (**put / laid /
prepared / developed**) so Mary could enjoy every corner of the garden in her wheelchair.

140 **Read the text. Some of the lines are correct and some have a word which should not
be there. If a line is correct, put a tick (✔) in the space provided.**

If a line has a word which should not be there, write it in the space provided.

SAFETY FIRST

0	*out*	0
00	✔	00
1		1
2		2
3		3
4		4
5		5
6		6
7		7
8		8
9		9
10		10
11		11
12		12
13		13
14		14
15		15

0 Every year, one out in five children in Britain is injured in an
00 accident serious enough to need hospital treatment.
1 Falls are the commonest cause of injury, other dangers are be cuts, burns
2 and poisoning. Of course, children also get hurt outside of
3 the home, especially while they playing near or walking across
4 the road. Children will always be prone to bumps and
5 bruises, but most injuries are preventable if the simple,
6 sensible safety measures are followed. For an example,
7 a safety gate be fitted at the top of the stairs will help prevent
8 falls. To avoid the possibility of children get poisoning
9 themselves, all tablets should be locked up out of
10 the reach. It should also be remembered that many house
11 plants are poisonous. Children are naturally curious for
12 and unaware of danger, so that never leave children in the
13 kitchen being alone, and keep hot irons away from them until they
14 will cool properly. Follow these guidelines and your home will
15 be a more safer place for your kids to grow up.

Practice test 2

PART 1

For questions 1 - 15, read the text below and decide which word A, B, C or D best fits each space. Mark your answers in the answer boxes provided.

STARTING A BUSINESS

Running your own business can **(0)** .... really high job satisfaction - the satisfaction of being in **(1)** .... of your own life and making your own **(2)** .... about how things should be done.

If you are ambitious, you may want to achieve **(3)** .... on a large scale and eventually to become rich. Or it may be **(4)** .... for you simply to enjoy work more and to achieve a modest increase **(5)** .... living standards at the same time.

It's important to take into **(6)** .... the less desirable aspects of the job as **(7)** .... . For instance, if problems **(8)** ...., it will be up to you to sort them **(9)** .... . You'll probably have to work harder and longer hours, especially in the **(10)** .... stages. You'll probably see less of your family and friends too. And, of course, you won't enjoy the security of a **(11)** .... pay packet.

If you see all this as a challenge **(12)** .... than a disadvantage, you have at **(13)** .... one of the qualities needed for success. Other qualities **(14)** .... : the ability to work on one's own, a refusal to **(15)** .... up, and a willingness to take on responsibility.

Do you have what it takes?

0	**A** make	**B** present	**C** provide	**D** suggest		**0**	A ☐	B ☐	C ▬	D ☐
1	**A** duty	**B** charge	**C** head	**D** position		**1**	A ☐	B ☐	C ☐	D ☐
2	**A** alterations	**B** proposals	**C** ideas	**D** decisions		**2**	A ☐	B ☐	C ☐	D ☐
3	**A** courage	**B** power	**C** success	**D** security		**3**	A ☐	B ☐	C ☐	D ☐
4	**A** many	**B** enough	**C** too	**D** lot		**4**	A ☐	B ☐	C ☐	D ☐
5	**A** at	**B** on	**C** in	**D** for		**5**	A ☐	B ☐	C ☐	D ☐
6	**A** account	**B** mind	**C** thought	**D** contemplation		**6**	A ☐	B ☐	C ☐	D ☐
7	**A** much	**B** also	**C** too	**D** well		**7**	A ☐	B ☐	C ☐	D ☐
8	**A** rise	**B** raise	**C** arise	**D** happen		**8**	A ☐	B ☐	C ☐	D ☐
9	**A** up	**B** in	**C** through	**D** out		**9**	A ☐	B ☐	C ☐	D ☐
10	**A** initiation	**B** early	**C** starting	**D** beginning		**10**	A ☐	B ☐	C ☐	D ☐
11	**A** permanent	**B** square	**C** regular	**D** usual		**11**	A ☐	B ☐	C ☐	D ☐
12	**A** rather	**B** instead	**C** otherwise	**D** other		**12**	A ☐	B ☐	C ☐	D ☐
13	**A** last	**B** least	**C** once	**D** most		**13**	A ☐	B ☐	C ☐	D ☐
14	**A** compose	**B** contain	**C** consist	**D** include		**14**	A ☐	B ☐	C ☐	D ☐
15	**A** give	**B** work	**C** turn	**D** draw		**15**	A ☐	B ☐	C ☐	D ☐

PART 2

For questions 16 - 30, read the text below and think of the word which best fits each space. Use only one word in each space. Write your answers in the answer boxes provided.

A TRIAL FLIGHT

It was a beautiful sunny day - perfect **(0)** .... what I had planned. I left home with my parents and we drove **(16)** .... the local airport, where we **(17)** .... booked a trial flight. It **(18)** .... £20 for half an hour. **(19)** .... we turned into the entrance, I felt a mixture of emotions. On the **(20)** .... hand, I felt confident and excited but, on the other, I felt a **(21)** .... scared.

The pilot greeted me **(22)** .... a friendly smile and led me to a small aeroplane. I got in, and was at once reminded **(23)** .... the time when I had had driving lessons. The plane had dual controls. The pilot briefly **(24)** .... the function of the **(25)** .... important instruments, and then we moved on to the runway. At this point, the instructor was **(26)** .... complete control. We sped down the runway and **(27)** .... off. We hit a little turbulence and my immediate reaction was to reach **(28)** .... the door handle! Then we settled down. We flew along the south coast, over land and sea, and gradually I took **(29)** .... of the plane, changing direction and altering the speed. **(30)** .... the pilot's guidance, I managed to land the plane. It was an unbelievably exciting experience!

0	*for*	0 ▭ ▬
16		16 ▭ ▭
17		17 ▭ ▭
18		18 ▭ ▭
19		19 ▭ ▭
20		20 ▭ ▭
21		21 ▭ ▭
22		22 ▭ ▭
23		23 ▭ ▭
24		24 ▭ ▭
25		25 ▭ ▭
26		26 ▭ ▭
27		27 ▭ ▭
28		28 ▭ ▭
29		29 ▭ ▭
30		30 ▭ ▭

PART 3

For questions 31 - 40, complete the second sentence so that it has a similar meaning to the first sentence. Use the word given and other words to complete each sentence. You must use between two and five words. Do not change the word given. Write your answers in the answer boxes provided.

0   I finished the book in two days.
   took
   It .... to finish the book.

| 0 | *took me two days* | ▢ 0 ▄ |

31   You ought to do something about this tap.
   time
   It's .... about this tap.

| 31 | | 31 ▢ ▢ |

32   He tries hard to keep up with the class.
   best
   He .... up with the class.

| 32 | | 32 ▢ ▢ |

33   Although he is rich, he is mean.
   wealth
   In ...., he is mean.

| 33 | | 33 ▢ ▢ |

34   I'm sure she was lying about her age.
   must
   She .... her age.

| 34 | | 34 ▢ ▢ |

35   Please check this document for misprints.
   sure
   Please .... misprints in this document.

| 35 | | 35 ▢ ▢ |

36   It takes two hours to fly from Athens to Rome.
   flight
   It's .... Athens to Rome.

| 36 | | 36 ▢ ▢ |

37   As you feel weak, you should cancel your trip.
   suggest
   I .... your trip as you feel weak.

| 37 | | 37 ▢ ▢ |

38   This is such bad news that I daren't tell anybody.
   so
   This .... that I daren't tell anybody.

| 38 | | 38 ▢ ▢ |

39   Can I speak to you in private?
   word
   Can I .... in private?

| 39 | | 39 ▢ ▢ |

40   Dogs are more of a responsibility than cats.
   such
   Cats .... as dogs.

| 40 | | 40 ▢ ▢ |

PART 4

For questions 41 - 55, read the text below and look carefully at each line. Some of the lines are correct and some have a word which should not be there. If a line is correct, put a tick (✓) by the number in the answer boxes provided. If a line has a word which should not be there, write the word in the answer boxes provided.

CHRISTMAS SHOPPING IN BRITAIN

0	There is usually a lot of rain in the streets of	
00	London, but as that does not stop British people from	
41	going to shopping, and no time is as busy as Christmas	
42	and January. January is that when the sales take	
43	place, and in London, which this is the most expensive	
44	city in Britain, the bargains are the best one. This means	
45	there are even more people than usual in the streets. Huge	
46	numbers of shoppers, be loaded with bags, push their	
47	way through the crowds. All British politeness is been	
48	forgotten. In January, the whole shops are trying to get	
49	rid of extra Christmas stock and the most shops	
50	offer huge discounts. From designer clothes	
51	up to household goods, the savings can be as high	
52	as 50%. British people love the sales and	
53	fight their way through the streets despite of	
54	the crowds and bad weather. There's nothing as	
55	like the thought of a bargain to send the British wild!	

0	✓	0
00	as	00
41		41
42		42
43		43
44		44
45		45
46		46
47		47
48		48
49		49
50		50
51		51
52		52
53		53
54		54
55		55

PART 5

For questions 56 - 65, read the text below. Use the word given in capitals at the end of each line to form a word that fits in the space in the same line. Write your word in the answer boxes provided.

TENNESSEE WILLIAMS

Tennessee Williams was born in 1914 and spent his (0) ....
in (56) .... Mississippi. His real name was Thomas Lanier
Williams, but like many people in the (57) .... of fame, he
adopted a pen-name. During his (58) .... he worked in various
(59) .... including a period as a shoe salesman.
However, it was of course as a (60) .... that he became famous.
His best work was based on the (61) .... of southern American
society with its pretence of well-mannered and (62) .... behaviour.
His most famous (63) .... include "A Street Car Named Desire"
and "Cat on a Hot Tin Roof". Both display a (64) .... of social
awareness and emotional tension. Many (65) .... films have been
made, based on his plays.

CHILD
EAST
PURSUE
YOUNG
OCCUPY
DRAMA
LIVE
ELEGANCE
ACHIEVE
COMBINE
SUCCESS

0	childhood	0
56		56
57		57
58		58
59		59
60		60
61		61
62		62
63		63
64		64
65		65

Pre - test 1

A   Choose the correct item.

1 He is a taxi driver, so he is accustomed to .... in the busy town centre.
A drive   B have driven
C be driven   D driving

2 He was offered the job because he was .... candidate.
A the best   B good
C better   D best

3 My doctor recommended me .... a week off work to recover from my illness.
A takes   B take
C to take   D took

4 He's .... helpful policeman I've met.
A least   B the least
C less   D little

5 I saw him .... the window and run away.
A breaking   B broke
C to break   D break

6 The sooner she moves out, ... it will be for all of us.
A the better   B the best
C better   D good

7 He means .... you for the damage he caused.
A to pay   B to have paid
C pay   D paying

8 He bought a(n) .... cottage in the country.
A stone, old, small   B old, small, stone
C small, old, stone   D stone, small, old

9 I've never heard such a loud voice .... his.
A than   B to
C as   D rather than

10 Jane would prefer to work as a secretary .... work as a typist.
A to   B rather
C from   D rather than

11 Can she really be so stupid as .... his lies?
A to believe   B believe
C to believing   D believing

12 Jane finished her maths homework and went on .... her English essay.
A doing   B to do
C to be done   D do

13 I saw him .... the cat.
A to chase   B chasing
C be chased   D to have chased

14 Please stop .... and give me your test papers.
A to writing   B to have written
C to write   D writing

15 She prefers washing clothes .... ironing them.
A to   B than
C rather   D from

16 It is very rude of him .... the teacher when she is speaking.
A interrupting   B to interrupting
C to interrupt   D interrupt

17 She's .... older than I thought.
A rather   B fairly
C quite   D pretty

18 He is known .... a lot of money to charity in the past.
A to donate   B donating
C to have donated   D donate

19 As well as .... at a school, she is a fashion model.
A to teach   B teach
C to have taught   D teaching

20 I .... to stay in tonight rather than go to the party.
A would rather   B would prefer
C prefer   D would

21 I wouldn't advise .... on the plane because you might feel sick.
A to smoke   B to have smoked
C smoke   D smoking

22 He is .... at football than his brother.
A best   B the best
C good   D better

23 She objects .... her younger sister so her parents can go out.
A to have looked after   B to looking after
C to look after   D looking after

24 She is looking for a .... suit.
A blue, dark, smart   B smart, dark, blue
C blue, smart, dark   D dark, smart, blue

B Put the verbs in brackets into the correct tense.

The Red Balloon Nursery School **1)** .... (open) last year, in an old building which **2)** ....
(be) empty for years. I **3)** .... (work) here for the last six months now. My day usually **4)** ....
(start) at 8 o'clock. This week I **5)** .... (look after) twenty-five toddlers whose parents **6)** ....
.... (want) some time to themselves during the day. By next year I hope the numbers **7)** ....
(rise) to nearly forty. Then maybe we **8)** .... (employ) another child-minder to help us.

C Put the verbs in brackets into the correct tense.

Mr McDermott **1)** .... (work) as a doctor. When he first **2)** .... (begin) his career in
1990, he **3)** .... (just/leave) medical school. He **4)** .... (open) his own doctor's
surgery in 1992 and since then he **5)** .... (work) as a doctor. He **6)** .... (enjoy) his
job and, at the moment, he **7)** .... (teach) young medical students in his spare time. He hopes
that in the future he **8)** .... (continue) to help sick people and his fellow physicians.

D Using the word given complete the sentences so that the second sentence has a similar meaning to the first sentence.

1   Smoking on trains is not allowed.
    mustn't   You .... on trains.
2   Shall we go to the party tonight?
    about   What .... the party tonight?
3   I'm sure they were covering something up.
    must   They .... something up.
4   She made the children tidy their room.
    were   The children .... their room.
5   She regrets leaving her job.
    wishes   She .... her job.
6   I need to buy a smart suit for the interview.
    ought   I .... a smart suit for the interview.
7   Take an umbrella; it might rain later.
    case   Take an umbrella .... later.
8   It's possible that they will be delayed in the traffic.
    may   They .... in the traffic.
9   They started restoring the old church a year ago.
    been   They .... the old church for a year.
10 You had better get some legal advice.
    were   If .... get some legal advice.
11 It wasn't necessary for you to be so rude.
    needn't   You .... so rude.
12 He said he was sorry he forgot their appointment.
    apologised   He .... their appointment.
13 You ought to go to bed.
    time   It .... to bed.
14 I advise you to take more exercise.
    should   You .... exercise.
15 Jane hasn't contacted me since she got married.
    heard   I .... Jane since she got married.
16 I'm sure it wasn't Susan that broke the vase.
    can't   It .... that broke the vase.
17 He paid £900 for his holiday abroad.
    cost   His .... £900.
18 The hospital in which I was born is being extended.
    where   The hospital .... is being extended.

19 She'll probably get the job.
likely   It is .... the job.
20 Sarah doesn't have as much free time as when she was single.
used   Sarah .... free time when she was single.

E ▶ Fill in the blanks with the correct particle(s).

1 When does school break .... for Easter?
2 She tried to cut .... smoking by only buying a packet of cigarettes a week.
3 They're carrying .... an experiment in the lab.
4 The situation called .... immediate action.
5 People believe this law should be done ....
6 Mum doesn't want to let me go to the party but I'll bring her ....
7 While she was tidying, she came .... an old photo of herself.
8 When she was told about Tim's accident, she broke .... in tears.

F ▶ Fill in the blanks with the correct preposition.

1 Anyone acquainted .... the music of Bach will appreciate that he was a genius.
2 That name sounds familiar .... me.
3 You can't put the blame .... me.
4 She's experienced .... handling money.
5 He is very attached .... his pet rabbit.
6 He died .... kidney failure.
7 He was charged .... speeding.
8 She was furious .... Sally for spending all her money.

G ▶ Correct the following sentences by taking out the inappropriate word.

1 I enjoy going to shopping.
2 Despite of her severe disability, she fulfilled her goals in life.
3 John is at the work.
4 He spends money as like if there was no tomorrow.
5 He works hard so that as to be promoted.
6 His latest novel, which is 500 pages long, it is a best-seller.
7 Being unemployed it is the worst thing that can happen to someone.
8 Susan used to be the happier than she is now.
9 He was caught shoplifting; needless is to say, he now has a criminal record.
10 He explained to us the more best ways of self-defence.
11 When one trying hard, people are more likely to succeed in life.
12 One hour later than she was enjoying a cup of tea in front of the TV.

1		1
2		2
3		3
4		4
5		5
6		6
7		7
8		8
9		9
10		10
11		11
12		12

H ▶ Fill in the correct word derived from the words in bold.

Detroit is renowned for the **(1)**... of cars.
If you make a good **(2)**... at the interview, you will get the job.
Teaching and medicine are more than **(3)**..., they're professions.
My history teacher has a vast **(4)**... of past events.
You are never too old to go to college and gain some **(5)**....
My greatest **(6)**... was graduating from university.
Henry Ford was a very **(7)**... businessman.
In Britain, most students spend about thirteen years in **(8)**....
The weatherman said there is a strong **(9)**... of rain today.
He was really **(10)**... at the casino; he lost all his money.
Some old laws are no longer **(11)**....
Athens is **(12)**... for its ancient buildings.

PRODUCT	1	1
IMPRESS	2	2
OCCUPY	3	3
KNOW	4	4
QUALIFY	5	5
ACHIEVE	6	6
SUCCESS	7	7
EDUCATE	8	8
POSSIBLE	9	9
LUCKY	10	10
EFFECT	11	11
FAME	12	12

Clauses / Linking Words

Billy, you're very late for school. **I won't let** you attend the class **until you give** me a good excuse.

I'm sorry, Miss. **I was banging** in some nails **when I hurt** two fingers.

But, I can't see any bandages.

Well, they weren't my fingers!

Time Clauses

- Time clauses are introduced by: **after, as, as long as, as soon as, for, just as, once, since, before, by the time** (= before, not later than), **when, while, until/till** (= up to the time when), **the moment (that), whenever, every time, immediately, the first time, the last time, the next time** etc.
  *George had to wait for half an hour **before** the doctor came.*

  <u>Main Clause</u>   <u>Time Clause</u>

- Time clauses follow the rule of the sequence of tenses; that is, when the verb of the main clause is in a present or future form, the verb of the time clause is in a present form and when the verb of the main clause is in a past form, the verb of the time clause is in a past form too.
  *I'll **stay** in the office **until I finish** the project.* (not: ~~until I will finish the project~~)
  *She **arrived before** the clock **struck** nine.* (not: ~~before the clock strikes nine~~)

- When the time clause precedes the main clause, a comma is used. When the time clause follows, no comma is used. ***When** he was in Washington, he met the President. He met the President **when** he was in Washington.*

- **Will** is never used in time clauses; we use a present form instead.
  *I'll cook dinner **after I tidy** the house.* (not: ~~after I will tidy~~)

- **when** (time conjunction) + present tense   *I'll see to it when I **have** time.*
  when (question word) + will/would   *Do you know **when** they **will** leave?*

141   **Underline the appropriate time phrase and put the verbs into the correct tense.**

1 I'm not leaving <u>until</u> / **by the time** I ...*finish / have finished* .... (finish) this job.
2 He promised to phone **while / the moment** he .... (arrive) in Orlando.
3 She had tidied the room **as soon as / by the time** her mother .... (get) home.
4 We'll have a party **when / while** the exams .... (be) over.
5 You can go home **whenever / before** you .... (want) to.
6 They were talking **as soon as / while** we .... (watch) the film.
7 Tom came home **just as / till** June .... (leave).
8 We went to sleep **after / until** we .... (eat) our meal.
9 **By the time / Until** I .... (arrive) home, George had already left.
10 Tell Jane I'll call her **by the time / as soon as** I .... (have) some news.
11 Ann didn't buy a car **until / since** she .... (save) enough money.
12 We had been waiting for six hours **until / by the time** the train .... (get) into the station.

- **If** is used for things which may happen. *Don't worry **if** I'm a little late.*
- **When** is used for things which are sure to happen. *I'll give you a ring **when** I reach London.*

142 Fill in: if or when.

Dear Mr Wong,

We would like to congratulate you once again on winning our first prize of a week's holiday in England. 1) ...**When**... you arrive at Heathrow airport, a limo will be waiting for you to take you straight to your hotel. You will probably want to go to bed 2) .... you get there as you will have had a long day. 3) .... you wake up the next day, you will be served a full English breakfast in bed. Then, you will have the rest of the week to explore London at your leisure or 4) .... you prefer, you can travel to one of the nearby towns. 5) .... you want to hire a car, remember to drive on the left and be especially careful 6) .... approaching or leaving roundabouts. Anyway, I'm sure you will find the English very helpful 7) .... you need any advice. 8) .... you have any questions before you leave, please do not hesitate to contact me.

Yours sincerely,
Mike Baldwin

- **By** is followed by time adverbs and means "before", "not later than". *You must finish this report **by** 8.00 tomorrow.*
- **By the time** is followed by a clause and means "before", "not later than". *He had watered the plants **by the time** she got back.*
- **Until** is followed by either a clause or a time adverb and means "up to the time when". *"Can you wait **until** I return?" "I can only wait **until** 10.30."*
- When the main clause is negative, we normally use **until**. *We **didn't** leave **until** Mary arrived.* (not: ~~by the time Mary arrived~~)

143 Fill in: by the time, until or by.

1   ...*By the time*... the last marathon runner crossed the finishing line, nearly everyone had gone home.
2   Don't try to show anyone this trick .... you have practised it a lot in front of a mirror.
3   If he carries on making investments like that, he'll be a millionaire .... he's 25.
4   We waited .... our parents had gone to bed, then we turned on the television.
5   The police station had burnt to the ground .... the fire brigade arrived.
6   The meeting had already finished .... 5.30.
7   They don't want to announce their engagement .... they have written to their parents.
8   Her father warned her to be home .... midnight.

144 Fill in: after, as soon as, since, before, by the time, while, until or whenever.

"So, Mrs Trumpton, welcome to your first driving lesson. I'd like to say a few words 1) ...*before*... we begin. The most important thing to remember is that the pedal in the middle is the brake - 2) .... you need to stop, you press it. Never start the engine 3) .... you get in the car, because it might be in gear and never drive off 4) .... you make sure the road is clear. You must continually check your mirror 5) .... you are driving, because it's important to know what is behind you. I will only take you out on the road 6) .... we have practised the basics in the car park for a couple of lessons. Don't worry Mrs Trumpton, I've been teaching people how to drive 7) .... 1982, so you're in good hands. I assure you that 8) .... you have finished this course, you will have become a safe and confident driver."

145 Underline the appropriate time phrase and put the verbs into the correct tense.

Gary didn't see the lorry stop in front of him **1)** <u>until</u>/**when** it
...*was*...(be) too late. He had been listening to music **2)** **while/since** he
.... (drive) home from work, hoping that his wife
would have dinner ready for him **3)** **whenever/by the time** he ....
(get) there. His wife is such an excellent cook that **4)** **whenever/as** he
.... (think) about her food, he can't concentrate on anything
else. **5)** "I .... (be) home **until/by** 6 o'clock," he thought happily.
So, **6)** **when/while** the lorry screeched to a halt in front of him he ....
.... (not/notice) it. In fact, he didn't realise anything was
wrong **7)** **until/since** his car .... (be) halfway underneath it.
Gary **8)** .... (lie) in hospital **since/for** that day. The
doctors aren't sure **9)** **for/when** he .... (be able) to go home.

146 Correct the sentences.

1 We waited for you by it got dark.   ...*We waited for you until it got dark.*
2 When the Queen will arrive, we must all stand up.   ....
3 As soon as I'll get home, I'll have something to eat.   ....
4 They didn't call by the time they had found the solution. ....
5 Can you phone me when you will be ready?   ....
6 Every time I will go shopping, I spend too much money. ....
7 I'll phone you if there will be a problem.   ....
8 The children cleared the table by the time they had finished eating. ....
9 Until we went to bed, it was nearly morning.   ....
10 I'll call you immediately as I reach my hotel.   ....

Oral Activity 7

Look at the pictures and make up sentences using the time words given. Work in teams or individually.

as

before

after

until

while

when

as long as

whenever

since

by the time

eg. A dog ran across the road as he was driving home / to the office. etc

I've found the perfect way **to get up** in the morning.

What's that?

At night I put a toaster under my bed **so that I can** pop up in the morning.

Expressing purpose · Clauses of Purpose

Purpose is expressed with

- **to-infinitive** (informal)/**in order to/so as to** (formal). *She wrote **to tell** him the news. (informal) She wrote **in order to tell** him the news. (formal) He studied hard **so as to be** the first.* (**"so as to"** is normally used when the verb "to be" follows)
- **so that + can/may** (present or future reference). *I'll help him **so (that)** he can finish early.*
  so that + could/might (past reference). *I helped him **so that** he **could** finish early.*
  The word "that" can be omitted in spoken English. *I left early **so** I could be there on time.*
- **for + noun/-ing form.** *Let's go out **for a meal**. A kettle is used **for boiling** water.*
- **with a view to + -ing form.** *We are gathered here **with a view to reaching** a decision.*
- **with the aim of + -ing form.** *He opened an account **with the aim of saving** money to buy a car.*
- **in case + present** (present or future reference) / **in case + past** (past reference). **Will/Would** are never used with "in case". *I'll take some sandwiches **in case I get** hungry. (not: ~~in case I'll get hungry~~) I **took** some water **in case I got** thirsty. (not: ~~in case I would get thirsty~~)*

Negative Purpose is normally expressed with

- **so as not/in order not + to-infinitive.** *He left early **so as not to miss** the train. (not: He left early ~~not to miss~~ the train.) She put on her raincoat **in order not to get** wet.(not: She put on her raincoat ~~not to get~~ wet.)*
- **so that + won't/can't** (present/future reference). *I'll pick you up from the station **so that you won't** need to take a taxi.*
  so that + wouldn't/couldn't (past reference). *He got a taxi **so that he wouldn't** be late.*
- **for fear + might.** *He locked all the windows **for fear (that) he might** be burgled.*
  for fear of sth/doing sth. *We don't go out at night **for fear of being** attacked.*
- **prevent + noun/pronoun + (from) + -ing form.** *He chained the dog up to **prevent it (from) biting** the children.*
- **avoid + -ing form.** *Ann got up early **to avoid being** late for work.*

- **Clauses of purpose follow the rule of the sequence of tenses.**
  *I'll bring a ball **in case** they **want** to play a game.*
  *She **ran** home **so that** she **could** watch the 6 o'clock news.*

147 Purpose can be expressed in various ways. Look at the examples, then rewrite the sentences in as many ways as possible.

1 He left early. He wanted to catch the train.
He left early so that he would/could catch the train. He left early to avoid missing the train. He left early to catch the train. He left early in order not to miss the train. He left early with the aim of catching the train. He left early so that he wouldn't miss the train. He left early with a view to catching the train. He left early in case he missed the train. He left early for fear he might miss the train. etc ....

2 She set her alarm clock. She wanted to get up early.
....
....
....
....

3 I won't leave the flat. John may call.
....
....
....
....

4 He revised hard for the test. He wanted to succeed.
....
....
....
....

148 Using the word in bold fill in the missing part of the second sentence so that it has a similar meaning to the sentences given. Do not change the word given.

1 She locked the money in the safe. Someone might steal it.
   prevent   She locked the money in the safe ....*to prevent it (from) being*........... stolen.
2 She made out a list of people to invite. She didn't want to leave anyone out.
   that   She made out a list of people to invite .... leave anyone out.
3 The doctor took his medicine bag. Someone might have been hurt.
   case   The doctor took his medicine bag .... hurt.
4 Jim didn't climb the tree. He didn't want to fall out of it.
   might   Jim didn't climb the tree .... out of it.
5 Alan bought some Coke. He wanted to have something to drink.
   to   Alan bought some Coke .... something to drink.
6 She put on suntan oil. She didn't want to get burnt.
   avoid   She put on suntan oil .... burnt.
7 They bought a double-decker bus. They intended to turn it into a mobile home.
   view   They bought a double-decker bus .... it into a mobile home.

149 Join the sentences using the purpose words given.

1 The bank contacted me. They informed me that I was overdrawn. (in order to)
   ...*The bank contacted me in order to inform me that I was overdrawn.* ....
2 The burglar wiped the gun. He didn't want to leave his fingerprints. (so that) ....
3 He doesn't carry a lot of cash. He might get robbed. (avoid) ....
4 She saved money. She intended to buy a house. (with a view to) ....
5 I ran. I wanted to catch the bus. (to) ....
6 Jane gave the police her phone number. Then the police could ring her. (so that) ....
7 Let's buy some Coke. We may have guests. (in case) ....
8 This is a tin opener. You use it to open tins. (for) ....
9 The little boy hid. He thought he would be punished. (for fear that) ....
10 She locked the diamond in the safe. Someone might steal it. (for fear of) ....

150 Underline the correct word.

It was midnight on Sunday 9th March and I was on duty. I had my walkie-talkie with me **1) for / so that** I could contact my partner if I needed him. I noticed that the door of number 14 Lime Avenue was open. I approached the house quietly **2) in order to / for fear** investigate. I entered cautiously **3) not to / so as not to** alert the intruder. He had a large sack **4) for / to** carry the stolen goods. I caught him by surprise and arrested him. I took him to the station **5) to / for** questioning. He admitted everything, but we recorded his statement **6) for fear that / so that** he might change his story later.

151 Fill in the appropriate purpose word and put the verbs into the correct form.

Dear Sir,

I am writing 1) ...*to apologise*... (apologise) for the damage I caused to your shop window last Saturday. I am terribly sorry but it wasn't completely my fault. I was driving rather fast because I was on my way to the hospital. My wife was pregnant and I needed to get to the hospital quickly 2) .... she .... (give) birth. As I was approaching your shop, a little boy suddenly stepped out in front of my car and I had to swerve 3) .... (not/hit) him. So you see, 4) .... (avoid) hitting the boy I crashed into your window. I have, however, written to my insurance company 5) .... the matter .... (be dealt) with promptly. I have also included details of the accident and your name and address 6) .... they .... (need) to contact you. I have been assured that you will receive a payment 7) .... (compensate) for the damage.

Yours faithfully,
John Miles

Oral Activity 8

There was a terrible storm at sea and a group of people were shipwrecked. Below are some pictures of objects they took with them in their lifeboat. In turn, students make a sentence stating the reason for taking the object of their choice. Each correct sentence gets one point.

a pair of binoculars

a box of matches

some tins of food

a compass

a radio

some blankets

an axe

some hats

a bucket

some fishing rods

a pack of cards

some rope

S1: *They took a pair of binoculars in order to look/so that they could look for ships.*

This is **such a** small diamond **that** I can't even see it.

That's right darling. It's **so** small **that** the glare won't hurt your eyes.

Clauses of Result

Clauses of result are introduced by: that (after such/so...), (and) as a result, (and) as a consequence, consequently, so etc. *There were **so** many people at the party **that** I didn't have time to talk to everyone.*

Main Clause ——————— Clause of Result

- **such a(n) + (adjective) + singular countable.** *It was **such a bad flight that** we'll never forget it.*
  Such is also used with **a lot of.** *There is **such a lot of** noise that I can't work.*
- **such + (adjective) + uncountable/plural noun.** *It was **such** nice weather **that** we went to the park.*
  *(not: such a nice weather) They were **such** cheap books **that** I bought them all.*
  So and **such** can be used without **that.** *He's **so** rude nobody speaks to him.*
- **so + adjective/adverb.** *I'm **so** hungry **that** I could eat a horse. He ran **so fast that** he won the race.*
  So is also used with **much, many, few** or **little.** *He's got **so little** patience with children **that** he can't be a teacher. She's got **so many** dresses **that** she can't decide which one to put on.*
- **so + adjective + a(n) + noun.** *It was **so nice a day that** we went to the beach. (not usual)*
- **as a result/therefore/consequently + clause.** *I had forgotten my passport and **as a result/therefore** I couldn't cross the border. He didn't work hard. **Consequently/Therefore** he lost his job. He didn't work hard. He, **therefore**, lost his job.*

- **Clauses of result follow the rule of the sequence of tenses. When the verb of the main clause is in a present or future form, the verb of the clause of result is in a present form too, and when the verb of the main clause is in a past form, the verb of the clause of result is in a past form too.**
  *It's such strong coffee that I **can't** drink it. She **was** so tired that she **couldn't** concentrate.*

Clauses of Reason

Clauses of reason are introduced by: as, since (= because), because, for (= because), as long as (= because), the reason for, the reason (why), on the grounds that. Because usually answers a **why-question.** *"**Why** did you come back early?" "**Because** there were no seats left." The clause of reason introduced by **for** never precedes the main clause. **For** always comes after a comma in written speech or a pause in oral speech. She didn't come on time **because** she was held up in a traffic jam. She didn't come on time, **for** she was held up in a traffic jam.*

- **When the clause of reason precedes the main clause, we separate the two clauses with a comma.**
  Since she isn't at home, we'll go out without her.
- **Reason can also be expressed with: Because of/Due to + noun/-ing form.** *Because of/Due to the fog all train departures were cancelled.* **Due to the fact/Because of the fact + that-clause.**
  Due to the fact/Because of the fact that there was fog, all train departures were cancelled.

152 **Underline the correct item.**

1 **For / Since** the children are staying at their grandmother's, let's go out for the evening.
2 Ben's **so / such a** charming that it's very difficult to refuse him anything.
3 The road is closed **as a result / because** there's been an accident.
4 Carla's **such / so** busy that she hasn't got time to see anyone.
5 **For / As** it's raining outside, let's take a taxi.
6 The hotel was fully booked. **Therefore / On the grounds that** we stayed at a guest house.
7 It's **so / such a** popular restaurant, you need to make a reservation.
8 **For / Since** I don't know the Becks very well, I've decided not to go to their party.
9 There were **so / such** few people around, the streets were almost deserted.
10 **Because / Due to** the traffic, I arrived at the office late.

153 **Fill in: so, such or such a(n).**

We were all **1)** ...*so*... excited about going on holiday that we had talked about little else for weeks. However, it was **2)** .... long since we had been abroad that I had forgotten all about the problems of travelling. Finally, our day of departure arrived. It was **3)** ...... long journey that we all had to get up at 2 o'clock that morning. When we arrived at the airport, our youngest son Tony was being **4)** .... naughty that, I'm sorry to say, I had to smack him. He screamed **5)** ...... loudly that lots of people came running to see what the matter was. Fortunately, he had quietened down by the time we boarded the plane. My husband ate **6)** ...... a lot of food that he gave himself terrible stomach-ache. The flight attendants thought he was having a heart attack and rushed to help him with oxygen. At that point he became **7)** .... upset that he knocked his meal all over my new dress. By this stage I was in **8)** .... bad mood that I burst into tears. Once my husband had recovered, he apologised **9)** .... sincerely to everyone that we all forgave him.

154 **Look at the examples, then rephrase the following sentences in every possible way.**

1 The shoes were so cheap that I bought three pairs.
   ...*They were such cheap shoes (that) I bought three pairs. They were very cheap shoes. Therefore I bought three pairs. Because of/Due to the fact that the shoes were so cheap, I bought three pairs. I bought three pairs of shoes because they were so cheap.* ....

2 It was such a long train journey that I fell asleep.
   ....
   ....
   ....

3 Due to the fact that the meal was so bad, we never went back to that restaurant.
   ....
   ....
   ....
   ....

4 The soup was so hot that she burnt her mouth.
   ....
   ....
   ....
   ....

5 Because the house is so big, it takes days to clean.

....
....
....
....

155 **Join the sentences with the words in brackets, then identify the clause they introduce.**

1 I missed the bus. I was late for work. (and as a result)
...*I missed the bus and as a result I was late for work. (clause of result)*.............................

2 The police didn't catch the thief. They were fooled by his disguise. (as)

....

3 Darren has a meeting. He can't baby-sit. (since)

....

4 Sharon doesn't listen. She makes mistakes. (consequently)

....

5 There were many people at the reception. They had to wait in line. (so...that)

....

6 The Raiders lost the game. Their best player was hurt. (as)

....

7 I don't like Roger. He is selfish. (The reason why...because)

....

8 It was a beautiful gesture. She nearly cried. (such...that)

....

9 It was cold. I couldn't feel my fingers. (so...that)

....

10 The weather is stormy. The plane is delayed. (such...that)

....

156 **Rewrite the underlined parts of the text using so or such.**

Many young musicians dream of fame without ever considering how long and painful the road to success can be. There are many things involved in being successful and if a young musician isn't aware of them all, failure is certain. Perhaps it is most important to remember the time and work needed to gain popularity. Most up-and-coming musicians spend a long time travelling, which means it is difficult for them to have a family life. In addition, new groups make very little money and musicians are often forced to live in poor conditions. Once the group is established, the next stage is to try and get a contract with a record company. However, this is difficult to obtain and only one group in thousands will actually receive a contract. Even that doesn't guarantee success and a record company will soon drop a group if it doesn't sell many records. To a great extent, sales are dependent on the musicians being seen on MTV. If MTV doesn't show their video, very few records will be sold. Most successful musicians admit that fame came as a surprise to them. They were always more concerned about producing good music. They say you must have a love for the music you are playing and success will automatically follow.

157 **Rephrase the following sentences using the words in bold.**

1 The cat is so fat that it can't walk.
   such   It is ...*such a fat cat that*... it can't walk.
2 He's such a lazy man that he seldom gets out of bed.
   so   He's .... he seldom gets out of bed.
3 The match was cancelled because it was raining.
   due   The match was cancelled .... it was raining.
4 It was so smoky on the bus that we could hardly breathe.
   consequently   The bus was .... we could hardly breathe.
5 It was such a noisy dog that I gave it away.
   therefore   The dog .... I gave it away.
6 He was always late so he lost his job.
   because   He lost his job .... always being late.
7 He placed an advertisement. He wanted to employ a cleaner.
   view   He placed an advertisement .... a cleaner.
8 She doesn't have many friends because she's rude and unpleasant.
   reason   The .... have many friends is that she's rude and unpleasant.
9 Nicole can't join the police force because she's very short.
   too   Nicole is .... the police force.
10 He got a promotion because he worked extremely hard.
   therefore   He worked extremely hard .... a promotion.

Oral Activity 9

The Miltons went on holiday abroad. They had some good experiences and some bad ones.
They went sightseeing every day./They did lots of shopping./They swam in the sea every day./They made lots of friends./They danced every night./They got bitten by mosquitoes./They got sunburnt./They couldn't eat the food, it was spicy./They couldn't sleep at night./They had a lot of luggage.
Now look at the pictures and make sentences using so, such, because, as a result etc to give reasons for the Miltons' good or bad experiences.

   eg. *There were so many interesting places to see that they went sightseeing every day.*
   or As there were a lot of interesting places to see, they went sightseeing every day.
   or Because there were a lot of interesting places to see, they went sightseeing every day. etc

Have you made the breakfast yet?

Not quite. **Even though** I've been boiling the eggs for fifteen minutes they're still hard.

Expressing concession · Clauses of Concession

Concession is expressed with

- **Although/Even though/Though (informal) + clause. ("Though" can also be put at the end of the sentence.)** *Although she spent all afternoon on the project, she didn't finish it. She spent all afternoon on the project. She didn't finish it, **though**.*
- **Despite/In spite of + noun/-ing form.** *Despite/**In spite of their wealth,** they aren't happy. **Despite/In spite of being rich** they aren't happy.* **Despite/In spite of the fact + that-clause.** *Despite the fact/**In spite of the fact that they are rich,** they aren't happy.*
- **While/Whereas/but/on the other hand/yet + clause** *He's tall **while/whereas/on the other hand/but** she is short.* **But/yet** always come between the two clauses. *Tom studied hard, **but** he failed the exam. Tom studied hard, **yet** he failed the exam.*
- **Nevertheless/However + clause.** *John's flat was on fire. **Nevertheless,** he didn't panic. John's flat was on fire. **However,** he didn't panic.*
- **However/No matter how + adjective/adverb + subject + (may) + verb.** *No matter how slowly he speaks, he can't make himself understood. **No matter how slowly he may speak,** he can't make ...*
- **Whatever/No matter what + clause.** *Whatever he said, she wasn't convinced. **No matter what** he said, she wasn't convinced.*
- **Adjective/Adverb + though + subject + verb/may + infinitive without to.** *Well-qualified **though he is/he may be,** he can't find a job. Early **though he left/he may have left,** he didn't arrive on time.*
- **Adjective/Adverb + as + subject + verb.** *Careful **as she is,** she had an accident.* **Clauses of concession express opposition or unexpected results. *Even though she is a careful driver,** she had a terrible accident.* (unexpected result) *In spite of the rain,** the game wasn't put off.* (opposition) **A comma is used either when the concessive clause precedes or follows the main clause.** *Even though she was tired, she worked overtime. She worked overtime, even though she was tired.*

158 ▸ Underline the correct item.

1 <u>However</u> / Although hard he studies, he doesn't get good marks.
2 My sister is dark, **whereas / despite** I am blonde.
3 **Despite / While** going on a diet, she put on five kilos.
4 Clever **whereas / as** he is, he failed the test.
5 **Even though / Despite** he had little money, he insisted on paying for the meal.
6 **In spite of / Whatever** you say, I won't believe you.
7 I invited Sue. She didn't come, **although / though**.

8 My mother is French **whereas / even though** my father is Polish.
9 Persuasive **though / but** he may be, I won't change my mind.
10 **Even though / Despite** we're good friends, we don't meet very often.

159 Fill in: although/though/even though, despite, while/whereas, but, however/no matter how, whatever/no matter what or as.

Mary is 16 and at school. **1)** ...*Despite*... being good at most subjects there are some that she still has problems with. **2)** .... hard she studies she doesn't seem to get good marks in maths, **3)** .... her father sits with her every week to try and help her understand it better. She loves art, **4)** .... she always gets good grades, **5)** .... she doesn't like sports at all **6)** .... she's quite athletic. Mary knows that **7)** .... she's still at school she has to keep working hard in all the subjects she's studying **8)** .... grades she gets. **9)** .... , she's optimistic that she'll improve overall.

160 Join the sentences using although, whereas, despite, but, while or in spite of.

A	B
1 Fiona is a company director.	a Fiona works long hours.
2 Fiona enjoys her job.	b Fiona's boyfriend likes rock music.
3 Fiona loves classical music.	c Fiona's mother is short with blonde hair.
4 Fiona owns a new Jaguar.	d Fiona's only 26.
5 Fiona is tall with dark hair.	e Fiona never drives to work.

1 ...*Fiona's a company director despite/in spite of being only 26*....
2 ....
3 ....
4 ....
5 ....

161 Look at the example, then rewrite the sentences in as many ways as possible.

1 The weather was bad. The ship departed.
...*Although/Even though the weather was bad, the ship departed. In spite of/Despite the bad weather, the ship departed. Bad though the weather was, the ship departed. Bad as the weather was, the ship departed. In spite of the fact that the weather was bad, the ship departed. The weather was bad. Nevertheless, the ship departed. etc*...

2 She had enough money for the dress. She didn't buy it.
....
....
....

3 She is sixty years old. She still goes jogging.
....
....
....

4 Tom arrived early. He didn't find a ticket for the concert.
....
....
....

5 The programme was boring. He continued to watch it.
....
....
....

162 **Complete the missing parts of the sentences.**

1 ...*Hard as she tried*..., she couldn't open the bottle.
2 .... you believe, I am innocent.
3 She loves animals while her younger sister ....
4 Despite going on a diet, ...
5 Even though she was only 7, ...
6 .... you offer me, I will never sell you my car.
7 Happy though he ...., he is actually depressed.
8 I enjoy eating meat, whereas my wife ....
9 She didn't take the job, ...
10 ...., he was still half an hour late.

163 **Rephrase the sentences using the words in bold.**

1 Although my mother is from Paris, I've never been there.
   fact   Despite ...*the fact that my mother*... is from Paris, I've never been there.
2 It sounds easy but it's really rather difficult.
   though   Easy .... it's really rather difficult.
3 In spite of having travelled the world, he is narrow-minded.
   travelled   Although .... he is narrow-minded.
4 However loudly you shout, Grandad won't hear.
   how   No .... Grandad won't hear.
5 Say what you like; I won't believe you.
   say   Whatever .... I won't believe you.
6 He is a sailor but he can't swim.
   being   In .... a sailor, he can't swim.
7 In spite of the restaurant being expensive, the food tasted terrible.
   though   Even .... expensive, the food tasted terrible.
8 Emma spent a year in Bonn but she can't speak German.
   fact   In spite .... a year in Bonn, Emma can't speak German.
9 He tried hard but he couldn't unlock the door.
   as   Hard .... he couldn't unlock the door.
10 He did his best. He came last.
   yet   He .... came last.

Oral Activity 10

Look at the pictures, then compare the two sisters using various words expressing concession.

*eg. **Sandra has dark hair, whereas Evelyn has fair hair. In spite of the fact they ...***

Clauses of Manner

- Clauses of manner are introduced by **as if / as though**. They come after the verbs: **act, appear, be, behave, feel, look, seem, smell, sound, taste.** *She **looks as if** she is sick. It **seems as though** there will be war soon.* Clauses of manner are also introduced by: **as, how, (in) the way, (in) the way that, the way in which, (in) the same way, (in) the same way as.** *Do it **as** I've told you to.*
- **Were** can be used instead of **was** in formal English in all persons in clauses introduced with **as if/as though.** *He speaks **as if he were** the boss. (formal English)*
- We can use **like** instead of as if/as though only in spoken English. *It looks **as if** it is going to snow. (written and spoken English). It looks **like** it is going to snow. (only in spoken English)*

The verb usage following **as if/as though** is normally similar to that in conditionals (see p. 142) and depends on whether the ideas are true or untrue.
Note the following examples:

Expressing similarity/probability (how sb/sth seemed)	**as if / as though + any tense form** *She behaves **as if** she **is** rich. (She may be rich, she may not - she seems to be rich anyway.)* *She felt **as if** she **had** a high temperature. (We don't know but she seemed to have a high temperature.)*
Unreal in the present	**as if / as though + Past Simple/Past Continuous** *She's not from Spain but she speaks Spanish **as if** she **were / was** from Spain. (not true - she is not from Spain.)*
Unreal in the past	**as if / as though + Past Perfect** *He looked **as if** he **had seen** a ghost. (not true - he didn't see a ghost.)*

164 Put the verbs in brackets into the correct tense.

1 He is very fit. He looks as if he ...*trains*... (train) every day; I wonder how he finds the time.
2 She looks as if his remark .... (hurt) her. He shouldn't have made it.
3 Try to live each day as if it .... (be) your last.
4 The tea was not made with sour milk, but it tasted as if it .... (be/made) with sour milk.
5 Tony knew nothing, but he acted as if he .... (know) something.
6 She isn't the Queen of England, but she talks as if she .... (be) the Queen of England.
7 The girl was staring at the car as if she .... (never/see) one before.
8 He behaves as if he .... (be) the boss of this company, but I'm glad to say he's not.

9 I don't think I'll bother taking a coat. It looks as if it .... (be) warm.
10 Do you know if Amanda is expecting a baby? She looks as if she .... (be) pregnant.
11 When he saw my new haircut, he looked at me as if I .... (just/step off) a spaceship.
12 It was so hot after the aerobics class I felt as though my face .... (be) on fire.
13 Bob hadn't received any news but he seemed really happy as if he ....
(just/receive) news of his promotion.
14 My father is so strict, he acts as if he .... (be) a general in the army.
15 His employees are not slaves but he treats them as if they .... (be).

165 Rephrase the following sentences using the words in bold.

1 She was tired. She felt like she had run a mile, but she hadn't actually.
   as   She was so tired she felt ....*as if / as though she had run*... .... a mile.
2 I think it is going to be a nice day.
   as   It looks .... to be a nice day.
3 We have met before. She behaved coldly towards me.
   never   She behaved coldly towards me .... met me before.
4 She is much thinner than when I last saw her.
   as   She looks .... weight since I last saw her.
5 He isn't a millionaire. He spends lots of money, though.
   if   He spends money .... millionaire.
6 I can smell dinner. I think we're having curry.
   though   It smells .... curry for dinner.
7 There were clouds in the sky. It would probably rain.
   looked   It .... going to rain.

166 Fill in: how, as though, the way that, as if, as or the same way as.

1 Stop arguing and just do ...*as*... you've been told.
2 She explained to us .... the machine worked.
3 I feel .... I've been waiting here all my life.
4 I wish you wouldn't treat me .... I were your slave.
5 I really hate .... Sylvia's decorated her flat.
6 Could you do my hair .... you did Sue's?

167 Find the mistake and correct it.

1 I'll go round to Pam's when I'll have time. ...*I'll go round to Pam's when I have time.*..................
2 I'm not going out until this film will be over. ....
3 Give me your number in case I will want to call you. ....
4 He set his alarm clock for 8.00 so not to oversleep. ....
5 I've got such much work to do I don't think I can finish it. ....
6 Mary was so upset that she can't stop crying. ....
7 For she was so good-looking she became a model. ....
8 Despite he was wearing a helmet, he was still badly injured. ....
9 Strict nevertheless he may appear, he's actually quite soft. ....
10 It was such a delicious food he asked for more. ....
11 Let's wait by the time it stops snowing. ....
12 In spite of she didn't feel like it, she went to the party. ....
13 He locked the door for fear someone broke into his house. ....
14 She worked hard with a view to get a promotion soon. ....
15 We arrived at the cinema early in case we would miss the start of the film.
....
16 We'll show our tickets when the inspector will come round. ....
17 He was so exhausted he felt as if he hasn't slept for weeks. ....

Could we have a bag to take my daughter's leftovers home to the dog, please?

Oh, Dad, how kind of you! What a wonderful surprise! Are we getting a dog, then?

Exclamations

- Exclamations are used to express anger, fear, shock, surprise etc. They always take an exclamation mark (!). Some exclamations are: **Oh dear!, Ah!, Good gracious!** etc. We can also use **what (a/an), how, such, so** or a **negative question** to form exclamatory sentences. *What a tall man he is!* *How tall he is!* *He is so tall!* *Isn't he tall!* Exclamatory sentences can also be formed with **here** or **there**. *Here comes the bus! Here it comes.* (Note in these two examples that the noun subject follows the verb while the pronoun subject precedes the verb.)

- **What + a(n) + (adjective) + singular countable noun.** *What a sweet girl!* (also: *How sweet a girl!* - not commonly used)
- **What + (adjective) + uncountable/plural noun.** *What horrible news!* *What lovely earrings!*
- **How + adjective/adverb.** *How polite he is!* *How fast she types!*
- **You + (adjective) + noun.** *You lucky man!* (also: *Lucky you! Lucky him!*)
- **such (a/an) + (adjective) + noun.** *It is such a nice day!* (also: *It is so nice a day!* - not commonly used)
- **so + adjective/adverb.** *He is so rude!* *He speaks so rudely!*
- **adverb/adverbial particle + subject + verb of movement.** *Away they marched!* *Off you go!*

168 **Rephrase the following exclamations in all possible ways as in the example:**

What a brilliant student you are! ...*You are such a brilliant student! Aren't you a brilliant student! You are so brilliant a student! How brilliant a student you are! You brilliant student!*...

1 What awful weather!
2 This box is so heavy!
3 What a clumsy girl!
4 Doesn't she look smart!
5 They have such bad manners!
6 How difficult the test was!
7 We're so close a family!
8 It's been such a tiring day!
9 You're such a lazy boy!

169 **Fill in: what (a/an), how, so or such.**

1 ...*What an*... odd man he is!
2 He's .... tired!
3 .... splendid idea!
4 .... gracefully she dances!
5 This is .... terrible news!
6 .... sad he looks!
7 .... wonderful view!
8 It's .... a long journey!
9 .... heavy rain!
10 He dresses .... smartly!

170 **Find the mistake and correct it.**

1 What wonderful she looks! ...*How wonderful she looks!*............................
2 What an exciting news! ....
3 How incredible story! ....
4 They sail off! ....
5 Tim is such good-looking! ....
6 The bus comes here! ....
7 How boring lecture! ....
8 What a slippery road is it! ....
9 It's so difficult exercise! ....
10 Goes there the last train! ....
11 She's so a liar! ....

Oral Activity 11

Divide the class into two teams. Teams in turn choose a box from the table below and make an exclamatory sentence. The first team to complete a line of three correctly in any direction wins.

what	how	such
what an	so	what a
so	such a	how

eg. **What bad news!**
How kind of you!
It's such bad weather! etc

171 **Rephrase the following sentences using the words in bold.**

1 When Ann left he started cooking.
until He waited ...*until Ann had left*... before he started cooking.
2 Eleven o'clock is the latest you can come home.
by You must .... eleven o'clock.
3 They wanted to avoid being seen, so they travelled at night.
order They travelled at night .... seen.
4 I failed the driving test because I panicked.
result I panicked during the driving test .... failed.
5 They wouldn't let us in, even though we had tickets.
despite They wouldn't let us in, ... had tickets.
6 She behaves like a crazy woman, but she isn't.
if She behaves .... crazy.
7 When Cynthia gets home, I'll tell you immediately.
soon I'll tell you .... home.
8 It's possible they'll be hungry, so I'll cook something.
case I'll cook something .... hungry.
9 The reason we're having this meeting is to appoint a new chairman.
view We're having this meeting .... a new chairman.
10 He is too tired to go on working.
so He is .... go on working.

Today I saw a baby **who** had put on 7 kilos in two weeks by drinking elephant's milk.

Do you know whose baby it was?

Yes. The elephant's!

Relative Clauses

Relative clauses are introduced by: a) relative pronouns i.e. **who, whom, whose, which** or **that** and b) relative adverbs i.e. **when, where** or **why** as follows:

Relative Pronouns

	Subject of the verb of the relative clause (cannot be omitted)	Object of the verb of the relative clause (can be omitted)	Possession (cannot be omitted)
used for people	**who / that** *That's the man **who**/**that** owns the place.*	**who / whom / that** *He's the man **(who**/**that**/**whom)** I met at the party.*	**whose** *This is Mr Brown, **whose** son has moved to Paris.*
used for things / animals	**which / that** *Give me the book **which**/**that** is behind you.*	**which / that** *Have a look at the stamps **(which**/**that)** I bought yesterday.*	**whose / of which** *That's the palace **whose** interior/the interior **of which** is being redecorated.*

- **Who, whom, which** or **that** can be omitted when they are the object of the relative clause, that is, when there is a noun or personal pronoun between the relative pronoun and the verb.
  When "who", "which" etc are subjects of the relative clause, they cannot be omitted.
  *The house (which/that) **they** bought is beautiful. ("which/that" is the object and can be omitted.)*
  *The students **who** failed the exam can sit it again in May. ("who" is the subject and can't be omitted.)*
- **Whom, which** or **whose** can be used in expressions of quantity with **of** (some of, many of, most of, none of, half of etc). *She bought a lot of dresses. Only a few of them were nice. She bought a lot of dresses, only **a few of which** were nice. She has a lot of money. Most of it was inherited from her aunt. She has a lot of money, **most of which** was inherited from her aunt.*
- **What** can be used as a subject or an object or to emphasise a word or phrase. *He did **what** I asked him. **What** we need is a holiday. **What** matters most in a relationship is honesty.*
- **That** can be used instead of **who, whom** or **which** but is never used after commas or prepositions.
  *He's the athlete **who**/**that** came first. That blue car, **which** is brand new, is my brother's. (not: ~~that is~~)*
  That usually follows superlatives and words such as: **something, nothing, anything, all, none, many** and **few**. *There's **something that** I don't understand. That's **all that** I have done.*

Relative Adverbs

Time	**when** (= in/on/at which)	*I'll never forget the day (**when**) I first saw the Alps from a plane.*
Place	**where** (= in/at/on/to which)	*The house **where** he lives is a Victorian one.*
Reason	**why** (= for which)	*That's the reason (**why**) he left his job.*

Prepositions in Relative Clauses

- **We do not normally use prepositions before relative pronouns.**
  *The meeting **to which** I went was very boring. (formal - not usual)*
  *The meeting **which** I went **to** was very boring. (usual)*
  *The meeting I went **to** was very boring. (more usual)*

172 Fill in: when, where, why, who, which, that or whose.

Jean Crowder, **1)** ...*who*... is 65, has a fascinating job. She works at a leisure centre, **2)** .... she teaches aerobics at classes **3)** .... attract women of all ages. Jean, **4)** .... slim figure and fashionable hairstyle make her look younger, first attended a keep-fit class 45 years ago **5)** .... she was a student. Then she heard about a class **6)** .... needed an instructor. That's **7)** .... she started this particular career. Jean's classes, **8)** .... last one hour, include dance and step exercises. Jean has some tips for those **9)** .... wish to stay young. "Eat plenty of fruit, **10)** .... is good for you. Try to spend time in places **11)** .... there is fresh air. Talk to young people, **12)** .... ideas can open your eyes." Jean will only stop teaching aerobics **13)** ....she is too old to walk. But, as she says, "I want to delay that day. That's the reason **14)** .... I look after my health."

- **A relative clause can be changed to a participle phrase. Note the examples:** *The woman **who is sitting** in front of you is my cousin. The woman **sitting** in front of you is my cousin. Anyone **who lies** will be punished. Anyone **lying** will be punished. Meals **which are served** cold are cheaper. Meals **served** cold are cheaper. The machine **which we bought** at the local shop was faulty. The machine **bought** at the local shop was faulty.*

173 Rewrite the following relative clauses as in the example:

1 The woman who is trying on the red shoes is an actress.
   ...*The woman trying on the red shoes is an actress*...
2 The man who is driving that bus is my brother. ....
3 The car which was broken into was a Porsche. ....
4 People who are caught stealing are imprisoned. ....
5 The woman who lives in this house is Russian. ....
6 The man who is playing the piano is blind. ....

174 Join the sentences as in the example:

1 My uncle has a large collection of antiques. Many of them are valuable.
   ...*My uncle has a large collection of antiques, many of which are valuable.* ....
2 I have ten cousins. None of them are girls. ....

3 There are some beautiful houses in the town. Some of them are more than two hundred years old.

....

4 She met lots of new people at the party. A few of them commented on her beautiful dress.

....

5 Ted planted lots of new rose bushes in his garden. Very few of them survived the cold winter.

....

6 The supermarket has thirty employees. Most of them work part-time.

....

Defining/Non-Defining Relative Clauses

● **A defining relative clause** gives necessary information and is **essential** to the meaning of the main sentence. It is not put in commas. *The teacher **who teaches maths** is popular in the school. (*The relative clause is necessary to identify which teacher is meant.)

● **A non-defining relative clause** gives extra information **not essential** to the meaning of the main sentence. The relative clause is put in commas. *Mr Jones, **who teaches science**, is very popular in the school. (*The relative clause isn't necessary because we know which teacher is meant.)

● **Note how the commas change the meaning** of the sentence. *The tourists, who had valid passports, were allowed into the country. (all the tourists had valid passports) The tourists who had valid passports were allowed into the country. (not all the tourists, only those whose passports were valid)*

● **Who, which** or **that** can be **omitted** when used as the object of the defining relative clause. *Here's the report **(which/that)** he brought us yesterday. (*"which/that" as an object can be omitted). *She's the woman **who/that** was promoted to Sales Manager last week. (*"who" as a subject cannot be omitted). **Who, Which** are not omitted in non-defining relative clauses. **That** cannot replace **who** or **which**. *David, **who** works really hard, got a promotion. (not: David, ~~that works really hard,~~ got a promotion.) He invited me to the party, **which** was very kind of him.*

175 Fill in the relative pronoun and put commas where necessary. Write (D) for defining, (ND) for non-defining and whether the relative pronoun can be omitted or not.

1 The food ...*that*... I like best of all is spaghetti. D .....*omitted*......
2 Fred, ...*whose*....... mother lives in Edinburgh, has gone to Scotland. ND ..*not omitted*..
3 The building .... was next to the school fell down. ....
4 Jane .... brother is also a doctor works at the hospital. ....
5 The restaurant .... we celebrated my birthday has closed. ....
6 Mrs Jones is the woman .... is in charge of this company. ....
7 The book .... I'm reading is about China. ....
8 Mr Smith .... runs our company is in hospital. ....
9 Neville .... family are rich has just bought a Mercedes. ....
10 The children .... I baby-sit for are twins. ....
11 This jumper .... I bought in Ireland is pure wool. ....
12 The priest .... married us has gone to work in Africa. ....
13 Emma .... sister is an actress is going on holiday to Hollywood. ....
14 The supermarket .... is near our house is open on Sundays. ....
15 The actor .... I most admire is Robert de Niro. ....
16 This vase .... he bought at a jumble sale is antique. ....
17 The dog .... Roger bought has just had six puppies. ....
18 The country .... my father was born is at war. ....
19 Anna .... cuts my hair has just bought her own shop. ....
20 There are some questions .... I cannot answer. ... .
21 My home town .... is near Birmingham is very small. ....
22 His uncle .... is a millionaire owns a house in the Bahamas. ....
23 The boy .... bicycle was stolen is at the police station. ....
24 The dog .... lives next door has had six puppies. ....
25 Sharon .... works at the Café Rousse spilt coffee on a customer. ....

176 **Use relatives to combine the following sentences as in the example:**

1 I spoke to a gentleman. He was very polite. ... *The gentleman (whom/that/who) I spoke to was very polite. The gentleman to whom I spoke was very polite.* ....
2 I'm writing about a film. It was made in 1958. ....
3 She's the girl. They were talking about her. ....
4 That's the restaurant. We go there every Saturday. ....
5 This is the island. We spent our holiday on it. ....
6 These are the Joneses. We went to the theatre with them. ....
7 That is the hotel. We used to stay at it every summer. ....
8 He's Mr Smith. I got all the information from him. ....
9 This is the knife. He cut the bread with it. ....
10 Mrs Andrews is the woman. I've received a letter from her. ....

177 **Join the sentences with the correct relatives.**

Last year I went to Paris. I stayed there for a week. It was a lovely experience. I will never forget it. I stayed with Louise. She is my French cousin. She introduced me to Pierre. His knowledge of Paris is amazing. I loved the boulevards. They are so wide and elegant. The Eiffel Tower is, of course, a great sight. It is famous all over the world. My favourite building, however, was the Invalides. It was built in the 17th century. At the end of the week I thanked Pierre. He had been very kind.

...*Last year I went to Paris where I stayed for a week.*...
....
....
....
....
....

178 **Find the mistake and correct it.**

1 I saw a TV programme about old people which go parachuting every weekend.
   ...*I saw a TV programme about old people who go parachuting every weekend.* ....
2 There's a door which leading to a secret passage at the end of the hall.
   ....
3 She's friendly with the two children whose their mother is the headmistress.
   ....
4 Sam works in Switzerland that is not in the European Union.
   ....
5 While on holiday I met a lot of people, some of which were really boring.
   ....
6 Do you know the name of the film which it won seven Oscars at last year's Academy Awards?
   ....
7 When I was in Australia, I visited my uncle which I had never met before.
   ....
8 Mr Collins is the man from who I bought my tape recorder.
   ....
9 The match about that you were talking ended in disaster.
   ....
10 They didn't have that I asked for.
   ....

179 Explain the meaning of the following as in the example:

1 The boys in my class who enjoyed the film saw it again.　　..only some boys in my class..
　The boys in my class, who enjoyed the film, saw it again.　...all the boys in my class ......
2 The drivers who were involved in the accident had to go to court.　...
　The drivers, who were involved in the accident, had to go to court.　...
3 The famous clubs which they go to are the most expensive.　...
　The famous clubs, which they go to, are the most expensive.　...
4 The German students, who I met at Jill's party, phoned me last night.　...
　The German students who I met at Jill's party phoned me last night.　...
5 My new records, which he borrowed last week, were ruined.　...
　My new records which he borrowed last week were ruined.　...

180 Rephrase the following sentences using the words in bold.

1 The building where I work caught fire yesterday.
　in　　　The building ...*in which I work/I work in*... caught fire yesterday.
2 It was very kind of Ted to lend me his car.
　which　Ted lent .... very kind of him.
3 The person I met was totally ignorant of the situation.
　who　　I met a .... totally ignorant of the situation.
4 The teacher was very angry because none of the students had done their homework.
　which　None of the students had done .... the teacher very angry.
5 The woman drinking tea over there is my mother.
　who　　The woman .... over there is my mother.
6 The person found guilty of murder was sent to prison.
　who　　The person .... of murder was sent to prison.
7 Joan came first, not Sally.
　who　　It ...., not Sally.
8 The lady in the pink dress is my aunt.
　wearing　The .... pink dress is my aunt.
9 The hotel in which we spent our summer holidays has been closed down.
　where　The hotel .... holidays has been closed down.
10 The stolen painting is a fake.
　which　The painting .... is a fake.
11 He's learning Spanish, not Portuguese.
　that　　It's ...., not Portuguese.
12 I wonder who owns this car.
　whose　I wonder .... is.

Oral Activity 12

Individually or in teams, give definitions of the following using relative pronouns or adverbs.

a builder	Shakespeare	a post office	an author
elephants	the seaside	a key	a professor
the theatre	a restaurant	a necklace	a pop singer
an axe	a blanket	a tailor	a school

eg. A builder is someone who builds houses.

Linking Words

Linking words show the logical relationship between sentences or parts of a sentence.

181 Say the sentences from the table in every possible way as in the example. Whenever this is not possible, make up a new sentence so that other linking words can be used.

eg. *She is both clever and rich. She's not only clever but she's also rich.   etc* ....

Positive Addition	and, both...and, not only...but (also/as well), too, moreover, in addition to, furthermore, further, also, not to mention the fact that, besides	She's clever **and** rich.
Negative Addition	neither...nor, nor, neither, either	**Neither** Barry **nor** Kevin knows how to drive. Barry doesn't know how to drive. **Nor** does Kevin.
Contrast	but, not...but, although, while, whereas, despite, even if, even though, on the other hand, in contrast, however, (and) yet, at the same time	Riding a bicycle may not be as comfortable as driving a car; **however** it is much more environmentally friendly.
Similarity	similarly, likewise, in the same way, equally	A glass of milk before you go to bed may help you sleep. **Similarly,** a hot bath could do the trick.
Concession	but, even so, however, (and) still, (and) yet, nevertheless, on the other hand, although, even though, despite/in spite of, regardless of, admittedly, considering, whereas, while, nonetheless	He carried on playing until the end of the game, **even though** he had a broken toe.
Alternative	or, on the other hand, either...or, alternatively	You could tell her the bad news, **or/ on the other hand/alternatively,** you could let her find out herself.
Emphasis	besides, not only this but...also, as well, what is more, in fact, as a matter of fact, to tell you the truth, actually, indeed, let alone	I'm afraid you are not qualified for this job and, **what is more**, you are far too young.
Exemplification	as, such as, like, for example, for instance, particularly, especially, in particular	All the performers were good, but Pavarotti **in particular** was magnificent.
Clarification	that is to say, specifically, in other words, to put it another way, I mean	She's angry. **Specifically,** she's angry at you.
Cause / Reason	as, because, because of, since, on the grounds that, seeing that, due to, in view of, owing to, for, now that, so	She decided to order a salad **now that** she had started her diet.

Manner	as, (in) the way, how, the way in which, (in) the same way (as), as if, as though	The coach explained **how** the team could beat their opponents.
Condition	if, in case, assuming (that), on condition (that), provided (that), providing (that), unless, in the event (that), in the event of, as/so long as, granted/granting (that), whether, whether...or (alternative condition), only if, even if, otherwise, or(else), in case of	The travel agency will contact you **in the event that/in case** your flight is changed.
Consequence of a condition	consequently, then, under those circumstances, if so, if not, so, therefore, in that case, otherwise, thus	You may be caught by the enemy. **If so,** tell them nothing.
Purpose	so that, so as (not) to, in order (not) to, in order that, for fear (that), in case, lest	Make a note of our appointment in your diary **in case** you forget about it.
Effect / Result	such/so...that, consequently, for this reason, as a consequence, thus, therefore, so	He was the only child of a rich banker and, **as a consequence**, he was very spoilt.
Comparison	as...as, than, half as...as, nothing like, the...the, twice as...as, less...than	Her second novel is **nothing like** her first.
Time	when, whenever, as, while, now (that), before, until, till, after, since	I like to visit the cathedral **whenever** I'm in Durham.
Place	where, wherever	Park your car **wherever** you want to.
Exception	but (for), except (for), apart from	We had a lovely holiday, **apart from** that one day when it rained.
Relative	who, whom, whose, which, what, that	There's the man **whose** house was burnt down.
Chronological	**beginning:** initially, first..., at first, to start/begin with, first of all **continuing:** secondly ..., after this/that, second..., afterwards, then, next, before this **concluding:** finally, at last, in the end, eventually, lastly, last but not least	**First of all,** I'd like to thank my mother ... **Then,** I must thank everyone involved in making this wonderful film ... **Finally,** I want to thank you, my fans.
Reference	considering, concerning, regarding, with respect/regard/reference to, in respect/regard/reference to this/to the fact that	**Considering** all the evidence, we find the accused "not guilty". I'm writing **with reference to** your report on whales.
Summarising	in conclusion, in summary, to sum up, as I have said, as (it) was previously stated, on the whole, in all, all in all, altogether, in short, briefly, to put it briefly	**To sum up**, the government must spend more money on public services.

182 **Replace the underlined words with synonymous ones.**

Sarah had had a terrific year **1)** <u>particularly</u> after she was given a promotion in the summer. She had worked hard all year and, **2)** <u>even though</u> she was exhausted, it had been worthwhile. She was happy because she had been given a rise. **3)** <u>On the other hand</u> she had a lot more responsibility than before. She didn't mind the change; **4)** <u>besides</u> it was a good challenge. **5)** <u>Apart from</u> opposition from one or two of her colleagues, she was really enjoying her new position. **6)** <u>As a matter of fact</u>, she had never been happier. Her home life had improved, **7)** <u>too</u>. She was now on friendly terms with **8)** <u>both</u> her mother <u>and</u> her father. They had come to an agreement and, **9)** <u>although</u> her parents still considered her their little girl, she was given more freedom **10)** <u>on the grounds that</u> she was, after all, 20!

1 ...*especially, in particular*...	4	7	10 ....
2	5	8	
3	6	9	

183 **Fill in: not ... but also, despite, unfortunately, because, even though, particularly, however, besides, seeing that or both ... and.**

Sally had a bad year, **1)** ...*particularly*... after she had lost her job in the spring. She was exhausted **2)** .... physically .... mentally and she needed a break. **3)** .... the fact that she was going alone, she was looking forward to her holiday. She had booked a hotel in a quiet resort **4)** .... she wanted to relax; **5)** ...., she couldn't stand crowded tourist resorts. It was supposed to be the holiday of a lifetime. **6)** .... that wasn't to be the case. **7)** .... only was the plane delayed for seven hours, ..., when she arrived at the hotel, her room had been double booked. **8)** .... they were to blame, the hotel owners offered her alternative accommodation. **9)** ...., the other hotel was in a noisy resort. **10)** .... she wasn't happy with the arrangement, she eventually had to accept their offer.

184 **Join the sentences, then identify the function of the linking words in brackets.**

1 I don't like doing the washing-up. My flatmate usually does the domestic jobs. (besides)
...*I don't like doing the washing-up; besides, my flatmate usually does the domestic jobs.*
(positive addition)...

2 I can't afford to lend her any more money. She already owes me £150. (moreover)
....

3 I enjoy my job. It's very well paid. (not only...but also)
....

4 He never does any homework. He managed to get a good mark in the test. (even though)
....

5 I'm afraid you're not tall enough to be a model. You're not very photogenic. (what is more)
....

6 He plays football like a professional. He isn't a professional though. (as if)
....

7 She's a very good teacher. She has no experience. (considering)
....

8 He has never bought anyone a present. He's totally mean. (in other words)
....

9 She is quite shy. She wants to be an actress. (and yet)
....

10 I'm going to phone him again. He doesn't want to speak to me. (even if)
....

185 Replace the underlined words with synonymous ones.

Dear Mr Greenlee,

I regret to inform you that your account is £1,560 overdrawn. 1) <u>Consequently</u>, I must ask you to return your credit cards immediately, 2) <u>in order not to</u> increase your debt. 3) <u>In addition</u>, you should not write any more cheques 4) <u>until</u> we have discussed the matter. 5) <u>In view of</u> the fact that you are currently unemployed, it may not be possible to extend your loan facilities. 6) <u>In fact</u>, arrangements must be made to pay off the amount as soon as possible. 7) <u>Initially</u>, the bank will assess your financial status. 8) <u>After this</u>, a weekly repayment will be decided upon. Your credit cards may be returned to you 9) <u>provided that</u> the repayments are kept up. 10) <u>In conclusion</u>, we sincerely hope we can deal with this matter to our mutual satisfaction.

Yours sincerely,
J. Cash
(Midway Bank PLC)

1 ...*Therefore, Thus*............   4 ....   7 ....   10 ....
2 ....   5 ....   8 ....
3 ....   6 ....   9 ....

186 Fill in: who, as...as, whenever, wherever, in this way, in particular, although, both ... and, such as, to sum up or specifically.

In all history there has never been a magician 1) ...*as*...famous ...*as*... Harry Houdini. 2) ...., he was well known for his incredible escape acts, 3) .... freeing himself from a locked safe at the bottom of a river. People recognised him 4) .... he went and 5) .... he performed, huge crowds gathered to watch. But, 6) .... he was a master of the art of illusion, he was a very honest man 7) .... fought for truth and justice. 8) ...., he campaigned against spiritualists and other people who claimed to have supernatural powers. 9) ...., he made quite a few enemies in the "entertainment" business. 10) ...., there have been few men this century who have combined 11) .... talent .... honesty in such an admirable way.

Oral Activity 13

In teams or individually students complete the sentences using an appropriate linking word.

1 We could stay in a hotel for a week, or ...*alternatively we could rent a villa.* ....
2 She never leaves the house ....
3 She is so confident she acts ....
4 My father was forced to retire early ....
5 I think French cheese is ....
6 I would like to spend a year travelling around the world ....
7 I have a lot of work to finish ....
8 You can leave the class early ....
9 She advised me to take traveller's cheques ....
10 She decided to go to the beach ....

187 Fill in: whether or not, alternatively, not only ... but also, what is more, as a matter of fact, however, owing to, neither ... nor, providing that, in order to, at the same time, firstly or thus.

There are many things you can do **1)** ...*in order to*... reduce pollution levels in the city. **2)** ...., to decrease the amount of traffic on the streets, you should ask yourself **3)** .... your car journey is really necessary. It could be cheaper and healthier to walk. **4)** ...., it could even be quicker, **5)** .... the amount of traffic at certain times of the day. **6)** ...., you could use public transport, **7)** .... avoiding the stressful experience of driving in the city and **8)** .... freeing yourself from the time-consuming necessity of finding a parking space. **9)** ...., when it comes to speed, health and convenience, **10)** .... walking .... the public transport system can compare with the simple bicycle. **11)** .... has it been proven to be faster than a car for most city journeys, ... you can park it almost anywhere **12)** .... you lock it securely.

188 Replace the underlined words with synonymous ones.

She had given her daughter permission to go on the trip **1)** provided that they were accompanied by an adult. She was worried sick that something would go wrong and constantly told Sally that **2)** in the event of an accident she should ring up immediately. She didn't want her daughter to go but, **3)** so as not to seem overprotective, she **4)** finally agreed. All Sally's friends were going on the trip **5)** apart from Julie and she knew what they all thought of her. Julie's parents wouldn't let her do anything **6)** for fear that something terrible might happen. **7)** Consequently she had very few friends. **8)** Whenever there was a party, she was never invited. **9)** On the whole, Sally's mother decided that **10)** despite the risks involved, she had to allow her daughter some freedom **11)** lest she too might become unpopular with her schoolmates.

1 ...*as long as*........	4	7	10 ....
2	5	8	11 ....
3	6	9	

189 Using the word in bold fill in the missing part of the second sentence so that it has a similar meaning to the first sentence. Do not change the word given.

1 There's someone waiting to speak to you.
   who   There's ...*someone who is waiting*... to speak to you.
2 Take some more money; you will need it.
   case   Take some more .... it.
3 The car was very expensive; he couldn't afford it.
   such   It was .... he couldn't afford it.
4 When they left she started tidying the room.
   until   She waited .... she started tidying the room.
5 She was early but she missed the beginning of the film.
   though   Early .... the beginning of the film.
6 He asked for a loan; he wanted to expand his company.
   view   He asked for a loan .... his company.
7 The man with the black umbrella is Mr Jones.
   carrying   The man .... the black umbrella is Mr Jones.

8 They locked the car; they were afraid someone might steal it.

fear   They locked the car .... it.

9 She's not from Italy but she speaks Italian like a native.

if   She speaks Italian .... from Italy.

10 She inherited some money; she gave most of it to charity.

which   She inherited some money, ... to charity.

11 I liked the whole film, but the last half hour was especially exciting.

particular   I liked the whole film, but the last half hour .... exciting.

12 There was thick fog so the plane couldn't take off.

due   The plane couldn't take off .... thick fog.

Oral Activity 14

Work in teams or individually and make up sentences combining the given ideas and the linking words as in the example. You may use any tense, provided the sentence is grammatically correct.

to buy (or not to buy) a new car   enough, a lot of, not much, little money

such ... that	consequently	although	when	yet ... still
even if	therefore	nevertheless	in case	as long as
unless	because of	but	otherwise	even though
despite the fact	as soon as	because	but ... anyway	whether ... or not
in spite of	so ... that	now that	since	neither .... nor

eg.   *He's got such a lot of money that he'll buy a new car.*
       Even if he has enough money, he won't buy a new car. etc

Oral Activity 15

The teacher sets the situation "Karen Lee had to apply for a new job." Students, one after the other continue the story using linking words.

Student A: *Therefore, she started sending letters to different companies.*
Student B: *A few days passed with no reply. Then, one day a letter arrived. etc*

Writing Activity 5

Read the CVs below then choose the most suitable applicant for the job of flight attendant. Support your decision using linking words.

Name:	Karen Lee	Susan Jones
Age:	22	25
Qualifications:	'A' Levels in French and Drama, First-aid certificate	University degree in Physics
Languages spoken:	English, French	English, French, Spanish, Italian
Previous experience:	waitress (1 year), tour guide (1 year)	secretary (6 months), nanny (3 months), sales assistant (6 months)
Marital status:	single	married - 1 child (2 months old)

To: The Company Director   *From P. Edwards*
Subject: Post of flight attendant with Cloud Nine Airlines

As instructed, I have interviewed two applicants for the post of flight attendant with Cloud Nine Airlines. Although both applicants are of a high standard, I have chosen ...

190 Complete the second sentence so that it has a similar meaning to the first sentence. Use the word given and other words to complete each sentence. You must use between two and five words. Don't change the word given.

1 They enjoyed playing football.
   time   They ...*had a good time playing*... football.
2 Write down my address; you may need it.
   case   Write down my address .... it.
3 This phone isn't working I'm afraid.
   out   This phone .... I'm afraid.
4 Let's sit on the terrace; the food isn't ready yet.
   until   Let's sit on the terrace .... ready.
5 Smoking isn't allowed here.
   smoke   They do .... here.
6 Operating a computer is difficult.
   operate   It .... a computer.
7 The examination lasted three hours.
   hour   It was .... examination.
8 Since it was very cold, we stayed at home.
   due   We stayed at home .... weather.
9 She won't buy him any chocolate if he doesn't stop crying.
   unless   She won't buy him any chocolate .... crying.
10 Can I stay with you for a week?
   put   Can .... for a week?
11 If there is a fire, you must not use the lift.
   event   In ...., you must not use the lift.
12 Mary hates vampire films and so does Paul.
   nor   Neither .... vampire films.
13 Would you like to come to the cinema with me?
   coming   How .... with me?
14 If he hadn't reacted so quickly, we would have been killed.
   reaction But ...., we would have been killed.

191 Look at Appendix 2, then fill in the correct particle(s).

1 Please **draw** ...*back*... from the edge of the cliff.
2 He went to the bank to **draw** .... some money.
3 Look! The train has just **drawn** ....
4 The lawyer **drew** .... the contract for the sale of the property.
5 I'm afraid you've **fallen** .... with your schoolwork.
6 He **fell** .... his father's point of view.
7 When John lost all his money, he **fell** .... his father for support.
8 The starving men **fell** .... the food greedily.
9 The roof is in danger of **falling** ....
10 He **fell** .... her at first sight.
11 They **got** .... the stolen goods.
12 Ann is **getting** .... her colleagues.
13 I don't understand what you are **getting** ....
14 He always **gets** .... me by buying me presents.
15 I tried to call you last night but I couldn't **get** .... you.
16 **Get** .... the train quickly, before it leaves.

Phrasal Verbs

1   in, on, back, up
2   on, out, up, in
3   in, out, back, on
4   out, on, in, up
5   for, in, behind, through
6   in with, into, off, out
7   apart, in, back on, on
8   out, upon, for, through
9   in, off, behind, back
10 through, out, through, for
11 off, on, through, away with
12 on, on with, by, round
13 in, at, through to, out
14 off, round, up, on with
15 on, over, across, through to
16 round, up, with, on

192 Look at Appendix 3, then fill in the correct preposition.

	Prepositions

1 He is **identical** ...*to*... his brother.
2 We were **impressed** .... her performance.
3 Claire made a bad **impression** .... Steve's parents.
4 She is **jealous** .... her well-off sister-in-law.
5 Mr Smith is **keen** .... photography.
6 This diet is **lacking** .... vitamins.
7 There is a **lack** .... iron in her blood.
8 Don't **lean** .... the window; it may break.
9 Sheila got **married** .... a pop singer.
10 There is no **need** .... more petrol.
11 The Browns are **new** .... this area.
12 It is **obvious** .... everyone that the painting is a forgery.
13 The accident victim has to be **operated** .... immediately.
14 He took no **notice** .... the warning and entered the building.

Prepositions

1 to, as, with
2 of, with, on
3 by, with, on
4 of, with, for
5 with, on, to
6 of, to, in
7 at, of, in
8 at, to, against
9 to, with, at
10 to, in, for
11 at, with, to
12 with, to, in
13 about, for, on
14 about, of, for

193 Think of the word which best fits each space. Use only one word in each space.

A MINOR ACCIDENT

James had been on his **(0)** ...*own*... for a few days now. His sister Anja, **(1)** .... is a florist, had had to go to Holland **(2)** .... business. Although James was quite **(3)** .... of cooking, it was Anja who usually cooked for them both and **(4)** .... she had left, she had prepared three meals for him **(5)** .... he only had to heat up. This meant that there would be **(6)** .... one day when James would have to make his own meal. He had decided on a tuna salad and toast - easy enough. James went to work at the advertising studio as usual and tried to concentrate on his work rather **(7)** .... on the fact that he was missing Anja terribly. At home in the evening, **(8)** .... James was making his toast and tuna salad, Anja rang. He was talking happily on the **(9)** .... when a strange smell floated under his nose. Shocked, he quickly **(10)** .... goodbye to Anja. He had forgotten **(11)** .... about the toast, which now had to be forced out of the toaster and the **(12)**............ room had filled **(13)** .... smoke before he realised it. "I'm **(14)** .... glad you're home!" exclaimed James when Anja returned. "Me too!" she replied. "But James **(15)** .... are the walls black?"

194 Use the words in capitals to form a word that fits in the space in the same line.

MUM'S HOBBY

My mother is a keen **(0)** ... who takes
every opportunity she can to practise.
She has a great deal of **(1)** ..., some
of which is very **(2)** ..., so she has
to be very **(3)** ..., especially if she goes
somewhere **(4)** ... . Some of her photos
have caused a great deal of **(5)** ...,
although the rest of us are sometimes
(6) ... with her, because she often
takes photos at **(7)** ... times.
However, we all **(8)** ... her skill
and her **(9)** ... to improve her
techniques. After all, having our
photos taken is not usually **(10)** ... .

PHOTOGRAPH	0	*photographer* 0
	1	1
EQUIP		
EXPENSE	2	2
CARE	3	3
DANGER	4	4
AMUSE	5	5
PATIENT	6	6
CONVENIENT	7	7
ADMIRATION	8	8
DETERMINE	9	9
BOTHER	10	10

195 Read the text carefully. Some of the lines are correct and some have a word which should not be there. If a line is correct, put a tick (✓) in the space provided. If a line has a word which should not be there, write it in the space provided.

FLYING

0	The most of us get on a plane excited about our	**0**	the
00	holiday. But after the flight we feel exhausted,	**00**	✓
1	which it is not the ideal way to start a holiday.	**1**	
2	How about can we stay fresh on a plane journey?	**2**	
3	Firstly, allow you yourself plenty of time to get	**3**	
4	to the airport and check in it. This cuts out	**4**	
5	stress. Don't eat rich, heavy food before you will	**5**	
6	board the plane, as this may make you to feel	**6**	
7	nauseous before you even have take off.	**7**	
8	Pass the time pleasantly by reading	**8**	
9	or watching the film provided. Free of drinks	**9**	
10	are usually provided on flights. Flying	**10**	
11	during the night can be to tiring, so try to get	**11**	
12	some sleep. Pillows and blankets are usually	**12**	
13	distributed to all passengers. Meals	**13**	
14	are as usually provided free and are generally	**14**	
15	of reasonable quality. Have a good flight!	**15**	

196 Choose the item which best explains the idioms, then make sentences using them.

1	a pain in the neck	(A)	sth/sb annoying	B	sth/sb embarrassing
2	a pet hate	A	a nasty pet	B	a major dislike
3	a piece of cake	A	an easy task	B	a part of something
4	a red letter day	A	a special day	B	a revolution
5	a rolling stone	A	a moving group	B	sb constantly on the move
6	a short cut	A	a shorter route	B	a small cut
7	a skeleton in the cupboard	A	a funny story	B	a hidden, unpleasant secret
8	a slip of the tongue	A	a swear word	B	an unintentional verbal mistake
9	a splitting headache	A	a painful headache	B	a broken head
10	a spoke in one's wheel	A	a flat tyre	B	an obstacle to one's plans

197 Put the verbs in brackets into the correct tense.

Dear Sarah,

Thanks for the Christmas card 1) ...**Did you enjoy**... (enjoy) yourself at Christmas? I wish I 2) .... (see) you but I 3) .... (be) too busy at the time. I 4) .... (work) in a shop for a few days. The shop 5) .... (belong) to Bob Smith. 6) .... (remember) him?

I 7) .... (go) to Spain in the summer. My parents 8) .... (recently/buy) a villa there. If you 9) .... (be) free in July, why 10) .... (not / you / come) with me? It 11) .... (be) great fun! Anyway, I'd better stop now. I 12) .... (invite) my cousin for lunch and I 13) .... (not/cook) anything yet! Write soon.

Love,
Sue

Passive Voice / Causative Form

Have all your cakes **been sold**?

There's one left. It **was** freshly **baked** this morning.

It looks as though it **has been eaten** by mice.

That's impossible, madam. The cat's been lying on it all morning.

Passive Voice

The **passive** is formed by using the appropriate tense of the verb **to be + past participle**. Present Perfect Continuous, Future Continuous, Past Perfect Continuous are not normally used in the passive.

	Active Voice	Passive Voice
Present Simple	They **serve** dinner at 6.00.	Dinner **is served** at 6.00.
Present Continuous	They **are serving** dinner now.	Dinner **is being served** now.
Past Simple	They **served** dinner.	Dinner **was served**.
Past Continuous	They **were serving** dinner.	Dinner **was being served**.
Future Simple	They **will serve** dinner.	Dinner **will be served**.
Present Perfect	They **have served** dinner.	Dinner **has been served**.
Past Perfect	They **had served** dinner.	Dinner **had been served**.
Future Perfect	They **will have served** dinner.	Dinner **will have been served**.
Present infinitive	They **should serve** dinner.	Dinner **should be served**.
Perfect infinitive	They **should have served** dinner.	Dinner **should have been served**.
-ing form	He likes people **serving** his dinner.	He likes his dinner **being served**.
Perfect -ing form	**Having served** dinner, ...	Dinner **having been served**...
Modals + be + p.p.	You **must serve** dinner.	Dinner **must be served**.

Note: **Get** is used in colloquial English instead of **be** to express something happening **by accident**.
*He **got hurt** last Monday. (more usual than: He **was** hurt last Monday.)*

The passive is used

- when the **agent** (the person who does the action) is **unknown, unimportant** or **obvious** from the context. *The door **had been locked**. (we don't know who locked it - unknown agent) Repairs **are being made** on the runway. (by the builders - obvious agent)*
- when we are interested more in the action than the agent, such as **in news reports, formal notices, instructions, processes, headlines, advertisements** etc. *The whole area **was evacuated**. (news report) Breakfast **is served** from 6.00 to 10.30. (formal notice)*
- to make **statements** more **formal** or **polite**. *"My new dress **has been ruined**." (more polite than saying "You ruined my dress.")*
- to put **emphasis** on the agent. *The Pyramids **were built by the ancient Egyptians**.*

198 Write sentences in the passive as in the example:

1 (The floor/not clean/yet) ....*The floor hasn't been cleaned yet.*...............
2 (The politician/interview/now) ....
3 (The Mona Lisa/paint/Leonardo da Vinci) ....
4 (My flat/burgle/last night) ....
5 (All tickets/sell/before we got there) ....
6 (The dog/not feed/yet) ....
7 (The presents/wrap/now) ....
8 (The prizes/award/President/tomorrow) ....
9 (Tea/grow/India) ....
10 (The prisoners/take/to prison/now) ....

199 Put the verbs in brackets into the correct passive form.

Something should **1)** ...*be done*... (do) to protect holidaymakers from awful experiences. So many articles **2)** ....(write) so far in newspapers and magazines warning tourists to guard against being victims of tricksters. The brochure advertisements ought to **3)** .... (approve) by ABTA before **4)** .... (publish) to ensure that the details which **5)** .... (give) aren't misleading or inaccurate. Mr and Mrs Brown had a typical bad holiday experience. They arrived at the old hotel which was situated in the middle of nowhere. The brochure claimed that it **6)** .... (build) recently, but it was obvious that it was old. It **7)** .... (not/decorate) for years and the paint was peeling off the walls. The previous owners had sold the hotel, which **8)** .... (buy) by an elderly couple. They **9)** ....(advise) by their children to employ staff to manage it but, unfortunately, people **10)** .... (still/interview) at the time when Mr and Mrs Brown arrived. Food **11)** .... (not/serve) in the restaurant and guests **12)** .... (expect) to make their own arrangements. As if that wasn't enough, when they went to their rooms, they found the bed linen **13)** .... (not/change) after the previous occupants. As far as Mr and Mrs Brown were concerned the hotel should **14)** ....(close) until adequate staff **15)** .... (employ). It is certainly nothing like the hotel which **16)** .... (describe) in the brochure.

200 Rewrite the newspaper headlines as complete sentences.

1 DEMONSTRATIONS AGAINST POLL TAX HELD LAST SUNDAY	**2 ALL-DAY STRIKE TO BE HELD BY ELECTRICITY WORKERS**	**3 MISSING PAINTING NOT YET RECOVERED**
4 CHILD RESCUED FROM QUICKSAND YESTERDAY	**5 £1,000,000 BEING RAISED FOR HOMELESS IN L.A.**	**6 MEXICO CITY TO BE HIT BY HURRICANE TOMORROW**

1 *Demonstrations against the Poll Tax were held last Sunday.* ....
2 ....
3 ....
4 ....
5 ....
6 ....

Changing from Active into Passive

● The object of the active verb becomes the subject in the new sentence. The active verb changes into a passive form and the subject of the active verb becomes the agent which

	Subject	Verb	Object	Agent
Active	*The mayor*	*opened*	*the new school.*	
Passive	*The new school*	*was opened*		*by the mayor.*

is either introduced with "by" or is omitted. The passive can be used only with transitive verbs (verbs which take an object such as give, write, take, open etc). Verbs such as happen, sleep, come, go, seem etc are not used in the passive.
● In the passive we use **by + agent** to say who or what did the action. We use **with + instrument** or **material** to say what the agent used. *She was hit on the head* **by** *the burglar* **with** *a piece of wood.*
● With verbs that take two objects, it is more usual to begin the passive sentence with the person. *They offered* **Ann** *a job.* → **Ann** *was offered a job.* (more usual than: **A job** *was offered to Ann.*)
● We put the agent (= person who performs the action) in the passive only if it adds information. When the agent is **unknown, unimportant** or **obvious** from the context, it is omitted. Agents such as **someone, people, I, you** etc are omitted. *King Lear was written* **by Shakespeare**. *(The agent is not omitted; it adds information.) Somebody helped him.* → *He was helped (by somebody). (unknown agent; by+ agent are omitted.)*
● **Make, hear, help, see** are followed by a **to-infinitive** in the passive. *They helped him tidy the garage.* → *He* **was helped to tidy** *the garage.* Note that **hear, see, watch** can be followed by a present participle in the active and passive. *I* **heard** *her* **practising** *the piano.* → *She* **was heard practising** *the piano.*
● The verbs **believe, expect, feel, hope, know, report, say, think** etc are used in the following passive patterns in personal and impersonal constructions.

a) **subject (person) + passive + to-infinitive** (personal construction)	*People believe he is a liar.* *He is believed to be a liar.*
b) **It + passive + that-clause** (impersonal construction)	*It is believed that he is a liar.*

● We use **be + past participle** or **have been + past participle** after modal verbs (will, can, may etc). *He* **can't repair** *the lock.* → *The lock* **can't be repaired**. *They* **may have painted** *the house.* → *The house* **may have been painted**.
● Verbs followed by a preposition (eg. accuse sb of, look after etc) take the preposition immediately after them when turned into the passive. *They accused him of murder.* → *He* **was accused of** *murder*.
● In **passive questions** with **who/whom/which** we do not omit **by**. *Who gave you this book?* → **Who** *were you given this book* **by**? *Who signed the letter?* → **Who** *was this letter signed* **by**?
● Participles like **amazed, broken, interested, pleased, worried** etc can be used either as adjectives or past participles in the passive. If these participles are used as adjectives, they cannot be turned into the active. Compare: *The first time I saw the building I was* **amazed**. *("amazed" is used as an adjective) I was* **amazed** *by your work. ("amazed" is used as a past participle - Your work amazed me.)*

201 **Change from the active into the passive. Omit the agent where it can be omitted. Justify the omission or inclusion of the agent.**

1 The Scots make the best fudge. ...*The best fudge is made by the Scots. (agent not omitted; emphasis on the agent)* ....
2 You should take these tablets before meals. ....
3 You must wash coloured clothes separately. ....
4 The teacher sent him out of the classroom. ....
5 Thousands of British tourists will visit Spain this summer. ....

6 The dentist pulled out my rotten tooth. ....
7 The police are questioning him now. ....
8 Someone has made a complaint. ....
9 They had left the lights on. ....
10 I broke my arm when I fell out of a tree. ....
11 The horrible old man was slowly poisoning the cat. ....
12 The snow will have covered the mountains by Christmas. ....
13 The waitress serves breakfast at 7 am. ....
14 Who delivered the parcel? ....
15 Her parents made her clean her room. ....
16 They will have finished the work by tonight. ....
17 Someone had warned her that she might lose her job. ....
18 Who discovered America? ....
19 Who is going to feed your dog? ....
20 Who answered the phone? ....
21 Who did they give the prize to? ....
22 Which building are they going to knock down? ....

202 Put the verbs in brackets into the correct passive form.

Last week a new leisure centre **1)** ...*was opened*... (open) in the town of Halden. The centre **2)** .... (believe) to be the largest in Europe and it **3)** .... (hope) that it **4)** .... (visit) by over 40,000 people a month. The centre **5)** .... (plan) for over ten years, but it **6)**...................(only/make) possible by a large government grant. Unfortunately, it **7)** .... (not/finish) yet, but it **8)** .... (think) that it **9)** .... (complete) by next month. The centre includes an Olympic-size swimming pool and fifty tennis courts which **10)**.......... .... (can/book) by phone. The gym **11)**..................... (claim) to be the most modern in the country. The equipment **12)** .... (buy) in Germany and training **13)** .... (provide) by five top instructors. Entrance fees are cheap because half the cost **14)** .... (pay) by the local council, so many local people will be able to afford them.

203 Fill in "by" or "with".

1 Most children are strongly influenced ...*by*... their parents.
2 The jam sandwiches were made .... white bread.
3 Jake was dismissed .... his boss.
4 The show was presented .... Mr Jones.
5 The parcels were tied .... string.
6 The meal was eaten .... chopsticks.
7 The song was performed .... Madonna.
8 This awful mess was made .... Carol's dog.

9 The football fans were observed .... the police.
10 My hair was cut .... a top stylist.
11 The goal was scored .... Liverpool's youngest player.
12 The beds were made up .... clean sheets.
13 The supermarket trolley was filled .... cat food.
14 My camera was loaded .... a black and white film.

204 Identify the word in bold as an adjective or past participle.

1 The audience were **amused** by the play. ....*past participle*.....................
2 The last time I went to the dentist I was **scared.** ....
3 She was **worried** all day after hearing the news. ....
4 The students were **bored** by the lecturer's long speech. ....
5 She was **exhausted** after cleaning the house all day. ....
6 Sue was **delighted** with all her birthday presents. ....

205 Complete the sentences using the passive and the verbs listed below.

must, shouldn't, might, can't

1 A: Has the rubbish been collected yet?
   B: Well, it's not here now so it ...*must have been collected.* ....
2 A: Did anyone tell David about the meeting?
   B: He's written it in his diary so he ....
3 A: Has someone repaired the telephone?
   B: I've just used it so it ....
4 A: Was Sue injured in the car accident?
   B: She .... I heard there were a few casualties.
5 A: Did anyone move the accident victim?
   B: Yes, but he .... It was a mistake to touch him.
6 A: Ted said someone stole his car. Is that true?
   B: No. It .... I've just seen him driving it.

206 Turn the following into the passive as in the example:

1 The policeman gave me a ticket.
   I *was given a ticket by the policeman*............
   A ticket *was given to me by the policeman.* ...
2 The waiter is serving them dinner now.
   They ....
   Dinner ....
3 The teacher won't show him his marks.
   He ....
   His marks ....

4 Ken offered Janet a ride.
   Janet ....
   A ride ....
5 Miss Price has taught Arnie a new dance step.
   Arnie ....
   A new dance step ....
6 They should have ordered you a taxi.
   You ....
   A taxi ....

207 Make sentences in the passive using infinitives or gerunds as in the example:

1 He expected people to have shown him more respect. ...*He expected to have been shown more...*
   respect. ....
2 I love people giving me flowers. ....
3 They can't stand people criticising them. ....
4 It seemed that the news shocked him. ....
5 She hates people keeping her waiting. ....
6 Someone ought to have told us about this. ....
7 Having eaten the dessert, we went on to drink coffee. ....
8 She likes people complimenting her on her work. ....

208 Rewrite the following passage in the passive.

My parents own the best restaurant in our town. Last weekend my father
dismissed the head waiter as he had stolen some stock from the cellar.
My father is going to hire a new waiter as he is doing all the work by
himself at the moment. He asked me to help serve the food. However, I
mixed up all the orders and the customers made several complaints. I'm
sure my father will never ask me to help him again!

....
....
....
....
....

209 **Use the active or the passive in any appropriate form of the verbs in brackets.**

1 Although the cheetah is the fastest animal in the world, it is in danger of becoming extinct if it continues ...*to be killed*... (kill) for its skin.
2 The children .... (frighten) by the story. It was about ghosts, witches and evil spirits.
3 Derek crashed his mother's car, and now they can't go on holiday. It ....(cannot/repair) quickly, because the front end .... (knock) into the wheel, making it unmoveable.
4 Yesterday we had a surprise party for Albert's birthday. While Mary .... (take) him to a show, we .... (gather) at his apartment. When they .... (return) home, Albert was surprised to see us all there.
5 The scandal is certain .... (report) in all the newspapers. The president .... (have) a difficult year.
6 Joan is an example of someone who can beat the odds. In 1980, she .... (tell) she had six months to live because she had cancer. After exercise, dieting and positive thinking she ....(recently/inform) that she .... (beat) the disease.
7 This newspaper .... (publish) by an Italian company. It ....(always/have) interesting stories.
8 Rice .... (grow) in this area for hundreds of years, but now the government.......................... (try) to find an alternative crop because rice .... (not/make) much profit last year.
9 My shoes .... (make) in Italy, but I .... (buy) them in France last May.
10 The Queen .... (not/see) since last July. The newspapers .... (say) that she is sick, but most people .... (not/believe) it.

210 **Rewrite the following passage in the passive.**

The Government made an important decision last night. They will ban all cars from the centre of town as pollution is seriously affecting people's health. They will allow only bicycles and buses to enter the town centre. They are making plans for a new environmental police force. After all, they must do something before it's too late.

....
....
....
....

211 **Rewrite the following passage in the passive.**

James Fitt witnessed a horrific plane crash last night. The fire brigade fought the wreckage fire while ambulance men rescued surviving passengers. Ambulances took all the survivors to hospital. No one knows yet what caused the plane to crash. Newspaper and TV reporters have already interviewed many of the survivors. The Civil Aviation Authority has launched a full investigation. They say that someone may have put a bomb on board the aircraft. They hope that the aircraft's "black box" will provide the vital information but they haven't found it yet. They are continuing the search.

....
....
....
....
....
....

6 Passive Voice / Causative Form

212 Rewrite the following sentences as in the example:

1 They say that the Loch Ness monster exists.
It is said that the Loch Ness monster exists.
The Loch Ness monster is said to exist. ...

2 They hope that a cure for the disease is imminent. ....
....

3 They believe that the hostage had died.
....
....

4 They expect that Jim will be offered a promotion.
....
....

5 They say that he was a dishonest man.
....
....

6 They believe that Elvis Presley is alive.
....
....

7 Everyone expects Rangers to win the cup.
....
....

8 People think that man is related to apes.
....
....

213 Rewrite the following sentences in the passive as in the example:

1 Police use trained dogs to find drugs. ...*Trained dogs are used by the police to find drugs.* ....
2 Nurses give the patients their medicine every morning. ....
3 A lifeguard rescued the drowning boy. ....
4 An electrician is repairing our water heater. ....
5 A defence lawyer will represent you. ....
6 They clean the rooms daily. ....
7 Customs officers searched her suitcases. ....
8 Hijackers were holding the plane passengers hostage. ....
9 A gas leak had caused the explosion. ....
10 An eyewitness gave the police a full report. ....
11 The government has increased the tax on cigarettes. ....
12 They are going to launch the product in May. ....

214 Make passive sentences using the words in brackets.

1 A: Were there many people invited to the party?
   B: Yes, *about 50 people were invited.* ... (about 50/people/invite)
2 A: Where is the accounts department?
   B: Oh, it .... (move/to the fifth floor).
3 A: What happened to that old woman?
   B: She .... (attack/and/rob).
4 A: Why does she look so happy?
   B: She .... (promote/to manageress).
5 A: What will happen to the old farmhouse?
   B: It .... (pull down).
6 A: Where are James and Simon?
   B: They .... (send/to the London office/last month).

215 Change from the passive to active.

1 His alibi may not be believed by the police. ...*The police may not believe his alibi.* ....
2 The missing person was located by the private detective. ....
3 Our leaking roof is being fixed by the builders. ....
4 Dinosaur remains have been found by a team of archaeologists. ....
5 You will be protected by a bodyguard 24 hours a day. ....
6 Air fares on all international flights have been increased by most major European airlines.
....
7 Plants are used by herbalists to cure common illnesses. ....

8 The offer will be confirmed by Jones Ltd tomorrow. ....
9 Tickets are checked by inspectors regularly. ....
10 Several members of the class were punished by the teacher. ....
11 The award is being presented by an eminent scientist. ....
12 She likes her paintings being admired. ....
13 This matter must be attended to immediately! ....
14 The window will have been replaced by the glazier by now. ....
15 Your flight may be delayed by a strike. ....

Oral Activity 16

Four young college students have bought an old double-decker bus and they are in the process of converting it into a mobile home so that they can tour Europe in it this summer. Look at the pictures and notes, then make sentences in the passive as in the example:

windows replaced, blinds put up, tyres repaired, door being put on, bus being painted, lights being repaired, roof removed, toilet and shower to be installed, new seats to be put in

Picture A

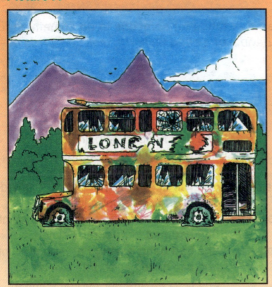

Picture B

eg. The windows have been replaced.   etc

Writing Activity 6

Write your friend a letter telling him what has been done, is being done or will be done to convert the double-decker bus into a mobile home and invite him on the tour round Europe.

Dear Sam,

    I can't tell you how excited we all are. Last month we bought an old double-decker bus to convert into a mobile home so that we can tour Europe in it this summer. So far the windows have been replaced ...

> I'm having my leg operated on tomorrow. I'm afraid I might **have it cut off**.

> Oh, good! Can I borrow your car then? You won't be needing it.

Causative Form

- **We use have + object + past participle to say that we arrange for someone to do something for us.** David **arranged for the builder** to build a shed. David **had a shed built**. (He didn't do it himself - the builder did it.)

Present Simple	She **paints** her portrait.	She **has** her portrait painted.
Present Continuous	She **is painting** her portrait.	She **is having** her portrait painted.
Past Simple	She **painted** her portrait.	She **had** her portrait painted.
Past Continuous	She **was painting** her portrait.	She **was having** her portrait painted.
Future Simple	She **will paint** her portrait.	She **will have** her portrait painted.
Future Continuous	She **will be painting** her portrait.	She **will be having** her portrait painted.
Present Perfect	She **has painted** her portrait.	She **has had** her portrait painted.
Present Perf. Cont.	She **has been painting** her portrait.	She **has been having** her portrait painted.
Past Perfect	She **had painted** her portrait.	She **had had** her portrait painted.
Past Perfect Cont.	She **had been painting** her portrait.	She **had been having** her portrait painted.
Infinitive	She can **paint** her portrait.	She can **have** her portrait painted.
-ing form	She likes **painting** her portrait.	She likes **having** her portrait painted.

- The verb **to have**, used in the causative, forms its **negations** and **questions** with **do/does** (Present Simple) and **did** (Past Simple). She **doesn't have** her hair dyed. **Did you have** your curtains put up?
- We can use the **causative** instead of the passive to express **accidents** or **misfortunes**. She **had** her car stolen. (= Her car was stolen.) He **had** his leg broken. (= His leg was broken.)
- **Get** can be used instead of **have** in the causative. I **had/got** my tooth taken out yesterday. **Get** is stronger in meaning than **have** and can be used to suggest difficulty.
  Get the door repaired, will you? He finally **got** the seats booked.

- **Make / have + object + bare infinitive** are used to express that someone causes someone else to do something, but their meaning is slightly different.
  He **made Ann type** the letter. (He **insisted** that Ann should type the letter.)
  He **had Ann type** the letter. (He **asked** Ann to type the letter.)
- **Get + object + to-infinitive** is used to show that someone **persuades** someone else to do something. He **got his mum to bake** him a cake. (He **persuaded** his mum to bake him a cake.)

216 **Tick the correct sentence for each picture.**

1 a Ben is cleaning the windows. ☑
b Ben is having the windows cleaned. ☐

2 a Peter is repairing his television. ☐
b Peter is having his television repaired. ☐

3 a Maria is shortening her jacket. ☐
b Maria is having her jacket shortened. ☐

4 a Melanie has filed her nails. ☐
b Melanie has had her nails filed. ☐

5 a Julie is piercing her ears. ☐
b Julie is having her ears pierced. ☐

6 a Mike is painting the door. ☐
b Mike is having the door painted. ☐

217 **Read the situations, then write sentences using the causative form.**

1 Our house is small. We need to build an extension. What should we do? ...*We should have an extension built.*...

2 Liz is at the beauty parlour. The beautician is painting her nails. What is she doing?
....

3 Wilf has written a novel and it's going to be published. What is Wilf going to do?
....

4 A jeweller has made a special wedding ring for Ann. What has Ann done?
....

5 Simon's suits are all made by a tailor. What does Simon do?
....

6 They have been burgled three times. Putting in a burglar alarm would help. What should they do?
....

7 Tina's boots have a hole in them. She can't wear them until they are mended. What should she have done? ....

8 Sonia is going to the optician for an eye test tomorrow. What's she going to do?
....

9 Trevor has paid a technician to install his computer. What has he done?
....

10 They had arranged for their house to be cleaned by the end of the week. Now it is clean. What had they done? ....

11 The grass has grown too much. What should they have done?
....

12 His tooth was filled yesterday. What happened to him?
....

13 No one has informed them of the meeting. What should he have done for them?
....

6 Passive Voice / Causative Form

218 Kate Gilmore is a poor young actress. Lily Showbourne is a rich star. Kate does everything herself while Lily pays other people to do it. Write what Lily says.

Kate Gilmore

Lily Showbourne

	Kate Gilmore		Lily Showbourne
1	I dyed my hair yesterday.	1	...I had my hair dyed yesterday...
2	I make all my costumes.	2	....
3	I enjoy entertaining people.	3	....
4	I'm going to cook dinner tonight.	4	....
5	I like doing my make-up.	5	....
6	I'll send some flowers to my mother.	6	....
7	I had painted my flat before I moved in.	7	....
8	I'll manicure my nails.	8	....
9	I write letters to my fans.	9	....
10	I make my bed every morning.	10	....

219 Complete the sentences with the verbs in brackets in the appropriate form.

1 Eating too much chocolate makes me ...*feel*... (feel) sick.
2 Mr Smith had his English lessons .... (pay) for by his company.
3 My mother had her skirts .... (shorten).
4 My mother had a dressmaker .... (shorten) her skirts.
5 Tom made Julie .... (help) him wash up.
6 I had an old dress .... (alter).
7 Emily got her friend .... (help) her move the sofa.
8 I had the optician .... (mend) my glasses.
9 I had my glasses .... (mend).
10 Tracy made George .... (wear) his glasses.
11 Nicky had Maria .... (tell) her the secret.
12 Joanne had the maid .... (make) her bed.

220 Complete the following conversation using the causative form.

A: We **1)** ...*are having the furniture rearranged*... (furniture/rearrange). We got tired of having it in the same place for so long.
B: That's a good idea. We **2)** .... (our furniture/replace) next week. I'm sick of it altogether!
A: We **3)** .... (new curtains/put up) tomorrow and we **4)** .... (the windows/clean) on Monday.
B: Oh, we **5)** .... (ours/do) last week.
A: Last week we **6)** .... (our new carpets/deliver), but I **7)** .... (not/the windows/clean).

221 **Write sentences in the causative form as in the example:**

1 John will have someone bring him the post. ...*John will have the post brought to him.* ....
2 Did Sheila ask the dressmaker to make her a dress? ....
3 When will his photographs be developed? ....
4 The decorators are decorating Tim's house at the moment. ....
5 Your car needs to be serviced. ....
6 The gardener was pruning Bob's bushes. ....
7 The manager had asked the secretary to book a room for him. ....
8 I paid someone to fix the roof of my house. ....
9 Let's ask the porter to carry the luggage to the taxi. ....
10 Larry has got the plastic surgeon to remove his tattoo. ....
11 A nurse took her temperature. ....
12 The make-up artist was applying the model's lipstick. ....
13 Ask the cook to prepare the vegetables. ....
14 Have you told the accountant to check the figures? ....
15 Jim hates the teacher correcting his mistakes. ....
16 Did the beautician paint Joanne's nails? ....
17 He told the maid to serve breakfast in his room. ....
18 Dad was late because the garage had been servicing his car. ....
19 Pam is going to tell someone to repair the pipes. ....
20 My parents' house was burgled last Monday. ....
21 He used to employ a chef who cooked his meals. ....
22 Does your mother ask for her shopping to be delivered to her house? ....
23 Did you pay an artist to paint a portrait of your family? ....
24 Do you employ someone to clean your house? ....
25 Did you tell the tailor to make a suit for you? ....

222 **Rephrase the following using have, make or get as in the example:**

1 He insisted that John should finish the report. ...*He made John finish the report.* ....
2 She asked him to fix the tap. ....
3 She persuaded her husband to cut the grass. ....
4 My teeth were polished yesterday. ....
5 He asked her to make his bed. ....
6 He insisted that the gardener should water the flowers. ....
7 The teacher asked them to rewrite the exercise. ....
8 The boss insisted that the secretary should type the letters. ....
9 Their new carpets were fitted yesterday. ....
10 She persuaded John to help her tidy the room. ....
11 He finally found a plumber to mend his toilet. ....
12 He persuaded his assistant to work late. ....

223 **Complete the sentences using the words in bold. You can use two to five words.**

1 Oxford beat Manchester United in the Cup Final yesterday.
   beaten   Manchester United ...*were beaten by Oxford*............................ in the Cup Final yesterday.
2 Now that I wear contact lenses, the optician tests my eyes every three months.
   have   Now that I wear contact lenses, I .... every three months.
3 It's possible to obtain concert tickets from most major music stores.
   obtained   Concert tickets .... from most major music stores.
4 Someone stole Mary's briefcase from her office while she was out.
   had   Mary .... from her office while she was out.
5 The headteacher insisted that all the pupils wear school uniform.
   made   The headteacher .... school uniform.

6 Someone should have already made all the arrangements for the business meeting.

been   All the arrangements .... for the business meeting.

7 The dentist extracted two of Steve's teeth yesterday.

got   Steve .... yesterday.

8 Peter had fed the dog by the time Sheila came back.

been   The dog .... by the time Sheila came back.

9 It is said that this diet is rich in vitamins.

be   This diet .... rich in vitamins.

10 Her dress needs shortening before the wedding.

shortened   She needs to .... before the wedding.

11 Flooding has damaged many major roads in the city.

have   Many major roads in the city .... flooding.

12 Most people think society's problems are the result of unemployment.

thought   It .... society's problems are the result of unemployment.

13 The bus driver insisted that the noisy passenger get off the bus.

made   The noisy passenger .... the bus.

14 He persuaded his brother to lend him his car.

got   He .... him his car.

15 Someone spilt fruit juice over Sophie's new white dress.

had   Sophie .... over her new white dress.

Oral Activity 17

The Town Hall is under restoration. It has to be opened by June. Look at the cues below, then make sentences using the causative form.

- alarm system / fit / recently
- new entrance hall / build / at this time
- central heating / install / already
- new furniture / deliver / before the next council meeting
- plumbing / renew / at the moment
- walls / paint / next month
- new carpet / lay / by May
- paintings / put up / in April
- outside of the building / clean / last week
- windows and doors / replace / already

eg. We have had an alarm system fitted recently. etc

Writing Activity 7

You are a secretary at the Town Hall. Write a report to the mayor informing him of the progress of the restoration work on the Town Hall.

To: The mayor   **From:**   Mrs Janet Jones

Subject: Restoration work on the Town Hall

Regarding the progress of the restoration work on the Town Hall, I have to report the following:
We have had an alarm system fitted recently and ...

224 Look at Appendix 2, then fill in the correct particle(s).

Phrasal Verbs

1 Her secret was **given** ...*away*... by her friend by mistake.
2 He has tried to **give** .... smoking twice.
3 When milk turns sour, it **gives** .... a horrible smell.
4 The teacher's patience finally **gave** ....
5 They were forced to **give** .... to the enemy.
6 Ricky **went** .... the flu.
7 My aunt has **gone** .... that pop quiz.
8 The fireworks **went** .... at midnight.
9 There wasn't enough cake to **go** ....
10 Before going to bed, we watched the fire slowly **go** ....
11 The detective carefully **went** .... the facts with the witness.
12 The film was so sad she couldn't **hold** .... her tears.
13 I was asked to **hold** .... while Mr Smith was fetched to the phone.
14 We were **held** .... on the motorway for three hours.
15 I **held** .... my anger until he'd left the room.

1 out, away, up, off
2 away, off, up, out
3 in, up, off, to
4 away, back, up, out
5 in, back, off, out
6 down with, up, over, away
7 along, back on, in for, by
8 into, off, on, out
9 for, down, through, round
10 out, off, up, with
11 away, by, back on, over
12 down, back, off, on
13 to, with, down, on
14 back, up, to, over
15 with, off, in, up

225 Look at Appendix 3, then fill in the correct preposition.

Prepositions

1 If you **persist** ...*in*... talking during class, I will have to punish you.
2 Our tour guide was very **pleasant** .... us during our holiday.
3 John was very **pleased** .... the way his painting turned out.
4 He took **pleasure** .... watching his grandchildren play in the garden.
5 May I have the **pleasure** .... your company at the dance tomorrow?
6 She is very **popular** .... her classmates.
7 Thick fog **prevented** the plane .... taking off.
8 His father was **proud** .... the way Tim performed.
9 They had a **quarrel** .... the date of the party.
10 I had a **quarrel** .... Stephen last night.
11 It took him a long time to **recover** .... the injuries.
12 There was no **reason** .... his reckless actions.
13 I tried to **reason** .... her, but she didn't pay attention.
14 There is a strong **relationship** .... smoking cigarettes and lung cancer.
15 Jim has a good **relationship** .... his parents.

1 on, in, at
2 for, to, about
3 to, in, with
4 in, on, of
5 at, of, with
6 in, about, with
7 from, of, in
8 by, of, in
9 about, with, of
10 to, with, against
11 after, of, from
12 of, for, at
13 for, on, with
14 in, between, of
15 between, in, with

226 Complete the sentences using the words in bold.

1 They took plenty of warm clothes so that they wouldn't be cold.
as   They took plenty of warm clothes ...*so as not to be* ....cold.
2 The au pair makes our beds every day
made   We .... the au pair every day.
3 People think that hard work is the key to success in life.
thought   Hard work .... the key to success in life.
4 I'm sure he wasn't lying when he told us the news.
can't   He .... when he told us the news.
5 His ill health made him give up his job as a miner.
because   He gave up his job as a miner .... his ill health.
6 If you let me know in time, I'll be able to book tickets.
long   I'll be able to book tickets .... me know in time.

7 Although he is inexperienced, he always puts forward good ideas.
lack Despite ...., he always puts forward good ideas.
8 The excursion was so relaxing that we felt refreshed afterwards.
such It was .... that we felt refreshed afterwards.
9 His story amused us and we all laughed.
found We .... and we all laughed.
10 Bad behaviour in the classroom is something I will not tolerate.
put I .... bad behaviour in the classroom.

227 Use the words in capitals to form a word that fits in the boxes provided.

WORKING ABROAD

Going to work abroad can prove to be quite a **(0)** .... experience. Learning how to adjust to **(1)** .... cultures is both character building and strengthening. Many people who give in to the **(2)** .... of living abroad, do so in search of a more **(3)** .... life. However, the whole concept of leaving your home country must be **(4)** .... thought out. Problems such as finding **(5)** .... and **(6)** .... procedures should be considered well in advance. For the first few weeks abroad, you may feel terribly **(7)** .... and homesick. **(8)** .... problems may also lead to unnecessary **(9)** .... with the locals, so it is always useful to **(10)** .... yourself with both the language of the country and its customs before you go.

VALUE	0	valuable
FOREIGNER	1	
	2	
TEMPT	3	
ADVENTURE		
CARE	4	
ACCOMMODATE	5	
IMMIGRATE	6	
LONELINESS	7	
COMMUNICATE	8	
UNDERSTANDING	9	
FAMILIAR	10	

228 Read the text carefully. Some of the lines are correct and some have a word which should not be there. If a line is correct, put a tick (✔) in the space provided. If a line has a word which should not be there, write it in the space provided.

TUTANKHAMEN'S TOMB

0 In April on 1922 the archaeologist Howard Carter and his	0	on
00 men discovered a tomb in the Valley of the Kings in	00	✓
1 Egypt. They had been working on for fifteen years and this	1	
2 was an incredible discovery. As far they were digging, they	2	
3 suddenly hit an underground doorway which it led to a	3	
4 tomb. It was the last resting place of an Egyptian Pharaoh,	4	
5 or king, who had been died thirty centuries before. The	5	
6 tomb contained of a rich collection of jewellery	6	
7 and one treasure which the Ancient Egyptians believed	7	
8 would be of a use to the dead ones in the afterlife. The	8	
9 Pharaoh's name was Tutankhamen. He died when	9	
10 he was a boy-king. His own body, which had been	10	
11 preserved in the traditional Egyptian way, was still in	11	
12 the tomb. The discovery of the tomb was been surrounded	12	
13 by a lot of suspicion. So many people believed that some	13	
14 of the strange things which they happened to people	14	
15 involved in it, were the result of a "Pharaoh's curse".	15	

Practice test 3

For questions 1 - 15, read the text below and decide which word A, B, C or D best fits each space. Mark your answers in the answer boxes provided.

PETER THE GREAT

Peter the Great was Russia's fourth Romanov Tzar and **(0)** .... 6 foot 7 inches, probably the tallest. He also had an enormous **(1)** .... for food and drink. Another "great" **(2)** .... of his personality was his **(3)** ...., which was fearsome. But it was his thirst for knowledge combined with his **(4)** .... of a new Russia that made him a great leader. In 1697, motivated by his desire to break **(5)** .... from the constrictions of old Russian customs, Peter travelled around Europe learning valuable military and industrial **(6)** .... .

When he returned to Russia, Peter was **(7)** .... to throw off the remnants of the past. He dramatically **(8)** .... the powers of the Russian aristocracy and abolished age-old **(9)** .... . In order to **(10)** .... his dream of a modernised Russia, he **(11)** .... universities, established the country's first newspaper and encouraged the development of industry. He also pushed back the empire's boundaries by **(12)** .... the armed forces. Before his death in 1725, Peter had had a new capital built and **(13)** .... it St Petersburg. It was **(14)** .... on the Western cities he most admired, like Paris and London, and **(15)** .... the capital until the First World War.

						A	B	C	D
0	**A** high	**B** with	**C** standing	**D** at	**0**	☐	☐	☐	■
1	**A** aptitude	**B** applause	**C** taste	**D** appetite	**1**	☐	☐	☐	☐
2	**A** face	**B** aspect	**C** view	**D** angle	**2**	☐	☐	☐	☐
3	**A** inclination	**B** temper	**C** mood	**D** disposition	**3**	☐	☐	☐	☐
4	**A** vision	**B** ambition	**C** jealousy	**D** greed	**4**	☐	☐	☐	☐
5	**A** free	**B** in	**C** up	**D** over	**5**	☐	☐	☐	☐
6	**A** professions	**B** studies	**C** designs	**D** skills	**6**	☐	☐	☐	☐
7	**A** convinced	**B** interested	**C** determined	**D** unwilling	**7**	☐	☐	☐	☐
8	**A** excluded	**B** eliminated	**C** reduced	**D** shortened	**8**	☐	☐	☐	☐
9	**A** heritage	**B** costumes	**C** means	**D** traditions	**9**	☐	☐	☐	☐
10	**A** make	**B** prepare	**C** fulfil	**D** produce	**10**	☐	☐	☐	☐
11	**A** began	**B** founded	**C** made	**D** found	**11**	☐	☐	☐	☐
12	**A** inflating	**B** spreading	**C** growing	**D** expanding	**12**	☐	☐	☐	☐
13	**A** entitled	**B** labelled	**C** named	**D** said	**13**	☐	☐	☐	☐
14	**A** modelled	**B** designed	**C** constructed	**D** copied	**14**	☐	☐	☐	☐
15	**A** remained	**B** kept	**C** settled	**D** retained	**15**	☐	☐	☐	☐

PART 2

For questions 16 - 30, read the text below and think of the word which best fits each space. Use only one word in each space. Write your answers in the answer boxes provided.

THE CHANNEL TUNNEL'S EURO-EXPRESS TRAINS

In November 1994, the first Eurostar passenger service departed **(0)** .... London's Waterloo International Station for the Gare du Nord, Paris. This high-speed, high-tech train is **(16)** .... flashiest thing in the entire British Rail network, although it will not be able to reach **(17)** .... top speed in Britain **(18)** .... the turn of the century, when the new rail link between London and Folkstone **(19)** .... completed.

But the British are more concerned about the safety of a link with France **(20)** .... about the time it **(21)** .... to get there and a lot of effort **(22)** .... gone into reducing British anxieties. For example, Eurostar's lightness minimises friction. In this **(23)** ...., the ride is made smoother and the passengers are given a greater sense of security.

Apart **(24)** .... giving an impression **(25)** .... safety, Eurostar, in its construction, has **(26)** .... carefully tested for fire safety, and the authorities believe that in the **(27)** .... of a fire, passengers could be evacuated long **(28)** .... there was a shortage of oxygen.

Perhaps the biggest test **(29)** .... Eurostar will be the effectiveness of its publicity, since financial success depends **(30)** .... winning the trust of the travelling public.

0	*from*
16	
17	
18	
19	
20	
21	
22	
23	
24	
25	
26	
27	
28	
29	
30	

PART 3

For questions 31 - 40, complete the second sentence so that it has a similar meaning to the first sentence. Use the word given and other words to complete each sentence. You must use between two and five words. Do not change the word given. Write your answers in the boxes provided.

0 I finished the book in two days.
took
It .... to finish the book.

| 0 | *took me two days* | 0 ▢ ■ |

31 The policeman insisted that the suspect should go to the station for further questioning.
made
The suspect .... to the station for further questioning.

| 31 | | 31 ▢ ▢ |

32 Shall we spend the day on the beach?
spending
How .... on the beach?

| 32 | | 32 ▢ ▢ |

33 I heard that Jeff and Holly ended their relationship last night.
broke
I heard that .... last night.

| 33 | | 33 ▢ ▢ |

34 He began designing the collection last week and has not finished yet.
has
He .... since last week.

| 34 | | 34 ▢ ▢ |

35 Your hair needs cutting.
have
You .... cut.

| 35 | | 35 ▢ ▢ |

36 She has never been so insulted before.
has
Never before .... insulted.

| 36 | | 36 ▢ ▢ |

37 There is a business meeting taking place on the third floor.
progress
There is .... on the third floor.

| 37 | | 37 ▢ ▢ |

38 The teacher asked the student to rewrite the composition.
had
The teacher .... the composition.

| 38 | | 38 ▢ ▢ |

39 June doesn't like staying up late and Terry doesn't either.
nor
Neither .... staying up late.

| 39 | | 39 ▢ ▢ |

40 Tom got his brother to do his project for him.
had
Tom .... his project for him.

| 40 | | 40 ▢ ▢ |

PART 4

For questions 41 - 55, read the text below and look carefully at each line. Some of the lines are correct, and some have a word which should not be there. If a line is correct, put a tick (✔) by the number in the answer boxes provided. If a line has a word which should not be there, write the word in the answer boxes.

THE BEST PLACE TO SWIM

0	Do you prefer swimming in the sea than to swimming in a	**0**	*than*
00	pool? Most people have a preference. Those who like	**00**	✓
41	the sea think this is a much more natural than a pool	**41**	
42	as there are no chemicals in it. The sea is being influenced	**42**	
43	by the weather, so that sometimes it is calm and sometimes	**43**	
44	rough, producing waves in which you can play with.	**44**	
45	However, a rough sea can to be dangerous, and a strong	**45**	
46	current in either a rough or a calm sea can pull	**46**	
47	swimmers away from land or under the water. Generally to	**47**	
48	speaking, a swimming pool is more safer than the sea. The	**48**	
49	chemicals are been there to keep the water clean and are not	**49**	
50	such as harmful as we think, and there is no current. Many pools	**50**	
51	have slides and even wave machines, which they make	**51**	
52	swimming fun. Moreover, there is always a lifeguard to watching	**52**	
53	the swimmers to make sure they are safe, and to help	**53**	
54	anyone who in trouble. You can also go to a pool all year	**54**	
55	round, whereas the sea is often freezing!	**55**	

PART 5

For questions 56 - 65, read the text below. Use the word given in capitals at the end of each line to form a word that fits in the space in the same line. Write your word in the answer boxes provided.

FINDING A JOB

In today's world of (0) .... hardship, finding a job is difficult. **(56)** .... has reached a record high, and even **(57)** .... qualified people are finding it **(58)** .... to find work. Despite this **(59)** .... news, there are certain things a person can do. Firstly, it is important to read the job **(60)** .... in as many newspapers as possible. Secondly, it is **(61)** .... to write letters to companies enclosing a copy of your CV. If your **(62)** .... is successful, it is imperative to impress the **(63)** .... . A smart **(64)** .... is essential along with some knowledge of the company. Above all, keep trying and you are sure to be **(65)** .... .

ECONOMY	**0**	*economic*
EMPLOYMENT	**56**	
HIGH	**57**	
DIFFICULTY	**58**	
DEPRESS	**59**	
ADVERTISE	**60**	
ADVISE	**61**	
APPLY	**62**	
INTERVIEW	**63**	
APPEAR	**64**	
SUCCESS	**65**	

7 Reported Speech

> I'm going to play football for my school team. I love football.

> You are going to play tennis? You **told me** that you loved football. You **said** you were going to play for the school team.

> Yes, I did, but after I let in the seventh goal, the team didn't like me.

Direct Speech is the exact words someone said. We use inverted commas in Direct Speech.
"I won't be back before 7.00," he said.

Reported Speech is the exact meaning of what someone said but not the exact words. We do not use inverted commas in Reported Speech.
*He said **he wouldn't be back before 7.00**.*

Say - Tell - Ask

- **Say** is used in Direct Speech. It is also used in Reported Speech when **say** is not followed by the person the words were spoken to.
  (Direct Speech) *"I can fix it," he **said**.* ➡ (Reported Speech) *He **said** he could fix it.*
- **Tell** is used in Reported Speech when it is followed by the person the words were spoken to.
  (Direct Speech) *"I can do it," he said **to me**.* ➡ (Reported Speech) *He **told me** he could do it.*
- **Ask** is used in reported questions and commands. **Ask** is also used in direct questions.
  He said to me, "Please, don't go!" ➡ *He **asked** me not to go.*
  *He **asked**, "Are you OK?"* ➡ *He **asked** me if I was OK.*
- We can use **say + to-infinitive** but never "say about". We use **tell sb, speak/talk about**, instead.
  *The boss **said to work** harder. He **spoke/talked about** his trips. He **told us about** his trips.*

Expressions with **say**	say good morning/evening etc, say something, say one's prayers, say a few words, say so, say no more, say for certain etc
Expressions with **tell**	tell the truth, tell a lie, tell (sb) the time, tell sb one's name, tell a story, tell a secret, tell sb the way, tell one from another, tell sb's fortune, tell sb so, tell the difference etc
Expressions with **ask**	ask a favour, ask the time, ask a question, ask the price etc

229 Fill in: say, tell or ask in the correct form.

First, the headmaster **1)** *...said...* good morning. Then he **2)** .... us that the police had been **3)** .... questions about hooliganism at school. The police **4)** .... that some pupils had been seen breaking windows. Several boys were **5)** .... if they knew anything, but of course they **6)** .... nothing. They were probably **7)** .... lies. The headmaster **8)** .... us all for information. He **9)** .... we must **10)** .... him the names of those involved. Well, I know who they were. But I can't **11)** .... him the secret. **12)** .... the truth is not always easy, is it?

230 Underline the correct item.

1 I can only help you if you **say / <u>tell</u>** me the problem.
2 My mother **said / told** to turn the oven on at 6 o'clock.
3 The doctor **said / told**, "You'd better stay in bed for two days."
4 My dentist **told / said** me to eat less chocolate.
5 Tom **told / said** he would be late home.
6 The teacher **said / told** us to do the exercise.
7 I like listening to him when he **says / talks** about his youth.
8 He won't be punished if he **says / tells** what happened.

Direct Speech		**Reported Speech**
"I **work** hard," he said.	➡	He said (that) he **worked** hard.
"I **am working** hard," he said.	➡	He said (that) he **was working** hard.
"I **have worked** hard," he said.	➡	He said (that) he **had worked** hard.
"I **worked** hard," he said.	➡	He said (that) he **had worked** hard.
"I **will work** hard," he said.	➡	He said (that) he **would work** hard.
"I **have been working** hard," he said.	➡	He said (that) he **had been working** hard.
"I **am going to work** harder," he said.	➡	He said (that) he **was going to work** harder.
"I **can work** harder," he said.	➡	He said (that) he **could work** harder.
"I **may work** harder," he said.	➡	He said (that) he **might work** harder.
"I **must work** harder," he said.	➡	He said (that) he **had to/must work** harder.
"I **should work** harder," he said.	➡	He said (that) he **should work** harder.
"I **ought to work** harder," he said.	➡	He said (that) he **ought to work** harder.
"**Do you work** hard enough?" she said to him.	➡	She **asked** him **if he worked** hard enough.
"**Work** harder!" she said to him.	➡	She told him **to work** harder.

Changing from Direct into Reported Speech (Statements)

- **Inverted commas** are omitted in Reported Speech. **That** is optional in the reported sentence.
  "I'm going out," he said. ➡ He said (that) he was going out.
- **When the reporting verb (said, told** etc) is in the past, all the following verbs usually change into a past form too. "I **enjoy** dancing," she said. ➡ She **said** she **enjoyed** dancing.
  However, the tenses do not change in Reported Speech when:
  a) the reporting verb (**said, told** etc) is in the Present, Future or Present Perfect tense.
      "The station **is** far from here," he **says**. ➡ He **says** the station **is** far from here.
  b) the speaker expresses general truths, permanent states and conditions.
      "Water **turns into** ice," he said. ➡ He said water **turns into** ice. (permanent truth)
  c) the speaker is reporting something immediately after it was said (up to date).
      "I **will** call you back," he said. ➡ He said he **will** call me back. (immediate reporting - up to date)
      "I **will** call you back," he said. ➡ He said he **would** call me back. (later reporting - out of date)
- If the speaker expresses something which is believed to be **true**, the tenses may **change** or **remain unchanged**. If something **untrue** is expressed, then the tenses definitely **change**.
  "She **likes** strawberries very much," he said. (true) ➡ He said she **likes/liked** strawberries very much.
  "Canada **is** a poor country," he said. (untrue) ➡ He said Canada **was** a poor country.
- The **Past Simple** changes into the **Past Perfect** or can remain the **same**. When the reported sentence contains a time clause, the tenses do not change. "I **was** early for the meeting," she said. ➡ She said she **was/had been** early for the meeting. "While I **was** staying in Madrid, I **met** Pedro twice," she said. ➡ She said she **had met/met** Pedro twice while she **was staying** in Madrid.
- The **Past Perfect** and the **Past Continuous** usually remain the same in Reported Speech. "I **was watching** TV while Ann **was reading** a book." ➡ He said he **was watching** TV while Ann **was reading** a book.
- If the reported sentence deals with **unreal past**, **conditionals type 2/type 3** or **wishes**, the tenses remain the same. "It's time we **went**," he said. ➡ He said it was time they **went**.
  "If I **were** you, I **would apologise**," he said. ➡ He said that if he **were** me, he **would apologise**.
- Personal pronouns and possessive adjectives change according to the context.
  "I will show **you my** new dress," she said. ➡ She said **she** would show **me her** new dress.
- Certain words change as follows depending on the context.

Direct Speech:	this/these	here	come	"Put that box down over **here**," she said.
Reported Speech:	that/those	there	go	She told him to put that box down over **there**.

● **Time words** and **tenses** can change or remain the same depending on the time reference. If the reported sentence is out of date, the tenses change. If the reported sentence is up to date, the tenses can remain the same. *"They **are** leaving **next week**," he said.* ➡ *He said they **were** leaving **the following week**. (speech reported after they had left - out of date) "They **are** leaving **next week**," he said.* ➡ *He said they **are** leaving **next week**. (speech reported before they have left - up to date)*

Direct Speech		**Reported Speech**
tonight, today, this week/month/year	➡	that night, that day, that week/month/year
now	➡	then, at that time, at once, immediately
now that	➡	since
yesterday, last night/week/month/year	➡	the day before, the previous night/week/month/year
tomorrow, next week/month/year	➡	the following day/the day after, the following/next week/month/year
two days/months/years etc ago	➡	two days/months/years etc before

231 **Jim met Ann while she was on holiday. Read Ann's words then report what she said.**

1 The weather is hot.
2 The food is delicious.
3 I go swimming every day.
4 I will always remember the place.
5 I hate going back to work.
6 I'm learning Spanish.
7 I've got a lovely sun tan.
8 I'm coming back again next year.
9 I've made a lot of friends.
10 The hotel is nice.

1 ...Ann said (that) the weather was hot.......
2 ....
3 ....
4 ....
5 ....
6 ....
7 ....
8 ....
9 ....
10 ....

232 **Turn the following sentences into Reported Speech.**

1 "A lot of English words are borrowed from other languages," the teacher said to us.
   ...*The teacher told us that a lot of English words are borrowed from other languages.*..............
2 "China is a densely populated country," she said. ....
3 "It's time they moved to a new house," Ann said. ....
4 "Water freezes below 0˚C," he said. ....
5 "I was reading the children a story last night when the lights went out," she said.

   ....
6 "I'll help you to repair your car tomorrow," he said to me. (out-of-date reporting) ....
7 "I didn't understand the meaning of the film," he said. ....
8 "You can come to me if you have any problems," she said to him. (out-of-date reporting) ....
9 "I saw the film you recommended last night," he said to her. ....
10 "I'm going to Spain next week," he said. (out-of-date reporting) ....
11 "She doesn't understand," he said. (up-to-date reporting) ....
12 "I would invite more people if I had a bigger flat," he said. ....
13 "I will not repeat this again," he said to us. (out-of-date reporting) ....
14 "I've applied for several jobs this week," he said. (out-of-date reporting) ....
15 "I'm afraid I can't come," he said to me. (up-to-date reporting) ....
16 "If I finish it this evening, we'll go out," he said to her. (out-of-date reporting) ....
17 "I saw him yesterday but he didn't recognise me," she said. ....

Reported Questions / Indirect Questions

- In **reported questions** we use the affirmative word order and the question mark becomes a full stop. To report a question we use: a) **ask + wh- word** (who, where etc) when the direct question begins with a wh- word, b) **ask + if/whether** when the direct question begins with an auxiliary verb (do, have, can etc). Pronouns, possessive adjectives, tenses, time expressions etc change as in statements.
  He said, "What are you doing?" ➡ He **asked what** I was doing.
  He said, "Did you enjoy the party?" ➡ He **asked if/whether** I enjoyed/had enjoyed the party.

- We use **Indirect questions** to ask for information/advice and **Reported questions** to report someone else's questions, suggestions, offers or requests. Indirect questions are introduced with: Could you tell me...?, Do you know...?, I wonder..., I want to know..., I doubt..., etc and their verb is in the affirmative. If the Indirect question starts with I wonder ..., I want to know ... or I doubt ..., then the question mark is omitted. Question words (**what, who, where** etc) or **whether** can be followed by an infinitive in the reported sentence.

Direct questions	Reported questions	Indirect questions
He asked me, "Shall I phone her?"	He asked me **whether he should phone her.**	I wonder **whether to phone her./ whether I should phone her.**
He asked me, "What time is it?"	He asked me **what time it was.**	Do you know **what time it is?**
He asked me, "Where can I put it?"	He asked me **where he could put it.** or He asked me **where to put it.**	Do you know **where he can put it?** or Do you know **where to put it?**

233 Fiona went for an interview last week. First read, then report Mr Roberts' questions.

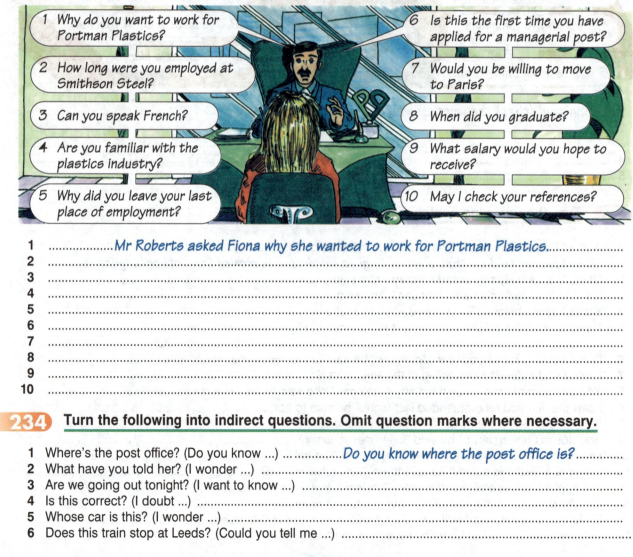

1 Why do you want to work for Portman Plastics?
2 How long were you employed at Smithson Steel?
3 Can you speak French?
4 Are you familiar with the plastics industry?
5 Why did you leave your last place of employment?
6 Is this the first time you have applied for a managerial post?
7 Would you be willing to move to Paris?
8 When did you graduate?
9 What salary would you hope to receive?
10 May I check your references?

1 ....*Mr Roberts asked Fiona why she wanted to work for Portman Plastics.*...............
2 ....
3 ....
4 ....
5 ....
6 ....
7 ....
8 ....
9 ....
10 ....

234 Turn the following into indirect questions. Omit question marks where necessary.

1 Where's the post office? (Do you know ...) ....*Do you know where the post office is?*...............
2 What have you told her? (I wonder ...) ....
3 Are we going out tonight? (I want to know ...) ....
4 Is this correct? (I doubt ...) ....
5 Whose car is this? (I wonder ...) ....
6 Does this train stop at Leeds? (Could you tell me ...) ....

Reported Commands / Requests / Suggestions

● To report **commands, requests, suggestions** etc, we use an introductory verb (**advise, ask, beg, offer, order, suggest, tell** etc) followed by a **to-infinitive**, an **-ing form** or a **that-clause** according to the introductory verb. (see pages 134 - 135)

*"**Touch** your toes,"* he said to us. ➡ He told us **to touch** our toes. (command)
*"**Don't** lie down,"* he said to us. ➡ He told us **not to lie** down. (command)
*"**Can** I go out?"* he said. ➡ He asked **to go** out. (request)
*"**Please, stay** with us tonight,"* he said to her. ➡ He asked her **to stay** with them that night. (request)
*"**Let's** play football,"* he said. ➡ He suggested **playing** football. (suggestion)
*"**You'd better** visit her,"* he said. ➡ He suggested **that I visit** her. (suggestion)

235 First read then report what the flight attendant told the passengers before takeoff.

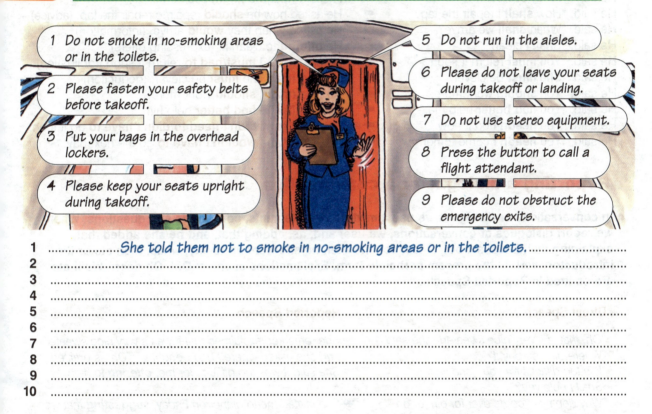

1 Do not smoke in no-smoking areas or in the toilets.
2 Please fasten your safety belts before takeoff.
3 Put your bags in the overhead lockers.
4 Please keep your seats upright during takeoff.
5 Do not run in the aisles.
6 Please do not leave your seats during takeoff or landing.
7 Do not use stereo equipment.
8 Press the button to call a flight attendant.
9 Please do not obstruct the emergency exits.

1   *She told them not to smoke in no-smoking areas or in the toilets.*
2   ....
3   ....
4   ....
5   ....
6   ....
7   ....
8   ....
9   ....
10 ....

236 Change the following from Direct into Reported Speech.

1 "Where have you been?" he said to me........................*He asked me where I had been.*
2 "Close your eyes and open the parcel," she said to me. ....
3 "I'm writing my autobiography," said Paul. (up-to-date reporting) ....
4 They said to her, "We hope you will lend us your car." (out-of-date reporting) ....
5 "Please sir, can I have some more food?" said Oliver. ....
6 "Go to your room and stay there!" said his father. ....
7 "Don't walk on the grass," the park attendant said to us. ....
8 "Did you pay the electricity bill?" he said to his wife. ....
9 "I'll phone you at seven o'clock tonight," she said to him. (out-of-date reporting) ....
10 "What size shoes do you take?" the shop assistant said to him. (out-of-date reporting) ......
11 "He's never written to me before," said Maria. (up-to-date reporting) ....
12 "Let's paint the walls blue!" said my little brother. ....
13 "Will Liza be safe on her own?" her father wondered. (out-of-date reporting) ....
14 My mother said to me, "Don't stay up reading too late!" ....
15 "I own two cars, a yacht and a private plane," said Roy. (untrue) ....

Modals in Reported Speech

- The forms of some modal verbs change in Reported Speech when the reported sentence is out of date. Will/Shall ➡ **would**, can ➡ **could/would be able to**, may ➡ **might/could**, shall ➡ **should** (asking for advice) or **would** (asking for information) / **offer** (expressing offers), must ➡ **must/had to** (obligation) (*must remains the same when it expresses possibility or deduction), needn't ➡ **didn't need to/didn't have to/wouldn't have to**.
- Would, could, used to, mustn't, should, might, ought to and had better remain the same.

Direct Speech		Reported Speech
He said, "I'**ll** see you later."	➡	He said (that) he **would** see me later.
He said, "I **can** lift weights."	➡	He said (that) he **could** lift weights.
He said, "I **can** do it tomorrow."	➡	He said (that) he **would be able to** do it the next day.
He said, "I **may** see John."	➡	He said (that) he **might** see John.
He said, "How **shall** I repair the tap?"	➡	He asked how he **should** repair/to repair the tap. (advice)
He said, "When **shall** we arrive?"	➡	He asked when they **would** arrive. (information)
He said, "**Shall** I clean it?"	➡	He **offered** to clean it. (expressing offers)
He said, "You **must** return it soon."	➡	He said (that) I **must/had to** return it soon. (obligation)
He said, "She **must** be clever."	➡	He said (that) she **must** be clever. (deduction)
He said, "You **should** work more."	➡	He said (that) I **should** work more.
He said, "You **had better** help me."	➡	He said (that) I **had better** help him.
He said, "You **needn't** do it now."	➡	He said (that) I **didn't need to/didn't have to** do it then.
He said, "You **needn't** come tomorrow."	➡	He said (that) I **wouldn't have to** go the next day.

Reporting a dialogue or a conversation

- In conversations or dialogues we use a mixture of statements, commands and questions. When we report dialogues or conversations, we use: and, as, adding that, and he/she added that, explaining that, because, but, since, so, and then he/she went on to say, while, then etc or the introductory verb in the present participle form. Exclamations such as: Oh!, Oh dear!, Well! etc are omitted in Reported Speech.

Direct Speech	Reported Speech
"Oh, that is a very nice sweater!" she said. "Where did you buy it?"	➡ She remarked/exclaimed that it was a very nice sweater **and** she asked where I had bought it. ("Oh" is omitted)
"It is too difficult for you," she said. "Shall I help you?"	➡ She said it was too difficult for me, **offering** to help.
"Why don't you come over for dinner on Friday?" she said. "We could discuss it then."	➡ She invited me to dinner on Friday, **suggesting** that we could discuss it then.

237 Rewrite the following conversations in Reported Speech.

A "How can I lose weight?" Alan said.
"You mustn't eat sweets or oily food. You can eat potatoes, though. You should also get plenty of exercise," said the doctor.
"Shall I join a gym?" said Alan.
"You needn't join a gym. You can go jogging every day," said the doctor.
...*Alan asked the doctor how he could lose weight.*..

B "How can I get a job?" Jane said.
"You can look through the newspapers at the job advertisements. You can also go to the Job Centre. I'm sure they could find you a job," said Julie.
"Shall I go to a private employment agency?" said Jane.
"You could, but it will cost you a lot of money and you don't have much," said Julie.
...*Jane asked Julie how she could get a job.*...

Exclamations · Yes/No short answers · Question tags

- **Exclamations** are introduced in Reported Speech with **exclaim, thank, wish, say, cry out in pain, give an exclamation of surprise/horror/disgust/delight** etc. The exclamation mark becomes a full stop. Exclamatory words such as **Oh!, Eee!, Wow!** etc are omitted in the reported sentence.
  "Ow!" she said as she hit her head on the door. ➡ *She **cried out in pain** as she hit her head on the door.*
- **Yes/No short answers** are expressed in Reported Speech with a **subject + appropriate auxiliary verb** or **subject + appropriate introductory verb**. *"Can you help me?" he said. "No," she said.* ➡ *He asked her if she could help him and she said **she couldn't**. or He asked her if she could help him, but she **refused**.*
- **Question tags** are omitted in Reported Speech. We can use an appropriate introductory verb to retain their effect. *"He isn't lying, is he?" she said.* ➡ *She **wondered** if he was lying.*

238 Turn the following into Reported Speech.

1 "You did steal the money, didn't you?" he said. ....*He insisted that I had stolen the money.*.........
2 "Will you leave the keys?" she asked. "Of course!" he said. ....
3 "Wonderful!" he said, when the bank manager agreed to lend him the money. ....
4 "Ouch!" he said, as the nurse gave him the injection. ....
5 "Would you like to come out with me?" he asked. "Not really," she replied. ....
6 "I don't suppose you could lend me any money, could you?" he asked me. ....
7 "Wow!" he said when he first saw the Pyramids. ....
8 "Would you like another piece of cake?" she asked. "Yes, please," he replied. ....
9 "You'll try not to be late, won't you?" he said to her. ....
10 "Ugh!" she said, as she stepped into the muddy puddle. ....

239 Rewrite the conversation in Reported Speech.

"Oh, Roger! What a surprise!" Lisa said at the sight of her husband.
"Hello, Lisa. Happy Birthday!" Roger said, giving her some flowers.
"Wow - they're lovely!" Lisa said. "Thank you."
"Would you like me to put them in water for you?" Roger asked.
"Yes, please," Lisa said.
"Let's go out tonight, shall we?" Roger said. "I've found a new restaurant which I think you'll like."

...*Lisa gave an exclamation of surprise at the sight of her husband.* ....
....
....

240 Rewrite the following conversations in Reported Speech.

A "Sally, would you like to go out tonight for a change?" Daniel asked.
"What a lovely idea! Why don't we go for a meal?" Sally said.
"Well ...mm... possibly, but I've already bought two tickets for the opera," Daniel said.
"Even better. But I'll walk out if you fall asleep like the last time!" Sally threatened.
"Not at all! I only had my eyes closed to enjoy the music," Daniel explained.
"All right then, I'll go, but you should keep your mouth closed if you're going to snore," Sally said.
...*Daniel asked Sally if she would like to* ....

B "John's late," said Mr Brown.
"He must have got stuck in traffic," said Sandra. "Shall I phone him?"
"No, you needn't phone him, but you'd better tell his secretary to check today's diary. He may have an appointment this morning," said Mr Brown.
...*Mr Brown said that John was late.* ....

7 Reported Speech

When we report a speaker's words we don't just apply rules mechanically, we interpret what we hear or read, so we use appropriate reporting verbs (introductory verbs) like the following:

Introductory verb	Direct Speech	Reported Speech
agree + to-inf	"Yes, I'll do it again."	➡ He **agreed to do** it again.
demand	"Tell me the truth!"	➡ He **demanded to be** told the truth.
offer	"Would you like me to drive you home?"	➡ He **offered to drive** me home.
promise	"I will pay you on Friday."	➡ He **promised to pay** me on Friday.
refuse	"No, I won't tell you her secret."	➡ He **refused to tell** me her secret.
threaten	"Keep quiet or I'll punish you."	➡ He **threatened to punish** me if I didn't keep quiet.
claim	"I witnessed the crime."	➡ He **claimed to have witnessed** the crime.
advise + sb + to-inf	"You should talk about your problem."	➡ He **advised me to talk** about my problem.
allow	"You can use my phone."	➡ He **allowed me to use** his phone.
ask	"Please, close the door."	➡ He **asked me to close** the door.
beg	"Please, please don't hit the dog."	➡ He **begged me not to hit** the dog.
command	"Move to your right."	➡ He **commanded me to move** to my right.
encourage	"Go ahead, say what you think."	➡ He **encouraged me to say** what I thought.
forbid	"You mustn't come home after eleven."	➡ He **forbade us to come** home after eleven.
instruct	"Mix the eggs with the flour."	➡ He **instructed me to mix** the eggs with the flour.
invite sb	"I'd like you to come to my party."	➡ He **invited me (to go)** to his party.
order	"Don't leave your room again."	➡ He **ordered me not to leave** my room again.
permit	"You may speak to the judge."	➡ He **permitted/allowed me to speak** to the judge.
remind	"Don't forget to turn the lights off."	➡ He **reminded me to turn** the lights off.
urge	"Try to have sympathy for the family."	➡ He **urged me to try** to have sympathy for the family.
warn	"Don't touch the wire with wet hands."	➡ He **warned me not to touch** the wire with wet hands.
want	"I'd like you to be kind."	➡ He **wanted me to be** kind.
accuse sb of + -ing form	"You acted as if you were guilty."	➡ He **accused me of acting** as if I were guilty.
apologise for	"I'm sorry I hurt you."	➡ He **apologised for** hurting me.
admit (to)	"Yes, I was wrong."	➡ He **admitted (to) being** wrong.
boast about	"I'm the fastest runner of all."	➡ He **boasted about being** the fastest runner of all.
complain to sb about	"You always argue."	➡ He **complained to me about** my arguing.
deny	"No, I didn't eat your cake."	➡ He **denied eating/having eaten** my cake.
insist on	"You must wear that blouse."	➡ He **insisted on me/my wearing** that blouse.
suggest	"Let's order a pizza."	➡ He **suggested ordering** a pizza.
agree + that-clause	"Yes, she's very kind."	➡ He **agreed that** she was very kind.
claim	"I saw the accident."	➡ He **claimed that** he had seen the accident.
complain	"You never ask my opinion."	➡ He **complained that** I never asked his opinion.
deny	"I have never met her!"	➡ He **denied that** he had ever met her.
exclaim	"It's a tragedy!"	➡ He **exclaimed that** it was a tragedy.
explain	"It's a complicated problem."	➡ He **explained that** it was a complicated problem.
inform sb	"Your request is being reviewed."	➡ He **informed me that** my request was being reviewed.
promise	"I won't be late."	➡ He **promised that** he wouldn't be late.
suggest	"You ought to give her a call."	➡ He **suggested that** I give her a call.
explain to sb + how	"That's how I succeeded."	➡ He **explained to me how** he had succeeded.

Introductory verb	Direct Speech	Reported Speech
wonder where/what/ why/how + clause (when the subject of the introductory verb is **not the same** as the subject in the indirect question)	He asked himself, "How old is she?" He asked himself, "Where are my keys?" He asked himself, "Why is she so cold?" He asked himself, "What is the right answer?"	➡ He **wondered how** old she was. ➡ He **wondered where** his keys were. ➡ He **wondered why** she was so cold. ➡ He **wondered what** the right answer was.
wonder + whether + to-inf or clause **wonder where/what/ how + to-inf** (when the subject of the infinitive is the **same** as the subject of the verb)	He asked himself, "Shall I invite them?" He asked himself, "Where shall I go?" He asked himself, "What shall I read first?" He asked himself, "How shall I tell her?"	➡ He **wondered whether** to invite them. ➡ He **wondered whether** he should invite them. ➡ He **wondered where** to go. ➡ He **wondered what** to read first. ➡ He **wondered how** to tell her.

241 Report the following using an appropriate introductory verb from the list below.

promise, apologise, remind, complain, deny, inform, order, allow, encourage, forbid

1 "The exam papers are still being marked, Jane," the teacher said.
.................*The teacher informed Jane that the exam papers were still being marked.* ....
2 "Don't forget to thank your mother," he said to Linda. ....
3 "You mustn't come here again," she said to the tramp. ....
4 "I didn't hit him," Sarah said. ....
5 "I'll tidy up when I return home, Mum," Tim said. ....
6 "I'm sorry I forgot to do the homework," she said to the teacher. ....
7 "You may see her for a few minutes," the nurse said to me. ....
8 "Get off the grass immediately!" he said to the kids. ....
9 "You're always forgetting to shut the fridge door," she said to her husband. ....
10 "Come on! Try it again," he said to me. ....

242 First write an appropriate introductory verb, then report the following situations.

1 "You should go to a doctor." ....*advise*.......... *He advised me to go to a doctor.*
2 "The bread is stale." ....
3 "I will buy you a present." ....
4 "You ought to tell her the news." ....
5 "I'm sorry I insulted you." ....
6 "Shall I help you?" ....
7 "Give me a statement or I'll detain you." ....
8 "Don't go near the fire!" ....
9 "That's why I didn't go." ....
10 "I didn't steal the money." ....
11 "Let's go out tonight." ....
12 "You must spend Christmas with us." ....
13 "Please, please give me some money!" ....
14 "Don't forget to tell Ann!" ....
15 "Yes, she's a good person." ....
16 "Shall I call her?" he asked himself. ....
17 "Can you pass me the salt, please?" ....
18 "Yes, I'll help you." ....
19 "Would you like a cup of tea?" ....
20 "I'll never forget your birthday again." ....

21 "No, I won't get out of bed." ....
22 "Tell me where he is." ....
23 "You ought to stop smoking." ....
24 "You mustn't be back later than ten." ....
25 "She's such a funny person!" ....
26 "Everybody be quiet!" ....
27 "You may see Mr Rogers." ....
28 "Go on, do as you want." ....
29 "Yes, I lied about my age." ....
30 "You made Sophie cry." ....
31 "I saw the murderer." ....
32 "I'm the fastest swimmer of all." ....
33 "That's how you can do it." ....
34 "What shall I do?" ....

243 Report the following conversation.

"Oh, I'm sorry to be early, Susan," said Jane. "Am I the first to arrive?"
"Yes, you are," Susan replied, "but it really doesn't matter."
"No, I am terribly sorry. The babysitter arrived early," said Jane.
"Well, why don't you help me in the kitchen?" said Susan.
"Of course. What would you like me to do?" replied Jane.
"Oh, no! I can smell the sausages burning," Susan cried, "I'd forgotten all about them. I hope they're not burnt."
"You must let me see to them," Jane said. "Go ahead and greet your guests. I think I can hear the first ones arriving."

...*Jane apologised to Susan for being early*......................................

Punctuation in Direct Speech

- We **capitalize** the first word of the quoted sentence. The **full stop**, the **question mark**, the **exclamation mark** and the **comma** come inside the inverted commas. The **comma** comes outside the inverted commas only when "he said/asked" precedes the quoted sentence.
  "She is on holiday," he said. He said, "She is on holiday." "She," he said, "is on holiday." **We do not use a comma after the question mark.** *"Shall we go out?" he asked.* but: *He asked, "Shall we go out?"*
- **The subject pronoun comes before the reporting verb (said, asked etc) whereas the noun subject often comes after "said", "asked" etc at the end or in the middle of the quoted sentence.**
  "She failed the test," he said. "She failed the test," said Tom. "She," said Tom, "failed the test."
  but: *He/Tom said, "She failed the test." (not: ~~Said Tom~~, "She failed the test.")*
- **Each time the speaker changes we normally start a new paragraph. (see Exs 239, 240,243)**

244 Punctuate the following making any other necessary changes.

1 Shall we play tennis on Saturday she asked
2 Colin his mother said is not here
3 He said stop it
4 Why are you late the teacher asked
5 Red is my favourite colour Tom said
6 Danny said I play the piano
7 Do you prefer basketball or football Peter asked
8 Barbara said I wasn't even there

245 Turn the following into a conversation. Mind the punctuation.

The policeman ordered the driver to step out of his car. The driver agreed, but he wondered what the matter was. The policeman inquired if the driver had been speeding, but the driver denied it. The policeman explained that it was illegal to drive at more than 50 km an hour on this stretch of road. The driver protested that he hadn't been speeding but the policeman insisted that he had. The policeman explained that he was obliged to give the driver a ticket for speeding. ....*"Step out of your car!" said the policeman.*...................................

Subjunctive

The bare infinitive form of the subjunctive is used after certain verbs and expressions to give emphasis. These are: advise, ask, demand, insist, propose, recommend, request, suggest, it is essential, it is imperative, it is important, it is necessary, it is vital followed by (that) + subject.
In British English we use should + simple form instead of the bare infinitive form of the subjunctive.
*He insists **(that) we be** here on time. (less usual) He insists **(that) we should be** here on time. (more usual)*

246 Give the correct form of the verb in brackets. Some of the verbs are passive.

1 It is vital that the new measures ....*should bring/bring*.......... (bring) hooliganism under control.
2 We demanded that he .... (change) the date of the meeting.
3 He asked that we .... (be) sure to include everything in the list.
4 She insisted that his identity .... (reveal) to the press.
5 We suggested she .... (consult) her lawyer.
6 It is important that he .... (remain) unseen for a while.
7 We requested that our luggage .... (deliver) to our hotel.
8 It is essential that no one else .... (get) involved in this affair.
9 The specialist recommended that she .... (take) some time off work.
10 It is necessary that negotiations .... (continue) on both sides.

247 Complete the sentences using the words in bold.

1 He reminded me to post the letter.
   told   He ....*told me not to forget*................................... to post the letter.
2 "Let's try that new Thai restaurant," she said.
   trying   She .... new Thai restaurant.
3 "Yes, I gave away your secret," she said.
   giving   She .... my secret.
4 "I'm sorry I lost the book you lent me," he said.
   apologised He .... the book I had lent him.
5 "Don't go too near the edge of the cliff," they said to us.
   warned   They .... too near the edge of the cliff.
6 "No, I didn't steal the company's money," the manager said.
   having   The manager .... the company's money.
7 "What shall I do?" she said.
   wondered   She .... do.
8 "You've caused a lot of pain to my family," she said to him.
   of   She .... a lot of pain to her family.
9 He told the manager he was dissatisfied with the service.
   about   He .... the service.
10 "You must apply for the teaching post," he said to me.
   on   He .... the teaching post.
11 "I'd like you to come to Paris with me," he said to her.
   go   He .... to Paris with him.
12 "Please, please don't give us any homework," they said to the teacher.
   not   They .... give them any homework.
13 "That's how I managed to escape," he said to me.
   how   He .... he had managed to escape.
14 "I'll never forget our anniversary again," he said.
   would   He .... their anniversary again.
15 "You should try to find another job," he said to me.
   me   He .... to find another job.
16 "Yes, it was a very dull lecture," she said.
   that   She .... a very dull lecture.
17 "No, I won't tell you where I was last night," he said to her.
   her   He .... where he had been the night before.

248 Find the mistake and correct it.

1 They suggested to see the film. ....*They suggested seeing the film.* ....
2 She asked me where was I going. ....
3 Can you tell me what time is it? ....
4 He told me to not touch the parcel. ....
5 I wonder why did he lie to me. ....
6 The suspect denied to murder the young woman. ....
7 They accused him to have committed the crime. ....
8 She asked me, "Where the bank is?" ....

249 Turn the following into a conversation. Mind the punctuation.

Christine complained that their house was too small. She suggested looking for somewhere bigger. Wayne asked her why she wanted to move. He pointed out they had only moved in a year before. She reminded him that he had said it would only be temporary. He agreed, but told her that his business hadn't been very successful so they couldn't afford to move yet. Christine asked if they would be able to move the following year. She said that the baby was growing up fast and that he needed his own room. Wayne admitted that she was right, but asked her to be patient. He promised that they would move as soon as they could afford it. ....*"Our house is too small," said Christine.*..

250 Rewrite the following sentences in Reported Speech.

1 "Can you make dinner tonight, Tom?" she said. "I'm working late." ...*She asked Tom to make dinner that night, explaining that she was working late.*..
2 "Don't play near the road," their mother said. "It's too dangerous." ....
3 "Can you take the dog for a walk?" he said to her. "I'm busy." ....
4 "Don't ask Simon how to use the computer," she said to me. "He doesn't know a thing about them." ...
5 "Can I borrow your pen, please?" he said to her. "I need to write something." ....
6 "Please don't talk!" said the teacher. "This is a test." ....
7 "Why don't you turn off the TV?" she said to him. "You aren't watching it." ....
8 "Come to our house tonight, Mary," he said. "Jim wants to see you." ....
9 "Have you read your newspaper?" he asked her." "I want to look at it." ....
10 "The baby should be asleep," she said. "It's ten o'clock." ....
11 "Why are you listening to this music?" he asked her. "It's awful." ....
12 "Do you want to go to the cinema?" he asked her. "There's a good film on." ....
13 "I don't want any more cake," she said. "I've had enough." ....
14 "I'm learning French," she said. "I'm going to Paris on holiday." ....
15 "I like Susan," he said. "She's very friendly." ....
16 "Tom is a good businessman," she said. "He works hard." ....
17 "I like learning English," she said. "It isn't too difficult." ....
18 "I'm teaching Jane's class," she said. "She's on holiday this week." ....
19 "You should open up your own restaurant," he said to Bill. "You are a very good cook." ....
20 "Sarah would like to own the house," he said. "She's lived here a long time." ....
21 "You could become famous, June," he said. "You're a very good singer." ....
22 "Are you going to take the job?" he asked Jane "or will you wait for a better one?" ....
23 "I need to buy some more oil," she said. "There is no more left." ....
24 "Can you phone Julie?" she asked me. "I heard she has had a fight with Mark." ....
25 "Do you know when May will be back?" she asked. "She's been away all week." ....
26 "Do you think we should try this new restaurant tonight?" he asked his wife. "I heard it's very good."

....
27 "If anyone phones," she said to me, "tell them I won't be here until tomorrow." ....
28 "If I can't come to the wedding," said John to Mary, "I'll let you know tomorrow." ....
29 "Shall I tell Tom about the trip?" he said to her, "or do you want to tell him yourself?" ....
30 "Sofia shouldn't have said that to the boss," said Julian. "He's very angry." ....
31 "I'd love to go to Venice," she said. "I've never been abroad." ....
32 "I must go now," said Samantha, "or I might miss the bus." ....

Oral Activity 18

Students are given one minute to look at the first of the pictures below. Use the picture as a stimulus to get students to prepare a short talk or story based on it. A student is then invited to the front of the class to tell his/her story while the rest of the class take notes. Then the students, using their notes, report what the speaker said. Continue in the same way with the other pictures.

A politician's speech

They were ready to go
on a week's holiday.

A strange dream I had

Oral Activity 19

In pairs, students use the first picture below as a stimulus to make up a short dialogue according to the situation given. Next, a pair of students act out the dialogue while the rest of the class take notes. Then, students report the conversation. Continue in the same way with the other two situations.

Yesterday Ann and Paul were talking in front of a shop window about some clothes they wanted to buy. What could they have been saying?

Last Monday Jim and Kristi had been waiting at the bus stop for a long time. What could they have been saying?

Kate and Bob went to a restaurant last Sunday. What could they have been saying?

Writing Activity 8

Imagine that you are a newspaper reporter who has been asked to write a short article about a recent campaign to improve literacy in your country. Remember to use verbs like add, warn, promise, explain etc.

Notes: literacy must be improved - standards of education need to be raised - we can improve things - this campaign can be a success - more money for schools - the literacy rate is unacceptably low - the country needs a change

A literacy campaign at this present time is essential to ......

English in use 7

251 Complete the second sentence so that it has a similar meaning to the first sentence. Use the word given and other words to complete each sentence. You must use between two and five words. Don't change the word given.

1 Simon hasn't been to York for two years.
last It's two years ....*since Simon last went to*........................ York.

2 I'll post it for you if you like.
like Would .... it for you?

3 They took a taxi because they didn't want to be late.
case They took a taxi .... late.

4 I paid £300 for the tape recorder.
me The tape recorder .... £300.

5 I'll call you if I need any information.
give I'll .... if I need any information.

6 They asked whose fault the breakage was.
blame They asked who .... the breakage.

7 Tim can run faster than Dan.
runner Dan isn't .... Tim.

8 I don't really want to see this film.
rather I .... this film.

9 She cycled from Paris to Calais in ten hours.
her It .... cycle from Paris to Calais.

10 I don't suppose you know where she is, do you?
happen Do .... where she is?

11 We were so shocked by the news we didn't know what to say.
shocking The news .... we didn't know what to say.

12 She obtained that vase quite by chance.
came She .... quite by chance.

252 Look at Appendix 2, then fill in the correct particle(s).

1 Cindy **kept** ...*back*... information from the police.
2 My boss told me to **keep** .... the good work.
3 If you don't **keep** .... all the homework, you might fail in the tests.
4 "You have to **keep** .... a word limit of 200," the teacher said.
5 He warned them to **keep** .... the freshly painted benches.
6 Darren was **let** .... by the judge as this was his first offence.
7 Vicky was often **let** .... by her forgetful sister.
8 Could you please **look** .... this contract? If you agree, sign it.
9 Ann has a nanny to **look** .... her children while she's at work.
10 **Look** .... all the unknown words in the dictionary.
11 **Look** .... this magazine and find the problem page.
12 She **looks** .... everyone who hasn't been to college.
13 We are all **looking** .... Christmas.
14 **Look** .... poisonous mushrooms.
15 We must **look** .... this problem and find out its cause.

Phrasal Verbs

1 in, out, back, on
2 out, up, after, at, on
3 down, in, up with, away
4 from, off, to, at
5 off, back, on, in
6 off, down, in, on
7 into, in, up, down
8 out, over, in, up
9 out, over, into, after
10 round, to, up, up to
11 through, out, on, for
12 into, onto, down on, in
13 back, on, forward to, up to
14 into, out for, onto, through
15 up to, on, out, into

253 Choose the item which best explains the idioms, then make sentences using them.

1 **be sick and tired**	A be ill and exhausted	(B) be annoyed at sth
2 **break one's word**	A admit sth one said is wrong	B not to keep one's promise
3 **break the ice**	A ease tension at first meeting	B accept coldly
4 **buy time**	A do sth to pass the time	B achieve a delay

254 Look at Appendix 3, then fill in the correct preposition.

Prepositions

1 The lifeguard **saved** the child ...*from*... drowning.
2 She's **sensitive** .... the needs of her daughter.
3 He was **sorry** .... the way he had behaved at the party.
4 Tom was **sorry** .... damaging his neighbour's fence.
5 Clare **spent** all her pocket money .... sweets.
6 Rod **sympathised** .... Delia's situation.
7 You weren't **sympathetic** .... that man.
8 Professor Reading **specialises** .... criminal law.
9 This bread **tastes** .... garlic.
10 She hasn't got a lot of **taste** .... clothes.
11 It's **typical** .... Jim to forget his keys.
12 Lisa was so angry that she **threw** a cup .... Mark.
13 The goalkeeper **threw** the ball .... his team-mate.
14 We made **use** .... Penny's flat while she was in France.
15 My residence permit is **valid** .... one more year.
16 This qualification is **valid** .... the United States.
17 She has **warned** her son .... talking to strangers.

	Prepositions
1	of, from, off
2	to, at, with
3	at, about, with
4	for, of, in
5	in, at, on
6	to, with, for
7	at, of, towards
8	in, at, on
9	in, of, from
10	in, on, at
11	from, for, of
12	to, at, for
13	off, to, on
14	for, of, at
15	of, in, for
16	in, at, with
17	of, about, in

255 Choose the correct item.

BARBADOS

Have you **(0)** ...*ever*... (ever / since / never/ for) been to Barbados? Life **(1)** ...... (by / at / on / over) Barbados is slow and peaceful. People there seem to **(2)** ...... (spend / pass / attend / follow) all their time eating and relaxing. You **(3)** ...... (almost / hardly / nearly / scarce) ever see anyone doing any real work. **(4)** ...... (Although / Nevertheless / Despite / Contrary) crowds of tourists are attracted **(5)** ...... (at / from / on / by) cheap package deals, the island, situated **(6)** .... (among / between / in / on) the Caribbean remains **(7)** .... (undisturbed / unattached / unspoilt / untouched). The temperature seldom falls **(8)** ...... (under / below / down / behind) 20˚C and you are unlikely to meet friendlier people anywhere in the world. In Bridgetown, the capital, you can sit on the balcony of a harbour-front restaurant **(9)** ...... (swallowing / sipping / biting / eating) fresh coconut cocktails, and watch the boats **(10)** ...... (unpacking / disembarking / unloading / delivering). It's also a great place to buy jewellery as not only is it beautifully made, but it is also tax-free. For the classiest hotels **(11)** ...... (face / head / turn / charge) north to the Platinum Coast, **(12)** ...... (called / termed / christened / named) after its white sandy beaches. The superb Glitter Bay Hotel is situated in flower-filled gardens with **(13)** ...... (careful / attentive / cautious / interested) staff and delicious food. As the sun **(14)** ...... (falls / jumps / sets / dives), enjoy your cocktail and start figuring out how to **(15)** ...... (take / earn / gain / possess) the money to get back to Barbados.

256 Put the verbs in brackets into the correct tense.

A **1)** ...*Have you ever noticed*... (you/ever notice) the scar on Bonnie's chin? She **2)** .... (get) it last year when she fell over. She **3)** .... (watch) a film on TV when the telephone **4)** .... (ring). As she went to answer it, she slipped on some water her husband **5)** .... (spill) on the floor.

B "If Amy **1)** .... (have) a party on Saturday, I can tell John to bring his flashing lights as I **2)** .... (see) him at work tomorrow. He **3)** .... (work) on the lights last night when I called round and I expect that he **4)** .... (fix) them by the weekend. Do you know if Amy **5)** .... (decide) whether to have a birthday party or not?"

Conditionals / Wishes / Unreal Past

Conditionals

	If-clause (hypothesis)	Main clause (result clause)	Use
Type 1 real present	if + any present form (Present S., Present Cont. or Present Perf.)	Future/Imperative can/may/might/must/should + bare inf Present Simple	true or likely to happen in the present or the future
	*If you **finish** work early, we**'ll go** for a walk.* *If you **have finished** your coffee, we **can pay** the bill.* *If you**'re** ill, **see** a doctor! If you **burn** yourself, it **hurts**.*		
Type 2 unreal present	If + Past Simple or Past Continuous	would/could/might + bare infinitive	untrue in the present; also used to give advice
	*If I **had** money, I **would travel** round the world. (but I don't have money - untrue in the present)* *If I **were** you, I **would take** an umbrella. (advice)*		
Type 3 unreal past	If + Past Perfect or Past Perfect Continuous	would/could/might +have + past participle	imaginary situation contrary to facts in the past; also used to express regrets or criticism
	*If we **hadn't left** so early, we **would have missed** the plane.*		

- Conditional sentences have two parts: the **if-clause** (hypothesis) and the **main clause** (the result clause). *If you post the invitations today, they will arrive on time.*
  if-clause   *main clause*
- There are three types of conditionals. **Type 1 - true in the present**, **Type 2 - untrue in the present** and **Type 3 - imaginary**, contrary to facts **in the past**. **For the usage of the verb forms in conditionals, see the chart above.** *If the weather **is** nice, we**'ll go** swimming. (true - It's possible.)*
  *If I **were** a bird, I **could fly**. (untrue in the present - I am not a bird.)*
  *If I **had been invited** to the party, I **would have gone**. (imaginary in the past - I wasn't invited, so I didn't go.)*
- When the if-clause precedes the result clause, we separate the two clauses with a comma.
  If you work hard, you will succeed. but: You will succeed if you work hard. (no comma)

- **Conditionals are usually introduced by if, unless** (= if not - normally used with 1st type conditionals). The following expressions can be used instead of "if": **providing, provided (that), as long as, in case, on condition (that), but for** (= without), **otherwise, or else, what if, supposing, even if, only if**.
  If you don't reserve a ticket, you won't get a seat.
  Unless *you reserve a ticket, you won't get a seat.* (not: ~~Unless you don't reserve~~...)
  You will get a seat **providing/provided (that)/as long as/only if** *you reserve a ticket.*
  Only if *you reserve a ticket,* **will you get** *a seat.* (When we begin the sentence with "only if", we invert the subject and the verb of the result clause.)
  Reserve a ticket, **otherwise/or else** *you won't get a seat.*
  What if *it rains, will you still go for a picnic with him?*
  Supposing *it rains, will you still go for a picnic with him?*
  Will you still go for a picnic with him **even if** *it rains?*
  But for *him, I wouldn't have been able to survive.* (**If it hadn't been for him** - *without his help*)
- **Future tense is not normally used with an if-clause.** *Unless you leave early, you will be late.* (not: ~~Unless you will leave~~ ...) *If you pay, you will get a receipt.* (not: ~~If you will pay~~...)
- **We do not normally use will, would** or **should in an if-clause. However, we can use will, would, should in conditionals to make a request or express insistence, annoyance, doubt** or **uncertainty.**
  If you **will/would** *calm down for a minute, I will be able to help you.* (request - *Will you please calm down?*)
  If you **will make** *a noise, I'll send you out.* (insistence - *If you insist on making a noise* ...)
  If you **should** *need any help, ask me.* (uncertainty - *I am not sure you will need help.*)
- **We can omit "if". When we omit "if" should, were** and **had** (Past Perfect) **come before the subject.**
  If he **should** *turn up, tell him to wait for me.* ➡ **Should he** *turn up, tell him to wait for me.*
  If I **were** *you, I would speak to her.* ➡ **Were I you,** *I would speak to her.*
  If he **had known,** *he would have told us.* ➡ **Had he known,** *he would have told us.*
- **After "if" we normally use were instead of was in all persons in type 2 conditionals in formal situations. Was is mainly used in spoken English.**
  If I **were/was** *you, I wouldn't buy such an expensive dress.*

---

257 **Match the parts of the sentences, then identify the type of conditionals.**

1 If Paul enters the competition,	A it wouldn't have been stolen.	1 ...*D (1st type)*.......
2 She won't go to work,	B if he had been on time.	2 ....
3 If he had locked his car,	C unless she's better.	3 ....
4 I would buy that vase	D he'll win.	4 ....
5 He wouldn't have missed the meeting	E if I had enough money.	5 ....

258 **Put the verbs in brackets into the correct form.**

Bob was getting very bored of lying in his hospital bed, so he was quite happy to see his Uncle Hamish come into the room. "Hello Bobby!" shouted Hamish. "How are you?" "I'd be better if I **1)** ...*weren't lying*... (not/lie) in this hospital," grumbled Bob. "Oh, cheer up!" said Hamish. "You **2)** .... (never/get) better if you have such a negative attitude." "You'd have a negative attitude too if you **3)** .... (be) stuck in this boring room with no TV for 24 hours a day!" "Well, you've no one to blame but yourself," said Hamish. "If you had not been driving so fast, you **4)** .... (not/crash) into that tree." "Oh no, Uncle Hamish. Don't say that. If one more person **5)** .... (say) that to me, I swear I'll punch them," said Bob. "Now, now Bobby! If I were you, I **6)** .... (be) more polite to my visitors. You're going to be in here for a  few weeks, and if you're rude to people, they **7)** .... (not/come) to see you," warned Hamish. "I'm sorry," Bob apologised. "I promise I'll be polite as long as you **8)** .... (not/mention) my careless driving again." "OK Bobby," agreed Hamish. "I'm sorry too. I wouldn't have mentioned it if I **9)** .... (know) how upset it makes you."

259 **Rephrase the following using "unless".**

1 If the neighbours don't stop shouting, I'll call the police.
...*Unless the neighbours stop shouting, I'll call the police.* ....
2 If he doesn't pay the fine, he may go to prison. ....
3 If the traffic isn't heavy, we should arrive by 10 pm. ....
4 If the Chinese restaurant isn't open, we'll go for a pizza. ....
5 If the athlete can't improve his speed, he won't break the record. ....

260 **Rewrite the following sentences omitting "if".**

1 If you drink too much coffee, you won't be able to sleep.
...*Should you drink too much coffee, you won't be able to sleep.* ....
2 If you'd brought a map, we wouldn't have got lost. ....
3 If I were you, I wouldn't tell anyone about it. ....
4 If he'd known about the meeting, I'm sure he would have come. ....
5 If you come across Paul, tell him I want to see him. ....

261 **Rephrase the following using the words in brackets.**

1 You can take photos in museums if you don't use a flash.   (only if, otherwise, as long as, unless)
2 If you eat sensibly, you won't put on weight.   (providing, unless, on condition that)
3 Should he invite me, I'll go.   (if, unless, provided, only if)

262 **Put the verbs in brackets into the correct tense.**

"If you don't work harder at school, you **1)** *'ll never get* (never/get) a good job." I remember my parents saying these words to me when I was at school. If I had listened to them then, I **2)** .... (not/become) what I am now. I **3)** .... (be) so much more if I had tried harder. I haven't always been a tramp actually; when I left school I had a job as a milkman and if the hours had been easier, I **4)** .... (do) it for much longer, but I hated getting up so early in the morning. When I lost my job, I **5)** .... (cannot/ pay) the rent, so my landlord said that if I **6)** .... (not/get) another job, I would be on the streets; and before I knew it, I was. I could have got another job if I **7)** .... (want) to, but at first I quite enjoyed the freedom of the outdoor life. If you sleep out in summer, it **8)** .... (not/be)

too bad, but in winter it's awful. If I **9)** .... (can/change) anything about my life now, I would get in touch with my family again, even though I know they would only say, "If you'd worked harder at school, you **10)** .... (not/get) yourself in this situation."

263 **Complete the following sentences with an appropriate conditional clause.**

1 If I won £1,000,000, ... *I would buy myself a villa by the sea.* ....
2 If you do well in the interview, ...
3 If you had caught the bus, ...
4 Should you see Jane tonight, ...
5 But for him, I ....
6 Unless he gets a promotion, ...
7 She would have gone to work ....
8 Only if you save your money, ...

264 **What do the if-clauses express: request, insistence, annoyance or uncertainty?**

1 If you will wash up afterwards, I'll make lunch. (...*request*...)
2 If you will listen to that awful music, you could at least wear headphones. (...)
3 If you will lend me the money, I can pay you back on pay-day. (...)
4 If you should drop out of college, you will have to look for a job. (...)
5 If the dog will keep barking, I'll let it out. (...)

Mixed Conditionals

All types of conditionals can be mixed. Any tense combination is possible if the context permits it.

	If - clause	Main clause	
Type 2	If they **were playing** all day, (They were playing all day,	they **will be** tired out now. so they are tired out now.)	**Type 1**
Type 2	If I **were** you, (You are not me, If he **were** a fast runner, (He is not a fast runner,	I **would have invited** her. so you didn't invite her.) he **would have won** the race. so he didn't win the race.)	**Type 3**
Type 3	If she **had saved** her money, (She didn't save her money,	she **would be going** on holiday. so she isn't going on holiday.)	**Type 2**

265 **Rewrite the following as mixed conditional sentences as in the example:**

1 She isn't at the meeting because she wasn't told about it.
...*She would be at the meeting if she had been told about it.* ....
2 I didn't apply for the job. I don't want to work there. ....
3 He didn't take his job seriously. He's unemployed now. ....
4 He didn't train every day. He won't win the race. ....
5 I didn't book seats. We can't go to the concert tonight. ....
6 You didn't warn me. Now I'm in a difficult situation. ....
7 I don't know him very well so I didn't give him any advice. ....

Implied Conditionals

● **An if-clause is not always stated; it is often implied and the rules for the verb usage are still followed in the result clause (main clause).**
He committed the crime, otherwise he wouldn't have been arrested. (implied conditional)
If he hadn't committed the crime, he wouldn't have been arrested.
I would have stayed longer, but he didn't ask me to. (implied conditional)
I would have stayed longer if he had asked me to.

266 **First underline the implied conditionals, then change them into if-clauses.**

1 I missed the early train, otherwise I wouldn't have been late.
...*If I hadn't missed the early train, I wouldn't have been late.* ....
2 The meal would have been lovely but you put the oven on too high. ....
3 I don't know anything about cars, otherwise I would have changed the tyre myself.

....
4 Michael would be celebrating but he didn't win the race. ....
5 They would be at the reception but they weren't invited. ....
6 The hotel wouldn't be overbooked but the receptionist made a mistake.

....
7 The film was very popular, otherwise the director wouldn't have won an Oscar.

....

> I wish I were rich.
> I wish I had enough money to buy a lot of food.

> I wish I hadn't put on so much weight.
> I wish I could go on a diet.

> Could you give me some food please?
> I haven't eaten anything for three days.

> If only I had your will-power!

Wishes

	Form	Use
I wish (if only) (wish/regret about the present)	**+ Past tense**	wish/regret about a present situation we want to be different
*I wish **you worked** more efficiently. (It's a pity you don't work more efficiently.)*		
I wish (if only) (wish/regret about the present)	**+ could + bare infinitive**	wish/regret in the present concerning lack of ability
*I wish I **could** drive a car. (But I can't.)*		
I wish (if only) (regret about the past)	**+ Past Perfect**	regret that something happened or didn't happen in the past
*I wish I **had attended** the seminar last Monday. (But I didn't. It's a pity I didn't attend it.)*		
I wish (if only) (impossible wish for a future change)	**+ subject + would + bare inf** (a. "wish" and "would" should have different subjects. We never say: ~~I wish I would, He wishes he would~~ etc b. wish + inanimate subject + would is used to express the speaker's lack of hope or disappointment)	wish for a future change unlikely to happen or wish to express dissatisfaction; polite request implying dissatisfaction or lack of hope

*I wish he **would drive** more carefully. (But I don't think he will. - wish for a future change unlikely to happen)*
*I wish the children **would be** more co-operative. (The children have refused to co-operate. - dissatisfaction)*
*I wish you **would be** more patient with Jim. (Please be more patient with him! - request implying lack of hope)*
*I wish it **would stop** raining. (But I'm afraid it won't stop raining. - wish implying disappointment)*

- In wishes, we go one tense back. This means that we use the Past Simple in the present or the Past Perfect in the past. *He's ill. He wishes he **weren't** ill. (present)*
  *I overslept yesterday. I wish I **hadn't overslept** yesterday. (past)*
- After **I wish** we can use **were** instead of **was** in all persons. *I wish I **was/were** richer.*
- **If only** means the same as **I wish** but it is more dramatic. *If only I **was/were** richer.*

267 Read what Irene says, then write what she wishes as in the example:

It rains all the time. I went camping and I regret it. The tent leaks; I didn't buy a new tent.
I'm going to catch a cold. I can't see my friends. I feel lonely. I wasted my holidays here.

1 .....I wish it would stop ....
.....raining all the time. ....

2 ....

3 ....

4 ....

5 ....

6 ....

7 ....

8 ....

268 Fill in the gaps with an appropriate auxiliary verb.

1 She can't type but she wishes she ...could....
2 They didn't buy the antique vase but they wish they ....
3 I'm not going to the concert but I wish I ....
4 I'm not very tall but I wish I ....
5 I didn't go to the meeting but I wish I ....
6 I can't tell him the truth but I wish I ....
7 I don't earn much money but I wish I ....
8 He probably won't listen but I wish he ....
9 She won't accept help but I wish she ....

10 They haven't got any children but they wish they
....
11 I didn't see the programme but I wish I ....
12 She's not qualified enough for the job but she wishes she ....
13 He can't afford to buy her a diamond ring but he wishes he ....
14 I don't live close to the office, but I wish I ....
15 She hasn't got a fax machine but she wishes she ....

269 Put the verbs in brackets into the correct tense.

Dear Beth,

I'm so desperate. I wish I 1) ...*hadn't moved*... (not/move) to this place. It's not a bad place but it's so quiet. If only there 2) .... (be) more people here my age, then I wouldn't feel so lonely. Even better, I wish my friends 3) .... (move) here from town. I thought I would enjoy the quiet life of the village but now I wish there 4) .... (be) some roads nearby so I could hear the traffic. I wish I 5) .... (afford) to move back to town but I don't have the money. Maybe it's the weather. I wish it 6) .... (stop) raining so at least I could go for long walks in the fields. Sometimes, when I'm really sad, I wish the village 7) .... (disappear) or my house 8) .... (collapse) so that I'd have to move. Maybe it will get better. If only I 9) .... (be) more patient. I wish I 10) .... (write) a more cheerful letter. It's made me even sadder. I look forward to hearing from you with some suggestions.

Best wishes,
Steve

270 Complete the following sentences using the words in bold.

1 She would have stayed longer, but the babysitter needed to leave at 9.00.
not If the babysitter ....*had not needed to leave*.......... at 9.00, she would have stayed longer.
2 We stopped at the service station. Otherwise, we would have run out of petrol.
not If .... at the service station, we would have run out of petrol.

3   Tim couldn't have found the treasure without the map.
   for   But ...., Tim couldn't have found the treasure.
4   I would have bought you a present but I didn't know that it was your birthday.
   wish   I .... it was your birthday; I would have bought you a present.
5   I grabbed his hand. Otherwise, he might have run into the road.
   case   I grabbed his hand .... into the road.
6   It's a pity I didn't read that book.
   wish   I .... that book.
7   Ann can organise the concert but somebody must help her.
   helps   Only if somebody .... the concert.
8   Helen would have lent you the money but you didn't ask her.
   asked   If ...., she would have lent you the money.
9   I didn't finish my assignment because I came down with a terrible cold.
   would   If I hadn't come down with a terrible cold, ... my assignment.
10 I learnt to swim because you encouraged me.
   never   I .... to swim if you hadn't encouraged me.
11 Lee didn't drive me to the airport and as a result I missed my flight.
   wish   I .... me to the airport; I wouldn't have missed my flight.
12 Kate will move to London but she must find a job first.
   finds   Only if Kate .... move to London.
13 You can't lose weight without doing some exercise.
   not   Unless you do some exercise, ... weight.

271 ▶ **Put the verbs in brackets into the appropriate form.**

The young reporter walked up to the table where Dora
Spangle was sitting and introduced himself. "Miss
Spangle, I'm Dan Quaid from *'Star International'*." The
actress smiled up at him charmingly. "If I **1)**...*had
known*... (know) you were coming, I'd have reserved a
bigger table," she said. "You're too kind," laughed Dan.
"You **2)** .... (not/say) that if you knew what
a huge appetite I have!" "Probably not," agreed Dora.
"Now, I have to go in ten minutes. So, if I were you, I **3)**
.... (start) asking your questions." "Very
well. Do you have any regrets about retiring from acting?"
asked Dan. "Not about retiring," she replied. "But I do
wish I **4)** .... (play) the role of Cleopatra
just once in my career." "If someone **5)** ....
(offer) you the part now, would you take it?" "No, it's too
late now. I've decided to retire and that's final." "What **6)**

.... (you/do) if you get bored?" "Oh, there's no chance of that," she assured him. "I might get
bored if I **7)** .... (not/have) all my animals to look after, though." "Do you ever wish you **8)**
.... (marry)?" Dan asked. "Not really," she replied. "Although I probably **9)** ....
.... (marry) John Rogers if he had asked me," she added sadly. "What if ..." "I'm sorry," Dora
interrupted. "I really must go now. It's time to feed my dogs and they get very upset if I **10)** .... (be)."

272 ▶ **Write sentences as in the example:**

1   You want to visit Australia but you're frightened of flying.
   ...*I wish I weren't frightened of flying. If I weren't frightened of flying, I could/would visit Australia.*
2   You wanted to go to the theatre but you couldn't find any tickets anywhere. ....
3   You wanted to ring Kelly but you lost her phone number. ....
4   You want to make a coffee but you've run out. ....
5   You want to go swimming but it's too cold. ....
6   You went on holiday; your camera was stolen. ....

If I **married** your daughter, I would make her very happy, sir.

Supposing she were poor, would you still want to marry her?

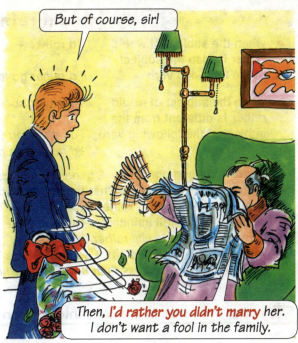

But of course, sir!

Then, **I'd rather you didn't marry** her. I don't want a fool in the family.

Unreal Past

● The Past Simple can be used to talk about imaginary, unreal or improbable situations in the present and the Past Perfect can be used to refer to imaginary, unreal or improbable situations in the past. This use of the Past forms is called the Unreal Past. We use the Unreal Past as follows:

Past Simple

● **Conditionals Type 2** (unreal in the present)
*If I **were** you, I would pay.*

● **wish** (present)
*I wish he **were** here now.*

● **Suppose/Supposing**
*Suppose you **were asked** to move out, what would you do?*

● **I'd rather/sooner sb ...** (present)
*I'd rather you **went** now.*

● **as if/as though** (untrue situation in the present) *He isn't French but he speaks French as if he **were** from France.*

● **it's (about/high) time** *It's time you **retired**.*

Past Perfect

● **Conditionals Type 3** (unreal in the past)
*If I **had seen** him, I would have told you.*

● **wish** (past)
*If only you **had taken** his advice when he gave it.*

● **Suppose/Supposing**
*Suppose he **had been seen** stealing the money, what would he have done?*

● **I'd rather/sooner sb ...** (past)
*I'd rather you **hadn't told** all those lies.*

● **as if/as though** (untrue situation in the past) *He hadn't been awarded the first prize but he behaved as if he **had been awarded** it.*

had better = should

I had better	+ present bare infinitive	(present/future reference)
*We had better **stop** smoking. (= We should stop smoking.)*		
It would have been better if	+ Past Perfect	(past reference)
*It would have been better if you **hadn't lied** to her. (= You shouldn't have lied to her.)*		

would rather = I'd prefer

● **when the subject of would rather is also the subject of the following verb**	**I'd rather +**	**Present bare infinitive** (present/future reference) **Perfect bare infinitive** (past reference)
		I'd rather go to the shops tomorrow. I'd rather not have gone yesterday.
● **when the subject of would rather is different from the subject of the following verb**	**I'd rather sb +**	**Past Simple** (present/future reference) **Past Perfect** (past reference)
	I'd rather you studied a little more.	
	I'd rather you had passed your driving test.	

- **prefer + gerund/noun + to + gerund/noun** (general) *I prefer (watching) TV to (going to) the cinema.*
- **prefer + full infinitive + rather than + bare infinitive** (general reference)
  I prefer to stay at home rather than go out.
- **would prefer + full infinitive + rather than + bare infinitive** (specific reference)
  I'd prefer to write to him rather than call him.
- **would rather + bare infinitive + than + bare infinitive**
  I'd rather buy a new dress than have this one taken in.

273 **Put the verbs in brackets into the correct form.**

1 I'd sooner you ...*did*... (do) something with your time rather than sit around all day.
2 He didn't win a prize, but he looked as though he .... (win) one.
3 If you hadn't seen the car in time, it .... (hit) you.
4 Supposing I offered you the job, ... (you/take) it?
5 It's about time you .... (go) on a holiday.
6 Suppose you .... (see) a mad dog, what would you do?
7 I'd rather you .... (not/drive) so fast, Pat.
8 It would have been better if you .... (tell) me the truth.
9 Sue went to France this year, but she says she would rather .... (go) to Spain.
10 It's a shame you missed the party; I would rather you .... (be) there.
11 John had better .... (not/speak) to me like that again.
12 He says he'd rather .... (cook) his own food than eat in restaurants.
13 I'd rather you .... (not/mention) this to anyone until next week.
14 Tim's mother would rather he .... (work) closer to home than he does.
15 The soup would have tasted better if you .... (not/put) so much pepper in it.
16 Greg says he would rather .... (not/leave) things as they are.
17 She would prefer to meet you personally rather than .... (talk) to you over the phone.
18 Sean prefers playing football to .... (watch) it.
19 Would you rather .... (write) in ink or in pencil?
20 Sheila prefers .... (get up) early in the morning rather than .... (oversleep).
21 Would he prefer .... (drive) to work tomorrow rather than cycle?
22 I would rather .... (speak) directly to the manager than .... (deal) with his rude secretary as I did.
23 My father prefers to have a beard rather than .... (have) a shave every day.
24 Tom prefers .... (ski) to .... (skate).
25 Wouldn't you prefer to sit on this seat rather than .... (stand) for the whole journey?
26 I wish I .... (be) as good as you at mathematics.
27 It seemed as if he .... (not/understand) the question.
28 I wouldn't have given him all that money if you .... (not/advise) me to.
29 Crime will continue to rise unless more police .... (be/put) on the streets.
30 If he .... (play) better, he would have won the game.
31 I wish Jim .... (not/move) to London last year as I hardly see him now.
32 If I .... (be) in the post office 5 minutes earlier, I would have witnessed the robbery.
33 I wish I .... (invite) more people to my fancy dress party last week.
34 If I .... (not/be) afraid of heights, I would try parachuting.
35 If you .... (not/let) her make her own decisions, she will never learn.
36 We'd better .... (take) some money for a taxi in case we miss the last bus home.

274 **Put the verbs in brackets into the correct form.**

A miner's life is a hard one. I wish it **1)** ...*weren't*... (not/be) so dirty and unhealthy. I also wish we **2)** .... (work) shorter hours and **3)** .... (have) better working conditions. If only I **4)** .... (not/leave) school so early. I wish I **5)** .... (do) something else, but the only thing I know is mining. I'd prefer **6)** .... (have) a job in the open air. There is nothing I'd rather **7)** .... (do) than work on a farm, for example - all that fresh air and open space! I wish the owners **8)** .... (make) my job a little safer. If only someone **9)** .... (invent) a machine to go underground, then I wouldn't have to do it. And I wish people **10)** .... (stop) complaining about how much money we earn because we deserve every penny we get. I wish I **11)** .... (be) a young boy again and **12)** .... (have) the chance to choose something else. My father was a miner, but I wish I **13)** .... (not/decide) to follow in his footsteps. My son had better **14)** .... (study) hard if he doesn't want to follow in mine!

275 **Rewrite the letter using wishes or if-clauses as in the example:**

Dear Mandy,

I'm writing to you feeling completely frustrated. As you know, I have to give a reception every year to entertain my husband's business associates so I have to go to a lot of trouble. Well, disaster struck again! In my attempt to appear an original hostess, I ordered some Chinese and Thai food to be served with chopsticks. Needless to say, my guests disapproved. I also booked a Latin band to come and play live, but our middle-aged guests found it hard to dance so energetically. My husband has no sympathy for me and is mad at my choice of entertainment. I must confess I want to get out of organising such social gatherings. It's a pity you weren't here; you missed out on a unique opportunity to see my husband dancing the salsa!

Yours,
Dorothy

eg. **I wish I didn't feel so frustrated. If I didn't have to give ...**

Oral Activity 20

Students in teams take turns to give their reactions to the following picture situations. The teams should be able to invent at least two situations per picture using conditionals and wishes as in the example:

Team A: *He wishes he could reach the island.*

Team A: *He wishes he hadn't been shipwrecked.*

Team B: *If he reaches the island, he might find something to eat.*

Team B: *If he hadn't been shipwrecked, he wouldn't be on a raft now.*

276 ▷ **Fill in: if, unless, provided or as long as.**

1 No one will be able to steal the jewels ...*unless*... they know the secret code.
2 You can't get into the club .... you're over 21.
3 Everyone wins a prize .... that they finish the game.
4 .... you change your address, you must let the post office know.
5 .... the boss has changed his mind, they will receive an extra Christmas bonus this year.
6 .... that you follow the map, you won't get lost.
7 Your father won't object to your going to the party .... you're back by 9 o'clock.

277 ▷ **Complete the following conversation with a suitable form of the verbs in brackets.**

Jane: Well, we **1)** ...*would have had*... (have) a great time if it **2)** .... (not/pour) with rain!
Sally: I **3)** .... (know). It really **4)** .... (spoil) the garden party. If we **5)** .... (know) it would rain, we **6)** .... (make) indoor plans.
Jane: Well, at least we **7)** .... (raise) a lot of money this time. If we **8)** .... (have) another successful fund-raiser later on in the year, we **9)** .... (have) enough money to buy the medical equipment required at the hospital.
Sally: Yes, and then if there **10)** .... (be) any money left, we **11)** .... (give) it to the old people's home.
Jane: That's a good idea. I'm sure that if we **12)** .... (donate) even a small amount, they **13)** .... (appreciate) it greatly.
Sally: I know it takes a lot of money to keep the home in good working order.
Jane: Yes. A friend of mine told me that if they **14)** .... (not/receive) any money from charity last year, the home **15)** .... (close) due to lack of funds.

Oral Activity 21

The Smiths are looking at two holiday advertisements. Imagine what they are thinking using conditionals, I'd rather, I'd prefer etc. Discuss this in pairs, then report back to your teacher.

Skiing in Austria

● travel by coach or train
● apartments
● magnificent views of mountains
● organised activities for evenings and nights
● delicious Austrian cuisine
● heated swimming pool

Package holidays to Hawaii

● daily flights
● variety of nightlife
● comfortable hotel rooms
● rooms with view of sea
● English food served daily
● magnificent beaches

eg. A: *If we choose the skiing holiday in Austria, we'll have to travel by coach or train.*
B: *We'd rather travel by plane because it's faster and safer.*

Writing Activity 9

The Smiths chose the package holiday to Hawaii. They are back now but they didn't have a good time as things didn't turn out the way they expected. Mrs Smith is writing her friend, Sue, a letter. Look at the ideas below, then write the letter using conditionals, wishes, had better, would rather.

hotel dirty and crowded, Mrs Smith was sick on the flight, sea polluted, beach crowded, rooms comfortable but noisy neighbours, food awful - Mr Smith was sick, no variety of entertainment

English in use 8

278 Put the verbs in brackets into the correct tense.

Frederick Stamp, a young man in his early twenties, **1)** ....*was committed*........ (commit) by his family to a psychiatric hospital. Frederick's best friend, a very wealthy man named Sir Ernest Frump, **2)** .... (be) greatly upset by this, so he started **3)** .... (spend) a great deal of time and money to secure Frederick's release. Sir Ernest strongly **4)** .... (believe) that Frederick was normal and **5)** .... (always/be). He finally 6) .... (persuade) three well known psychiatrists to assess Frederick, in the hope that they would realise what a huge mistake 7) .... (make). "If you 8) .... (talk) to him, you 9) .... (see) what a completely sane man he is," insisted Sir Ernest. "I 10) .... (try) for years to set my friend free. I wish someone **11)** .... (listen) to me!" The day of the assessment finally **12)** .... (arrive). Frederick **13)** .... (sit) perfectly relaxed while the three doctors **14)** .... (ask) him questions. "What **15)** .... (you/do) when you leave here?" one of them asked. "**16)** .... (you/get) a job?" "Well, I **17)** .... (think) about it," replied Frederick. "I **18)** .... (not/make up) my mind yet, though. Perhaps I **19)** .... (write) a book or I may **20)** .... (take up) painting again." He **21)** .... (pause) and **22)** .... (smile) at the doctors, who **23)** .... (listen) carefully to his

279 Look at Appendix 2, then fill in the correct particle(s).

		Phrasal Verbs

1. Without my glasses I can hardly **make** ...*out*... the words on this page.
2. She must have **made** .... that story; it can't be true.
3. They are **made** .... each other; I'm sure they'll get married.
4. They didn't **make** .... after their quarrel.
5. Can you **make** the cheque .... for £100?
6. He bought her some flowers to **make** .... his bad behaviour.
7. His grandmother **passed** .... in March last year.
8. At the party he **passed** himself .... a rich businessman.
9. Help me to a seat; I think I'm going to **pass** ....
10. Don't worry, I'm going to **pay** him .... for what he did to you.
11. Ten employees were **paid** .... as there wasn't enough work for all.
12. At the last moment, Bill **pulled** .... the deal.
13. **Pull** yourself .... and stop behaving like a child.
14. The train **pulled** .... at the station 20 minutes late.
15. We arrived just in time to see the train **pull** .... the station.

Phrasal Verbs

1. for, out, off, up
2. up, up for, for, over
3. off, up to, up, for
4. up, for, off, over
5. up to, off, out, up for
6. up for, off, up, over
7. away, by, off, over
8. out, through, off as, by
9. off, up, out, back
10. down, back, up, off
11. down, off, up, back
12. up, out of, back, through
13. together, in, down, out
14. back, down, out, in
15. off, in, out of, from

280 Complete the sentences using the words in bold.

1. It's only a twenty-minute drive to the airport.
   takes   It only ....*takes twenty minutes to drive*................................ to the airport.
2. She will have her book published next month
   brought   Her .... next month.
3. It was careless of him to leave the oven on.
   should   He .... the oven on.
4. "Will I ever get rich?" Tom wondered.
   if   Tom .... get rich.
5. The weather was so cold that we couldn't go out.
   such   It .... we couldn't go out.
6. After his retirement he started playing golf.
   took   After his retirement .... golf.

7 Although he was tall, he couldn't reach the shelf.
his   Despite .... reach the shelf.
8 Sheila doesn't agree with John's way of thinking.
approve   Sheila .... way of thinking.
9 Jane's stories amused everybody last night.
found   Everybody .... last night.
10 Cynthia is a better typist than Betty.
well   Betty .... as Cynthia can.

281 Look at Appendix 3, then fill in the correct preposition.

Prepositions

1 on, by, in
2 by, at, on
3 on, with, at
4 in, by, at
5 by, with, of
6 in, by, at
7 at, in, on
8 of, by, at
9 for, at, of
10 with, in, by
11 In, At, On
12 At, By, In

1 We usually go ...*by*... bus because it's cheaper than the train.
2 I left my purse .... the bus when I got off.
3 She was .... a plane to Madrid when the bomb exploded.
4 I must pass my tests .... all costs.
5 I'm sorry, I put milk in your coffee .... mistake.
6 The bus only stops here .... request.
7 She came .... his request.
8 I know him .... sight, but I've never spoken to him.
9 I was .... a loss for words when I saw him.
10 Mum made the skirt .... hand.
11 .... the end of the programme, she turned the television off.
12 .... the end they got married, but we had thought they never would.

282 Think of the word which best fits each space. Write only one word in each space.

ADVICE TO FIRST-TIME AIR TRAVELLERS

Travelling **(0)** ...*by*... aeroplane can be a tiring business if you are new to it, so it's best to be well-prepared. If your destination is a foreign country **(1)** .... you don't know at **(2)** ...., it's best to arrange for someone who is familiar **(3)** .... the place to meet you at the airport. Be sure to **(4)** .... him the name of the airport or terminal and the flight number, as **(5)** .... as the estimated arrival time. Specify a meeting place and have his phone number in **(6)** .... something goes wrong. It is not unknown for luggage to **(7)** .... lost so it is **(8)** .... taking out travel insurance. You should also **(9)** .... sure your luggage can be easily identified so **(10)** .... you won't miss it or confuse it **(11)** .... someone else's at baggage reclaim. When you set **(12)** .... for the airport, double-check that you have everything - tickets, passports, visas, insurance and foreign currency. Give yourself **(13)** .... of time for the journey. You'll need to arrive at **(14)** .... two hours before takeoff. Once you're at the airport, never agree **(15)** .... carry anyone else's luggage.

283 Use the words in capitals to form a word that fits in the space in the same line.

CHINA

Two centuries ago China was seen as a **(0)** ...... of mystery and wasteland. Its only **(1)** ...... export was tea. However, over the years **(2)** ...... in China has changed. Many have noted the change in Chinese **(3)** ...... especially the **(4)** ...... of its people.
A **(5)** ...... of the West and the East is now found in modern businesses. The **(6)** ...... of weapons and the growth of its army have made China a world power. But urban development has been **(7)** ...... to the Chinese. Thousands of **(8)** ...... peasant farmers have been attracted to the new cities. Their **(9)** ...... of the land is forgotten and many die homeless. China's future is **(10)** ......; no one knows what will happen next.

COMBINE	0	*combination*
FAME	1	
LIVE	2	
SOCIAL	3	
TREAT	4	
MIX	5	
PRODUCT	6	
HARM	7	
LUCKY	8	
KNOW	9	
PREDICTABLE	10	

Practice test 4

For questions 1 - 15, read the text below and decide which word A, B, C or D best fits each space. Write your answers in the answer boxes provided.

BODY LANGUAGE

Language is commonly believed to be a system of communication that **(0) ....** of sounds and written symbols. However, we can also communicate **(1) ....** other ways by using our facial **(2) ....**, our tone of voice and even our **(3) ....** body. In fact, in many situations, non-verbal communication can **(4) ....** more accurately what a person is feeling. Body language always speaks the truth, **(5) ....** words can often be **(6) ....** .

For successful communication both at the office and at home, an understanding of body language is important. At work, non-verbal communication is **(7) ....** to power. People **(8) ....** charge tend to lean **(9) ....** in their chairs, fold their hands behind their heads and **(10) ....** their feet up on the desk. They usually **(11) ....** conversations, both talking and interrupting more than others. Those who **(12) ....** orders, on the other hand, are much less relaxed and tend to sit on the **(13) ....** of their chairs with their arms tightly folded.

Body language plays an equally important role at home. Children are particularly quick to pick **(14) ....** on non-verbal signals and can distinguish **(15) ....** what is said and what is really meant.

0	A exists	B consists	C contains	D includes
1	A to	B for	C in	D by
2	A expressions	B shapes	C looks	D aspects
3	A full	B whole	C partial	D total
4	A explain	B announce	C reveal	D publish
5	A whereas	B so	C except	D therefore
6	A senseless	B hopeless	C mistrustful	D misleading
7	A associated	B related	C combined	D reserved
8	A at	B on	C by	D in
9	A back	B behind	C away	D against
10	A put	B lay	C deposit	D lie
11	A overwhelm	B master	C dominate	D hold
12	A do	B give	C lead	D follow
13	A top	B edge	C limit	D border
14	A out	B over	C up	D at
15	A between	B among	C from	D that

	A	B	C	D
0		■		
1				
2				
3				
4				
5				
6				
7				
8				
9				
10				
11				
12				
13				
14				
15				

PART 2

For questions 16 - 30, read the text below and think of the word which best fits each space. Use only one word in each space. Write your answers in the answer boxes provided.

EXTREME SKIING

Most people would rather take up a sport that involves **(0)** .... or no risk and would certainly not choose a sport **(16)** .... extreme skiing, which is **(17)** .... of the most dangerous in the world. Extreme skiing is **(18)** .... for those who **(19)** .... for adventure. Invented by the French, **(20)** .... is a sport which attracts brave skiers **(21)** .... would rather ski down a 60-degree slope and tackle hair-raising jumps **(22)** ....experience the relaxing pleasures of conventional skiing. The ultimate goal of most extreme skiers is to win the World Extreme Ski Championship, **(23)** .... skiers have to tackle the most challenging terrain and can only survey the course **(24)** .... the bottom of the mountain. One successful competitor said that he was glad that he had had a good look at the course beforehand, as a fall could **(25)** .... been fatal. Another, who was not **(26)** .... lucky, explained that she could have waited **(27)** .... the conditions were better, but then the danger would have been eliminated.

(28) .... people who enjoy putting their lives at risk are drawn to extreme skiing, their families would rather they hadn't chosen **(29)** .... a dangerous sport. There must be **(30)** .... more worrying than seeing someone you love fling themselves off a cliff face.

0	*little*
16	
17	
18	
19	
20	
21	
22	
23	
24	
25	
26	
27	
28	
29	
30	

PART 3

For questions 31 - 40, complete the second sentence so that it has a similar meaning to the first sentence. Use the word given and other words to complete each sentence. You must use between two and five words. Do not change the word given. Write your answers in the answer boxes provided.

0   I finished the book in two days.
took
It .... to finish the book.

| 0 | *took me two days* | 0 ▬ |

31   The town where I live is close to the sea.
in
The town I .... is close to the sea.

| 31 | | 31 |

32   Sally behaves better than Sue.
well
Sue is .... Sally.

| 32 | | 32 |

33   It was difficult for Jim to overcome his problems.
difficulty
Jim .... his problems.

| 33 | | 33 |

34   All flights were cancelled because there was a strike.
due
All flights .... strike.

| 34 | | 34 |

35   Tom fell in love with the place at first sight.
for
Tom .... straight away.

| 35 | | 35 |

36   How long ago did he move in?
since
How long .... in?

| 36 | | 36 |

37   I like travelling by car more than by train.
rather
I prefer to .... by train.

| 37 | | 37 |

38   I'm sure she didn't lie to you.
have
She .... to you.

| 38 | | 38 |

39   Paul tried as hard as he could to win the race.
best
Paul .... the race.

| 39 | | 39 |

40   He doesn't drive because he's afraid of having an accident.
fear
He doesn't .... an accident.

| 40 | | 40 |

PART 4

For questions 41 - 55, read the text below and look carefully at each line. Some of the lines are correct and some have a word which should not be there. If a line is correct, put a tick (✔) by the number in the answer boxes provided. If a line has a word which should not be there, write the word in the answer boxes provided.

BEING SUPERSTITIOUS

	Text		Answer	
0	Many people are superstitious about different things.	0	✔	0
00	One particular superstition, however, which it is shared	00	it	00
41	by the many people all over the world, is the belief that	41		41
42	the number 13 is an unlucky number. This is why some	42		42
43	buildings do not have a 13th floor, and why some of	43		43
44	people do not like to sit at a table with 12 other people.	44		44
45	Despite this, no one really knows why so many people	45		45
46	do not like the number 13, although there are several of	46		46
47	theories. Another of common superstition is for people	47		47
48	to touch or knock on something made of wood if	48		48
49	when they want good luck to come their way or to	49		49
50	prevent anything bad from happening to them. People	50		50
51	used to believe that certain gods lived inside a trees	51		51
52	and, whenever they were faced with a difficult situation,	52		52
53	they would knocked on the wood of a tree to ask	53		53
54	for god's help and protection. Although of this practice	54		54
55	continues on today, we often just say "touch wood".	55		55

PART 5

For questions 56 - 65, read the text below. Use the word given in capitals at the end of each line to form a word that fits in the space in the same line. Write your word in the answer boxes provided.

LEARNING A FOREIGN LANGUAGE

Most people have the (0) .... to learn a foreign language. They simply need constant (56) .... in order to overcome their fears. (57) .... seems to be the most difficult aspect for some students, while for others it is (58) .... of the spoken word. This feeling is not (59) .... to those who feel least (60) ...., as even the most outgoing students are sometimes (61) .... to speak. One reason for this reluctance may be (62) .... . Students may be (63) .... of their accent. We could say that the root of this problem might be the student's desire for (64) ...., but no one can have perfect (65) .... without practice.

Word		Answer	
ABLE	0	ability	0
ENCOURAGE	56		56
CONVERSE	57		57
COMPREHEND	58		58
EXCLUDE	59		59
CONFIDENCE	60		60
RELUCTANCE	61		61
SHY	62		62
SHAME	63		63
PERFECT	64		64
PRONOUNCE	65		65

A Choose the correct item.

1 I'd be grateful if you'd .... me the secret of making perfect pastry.
   A say   B speak
   C talk   D tell

2 If only I .... a motorcycle instead of a car. I wouldn't have to spend so much on petrol.
   A had bought   B buy
   C have bought   D bought

3 Even though he objected to violence, he was made .... in the army.
   A serving   B serve
   C to serve   D had served

4 I won't telephone you .... I know for sure.
   A by the time   B when
   C until   D by

5 Even if I .... all night, I still wouldn't be properly prepared for tomorrow.
   A will study   B have studied
   C would study   D studied

6 He didn't want to wash the family car but his father made him .... it.
   A doing   B have done
   C did   D do

7 He arrives .... punctually you can set your watch by him.
   A such   B so
   C very   D too

8 These letters haven't been typed. Have the typists .... them right away!
   A do   B to do
   C doing   D to doing

9 She wouldn't forgive him .... all his apologies.
   A even though   B despite
   C in spite   D although

10 Make sure you know the answer in case he .... you.
   A will ask   B asks
   C would ask   D has asked

11 Will you get my husband .... me as soon as he arrives at work?
   A ring   B ringing
   C have rung   D to ring

12 .... tasteful furniture you have bought!
   A What a   B What
   C So   D How

13 It's time you .... up your mind about what you're going to do with your life.
   A have made   B made
   C make   D had made

14 Suppose I didn't have enough money, ... me some?
   A would you lend   B do you lend
   C have you lent   D did you lend

15 She was heard .... that she was planning to move to Swansea.
   A to saying   B say
   C to say   D said

16 I'd prefer to see him personally .... write him a letter.
   A from   B to
   C rather than   D rather

17 I'd rather he .... me to my face rather than behind my back.
   A criticised   B criticising
   C has criticised   D to criticise

18 Sandra works .... a computer programmer for IBM.
   A like   B as
   C as if   D for

19 He was stabbed .... a knife.
   A by   B from
   C with   D of

20 .... she nor her husband will have an animal in the house.
   A Neither   B Or
   C Either   D Nor

21 I'd better .... slowly in this icy weather.
   A drive   B have driven
   C drove   D to drive

22 I prefer watching TV .... listening to music.
   A than   B rather than
   C to buy   D from

23 He collects not only stamps .... old coins.
   A while   B though
   C whereas   D but also

24 Few people like him because he has .... bad manners.
   A so   B that
   C such   D such a

B **Using the word given complete the sentences so that the second sentence has a similar meaning to the first sentence.**

1 I'll mow the lawn tomorrow but only if it's fine.
is   Only if it .... mow the lawn tomorrow.
2 Although he doesn't have much money, he seems happy.
lack   Despite .... he seems happy.
3 "You'd better think carefully before you make a decision," he said.
warned   He .... carefully before I made a decision.
4 "You would have enjoyed the film but you didn't see it," she said.
seen   If .... the film, you would have enjoyed it," she said.
5 It was unwise of him to believe the weather forecast.
should   He .... the weather forecast.
6 The information was so complicated that I couldn't understand it.
such   It .... I couldn't understand it.
7 He persuaded Mary to go shopping for him.
got   He .... shopping for him.
8 "You simply must let me pay for the meal," he said.
insisted   He .... the meal.
9 When he left, she started typing the letters.
until   She waited .... she started typing the letters.
10 I'm sure he wasn't serious when he said he'd resign.
can't   He .... when he said he'd resign.
11 Vandals sprayed graffiti on his car.
had   He .... his car by vandals.
12 Jim is a better storyteller than Alan.
well   Alan doesn't .... as Jim.
13 It is said that this juice has a high sugar content.
have   This juice .... a high sugar content.
14 He would never have bought the car without the generous discount.
for   But ...., he would never have bought the car.
15 I met a man; he's the owner of Pueblo Restaurant.
who   The man .... is the owner of Pueblo Restaurant.
16 "Will you have lunch with me today?" he said. "I'm afraid I can't," she replied.
down   She .... his invitation to have lunch with him that day.
17 Experts believe excessive sunbathing causes skin cancer.
believed   Excessive sunbathing .... skin cancer.
18 The man who owns this car will be arrested.
whose   The man .... will be arrested.
19 Since there were several strikes, production fell last year.
due   Production fell last year .... strikes.
20 I didn't lose weight so my new swimsuit still doesn't fit.
wish   I .... so that my new swimsuit would fit.

C **Fill in the correct particle(s).**

1 A snob always looks .... people who have little money.
2 Although I didn't fully agree, I fell .... his plans.
3 Rotting rubbish gives .... a most unpleasant smell.
4 Your writing is so small it's difficult to make .... the words.
5 Please keep .... the grass.
6 He was sorry to hear that Aunt Sheila had passed .... last Monday.
7 John gets .... well with his colleagues. Everyone likes him.
8 Hold .... a moment while I fetch the money to pay you.

D Fill in the correct preposition.

1 I'm studying three subjects now, but later I'll specialise .... one.
2 This message must get through .... all costs.
3 Coffee shops will always be popular .... retired people.
4 He'd be a valuable employee if he wasn't lacking .... common sense.
5 I know him .... sight.
6 They always quarrel .... how to spend their money.
7 Dress smartly to make a good impression .... others.
8 We sympathised .... Tim when he told us he had been fired.

E Put the verbs in brackets into the correct tense.

Barry Kent lives in a small house. He wishes he 1) .... (own) a nice flat, but he can't afford it. If he 2) .... (have) a job, he could save some money. But Barry has no qualifications. "I wish I 3) .... (work) harder at school," he says. "If I 4) .... (pass) a few exams, I could have gone to college. If I can, I 5) .... (go) to evening classes. I hate this bedsit. I wish I 6) .... (never/leave) home. But mum was always nagging me." Barry has some advice for people at school. "If I 7) .. .. (be) you, I'd study hard. I wish I 8) .... (listen) to my teachers' advice years ago."

F Put the verbs in brackets into the correct tense.

Gordon Jones lives and works in Greenland. He wishes he 1) .... (live) somewhere warmer though. If he 2) .... (work) in Portugal, for example, he wouldn't have to wear such warm clothes all the time. "I wish I 3) .... (take) that job in Portugal," he says. "It didn't pay so well, but at least I could have enjoyed the sunshine. I 4) .... (never/get) a suntan in this country. I wish I 5) .... (think) about it more carefully at the time." If he 6) .... (not/be) so worried about money, he would have made the right decision. He has some advice for people thinking of emigrating. "If I 7) .... (be) you, I would try to be sure you know where you really want to go. If I 8) .... (know) Greenland was so cold, I'd never have come."

G Find the word which should not be in the sentence.

1 Many of people believe he is a liar.
2 Don't finish the meal. Instead of I'll order a sweet.
3 Please show your boarding pass while you boarding the plane.
4 Flying is much more safer than driving.
5 Passengers who are delayed will be offered free of meals.
6 I think it's those meatballs I ate which they made me feel sick.
7 The traffic is sometimes very bad, so allow to yourself plenty of time.
8 You'll find the most of these questions easy to answer.
9 Exercise makes you to feel good but it can also harm you.
10 It's not as far away such as you might think.
11 I prefer playing sport than to watching TV.
12 It's a fine day today so that we'll go swimming.

H Fill in the spaces with the form of the words in bold.

1 Spain is .... for its beaches.
2 In his .... to be first, he pushed everyone else aside.
3 She was so .... that she lost all her money at the casino.
4 Water is a .... of hydrogen and oxygen.
5 Not all antiques are as .... as they look.
6 His refusal to give up won the .... of everyone.
7 The .... of an explorer is thrilling.
8 He's in Africa now. He's always had an .... spirit.
9 A teacher should be .... with his students.
10 The window was so dirty it was .... to see out of it.
11 Look .... through the notes before you start writing.
12 Drive the car around the car park to .... yourself with the controls.

FAME
DETERMINE
LUCKY
COMBINE
VALUE
ADMIRE
LIVE
ADVENTURE
PATIENCE
DIFFICULTY
CARE
FAMILIAR

9 Nouns / Word Formation / Articles

- Nouns are: **abstract** *(art, belief etc)*, **concrete** *(artist, believer etc)*, **proper** *(Jill, Peter, Portugal etc)*, **collective** *(group, crowd, team, flock, herd, family etc)* **and common** *(woman, dog etc)*.
- There are three genders of nouns: **masculine** (**He** - men and boys, animals when we know their sex), **feminine** (**She** - women and girls, countries, ships, vehicles when regarded with affection or respect, animals when we know their sex) and **neutral** (**It** - things, babies and animals if we don't know their sex).
- Most nouns describing people have the same form whether they are male or female. *teacher, student etc.* Some nouns have different forms, though. *actor - actress, groom - bride etc.*

The Plural of Nouns

Nouns are made plural by adding:
- **-s** to the noun. *(chair - chairs)*
- **-es** to nouns ending in **-s, -ss, -x, -ch, -sh, -z.** *(bus - buses, glass - glasses, fox - foxes, torch - torches, brush - brushes, buzz, buzzes)*
- **-ies** to nouns ending in **consonant + y** *(lady - ladies)* but **-s** to nouns ending in **vowel + y** *(day - days)*
- **-es** to nouns ending in **consonant + o** *(potato - potatoes)*
- **-s** to nouns ending in **vowel + o** *(studio - studios)*, **double o** *(zoo - zoos)*, **abbreviations** *(photograph / photo - photos, autos, kilos, memos)*, **musical instruments** *(piano - pianos)* **and proper nouns** *(Eskimo -Eskimos)*. **Some nouns ending in -o can take either -es or -s. These are: buffaloes/buffalos, mosquitoes/mosquitos, volcanoes/volcanos, zeroes/zeros, tornadoes/tornados etc.**
- **-ves** to some nouns ending in **-f/-fe.** *(calf - calves, half - halves, knife - knives, leaf - leaves, life - lives, self - selves, thief - thieves, wolf - wolves)* **(but: belief - beliefs, chief - chiefs, cliff- cliffs, handkerchief - handkerchiefs, hoof - hoofs/hooves, roof - roofs, safe - safes)**
- Some nouns of Greek or Latin origin form their plural by adding Greek or Latin suffixes. *basis - bases, crisis - crises, terminus - termini, criterion - criteria, phenomenon - phenomena, stimulus - stimuli, datum - data, medium - media etc.*

Compound nouns form their plural by adding **-s/es**:
- to the **second noun** if the compound consists of two nouns. *ball game - ball games*
- to the **noun** if the compound consists of an adjective and a noun. *frying pan - frying pans*
- to the **first noun** if the compound consists of two nouns connected by a preposition or to the noun if the compound has only one noun. *mother-in-law —mothers-in-law, passer-by —passers-by*
- **at the end** of the compound if it does not include any nouns. *letdown - letdowns*

● **Irregular Plurals:** man - **men**, woman - **women**, foot - **feet**, tooth - **teeth**, louse - **lice**, mouse - **mice**, child - **children**, goose - **geese**, sheep - **sheep**, deer - **deer**, fish - **fish**, trout - **trout**, ox - **oxen**, salmon - **salmon**, spacecraft - **spacecraft**, aircraft - **aircraft**, means - **means**, species - **species**, hovercraft - **hovercraft**

284 <u>Write the plural of the following nouns.</u>

1	nanny	...*nannies*....	11	bush	....	21	ferryboat	....
2	father-in-law	....	12	pen-friend	....	22	watch	....
3	headache	....	13	video	....	23	medium	....
4	dictionary	....	14	pillowcase	....	24	bay	....
5	pincushion	....	15	violin	....	25	flamingo	....
6	phone	....	16	wife	....	26	taxi-driver	....
7	hoof	....	17	volcano	....	27	potato	....
8	radio	....	18	mouse	....	28	safe	....
9	train robbery	....	19	godfather	....	29	onlooker	....
10	painkiller	....	20	wish	....	30	walking-stick	....

285 <u>Fill in the plural as in the example:</u>

I wonder who decides what sort of 1) ...*animals*... (animal) are kept in 2) .... (zoo)? You expect to see a lot of 3) .... (monkey), 4) .... (rhino), and 5) .... (lion), but you rarely see 6) .... (ox), 7) .... (sheep), 8) .... (deer) or 9) .... (goose), probably because these can be seen commonly enough in the wild. Each day large 10) .... (delivery) of food arrive for the 11) .... (beast) to eat. Not expensive items like 12) .... (salmon) or 13) .... (trout), but ordinary things like 14) .... (potato) and 15) .... (tomato) - although the 16) .... (panda) like 17) .... (bamboo). The whole family, 18) .... (man), 19) .... (woman) and 20) .... (child) can take 21) .... (photo) or make 22) .... (video) of them eating with their 23) ....(paw) and 24) .... (tooth), since animals do not use 25) .... (knife) and 26) .... (fork) to eat.

286 <u>Fill in the plural as in the example:</u>

Dear Manager,

I'm writing to complain about the terrible evening I had at your restaurant. We had reserved a table but when we arrived, there weren't enough 1) ...*chairs*... (chair) for us to sit on. Even though we'd checked beforehand, we were told that there were no 2) .... (meal) especially for 3) .... (child). We had to keep asking the waiter to bring us some 4) .... (glass) and when he gave us our 5) .... (knife) and 6) .... (fork), they were dirty. We were informed that not all the 7) .... (dish) were available that evening and, when we did receive our food, the 8) .... (potato) were raw and the meat was so tough I nearly broke my 9) .... (tooth) when I bit into it. However, that was nothing! The real horror was when I saw two 10) .... (mouse) running across the floor. I think I'm entitled to some compensation as long as it doesn't include free 11) .... (meal) at your restaurant! I look forward to hearing from you.

Yours sincerely,
M. Bennet

Countable · Uncountable Nouns

- Nouns can be **countable** (those that can be counted) *1 book, 2 books etc* or **uncountable** (those that can't be counted) *flour.* Uncountable nouns take a singular verb. *Information **is** available at the front desk.* **They are not used with a/an. Some, any, no, much** etc can be used with them. *I need **some** advice. (not: ~~an advice~~).* But we say: **a** relief, **a** pity, **a** shame, **a** wonder, **a** knowledge (of sth), **a** help although they are uncountables. *What **a pity**! It's such **a shame**!*
- The most common uncountable nouns are: **Mass nouns: (fluids:** *blood, coffee, milk, oil, tea, water,etc,* **solids:** *bread, butter, china, coal, fish (meaning food), food, fruit, glass, ice, iron, meat, soap,* **gases:** *air, oxygen, pollution, smoke, smog, steam etc,* **particles:** *corn, dust, flour, hair, pepper, rice, salt, sand, sugar, wheat etc)*
  Subjects of study: *chemistry, economics, history, literature, mathematics, physics, psychology etc*
  Languages: *Chinese, English, French, German, Greek, Italian, Spanish, Turkish etc*
  Games: *baseball, billiards, chess, football, golf, poker, rugby, soccer, tennis etc*
  Diseases: *cancer, flu, measles, mumps etc*
  Natural phenomena: *darkness, fog, gravity, hail, heat, humidity, light, lightning, rain (but: the rains = season of continuous rain in tropical countries), snow, sunshine, thunder, weather, wind etc*
  Some abstract nouns: *accommodation, advice, anger, applause, assistance, behaviour, business, chaos, countryside, courage, damage, dirt, education, evidence, housework, homework, information, intelligence, knowledge, luck, music, news, peace, progress, seaside, shopping, traffic, trouble, truth, wealth, work etc*
  Collective nouns: *baggage, crockery, cutlery, furniture, jewellery, luggage, machinery, money, rubbish, stationery etc*
- Many **uncountable nouns** can be made **countable** by adding a partitive:
  *a **piece** of paper/cake/information/advice/furniture; a **glass/bottle** of water; a **jar** of jam; a **rasher** of bacon;a **box/sheet** of paper; a **packet** of tea; a **slice/loaf** of bread; a **pot** of yoghurt; a **pot/cup** of tea; a **kilo/pound** of meat; a **tube** of toothpaste; a **bar** of chocolate/soap; a **bit/piece** of chalk; an ice **cube**; a **lump** of sugar; a **bag** of flour; a **pair** of trousers; a **game** of soccer; a(n) **item/piece** of news; a **drop/can** of oil; a **can** of Coke; a **carton** of milk; a **block** of wood; a **flash/bolt** of lightning; a **clap/peal** of thunder etc*
- Some nouns take only a plural verb. These are objects which consist of two parts: **garments** *(pyjamas, trousers etc)*, **tools** *(scissors etc)*, **instruments** *(binoculars, compasses, spectacles etc)* or **nouns** such as: arms, ashes, barracks, clothes, congratulations, earnings, (good) looks, outskirts, people, police, premises, riches, stairs, surroundings, wages etc.
- **Group nouns** refer to a group of people. These nouns can take either a singular or a plural verb depending on whether we see the group as a whole or as individuals. Such **group nouns** are: army, audience, class, club, committee, company, council, crew, crowd, headquarters, family, jury, government, press, public, staff, team etc. *The **team was** the best in the country. (= the team as a group) The **team were** all given medals. (= each member separately as individuals)*
- With expressions of duration, distance or money meaning "a whole amount" we use a singular verb. *Two weeks **isn't** long to wait. Ten miles **is** a long way to ride. Ten thousand pounds **is** too much to spend on this house.*

Some nouns have a different meaning in the plural.

Singular	Plural
*Give me a piece of **paper**, please!*	*The police asked to see his **papers**. (documents)*
*The needle of a **compass** always points North.*	*You can draw a perfect circle with **compasses**.*
*It is a **custom** to give presents at Christmas.*	*All plane passengers were searched at **customs**.*
*She has a lot of **experience** in teaching.*	*We had lots of exciting **experiences** on our trip.*
*Would you like a **glass** of milk?*	*He can't see very well without his **glasses**.*
*She has got long, blonde **hair**.*	*There are two **hairs** in your milk!*
*They were shocked at the **scale** of the disaster.*	*She weighed herself on the **scales**.*
*The bowl is made of **wood**.*	*The girls got lost in the **woods**.*
*He goes to **work** every day except Sunday.*	*Picasso's **works** are really fascinating.*
*There were many **people** waiting outside.*	*All **peoples** of the world should be peaceful. (nations)*
*Don't go out in the **rain** without an umbrella.*	*In some climates the **rains** come twice a year.*

287 Fill in: is or are.

1 Your jeans ...*are*... hanging in the wardrobe.
2 Where .... my scissors?
3 There .... a lecture on economics today.
4 The shopping .... extremely heavy.
5 Where .... my boxing gloves?
6 This information .... incorrect!
7 Her hair .... beautiful.
8 Your socks .... in the drawer.
9 Her furniture .... very expensive.
10 His accommodation .... luxurious.
11 Evidence .. needed before the trial can continue.
12 The news .... very exciting.
13 Mumps .... a common illness among young children.
14 Where .... my glasses?
15 German .... difficult to learn.
16 Where .... the kitchen scales? I want to weigh some flour.
17 Chess .... a popular game.
18 Her work .... very tiring.
19 People .... starving in many countries.
20 Happiness .... the key to her success.

288 Write the correct form of the verbs in brackets. Use only the Present Simple.

1 Wild geese ...*fly*... (fly) south for the winter.
2 The press .... (be) often unfair to political candidates.
3 Six months .... (be) a long time to spend in hospital.
4 Two miles .... (be) not a long way to walk to school.
5 Economics .... (be) difficult for people with poor maths skills.
6 American Airlines .... (be) one of the largest carriers in the United States.
7 The stairs .... (be) too steep for me to climb.
8 Two-thirds of the food produced on the farm .... (be) used to feed people in that region.
9 .... (be) the number of students studying French falling?
10 Bus trips to and from New York .... (take) two hours either way.
11 International news .... (rely) on correspondents in every major city.
12 Five pounds .... (be) quite a lot of money to lose.
13 In the Philippines, there .... (be) heavy rains each year.
14 Two hours per week .... (be) not enough to learn a foreign language.

289 Write the correct form of the verbs in brackets.

I sometimes think that society 1) ...*throws*... (throw) away things without even thinking of repairing them. Trousers 2) .... (be) easy to mend or can be made into shorts which 3) .... (look) nice on most people. Pliers that 4) .... (be) broken or scissors that 5) .... (be) blunt can be fixed or sharpened. Clothes 6) .... (be) expensive and household goods always 7) .... (prove) useful so why 8) .... (be) these belongings often thrown away? Intelligence 9) .... (be) not really needed, just common sense. Congratulations 10) .... (be) in order for those who 11) .... (use) their heads in this way. An old pair of jeans which 12) .... (be) used for gardening, pyjamas which 13) .... (become) dishcloths and tights which 14) .... (strain) food, all make our earnings 15) .... (go) further.

290 Underline the correct item. Sometimes both of them are correct.

1 The advice she gave me **was**/**were** very helpful.
2 Her earnings **are**/**is** very low.
3 The weather **are**/**is** very unpredictable in England.
4 Sugar **is**/**are** bad for your teeth.
5 Most people **go**/**goes** on holiday at least once a year.
6 Physics **is**/**are** the study of natural laws.
7 Football **are**/**is** a popular sport.

8 All of his clothes **was/were** on the floor.
9 Her stunning looks **is/are** the key to her success.
10 Her brother's death **was/were** traumatic.
11 Athletics **is/are** challenging.
12 Her love of money **was/were** almost an obsession.
13 His luggage **was/were** extremely heavy.
14 **Is/Are** the information correct?

15 The old couple **is/are** moving to the coast.
16 The staff of the hospital **is/are** very helpful.
17 Billiards **is/are** played by many people.
18 There **is/are** a lot of sheep in that field.
19 The company headquarters **is/are** in London.
20 Darts **is/are** a popular game in Britain.
21 The news **is/are** on at 6 o'clock.

291 Make the following uncountable nouns plural as in the example:

1	furniture	two	...*pieces of furniture*......	8	tea	three	....
2	chalk	three	....	9	water	two	....
3	rice	two	....	10	butter	three	....
4	thunder	two	....	11	flour	three	....
5	paper	two	....	12	lightning	two	....
6	fruit	three	....	13	scissors	four	....
7	tennis	three	....	14	news	two	....

> **A couple of, several, a few, many, a (large, great, good) number of, both** are followed by a countable noun. **(Too) much, a little, a great/good deal of, a large/small amount/quantity of** are followed by an uncountable noun. **A lot of, lots of, hardly any, some, no, plenty of** are followed by a countable or uncountable noun.

292 Underline the expressions which can be used with the nouns as in the example:

1 She has bought <u>a couple of</u>, <u>several</u>, too much, <u>a few</u>, a little, <u>lots of</u> dresses.
2 She's got **a little, a lot of, hardly any, several, a few** experience in typing.
3 He drank **two, both, some, several, too much** glasses of water.
4 She is wearing **several, too many, hardly any, too much, no** jewellery.
5 The fire is going out - you'll have to fetch **a little, several, a couple of, some, plenty of** wood.
6 I've been shopping and I've got **no, a few, a little, hardly any, too many** money left.
7 Everyone needs **too much, a little, a few, a couple of, a number of** friends.
8 Flowers need **plenty of, a number of, too many, a great deal of, a lot of** water.
9 Could you move along to give me **a few, some, several, a little, plenty of** space?
10 I'm afraid I can't come for **a great deal of, several, a number of, too much, a little** reasons.
11 I can finish it only if you give me **plenty of, a number of, too many, some, a little** time.
12 **Too much, Plenty of, A few, Hardly any, A little** people were standing at the bus-stop.
13 I like **both, a little, plenty of, a couple of, too much** your ideas.
14 There are **a little, a great deal of, too much, hardly any, not many** things I'd like to say.

Oral Activity 22

The teacher divides the class into two teams and gives them countable or uncountable nouns. The teams in turn add "a/an" or "some". Each correct answer gets 1 point. The team with the most points is the winner.

Words to be used: paper, book, people, elephant, homework, machinery, village, church, sugar, biscuit, oil, furniture, match, actor, chalk, cheese, news, oyster, flower, water etc

eg. Teacher: paper   Teacher: book
    Team A S1: some paper   Team B S1: a book etc

Word Formation

- There are certain **prefixes** (syllables put at the beginning of words) and **suffixes** (syllables put at the end of words) which are used to form new words. However, there are no certain rules to follow to form one word from another.

Prefixes

anti-	= against	eg. **anti**nuclear	**pre-**	= before	eg. **pre**judge
bi-	= two	eg. **bi**lingual	**pro-**	= in favour of	eg. **pro**-American
co-	= with	eg. **co**operation	**re-**	= again	eg. **re**arrange
de-	= acting against	eg. **de**composition	**semi-**	= half	eg. **semi**circle
ex-	= before, former	eg. **ex**-general	**sub-**	= under	eg. **sub**conscious
inter-	= between	eg. **inter**mediate	**super-**	= above	eg. **super**natural
mono-	= one	eg. **mono**lingual	**trans-**	= across	eg. **trans**atlantic
non-	= not	eg. **non**-stop	**tri-**	= three	eg. **tri**cycle
over-	= too much	eg. **over**eat	**under-**	= not enough	eg. **under**estimate
post-	= after	eg. **post**graduate	**uni-**	= one	eg. **uni**cycle

- There are certain **prefixes** which mean **not** or show an **opposite** state or process. These are:

un-	eg. **un**believable	**ir-** (before r)	eg. **ir**resistible	**in-**	eg. **in**competent
im-	eg. **im**possible	**il-** (before l)	eg. **il**legal	**dis-**	eg. **dis**agree
mal-	eg. **mal**function				

Suffixes

-ee	(with passive meaning)	eg. employ**ee**	**-ish**	a) = with the quality of	eg. child**ish**
-er	(with active meaning)	eg. employ**er**		b) = rather	eg. small**ish**
-ful	a) = with	eg. care**ful**	**-less**	without	eg. care**less**
	b) : indicates quantity	eg. spoon**ful**	**-proof**	safe against	eg. water**proof**

- To describe people we add **-ar, -er, -or** to the end of the verbs or **-ist, -ian** to the end of nouns or verbs making any necessary spelling changes. *lie - liar, rob - robber, create - creator, type - typist, music - musician*

- **Nouns formed from verbs**

-age	eg. break - break**age**	**-ence**	eg. prefer - prefer**ence**	**-sis**	eg. analyse - analy**sis**
-al	eg. propose - propos**al**	**-ion**	eg. confuse - confu**sion**	**-tion**	eg. direct - direc**tion**
-ance	eg. annoy - annoy**ance**	**-ment**	eg. amuse - amuse**ment**	**-y**	eg. perjure - perjur**y**
-ation	eg. organise - organis**ation**	**-sion**	eg. suspend - suspen**sion**		

- **Nouns formed from adjectives**

-ance	eg. tolerant - toler**ance**	**-ion**	eg. desperate - despera**tion**	**-ment**	eg. content - content**ment**
-cy	eg. fluent - fluen**cy**	**-iness**	eg. happy - happ**iness**	**-ty**	eg. royal - royal**ty**
-ence	eg. obedient - obedi**ence**	**-ity**	eg. popular - popular**ity**	**-y**	eg. honest - honest**y**

- **Adjectives formed from verbs**
- **Verbs formed from adjectives/nouns**

-able eg. bear - bear**able**	**-ive** eg. decide - decis**ive**	**-en** eg. dark - dark**en**	fright - fright**en**

293 Make nouns from the following words.

1	employ	...employee, employer..............	6	publish	....
2	post	....	7	develop	....
3	except	....	8	combine	....
4	expand	....	9	drive	....
5	accept	....	10	inspire	....

11	instruct	....	**21**	lonely	....
12	portray	....	**22**	reluctant	....
13	translate	....	**23**	excellent	....
14	injure	....	**24**	intelligent	....
15	refer	....	**25**	accurate	....
16	apologise	....	**26**	excited	....
17	examine	....	**27**	fragile	....
18	pollute	....	**28**	regular	....
19	judge	....	**29**	stupid	....
20	use	....	**30**	isolate	....

294   **Fill in the right form of the words in brackets.**

The **1)** ...*length*... (long) of the journey was beginning to cause a lot of **2)** .... (frustrate) for everyone involved. Unfortunately, father got the blame, as he had been responsible for the **3)** .... (organise) of the trip. **4)** .... (impatient) had begun to set in when we realised we'd been given the wrong **5)** .... (direct) by a well-meaning pedestrian. What is more, father's **6)** .... (popular) was not **7)** .... (increase) by his **8)** .... (insist) that we stop every hour or so to observe the scenery. The trip to France, he'd said, would **9)** .... (broad) our horizons and provide us with both **10)** .... (amuse) and **11)** .... (educate). However, in **12)** .... (real), it turned out to be an **13)** .... (bear) waste of time and effort. It was then that we made the **14)** .... (decide) never to listen to one of father's **15)** .... (propose) again.

295   **Add the correct prefixes to the beginning of the words.**

1   The ...*anti-*... **government** protesters marched to parliament.
2   John .... **slept** and was late for work.
3   Many people who wanted tickets were disappointed because the organisers had .... **estimated** the singer's popularity.
4   He is taking a .... **atlantic** flight from London to New York.
5   When the ambulance came, the man was .... **conscious** after being knocked down by a car.
6   The .... **president** of the United States was honoured at a ceremony, five years after he resigned.
7   People who can only speak their own language are called .... **lingual**.
8   Superman is a comic strip character who has .... **human** strength.
9   There were violent scenes as .... **government** and anti-government demonstrators fought outside parliament.
10   .... **racial** fighting between the two minorities had led to civil war in the country.
11   John left his job because he was .... **able** to deal with such a large amount of work.
12   The two countries .... **operated** to prevent the shipment of drugs from one to the other.
13   That child looks very thin. I think he must be .... **fed**.
14   Don't .... **feed** the dog or it'll get fat.
15   The media gave her so much attention she became a .... **star** overnight.
16   He never goes out or talks to people; he's so .... **social**.
17   Tom knew the information was somewhere in his .... **conscious**, but he couldn't remember it.
18   I always find the day after Christmas an .... **climax**.
19   The man had to .... **apply** the paint because the first coat wasn't sufficient.
20   Ghandi achieved a lot through .... **violent** action.
21   The neighbouring tribes found it difficult to .... **exist** peacefully.
22   We caught the .... **continental** train from Paris to Istanbul.
23   As these programmes are .... **changeable**, they can be used with any computer system.
24   We weren't allowed onto the ferry because it had been .... **booked**.

> Mummy, there's **a** black cat in **the** kitchen.

> That's alright dear. **Black cats** bring good luck.

> Not **the** black cat in our kitchen. It's just eaten **the** cake on **the** table.

Articles

Indefinite article (A/An)

● **A/An** is used only with singular countable nouns to talk about indefinite things. *I can't find **a** taxi. (Which taxi? Any taxi; indefinite)* **Some** is used instead of **a/an** with plural countable nouns. *There are **some** taxis at the taxi rank.* **Some** is also used with uncountable nouns. *Give me **some** sugar please.* **A/An** is often used after the verbs **be** and **have**. *She's **a** teacher.*

● **A/An** is used to mean **per**. *He works five days **a** week.* **A/An** is also used before **Mr/Mrs/Miss + surname** when we refer to an unfamiliar person. *There's **a Mr Smith** waiting for you.*

● **A/An** can also be used with: **money** *(a/one dollar)*, **fractions** *(a/one quarter)*, **weight/measures** *(an/one inch)*, **whole numbers** *(a/one million)*, **price/weight** *(£1 a litre)*, **frequency/time** *(twice a day)*, **distance/fuel** *(50 miles a gallon)*, **distance/speed** *(100km an hour)* and **illnesses** *(a headache, a fever, have a cold, catch a cold, (a) toothache, (a) backache, a temperature).*

● We use **a/an + noun** meaning only **one** *(There's **a** pen on the desk.)* and **one + noun** when we want to emphasise that there is only one *(There's **only one** pen on the desk, not two.).*

Definite article (The)

● **The** is used with singular and plural nouns, countable and uncountable ones, to talk about something specific or when the noun is mentioned for a second time. *Can you give me **the** book over there? (Which book? The one over there; specific) The farmer found **a gold cup** in his field. He took **the cup** to the police station. (the word "cup" is mentioned for a second time)*

● **The** can also be used with the words beach, cinema, coast, country(side), earth, ground, jungle, radio, sea, seaside, sky, theatre, weather, world etc. *What's **the** weather like today?* We usually say **"television" without "the"**. *I like watching TV but: Turn off **the** television.* **Note:** *We've got a house near **the** sea. but: Tom is **at sea** (he's sailing).*

● **The** is optional with seasons. *Where are you going in **(the)** summer?*

● We can use **a/an** or **the** before singular countable nouns to refer to a group of people, animals or things. *A/The tiger lives in the jungle. (We mean all tigers.)* The word "man" is an exception. *Man is mortal. (not: ~~The man~~)* We omit **a/an** or **the** before a noun in the plural when it represents a group. *Tigers are dangerous. (not: ~~The tigers~~ are dangerous.)*

296 Fill in: a, the, some where necessary in the spaces below.

1 He has ~~a~~ sunstroke after spending too much time on ...*the*... beach.
2 We went for .... walk along .... coast.
3 "I'll give you .... advice: don't be late again."
4 .... people think .... climate in the Mediterranean is .... best in .... world.

297 **Fill in: a, an or the where necessary.**

In **1)** ...*the*... days before **2)** .... invention of **3)** .... radio or television, **4)** .... majority of people made their own entertainment at home. Many **5)** .... evenings were spent reading **6)** .... novel, playing the piano or painting **7)** .... picture. In many ways, people were almost forced to find **8)** .... creative outlet in one form or another. Things have changed a lot since then, however. Now, **9)** .... typical evening's entertainment would be to spend **10)** .... few hours in front of **11)** .... television. This is not really **12)** .... very productive use of one's time or energy and has maybe contributed to **13)** .... breakdown of communication within **14)** .... family.

298 **Fill in: a, an or some where necessary.**

When David went to **1)** ...*a*... travel agent's to ask for **2)** .... information about cruises to South America he was given **3)** .... brochure and told that if he wanted to go, he would have to make **4)** .... booking as soon as possible, as the next cruise was leaving in **5)** .... fortnight. He looked at the brochure and, after **6)** .... thought, decided to go, provided he could make **7)** .... arrangement with his boss to get **8)** .... time off. He gave the travel agent **9)** .... money as a deposit, then went to his office as he had **10)** .... important work to do. After **11)** .... hour or so, his boss came in and David asked him if he could take **12)** .... three weeks off as he hadn't had **13)** .... holiday for nearly **14)** .... year. His boss was quite agreeable, though he had at first had **15)** .... doubts about letting David go for such **16)** .... long time. In the end he agreed to give him **17)** .... entire month off, and wished him **18)** ...... wonderful holiday.

299 **Finish the sentences as in the example:**

1 They called in the police to deal with the situation.
The police ...*were called in to deal with the situation.* ....
2 We had lovely weather last week. The weather ....
3 He needs more experience. More experience ....
4 She looks very striking. Her looks ....
5 Have you seen the scissors? Do you know where ....
6 We were late because of the bad traffic. We were late because the ....
7 They prefer to live on the outskirts. The outskirts ....
8 He gave me very helpful advice. The advice he gave me ....
9 She didn't make very impressive progress. The progress she made ....
10 They are developing the city centre. The city centre ....
11 They gave me incorrect information. The information ....
12 These trousers are too small. This pair ....
13 She told us some good news. The news ....
14 They are installing new machinery in the factory. New machinery ....
15 They lost their luggage during the flight. Their luggage ....
16 They need to redecorate their premises. Their premises ....
17 He likes mathematics more than any other subject. Mathematics ....
18 They found very cheap accommodation. The accommodation ....
19 The house is in beautiful surroundings. The surroundings ....
20 She's got dark, curly hair. Her hair ....
21 He's only interested in tennis. Tennis ....
22 Many students consider chemistry a difficult subject. Chemistry ....
23 They often play soccer in England. Soccer ....

The is used before

- **nouns which are unique.** *the moon, the Acropolis*

- **names of cinemas** *(The Odeon)*, **hotels** *(The Ritz)*, **theatres** *(The Lyceum)*, **museums** *(The Louvre)*, **newspapers/magazines** *(The Telegraph)*. ***but:*** *Newsweek)*, **ships** *(The Bounty)*, **institutions** *(The UN)*, **galleries** *(The National Gallery)*

- **names of rivers** *(the Mississippi)*, **seas** *(the Red Sea)*, **groups of islands/states** *(the Virgin Islands, the USA)*, **mountain ranges** *(the Urals)*, **deserts** *(the Gobi desert)*, **oceans** *(the Pacific)*, **canals** *(the Panama Canal)* **and names or nouns with "of".** *(the Tomb of the Kings, the Garden of Eden)* **Note:** *the equator, the North/South Pole, the north of England, the South/West/North/East*

- **musical instruments, dances.** *the guitar, the waltz*

- **names of families** *(the Simpsons)*, **nationalities ending in -sh, -ch or -ese** *(the Welsh, the Dutch the Chinese etc)*. **Other plural nationalities are used with or without the** *(the South Africans, the Swiss etc)*.

- **titles** *(the Pope, the Duke of Norfolk, the Queen)*. **but: "The" is omitted before titles with proper names.** *Queen Alexandra*

- **adjectives used as plural nouns** *(the old, the sick, the privileged, the deaf etc)* **and the superlative degree of adjectives/adverbs** *(the worst)*. *She's the **most sensible** girl in the class.* **Note: "most" used as a determiner followed by a noun, does not take "the".** *Most children like animals.* **but:** *Of all European cities Rome has **the most** careful drivers.*

- **the words: station, shop, cinema, pub, library, city, village etc.** *She went to **the library** to return some books.*

- **morning, afternoon, evening, night.** *I'll be at work in **the** morning.* **but: at night, at noon, at midnight, by day/night, at 4 o'clock etc**

- **historical references/events.** *the French Revolution, the Dark Ages, the Thirty Years' War* **(but:** *World War I)*

- **only, last, first (used as adjectives).** *He was **the only** person to disagree.*

The is omitted before

- **proper nouns.** *Paul comes from **London**.*

- **names of sports, games, activities, days, months, holidays, colours, drinks, meals and languages (not followed by the word "language").** *She plays tennis well. She likes blue. We speak French.* **but: The Latin language is hardly used now.**

- **names of countries** *(Portugal)*, **but: the Argentine, the Netherlands, (the) Sudan, the Hague, the Vatican City, cities** *(Lisbon)*, **streets** *(Regent Street, **but:** the High Street, the Strand, the Mall, the Bristol road, the A4, the M1 motorway)*, **squares** *(Constitution Square)*, **bridges** *(London Bridge **but:** the Bridge of Sighs, the Forth Bridge, the Severn Bridge, the Golden Gate Bridge)*, **parks** *(Regent's Park)*, **stations** *(Waterloo Station)*, **individual mountains** *(Everest)*, **islands** *(Malta)*, **lakes** *(Lake Ontario)*, **continents** *(Asia)*

- **possessive adjectives.** *This isn't your bag.*

- **two-word names whose first word is the name of a person or place.** *Charles de Gaulle Airport, Buckingham Palace* **but:** *the White House, (because the first word "White" is not the name of a person or place)*

- **pubs, restaurants, shops, banks and hotels which have the name of their founder and end in -s or -'s.** *Selfridges, Barclays Bank, Harry's Pub* **but:** *the Black Swan (pub) (because "Black Swan" is not a name of a person or place)*

- **bed, church, college, court, hospital, prison, school, university, when we refer to the purpose for which they exist.** *John went to university. (He is a student.)* **but:** *His mother went to **the university** to see him last week. (She went to the university as a visitor.)* **Work (= place of work) never takes "the".** *She is at **work**.*

- **the words home, Father/Mother when we talk about our own home/parents.** *Mother is at **home**.*

- **means of transport: by bus/by car/by train/by plane etc but: in the car, on the bus/train etc.** *He travelled **by train**.* **but:** *He left **on the 6 o'clock train** yesterday.*

- **We say: flu/the flu, measles/the measles, mumps/the mumps but:** *He's got **diabetes**.*

300 **Fill in "the" where necessary.**

My father owns a shop in **1)** ...*the*... village where we live. His shop is **2)** ...... only newsagent's in our village. It's next to **3)** ..... post office and **4)** ..... station, and only two minutes walk from **5)** ...... home. **6)** ...... shop has been in our family for two generations. When my grandfather owned it, I was only very young. I used to help him on **7)** .... Sunday afternoons by weighing **8)** .... sweets and putting them in **9)** ...... bags. Sometimes he would even let me use **10)** ...... ice-cream machine, which I loved. My mother used to get angry with him though, because he would leave me alone to look after **11)** ...... shop while he went to talk to **12)** ...... friends at **13)** ...... pub. One afternoon I was in **14)** ...... shop tidying **15)** .... newspapers when a man came in. **16)** .... man was very tall and looked very serious. He asked me if my grandfather was around. I said he was in **17)** ...... back room and went to get him. When my grandfather came out, he saw **18)** ...... man and suddenly started to cry. **19)** ...... two men hugged and talked in **20)** ..... quiet voices. Eventually they remembered me in **21)** .... corner of **22)** ...... shop. My grandfather turned to me and introduced **23)** ...... man to me. He was my grandfather's brother who had moved to **24)** ...... Australia after **25)** ...... war and they hadn't seen each other for 20 years.

301 **Fill in: a, an or the where necessary.**

1 ...*The*... Tower of London is ...*a*... popular tourist attraction.
2 Newcastle is ...... town in ...... north of ...... England.
3 ...... Princess lives in ...... palace in ...... London.
4 ...... Buckingham Palace is where ...... Queen of England officially lives.
5 She bought ...... expensive necklace at ...... Harrods.
6 They went for ...... stroll around ...... St James' Park.
7 The supermarket is in ...... Kendell Street opposite ...... Lloyds Bank.
8 ...... hotel where they held their wedding reception was called ...... Grand Hotel.
9 Anna was born in ...... Italy but she lives in ...... USA now.
10 The convict is in ...... prison on ...... outskirts of town.
11 His favourite newspaper is ...... Guardian.
12 ...... Gatwick Airport is in ...... southern England.
13 ...... Duchess of York opened ...... new hospital in ...... centre of London.
14 He went on ...... expensive holiday to ...... Bahamas.
15 ...... Statue of Liberty is in ...... New York.
16 ...... National Park was opened ...... last week by ...... mayor.
17 ...... expedition to ...... South Pole needs a lot of careful planning.
18 ...... Odeon cinema is in ...... Appleton Street just past ...... library.
19 Last month I saw ...... film and then went to ...... concert. ...... film was brilliant but ...... concert was boring.
20 There are three cars parked outside: ...... Mercedes, ... Jaguar and ...... Fiat. Mine is ...... Fiat.
21 ...... Harrods is a huge department store near ...... Kensington Gardens.
22 Sam lives in ...... little flat in ...... middle of the city. There is ...... hotel nearby and ...... noise keeps him awake at night.
23 ...... Hilton Hotel is situated near ...... River Thames.
24 I applied for ...... job last week. ...... job involved driving ...... van around the country.
25 ...... Tate Gallery is quite far from ...... Science Museum, so you'd better take a bus.
26 ...... Sales Manager has ...... cold, so he can't come to ...... meeting this afternoon.
27 I have ...... appointment at ...... dentist's this afternoon because I've got ...... toothache.
28 We spent ...... last summer on ...... island of Crete.

302 Fill in "the" where necessary.

1) ..—.. Last year we went on holiday to Spain where my father was born. We had never been before as a family so I couldn't wait. We travelled by 2) ...... plane and when we got to 3) ...... airport in 4) ...... Madrid I was very excited. We saw many interesting sights and we visited 5) ...... Prado Museum and 6) ...... Escorial Palace where 7) ...... King of Spain lives. We also watched a bullfight. It was thrilling. We stayed in Spain all 8) .... summer and we toured some of 9) .... Spanish islands, too. I liked 10) ...... Spaniards but I found 11) ...... Spanish language rather difficult to understand. 12) ...... people there spoke very quickly and, although I had taken 13) .... Spanish lessons at school, I was by no means fluent. We also met members of 14) .... family whom we had never seen before and we went out with them a lot. My cousins took us to 15) .... cinema one night but 16) .... film was in 17) .... Spanish so we didn't understand very much! All in all, we had a good holiday and we have invited our cousins to come and stay at our house 18) .... next year.

303 Fill in "the" where necessary.

Dear Sally,

I've been in England for a month now and I'm really enjoying it. 1) ...*The*... English family I'm staying with are very kind, but they are very different from my family. Mrs Taylor stays at 2) ...... home every day doing 3) ...... cooking and cleaning and looking after 4) .... children. Jane goes to 5) ...... school but Johnny is only two and he doesn't even go to 6) ...... nursery school yet. Mr Taylor is a writer. At the moment, he is writing a book about 7) ...... World War II. He is doing research and he goes to 8) ...... library every day to get 9) ...... information. When he is at 10) ...... home, he locks himself in 11) ...... study and won't let anyone disturb him. He has been working on 12) ...... book for over two years and he hopes that it will be ready in 13) ...... spring. On Sundays they all go to 14) ...... church and in 15) ...... afternoon they visit 16) ...... children's grandparents. 17) ...... rest of 18) ...... week is spent indoors either watching 19) ...... television or reading one of 20) ...... many books that they have collected over the years. They have really made me feel welcome. Write back to me soon with all your news.

Regards,
Julie

304 Fill in the correct form of the words in brackets.

Learning a language is full of 1) ...*difficulties*... (difficult). It's important to have a good 2).............................. (understand) of the 3) .... (grammar) structures as well as a 4) .... (commit) to learning vocabulary. It's almost 5) .... (possible) to improve one's skills without time spent in the company of native 6) .... (speak). When you first begin to learn, you may feel 7) .... (competent) because you're making so many mistakes. You can sometimes scream in 8) .... (frustrate) at how long it takes to build up 9) .... (confident). It's 10) .... (essence) to have a 11) .... (teach) that has a lot of 12) .... (tolerant) and makes a particular effort to be 13) .... (help). Eventually your hard work will pay off and your 14) .... (dedicate) will lead to complete 15) .... (fluent).

305 Fill in "the" where necessary.

1) ...*The*... Peters are a very interesting family. Mr Peters has sailed around 2) ...... world on his yacht 3) ...... "Bella". Mrs Peters has travelled around 4) .... India and seen many exciting things. Their son, John, works for a newspaper and he has interviewed many famous people including 5) ...... Pope and 6) ...... Princess Anne. Sally, their daughter, is very ambitious. She is training to be a lawyer. One day she hopes to be 7) ...... most successful lawyer in 8) ...... country. As a family, they spend very little time together. They only see each other for a short time in 9) .... mornings before they all go their separate ways. At the moment Mrs Peters is writing a book about 10) ...... famous

buildings. She is doing research on 11) ...... Westminster Abbey and 12) ...... St Paul's Cathedral. She hopes to publish 13) ...... book by the end of 14) ...... year. Mr Peters is getting ready for a trip around 15) ...... Europe. This time however he has decided to go by 16) .... bus and not by 17) .... boat. John is preparing for a trip to 18) ...... USA where he will be meeting 19) ...... President. Sally, of course, doesn't have much spare time as her studies take up most of 20) ...... day.

306 Fill in "the" where necessary.

1 It was getting late, so we went to .---. bed.
2 My aunt buys her vegetables at ...... market in John Street.
3 ...... Heathrow Airport is one of ...... busiest in the world.
4 He was taken to ...... hospital when he broke his leg.
5 Jenny works in ...... hospital in ...... centre of town.
6 Her brother has been to ...... prison twice for robbery.
7 Although he didn't go to ...... university, he's a very clever man.
8 There's a concert at ...... university tonight.
9 My grandmother was religious and went to ...... church every Sunday.
10 Sarah's not home - she's at ...... work.
11 We travelled round France by ...... car.
12 William crashed ...... car into a lamp-post.

307 Write the unnecessary word in the boxes provided, otherwise put a tick (✓).

1 What a beautiful scenery!
2 Let's meet at the Victoria Station.
3 The Alps extend over 1,000 kilometres.
4 The coffee is expensive nowadays.
5 Selfridges is in the Oxford Street.
6 She's very good at the painting.
7 Have you ever been to the New York?
8 The plane hit a bad weather.
9 We spent three months in the West Indies.
10 The many people are afraid of snakes.
11 The countryside we drove through was very beautiful.
12 They gave me an information about bargain flights.
13 An elephant is a very large animal.
14 I've got a good news.
15 After his accident he spent a month in the hospital.

#		#
1	*a*	1
2		2
3		3
4		4
5		5
6		6
7		7
8		8
9		9
10		10
11		11
12		12
13		13
14		14
15		15

308 Fill in "the" where necessary.

Welcome, ladies and gentlemen, to our coach tour of **1)** .—. Portsmouth, **2)** ...... most exciting resort on **3)** ...... south coast of England. First, we will be visiting **4)** ..... St John's Cathedral and **5)** ..... Cathedral of **6)** ...... St Thomas. Guidebooks can be purchased from one of **7)** ...... gift shops. As you may know, **8)** ...... Charles Dickens was born in this city and we shall visit **9)** ..... Charles Dickens' Museum, so you can see where **10)** ..... man himself lived and died. Around 1 o'clock, we will eat in **11)** ..... Orangery Restaurant. In **12)** ...... afternoon, there is an optional trip by **13)** ...... boat around **14)** ...... harbour. Alternatively, you can visit **15)** ...... historic ships of **16)** ...... Portsmouth. Feel free to leave **17)** ...... your bags on **18)** .... coach if you wish. The tour commentary will be in **19)** ...... English and **20)** ...... French.

309 Fill in "the" where necessary.

1 .—. Manila is the capital of ...*the*... Philippines.
2 ...... Andes is a mountain range in ...... South America.
3 ...... China is ...... most populated country in ...... world.
4 A tunnel has been built beneath ...... English Channel.
5 The longest river in the world is ...... Nile.
6 Many people have climbed ...... Everest.
7 ...... Sicily is an Italian island.
8 The capital of ...... Italy is ...... Rome.
9 ...... Panama Canal joins ...... Atlantic and Pacific oceans.
10 ...... North Sea is between ...... Britain and ...... Norway.
11 Do you know where ...... Rocky Mountains are?
12 ...... Trafalgar Square is in ...... London.
13 ...... Severn Bridge is in ...... Wales.
14 ...... Australia is in ...... southern hemisphere.
15 ...... Hotel Ascot is situated in ...... central London.
16 I learnt to play ...... cello when I was at ...... school.
17 She spent ...... morning working in ...... library.
18 I plan to study ...... French at ...... university ...... next year.
19 ...... Smiths have just bought a holiday home near ...... Lake Geneva.
20 I usually go to ...... work by ...... bus.
21 A fire at ...... Windsor Castle destroyed all ...... Queen's paintings.

Oral Activity 23

The teacher divides the class into two teams and gives them nouns. The teams in turn add "the" where necessary. Each correct answer gets 1 point. The team with the most points is the winner.

Words to be used: **Panama Canal, London Bridge, Waterloo Station, Lloyds Bank, Bahamas, Regent Street, Argentine, Louvre, Guardian, High Street, piano, Middle Ages, New York, Sicily, Lake Superior, Amazon, Suez Canal, United Kingdom, Asia, Alps, Red Sea, Indian Ocean, Hilton Hotel, Bombay Restaurant, Odeon Cinema, Harrods, Tate Gallery, Great Wall of China, Tower of London, Evening Post, Downing Street, Orly Airport, Prince of Wales, Westminster Abbey, St Paul's Cathedral, Hyde Park etc**

eg. Teacher: *Panama Canal*   Teacher: *London Bridge*
    Team A S1: *the Panama Canal*   Team BS1: *London Bridge* etc

310 **Put the verbs in brackets into the correct form.**

Becky **1)** ...had... (have) an interesting experience when she was a student. She **2)** .... (be) at Bristol University for nine months and she **3)** .... (begin) to worry about money. She **4)** .... (know) that, if she wanted to continue her studies, she **5)** .... (have to) earn some extra cash. "If I **6)** .... (be) you," her friend said, "I **7)** .... (do) some nude modelling for the art school. It's easy work and the models **8)** .... (pay) quite well." "That's a good idea," said Becky. "I think I **9)** .... (do) that." On **10)** .... (arrive) at the art school for her first session, Becky **11)** .... (show) to the dressing-room where she **12)** .... (take off) all her clothes and **13)** .... (put on) a robe. Then she entered the studio where about twenty art students **14)** .... (sit) in front of an empty chair. She walked up to it, took off her robe and sat down. Some of the students started **15)** .... (giggle) and Becky **(16)** .... (cannot/understand) why. She **17)** .... (sit) there for three minutes when a professor ran into the room. "You **18)** .... (make) a mistake," he said. "You are in the wrong room!" She **19)** .... (enter) the class where the students were supposed **20)** .... (paint) an empty chair!

311 **Look at Appendix 2, then fill in the correct particle(s).**

Phrasal Verbs

1 We **put** ...aside... £200 to buy Christmas presents.
2 The teacher **put** .... his ideas well, helping us a lot.
3 I **put** his bad mood .... his losing that money last night.
4 We'd better **put** .... our meeting until tomorrow; I'm busy now.
5 Our class is **putting** .... "Cinderella" as the school play.
6 The firemen tried hard to **put** the fire ....
7 Could you **put** me .... to the manager, please?
8 I can't **put** .... those children any longer. They're very noisy.
9 He **ran**.................... his old friend, Tom, in Oxford Street last week.
10 If you **run** .... your friends unnecessarily, you risk losing them.
11 We've **run** .... sugar; could you go and buy some?
12 He **ran** .... such big bills he couldn't afford to pay them.

1 down, aside, in, on
2 back, down, across, through
3 up to, up with, down to, out
4 off, in, on, up
5 across, on, forward, off
6 back, in, down, out
7 through, on, forward, by
8 down, up with, on, off
9 up, in, across, through
10 down, off, through, up
11 in, off, out of, on
12 away, after, down, up

312 **Look at Appendix 3, then fill in the correct preposition(s).**

Prepositions

1 Help! The house is ...on... fire.
2 After running up the hill, I was .... breath.
3 The miners have been .... strike for two months.
4 John Prior isn't here; he's .... duty.
5 The police have got the riot .... control.
6 She is away .... business in America.
7 The lift has been .... order for two days.
8 The new rules are still .... discussion.
9 What you're saying is .... the point; it's not relevant at all.
10 The thief was .... arrest for stealing a woman's handbag.

1 at, of, on
2 in, out of, off
3 on, at, for
4 in, off, at
5 under, in, off
6 at, on, for
7 off, at, out of
8 at, under, for
9 out of, at, off
10 under, in, with

313 **Complete the sentences using the words in bold.**

1 I haven't ridden a bicycle for years.
   rode   It's years ....since I rode.. a bicycle.
2 Bill worked in a factory all summer.
   spent   Bill .... in a factory.
3 We bought more vegetables than we needed.
   have   We .... many vegetables.

4 I'd rather speak to him tonight.
prefer I .... him tonight.
5 Bob hardly ever walks to work.
used Bob .... to work.
6 I tried speaking French, but no one could understand me.
make I couldn't .... when I tried speaking French.
7 She has decided to start her own business and we can't stop her.
prevent We can't .... her own business.
8 Please close the windows before you leave.
without Please don't .... the windows.
9 They failed to reach the top of the mountain.
succeed They .... the top of the mountain.
10 Mrs Smith is over 70, but she still works full-time.
her In ...., Mrs Smith still works full-time.

314 Read the text carefully. If a line is correct, put a tick (✓) in the space provided. If a line has a word which should not be there, write it in the space provided.

SHOPPING

0	✓	0
00	*to*	00
1		1
2		2
3		3
4		4
5		5
6		6
7		7
8		8
9		9
10		10
11		11
12		12
13		13
14		14
15		15

0 On Saturdays I usually try to avoid
00 going to shopping. The town centre is full
1 of shoppers who loaded with bags and parcels.
2 The shops are so many crowded that it can
3 take hours to be served. Yet, despite of the
4 crowds, parents, children and groups of friends
5 fill the whole shops from opening to closing
6 time, searching frantically for something to buy
7 as like if there was no tomorrow. Having once
8 wasted a whole day with looking for a pair of shoes,
9 I have been decided that Saturday shopping
10 is an experience which I do not wish to repeat it.
11 I now prefer shopping on a weekday so that
12 as not to be disturbed by the crowds. I can find
13 what I'm looking for straight away and, in one hour
14 later than, I am back home relaxing with a cup of
15 tea feeling of sympathy for those still on the run.

315 Choose the correct item.

Many girls who love sport dream of **(0)** ...*representing*... **(representing/seeming/standing/presenting)** their country in an international competition. However, as any successful sports star will **(1)** ...... **(say/tell/mention/announce)** you, it is not all glamour. To begin with, she needs a lot of **(2)** ...... **(fortune/chance/luck/probablity)**. Once she has been discovered, she must **(3)** ...... **(spend/take/hold/pass)** a lot of time waiting for the right opportunity. She must be able to **(4)** ...... **(practise/exercise/train/coach)** her sport even when she feels tired, and carry **(5)** ...... **(at/on/away/over)** training even if she isn't in the mood. As part of a team, she must be able to **(6)** ...... **(agree/match/suit/fit)** in and not think too much **(7)** ...... **(in/to/on/about)** herself. In addition, she will have to overcome any physical problems that **(8)** ...... **(lift/raise/arise/rise)**. It is not unusual for sportsmen or women to become **(9)** ...... **(sick/awful/bad/poor)** or injured, particularly if they do a sport in which there is a lot of **(10)** ...... **(touch/feeling/contact/communication)** with other athletes. Illnesses or accidents can mean **(11)** ...... **(delay/lateness/failure/loss)** of training time. Even sharp spikes on running shoes are to be blamed for **(12)** ...... **(causing/having/doing/resulting)** problems for athletes! Once a sportswoman becomes successful, she becomes **(13)** ...... **(responsible/certain/sure/marked)** to her fans as her life becomes public and any action may be **(14)** ...... **(mistaken/confused/understood/misinterpreted)** by the media. Many sports players get involved in **(15)** ...... **(work/job/occupation/tasks)** for charity.

10 Emphatic Structures / Inversion

Who was it that painted my car red and green?

It was me that did it.

Well ..er.. I just wanted to say that **not only does it look lovely but it's also drying** beautifully.

We use emphatic structures when we wish to emphasise a particular part of a sentence in spoken English or written English.

- We can use **it is/was (not) + subject/object + that** or **who(m)** in statements/negations or **is/was it + subject/object + that or who(m)** in questions. If the object is a person, we use **that, who** or **whom,** otherwise **that** is the correct form.

   It was the headmaster that/who organised the school bazaar. *It wasn't me that/who organised it.*
   It is me that/who you're talking to, so don't lie.
   Was it here that you met him? ("who" is not possible because "here" is not a person)
   It wasn't Sophie that/who prepared this meal. *It **was the TV that** woke me up.*

- We can use **that is/was + question word** in statements or **is/was that + question word** in questions.

   That is (That's) what he told the police.
   That was how he became a successful businessman.
   Is that where he's living now?
   Was that why he resigned?

- We can also use **question word + is/was it + that** in questions.

   Where is it that you're planning to go?
   Who was it that sent you those flowers?
   When was it that you realised you were being followed?

- We can use **question word + subject + verb + is/was.**

   What I need is some good advice. *What I don't need is criticism.*

- We can ask emphatic questions with **ever** expressing **admiration, anger, concern** etc.

   Wherever did you find it?
   Whoever did you talk to?
   Whatever are you doing there?

- In the Present Simple, Past Simple or Imperative we can use the construction **do/does/did + bare infinitive** to give emphasis. *I **do care** for you. He **did tell** me he was leaving. **Do sit** down, please!*

316 <u>Rewrite the sentences using emphatic constructions starting with the words given.</u>

1   He promised not to do it again. He ...*did promise not to do it again.* ....
2   She was promoted a year after she had been hired. It was ....
3   When did you accept his proposal? When was ....
4   Have some more cake! Do ....
5   I need a good night's sleep. What ....

317 Rewrite the sentences putting emphasis on the highlighted words.

1 **Tom** spread those rumours about his boss. *It was Tom that spread those rumours about his boss.*
2 Are you going to wear **this dress** at the reception? ....
3 **Ann** put up the Christmas decorations. ....
4 Why can **you** never be at work on time? ....
5 **John** looks after the children when Sheila is at work. ....
6 **Where** did you spend your holidays last summer? ....

318 Rewrite the politician's speech using "what" to emphasise the important parts.

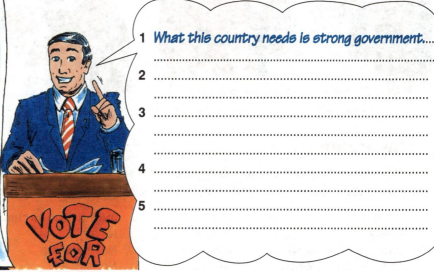

1 This country needs strong government.
2 I worry about the present economic situation.
3 People want public money to be spent on public services.
4 It is important that policy decisions are made on the basis of what is right for this nation.
5 Our policies reflect the importance we attach to education.

1 *What this country needs is strong government....*
....
2 ....
....
3 ....
....
4 ....
....
5 ....

319 Rewrite these fire drill instructions. Use "what" to emphasise the important parts.

1 You should remember not to panic. ...*What you should remember is not to panic.* ....
2 You must concentrate on leaving the building quickly...
3 You have to ensure that someone has called the fire brigade. ....
4 You need to check that everyone is safely out of the building. ....
5 You should not worry about your personal possessions. ....

320 Look at Mrs Jones' answers, then rewrite them using emphatic structures.

1 "Who did you go shopping with?" "Mrs Regan." ...*It was Mrs Regan who I went shopping with.* ....
2 "Where did you leave your purse?" "At the grocer's." ....
3 "When did you realise you'd left it there?" "Just now." ....
4 "Is it certain that you left it there?" "Yes." ....
5 "Should we telephone the police or the shop?" "The shop." ....
6 "Who should telephone them?" "You, of course." ....

321 Read this information, then rewrite it emphasising the words in bold.

1 **The Beatles** recorded *Let it Be*. ...*It was the Beatles who/that recorded Let it Be.*...........................
2 **Paul McCartney** sang the lead. ....
3 The video was recorded **on a rooftop**. ....
4 The record was released **in 1969**. ....
5 **John Lennon** played lead guitar. ....
6 The Beatles broke up **shortly after this**. ....

Last year I opened a jeweller's shop.

Oh really? Were you successful?

Not really. No *sooner had I* opened the door *than* the police arrived!

Inversion

We invert the subject and auxiliary verb in the sentence to give emphasis. This happens:

● **after certain expressions when they are at the beginning of a sentence.**

Seldom	**Little**	**In/Under no circumstances**	**Only in this way**
Rarely	**Barely**	**Never**	**Only by**
Scarcely (ever) ... when	**Nowhere**	**Never before**	**Nor/Neither**
Hardly (ever) ... when	**Not till/until**	**Not since**	**Only then**
No sooner ... than	**On no occasion**	**Not even once**	
Not only ... but also	**In no way**	**On no account**	

*Rarely **do we see** him these days.*
*No sooner **had we got** into the house **than** he phoned us.*

Note: When the following expressions begin a sentence, we use inversion in the main clause.
   only after, only by, only if, only when, not till/until, not since
   *Only after he had graduated, **did he start** looking for a job.*
   *Only if you invite her, **will she come** to your party.*
   *Not until all tests had been completed, **were we told** the results.*

● **after so, such, to such a degree (in result clauses) when they are at the beginning of a sentence.**
*So careful **is he** that he never makes any mistakes.*
*Such a brilliant student **was he** that he was offered a scholarship.*

● **with should, were, had in conditionals at the beginning of the sentence when "if" is omitted.**
Type 1:   *Should you see him, tell him to call me. (= If you should see ...)*
Type 2:   *Were I you, I would cancel my trip. (= If I were you ...)*
Type 3:   *Had he known, he would have made arrangements. (= If he had known ...)*

● **after so, neither/nor, as when expressing agreement.**
*"I hate horror films." "**So do I.**" ("So" is used to agree with an affirmative statement.)*
*"Jane hasn't returned our calls." "**Neither/Nor has** her husband." ("Neither/Nor" are used to agree with a negative statement). His colleagues respected him **as did** his boss.*

The subject and the main verb are also usually inverted in the following structures:
● **after adverbs of place.**
***Here comes** the bride! **Away ran** the thief!*
● **in Direct Speech when the reporting verb comes after the quote and the subject is a noun.**
*"I've never seen him," **said Helen.***

322 **Complete the sentences using the words in bold.**

1 She remembered the man's name after he'd walked away.
remember Only after he'd walked ...*away did she remember*................................. the man's name.
2 They had no idea it was a classical concert.
know Little .... it was a classical concert.
3 There's no way I can come to the meeting on Friday.
can In no way .... to the meeting on Friday.
4 They could only keep the children quiet by giving them sweets.
by Only .... they keep the children quiet.
5 She's a talented dancer and a good singer as well.
only Not .... dancer but she's also a good singer.
6 Don't show these figures to anyone on any account.
should On no account .... to anyone.
7 If I had realised how unhappy she was, I wouldn't have been so abrupt.
realised Had .... was, I wouldn't have been so abrupt.
8 I haven't seen better service anywhere.
else Nowhere .... better service.
9 You must not open this door under any circumstances.
no Under .... this door.
10 He'd never seen such a professional performance before.
before Never .... such a professional performance.
11 As soon as he had eaten, he jumped up and began to dance.
sooner No .... he jumped up and began to dance.
12 She wasn't pretty; she didn't have a nice personality either.
nor She wasn't pretty .... a nice personality.
13 You will finish this work if you start now.
will Only if you .... this work.
14 The papers blew away.
blew Away .... papers!
15 They didn't see the sign until it was too late.
did Not until it was .... the sign.
16 It was only after he'd left the house that he realised he'd forgotten his key.
did Only after he'd left the house .... forgotten his key.
17 If I were you, I'd just ignore her cruel remarks.
you Were .... ignore her cruel remarks.
18 They didn't arrive on time; they didn't apologise either.
nor They didn't arrive on time; .... apologise.
19 He laughed so much that tears rolled down his cheeks.
laugh So much .... tears rolled down his cheeks.

323 **Rewrite the sentences starting with so or such.**

1 Being tired, Don slept for twelve hours. So ...*tired was Don that he slept for twelve hours.*...............
2 He had such a fierce dog that we were terrified. Such ....
3 I got so angry that I screamed. So ....
4 We received such a big telephone bill that we couldn't pay it. Such ....
5 The sea looked so lovely that we dived in. So ....

324 **Respond to the sentences below.**

1 "I've got a headache!" "So ....*have I*.....""
2 "I didn't pass my driving test." "Nor ...."
3 "We went to Corfu last summer." "So ...."
4 "I can speak Italian." "So ...."
5 "I'm not going out tonight." "Nor ...."

10 Emphatic Structures / Inversion

325 Complete the sentences using the words in bold.

1 I won't lend Joe money on any account.
   account   On .... *no account will I lend* .... Joe money.
2 I lost my handbag and my keys too.
   only   Not .... handbag but I also lost my keys.
3 Uncle John doesn't visit us often.
   does   Rarely .... us.
4 As soon as she took out insurance, her house mysteriously burnt down.
   sooner   No .... insurance than her house mysteriously burnt down.
5 Stanley was so happy that he threw his hat in the air.
   happiness   Such .... that he threw his hat in the air.
6 It was the first time I had visited London.
   before   Never .... London.
7 Had he apologised, I'd have forgiven him.
   if   I'd have forgiven .... apologised.
8 She wasn't old enough, or experienced enough to get the job.
   nor   Neither .... experienced enough to get the job.
9 Bill had no idea that the car was stolen.
   know   Little .... that the car was stolen.
10 You should never lend Tony your car.
   circumstances   Under .... lend Tony your car.
11 I've never seen Chris pay for a drink.
   occasion   On .... Chris pay for a drink.
12 She won't do it unless you make her.
   will   Only if .... do it.
13 He had to break the window to get into his car.
   could   Only by .... get into his car.

326 Fill in the blanks using "nor..." or "so..." as in the example:

Bert and Bill were helping me move a big old wardrobe of mine. When we got upstairs, Bill suddenly disappeared. "I can't find Bill anywhere," said Bert. **1)** "...*Nor can I...*," I replied. "Perhaps he went downstairs." We decided to start without him. "I can't lift it," Bert said. "I'm not strong enough." **2)** "......................," I replied. "We'd better wait for Bill." "I would like to know where he is, though," said Bert. **3)** "...................," I said. "We'll just have to wait a bit longer." Just then we heard a noise inside the wardrobe. "I can hear someone inside," I said, opening the wardrobe. **4)** "......................!" cried Bert, on seeing Bill standing there. "I'll kill you, Bill!" **5)** "......................," I screamed. "What on earth are you doing?" "I was trying to help," Bill said apologetically. "I thought I'd stay in here and carry the clothes!"

327 Put the verbs in brackets into the correct form.

In no other country in the world **1)** .....*is there*.... (there be) such a high regard for wit as in Britain. One quality which they all possess is their sense of humour. As John Cleese once said, "Under no circumstances **2)** .... (you/should/tell) an Englishman that he has no sense of humour. Only in Britain **3)** .... (we/can/make) a virtue of the ridiculous; nowhere else **4)** .... (I/eat) such absurdly named dishes as 'Toad-in-the-Hole' or 'Bubble-and-Squeak'. Not only **5)** .... (it/have) the world's most depressing weather but also the longest queues. Nevertheless, as long as it retains its humour and politeness, Britain will always be 'home' to me."

328 Think of the word which best fits each space. Use only one word.

THE CHANGING FACE OF BRITISH TOWN CENTRES

These days, most town centres look similar (0) ...*to*... each other. This is largely because they have the same shops, belonging (1) .... the same companies. There are, of course, advantages to this situation. (2) .... instance, if you buy something from a chain store while you are (3) .... holiday which you later wish to return or have replaced, you can take it back to your local branch. However, many people have little to say in favour of the modern high street. In the past, the high street was (4) .... of small, independent shops, most of (5) .... specialised (6) .... one type of service or product. So, there would (7) .... been a baker's, a cobbler's, a hardware shop and so on. They not (8) .... offered a more personal service, but also a more friendly (9) .... Nowadays, shops sell a wide (10) .... of goods, but they don't often have those little extras, (11) .... a handle for the food mixer you (12) .... had since you were first married and do not want to (13) .... away. (14) .... contrast, a shop in the old high street would have had that handle and it would have checked the food mixer to make

329 Look at Appendix 2, then fill in the correct particle.

1 If you'd like to take a seat, I'll **see** ...*about*... changing your ticket.
2 I took my parents to the airport and **saw** them ....
3 He tried to convince us he was an actor but we **saw** .... him.
4 You clear the table and I'll **see** .... the washing-up.
5 Make sure you **see** .... the property before you agree to buy it.
6 The cold weather has finally **set** ....
7 They **set** .... at 5.00 in the morning and returned at 9.00 in the evening.
8 John insisted he was innocent and that somebody had **set** him ....
9 He decided to **set** .... his own business.
10 He was **set** .... finishing the project before Monday.

Phrasal Verbs
1 off, about, for, into
2 out, over, off, to
3 to, about, for, through
4 for, to, with, at
5 to, over, out, about
6 about, down, in, up
7 out, to, back, by
8 down, off, on, up
9 up, back, off, to
10 aside, down, on, out

330 Look at Appendix 3, then fill in the correct preposition(s).

1 Everybody has to do overtime because we are ...*behind*.. schedule.
2 .... our astonishment, he managed to win the race.
3 Break the chocolate .... pieces so that everyone can have some.
4 It's .... the law to drive a car without wearing a seatbelt.
5 They built a road round the city .... a view to decreasing pollution.
6 The injured man had to be taken to hospital .... delay.
7 He enjoys walking .... the hills.
8 We stayed on the platform until the train was .... sight.
9 You can't go that way because the road is .... repair.
10 Actors and actresses have to learn their parts .... heart.
11 She can tell you the names of all the world's capital cities .... memory.
12 Some species are .... danger of extinction.

Prepositions
1 back, off, behind
2 At, To, In
3 in, at, into
4 against, on, off
5 of, in, with
6 against, without, in
7 at, on, in
8 at, out of, on
9 under, in, behind
10 from, of, by
11 by, of, from
12 at, by, in

331 Complete the sentences using the words in bold.

1 A famous poet once lived in that house.
   where   That's ....*the house where*... a famous poet once lived.
2 Helen regretted selling her grandmother's house.
   wished   Helen .... her grandmother's house.

3 Shirley hasn't seen her parents since her brother's wedding.
   last   Shirley .... her brother's wedding.

4 The washing machine still needs repairing.
   been   The washing machine .... yet.

5 As they couldn't stop the car, they panicked.
   able   Not .... the car, they panicked.

6 Vanessa will be twenty-five on Tuesday.
   birthday   It .... on Tuesday.

7 No one in the school can beat him at tennis.
   player   He is .... in the school.

8 The doctor was still examining the patient when I called.
   examined   The patient .... when I called.

9 Simon has done very little work today.
   hardly   Simon .... work today.

10 The honey was so good that she bought 5 kilos.
   such   It .... that she bought 5 kilos.

332 **Read the text carefully. If a line is correct, put a tick (✓) in the space provided. If a line has a word which should not be there, write it in the space provided.**

TRAVELLING

0 When I left university I went travelling all over	**0**	✓
00 in the world. I was so fascinated by New Zealand	**00**	*in*
1 that I decided to spend a year there. In order that	**1**	
2 to do so I had to find a job. However, I had very enough	**2**	
3 money to get by for a few of months, so needless to	**3**	
4 say, I took the opportunity to travel around and see the	**4**	
5 country. Everywhere I went, the people were the friendlier	**5**	
6 than anywhere else I had ever been at, which is important	**6**	
7 when one travelling. The landscape was wonderful as well,	**7**	
8 with the more richest variety of plant life I had	**8**	
9 ever seen. I was also fascinated by the traditions	**9**	
10 of the Maori natives and took every opportunity to talk	**10**	
11 to them. My journey it was very enjoyable and I wanted	**11**	
12 more than ever to stay, but that was been dependent on	**12**	
13 my finding a job. I hadn't had been looking for more than	**13**	
14 a few days when I found a job as a waiter. Everyone person	**14**	
15 at the work was great and I really enjoyed my time there.	**15**	

333 **Use the words in capitals to form a word that fits in the space in the same line.**

THE JOB INTERVIEW

It is important to make a good **(0)** ...... when going
for a job interview. Interviewers usually ask a **(1)** ...... of
questions, many of which concern **(2)** .... However, they
also usually like to ask questions about previous **(3)** ...... as
well as **(4)** ...... not connected to the work place. Often, the
(5) ...... candidate is not the one with the most impressive
(6) ...... but the one who shows that he or she has made
the most **(7)** ...... use of their time. Few employers want
employees who are **(8)** ...... to think for themselves. The
(9) ...... of advancement in any job very rarely depends on
the **(10)** ...... of work but more on the enthusiasm and
dedication of the employee.

IMPRESS	**0**	*impression*
VARIOUS	**1**	
QUALIFY	**2**	
OCCUPY	**3**	
ACHIEVE	**4**	
SUCCESS	**5**	
EDUCATE	**6**	
EFFECT	**7**	
ABLE	**8**	
POSSIBLE	**9**	
ACCURATE	**10**	

PART 1

For questions 1 - 15, read the text below and decide which word A, B, C or D best fits each space. Write your answers in the answer boxes provided.

TATTOOING: AN ANCIENT TRADITION

Tattooing is an **(0)** .... art. In ancient Greece, people who had tattoos were **(1)** .... as members of the **(2)** ...., classes. On the other hand, tattooing was **(3)** .... in Europe by the early Christians, **(4)** .... thought that it was a sinful thing to **(5)** .... .

It was not **(6)** .... the late 18th century, when Captain Cook saw South Sea Islanders decorating their bodies with tattoos, that attitudes began to **(7)** .... . Sailors came back from these islands with pictures of Christ on their backs and from then on, tattooing **(8)** .... in popularity. A survey by the French army in 1881 **(9)** .... that among the 378 men **(10)** .... there were 1,333 designs.

Nowadays, not **(11)** .... finds tattoos acceptable. Some people think that getting one is silly because tattoos are more or less permanent. There is also some **(12)** .... about **(13)** .... blood disease from unsterilised needles. Even for those who do want a tattoo, the **(14)** .... of getting one is not painless, but the final result, in their eyes, is **(15)** .... the pain.

						A	B	C	D
0	A elderly	B old	C original	D outdated	**0**	☐	■	☐	☐
1	A supposed	B realised	C regarded	D held	**1**	☐	☐	☐	☐
2	A greater	B upper	C high	D extreme	**2**	☐	☐	☐	☐
3	A banned	B exported	C blamed	D finished	**3**	☐	☐	☐	☐
4	A whose	B that	C they	D who	**4**	☐	☐	☐	☐
5	A be	B create	C make	D do	**5**	☐	☐	☐	☐
6	A by	B until	C for	D since	**6**	☐	☐	☐	☐
7	A vary	B convert	C change	D move	**7**	☐	☐	☐	☐
8	A gained	B won	C earned	D made	**8**	☐	☐	☐	☐
9	A declared	B said	C explained	D showed	**9**	☐	☐	☐	☐
10	A inquired	B questioned	C demanded	D spoken	**10**	☐	☐	☐	☐
11	A everybody	B every	C each	D nobody	**11**	☐	☐	☐	☐
12	A danger	B trouble	C concern	D threat	**12**	☐	☐	☐	☐
13	A gaining	B catching	C having	D infecting	**13**	☐	☐	☐	☐
14	A progress	B system	C pace	D process	**14**	☐	☐	☐	☐
15	A due	B worth	C owed	D deserved	**15**	☐	☐	☐	☐

PART 2

For questions 16 - 30, read the text below and think of the word which best fits each space. Use only one word in each space. Write your word in the answer boxes provided.

TUSCANY

Tuscany has much to offer the visitor as it has **(0) ....** beautiful countryside and a number of historic towns. One of its **(16) ....** famous cities is Florence, **(17) ....** is known for its cathedral and the beautiful bridge, Ponte Vecchio. In **(18) ....**, there are some colourful markets, which are quite cheap considering **(19) ....** expensive Italy can be. Another city most people will have heard **(20) ....** is Pisa, famous **(21) ....** its Leaning Tower. That is not the only attraction **(22) ....** seeing in Pisa, as there is also an eleventh-century cathedral. Bargo, on the other **(23) ....**, is a town that may not **(24) ....** known to the average visitor. Nevertheless, it should not be missed by **(25) ....** who is interested **(26) ....** seeing the best of Tuscany. It is full of old buildings which have all **(27) ....** painted red, ochre, pale blue or green. The streets are lined with trees and there are **(28) ....** restaurants and pavement cafés **(29) ....** you can sit and admire the cathedral and Mount Panio, which lies just behind the town. The atmosphere in this place is **(30) ....** charming and restful.

0	*both*	0
16		16
17		17
18		18
19		19
20		20
21		21
22		22
23		23
24		24
25		25
26		26
27		27
28		28
29		29
30		30

PART 3

For questions 31 - 40, complete the second sentence so that it has a similar meaning to the first sentence. Use the word given and other words to complete each sentence. You must use between two and five words. Do not change the word given. Write your answers in the answer boxes provided.

(0) I finished the book in two days.
took
It .... to finish the book.

| 0 | *took me two days* | 0 ▭ ▬ |

(31) He will probably fail the exams this year.
unlikely
He is .... the exams this year.

| 31 | | 31 ▭ ▭ |

(32) I don't suppose you know what time the ferry leaves, do you?
happen
Do .... what time the ferry leaves?

| 32 | | 32 ▭ ▭ |

(33) He lost his luggage in the airport.
lost
His... in the airport.

| 33 | | 33 ▭ ▭ |

(34) It was after midnight when Jim finally arrived.
turn
Jim .... until after midnight.

| 34 | | 34 ▭ ▭ |

(35) Women are said to be safer drivers than men.
drive
Women are said .... men.

| 35 | | 35 ▭ ▭ |

(36) Margaret doesn't like working nights.
have
Margaret wishes .... work nights.

| 36 | | 36 ▭ ▭ |

(37) She didn't come to my party; she didn't call me either.
nor
She neither came to my party .... me.

| 37 | | 37 ▭ ▭ |

(38) Tom spends so much time at work that I hardly see him.
such
Tom spends .... at work that I hardly see him.

| 38 | | 38 ▭ ▭ |

(39) How long have your parents been married?
get
When .... married?

| 39 | | 39 ▭ ▭ |

(40) John is in the habit of getting up early every day.
used
John .... early every day.

| 40 | | 40 ▭ ▭ |

PART 4

For questions 41 - 55, read the text below and look carefully at each line. Some of the lines are correct, and some have a word which should not be there. If a line is correct, put a tick (✔) by the number in the answer boxes provided. If a line has a word which should not be there, write the word in the answer boxes provided.

LONELINESS

0	Loneliness is a disease of modern living, a result of	0	✔
00	which people being more mobile and having more opportunities.	00	which
41	With the break-up of family units, there is little of	41	
42	stability on which to build good relationships. Loneliness	42	
43	isn't something that can be solved itself simply by	43	
44	seeing a counsellor, speaking to someone that on the	44	
45	telephone or to being in the company of a lot of people.	45	
46	Advice been often given includes: joining clubs, taking up a	46	
47	sociable hobby or even by trying a part-time job if you	47	
48	don't work outside from the house. However, none of this	48	
49	advice will provide with an easy answer. To ease the	49	
50	feeling of emptiness it takes time. Friendships have	50	
51	to be allowed to grow on and deep bonds can't be	51	
52	formed with just anyone. Anyone might be like a	52	
53	victim of loneliness at some time or other in their	53	
54	lives. If you change jobs, get married to or move,	54	
55	you too might have had problems in a new environment.	55	

PART 5

For questions 56 - 65, read the text below. Use the word given in capitals at the end of each line to form a word that fits in the space in the same line. Write your word in the answer boxes provided.

COFFEE HOUSES

Coffee houses are a **(0)** .... of Viennese life. Each one serves a huge **(56)** .... of exotic coffees, so you should consult the menu. The most popular coffee is Brauner, which is **(57)** .... to espresso. The waiters are **(58)** .... polite and must be spoken to **(59)** .... . Most regulars sit for hours over one cup of coffee and do not feel obliged to order further **(60)** .... .
Tourists often cause **(61)** .... and are seen as
(62) .... who try to strike up conversations. The Viennese do not go to coffee houses to be **(63)** ....; they go to be seen in public. Upon leaving, it isn't **(64)** .... to leave a very large tip.
The **(65)** .... coffee drinker usually rounds the bill up to the nearest schilling.

SPECIAL	0	speciality
SELECT	56	
SIMILARITY	57	
EXTREME	58	
RESPECT	59	
REFRESH	60	
ANNOY	61	
INVADE	62	
SOCIAL	63	
NECESSITY	64	
KNOWLEDGE	65	

Pronouns / Determiners

How would **you** like **your** hair cut? Shall **I** cut **it** like **your** father's?

Oh no! I don't want **mine** to look like **his**. **His** hair has got a hole on top!

Pronouns

Personal pronouns		Possessive adjectives	Possessive pronouns	Reflexive-Emphatic pronouns
before verbs as subjects	**after verbs as objects**	**followed by nouns**	**not followed by nouns**	
I	me	my	mine	myself
you	you	your	yours	yourself
he	him	his	his	himself
she	her	her	hers	herself
it	it	its	---	itself
we	us	our	ours	ourselves
you	you	your	yours	yourselves
they	them	their	theirs	themselves

Personal Pronouns

● **We use personal pronouns to refer to people, things or animals. *We*'ve met the manager. *He*'s really young. We don't use a noun and a personal pronoun together. *Your* coat is in the wardrobe. (not: *Your coat it's in the wardrobe.*) *My* uncle bought me a present. (not: *My uncle he bought me a present.*)**

● **We use I, you, he, she etc before verbs as subjects and me, you, him, her etc after verbs as objects. *I* lent *him* my dictionary but *he* lost *it*.**

334 **Fill in the correct pronouns or possessives.**

Dear Fiona,

Thanks very much for your last letter. It was great to hear from 1) ...*you*... . Has 2) .... husband decided whether or not to accept the promotion 3) .... boss offered 4) .... yet? 5) .... would be brilliant for both of 6) .... if 7) .... did. Tom and Sarah visited 8) .... last month. I hadn't seen 9) .... since the summer, when 10) .... all went to Anna's wedding, so 11) .... was a special weekend. Sarah said 12) .... might go to America in May to see some friends of 13) ...., who the rest of 14) .... haven't met, but 15) .... isn't sure. Well, that's 16) .... most important news for now. I look forward to receiving 17) .... when 18) .... have time.

Love,
Janet

- **There + be** is used for something mentioned for the first time or to say that something or someone exists. *There are* some messages for you on your desk.
- **Personal pronoun + be/other verb** is used to give more details about something or someone already mentioned. *There's* a woman at the door. *She* wants to talk to you.
- **It + be** is used for **identification**. *There's a man on the phone. It's your husband.*
- **It + be** with **to-infinitive** or **that-clause** is used to begin a sentence. *It's nice to be back. It's a shame that he didn't call us. It* is also used for weather, distance, temperature, time expressions and in the following expressions: It seems that, It appears that, It looks like, It is said that, It doesn't matter etc. *It's sunny today, isn't it? It appears that they are going to move. It seems that there is a mistake in these figures. But we also say: There seems to be a mistake in these figures.*

335   <u>Fill in: there or it.</u>

Tom: Look, **1)** ...*there*... isn't much time left. Have you made a decision?

Sandra: I have, but I'm not sure you're going to like **2)** .... **3)** .... are a lot of things to take into consideration.

Tom: What do you mean? **4)** .... 's not that hard to choose a holiday.

Sandra: No, but **5)** .... seem to be so many choices and we've only got a limited amount of money. Anyway, I've decided **6)** .... 's only one place for us.

Tom: Where is **7)** ....? France, Italy, Spain?

Sandra: No.

Tom: Is **8)** .... Germany then? I've always wanted to go there.

Sandra: I think we should go to Grandma's house in Blackpool for a week.

336   <u>Fill in: there or it.</u>

1 "Is ...*it*... mother's birthday tomorrow?" "No, her birthday is next week."
2 ....'s Christmas Day and everyone is happy.
3 I'll never make it to work on time. .... takes half an hour to get there and I'm already late.
4 ....'s no need to worry. I'm sure .... won't matter if you are a little late.
5 ....'s no light on in the house - something must be wrong.
6 Shall we take a taxi? ....'s much too far to walk.
7 .... was a party at Sally's last night. .... were lots of people and ...... went on until the early hours.
8 "Will .... matter if I'm a bit late for the meeting?" "Well, ... might be a good idea to warn the manager."

Possessive adjectives/pronouns

- **Possessive adjectives/pronouns** express possession. Possessive adjectives go before nouns, whereas possessive pronouns do not go before nouns. *This is **my** diary. It's **mine**. Sometimes possessive pronouns go at the beginning of a sentence. **Theirs** is the blue car.*
- We use **the** rather than a possessive adjective with parts of the body after prepositions. Verbs used in this pattern include: hit, kiss, punch, slap, bite, touch, pat, sting etc. *She **kissed** the baby on **the** cheek. He **punched** me on **the** nose.(not: on my nose)*
- **Own** is used with possessive adjectives to emphasise the fact that something belongs to one person and no one else. *She's got **her own** chauffeur. or She's got a chauffeur **of her own**.*

337   <u>Fill in the blanks with a possessive adjective or a possessive pronoun.</u>

1 This is ...*my*... (I) bag but that one over there is ...*yours*... (you).
2 .... (she) score was better than .... (I).

3 .... (they) holiday starts the week after .... (we).
4 Can we have .... (you) suggestion first and then we'll hear .... (he)?
5 I didn't bother going to .... (he) party and he won't be coming to .... (I).
6 .... (we) flight was delayed but .... (they) took off on time.
7 I wish .... (I) voice was as good as .... (she).
8 Unfortunately, ... (they) team played better than .... (we) so we lost the match.
9 If you're a friend of .... (he), then you're a friend of .... (I) too.
10 We'll leave .... (she) house after dinner, so we should be at .... (you) before 10.00.

> What's your **baby's name**?
>
> Caffeine.

> That's a strange name.
>
> Yes. You see, she keeps us awake all night!

Possessive case with 's or s' for people or animals

- **singular nouns (person or animal) + 's** *the boy's racket, the dog's ears, the queen's limousine*
- **regular plural nouns + '** *the passengers' luggage*
- **irregular plural nouns not ending in s + 's** *the children's toys, the women's magazines*
- **compound nouns + 's** *my sister-in-law's house*
- **'s after the last of two or more names to show common possession**
  Kate and Alan's yacht (They own a yacht.)
- **'s after each name to show individual possession** *Sonia's and Marisa's yachts (Each owns a yacht.)*

Possessive case with "of" for inanimate things

- **of + inanimate things or abstract nouns** *the windows of a house, the price of success*
- **of + possessive case/possessive pronouns when there is a determiner (this, some etc) before the noun.** *Listen to this song of Eric's. (one of Eric's songs), a friend of mine (one of my friends)*
  Note: phrases of place + 's *(at the dentist's, the building's entrance),* **time or distance expressions + 's/'** *(last year's reports, two days' work, a mile's walk).* **We can use either 's or of when we talk about places or organisations.** *(York's monuments or the monuments of York).* **We use of with people in longer phrases.** *(That's the sister of one of my colleagues.)*

338 ▶ **Rewrite the following using the correct possessive form.**

1 at the baker - the shop ...*at the baker's*...........
2 the princess - the ring ....
3 the couple - the honeymoon ....
4 the honey - the taste ....
5 the tree - the roots ....
6 the children - the toys ....
7 the line - the end ....
8 my mother-in-law - hat ....
9 the cats - collars ....

10 the dog - the basket ....
11 the room - the emptiness ....
12 the world - the wonders ....
13 the man - the wallet ....
14 the prisoners - the escape ....
15 the view - the beauty ....
16 the monkey - the tail ....
17 the bride - the mother ....
18 the girls - father ....

339 **Rewrite the following using the correct possessive form.**

1   The fashionable colour this year is blue. ...*This year's fashionable colour is blue.*....................
2   She had a hard day of work. ....
3   You will receive this a month from now. ....
4   They weren't at the celebrations last year. ....
5   The walk to the village is a mile long. ....
6   We must look at the timetable for this week. ....
7   I read the article in the paper - Sunday. ....
8   The writer showed us a poem - his. ....
9   We had a party in Sue - Sally - flat. ....
10 Mr Brown - Miss Green - offices are being refurnished. ....
11 You should follow your parents - the advice. ....
12 I am to be bridesmaid at Harry - Renata - the wedding. ....
13 The roof - the tiles are falling off. ....
14 Simon is certainly no friend - my. ....
15 The Porsche drew up at the restaurant - the entrance. ....
16 A security guard checked the passengers - the bags. ....

Reflexive/Emphatic Pronouns (myself, yourself etc)

● **Reflexive pronouns** are used after certain verbs (**behave, burn, cut, enjoy, hurt, kill, look at, laugh at, introduce, dry, teach** etc) when the subject and the object of the verb are the same. *Did you enjoy yourself? He taught himself how to drive.*

● **Reflexive pronouns** can be used after **be, feel, look, seem** to describe emotions or states. *He doesn't seem himself these days.* They are also used after prepositions but not after prepositions of place. *He is so proud of himself.* but: *He looked behind him.* (not: ~~behind himself~~)

● Certain verbs do not normally take a reflexive pronoun. These are: **wash, shave, (un)dress, afford, complain, meet, rest, relax, stand up, get up, sit down, wake up** etc. *He got up and shaved.* **We don't say:** *He got up ~~himself~~ and shaved ~~himself~~.* **However we can use a reflexive pronoun with wash or dress when we talk about young children or animals.**
 I'm teaching my son how to **wash himself.** *Those monkeys are* **dressing themselves!**

● **Emphatic pronouns** have the same form as reflexive pronouns but a different meaning. They emphasise the noun, or the fact that one person, and not another, performs an action. *He himself conducted the interview.* They also mean "without help". *She fixed the leak herself.* (without help) They go after nouns, pronouns or after "but" and "than". *She'd like to marry someone older than herself.*

● Note these idioms: **Enjoy yourself!** (= Have a good time!) **Behave yourself!** (= Be good!) **I like being by myself.** (= I like being alone.) **She lives by herself.** (= She lives on her own.) **By myself, by yourself, by himself etc** (= on my own, on your own, on his own etc) **Help yourself to coffee.** (= You're welcome to take some coffee if you want some.) **Do it yourself.** (= Do it without being helped.) **Make yourself at home!** (= Feel comfortable.) **Make yourself heard.** (= Speak loudly enough to be heard by others.) **Make yourself understood.** (= Make your meaning clear.)

340 **Fill in the correct pronouns then identify them: reflexive or emphatic?**

1 They're not behaving
...*themselves*... .
(reflexive)

2 He made this raft
....
....

3 Oh, no! I've ruined
my dress ....
....

4 The cat is licking
....
....

5 Look out! You'll hurt

....

....

6 She has poisoned

....

....

7 He built this house

....

....

8 They are enjoying

....

....

341 **Complete the sentences using words from the list below and a -self pronoun.**

draw, bake, make, fix, prepare, cut, organise, decorate

1 Sue didn't buy a cake for her birthday. She ...*baked one herself.* ...

2 My brother's a mechanic, so he doesn't have to pay somebody to repair his car. He ....

3 Her cousins are excellent dressmakers. They ....

4 Do you like the salad? I ....

5 John didn't go to the hairdresser's. He ....

6 We didn't go to a travel agent's to organise our holiday. We ....

7 What do you think of my aunt's new house? She ....

8 Do you like this picture? I ....

342 **Put the verbs in brackets in the correct form with or without a reflexive pronoun.**

James: You don't look well this morning Julie.

Julie: I know. When I **1)** ...*saw myself*... (see) in the mirror this morning, I got a shock.

James: How **2)** .... (you/feel)?

Julie: Pretty bad. I **3)** .... (give) a treat last night and went to a restaurant for a meal.

James: And **4)** .... (you/enjoy) it?

Julie: At the time, yes. But now I'm **5)** .... (ask) if the food was really fresh.

343 **Fill in the appropriate pronoun or possessive adjective.**

Paul: Suzie, **1)** ...*I*... 've cut **2)** .... Can **3)** .... bring **4)** .... a plaster, please?

Suzie: Oh, dear! How did you do **5)** ....?

Paul: I was cutting some bread to make **6)** .... a sandwich. That knife's really sharp, isn't **7)** ....?

Claire: What's happening? Oh, Paul, what's wrong with **8)** .... finger?

Suzie: **9)** ....'s cut **10)** ....

Claire: Put **11)** .... hand in some cold water.

Suzie: Yes, do as **12)** .... says. **13)** .... will stop the pain.

Paul: OK. Agh! **14)** ....'s freezing!

Claire: **15)** ....'s such a baby! I don't know how you put up with **16)** ...., Suzie!

Suzie: Men always make a fuss. **17)** .... act like children when they hurt **18)** ....

Claire: Shall we take you to hospital? You needn't drive your car. I'll take you in **19)** ....

Paul: No, no. I'll be alright.

Suzie: Yes, just calm **20)** .... down. I think you'll live.

344 Fill in with: of one's own, on one's own or one's own in the correct form.

1 Can you help me with these suitcases? I can't lift them ...*on my own*... .
2 He always does what other people tell him. He hasn't got a mind ....
3 Why do you always drink my milk? Don't you get any ....?
4 They desperately need a place .... since they have two small children and her parents' house is very small.
5 Is this all .... work, or did someone help you?
6 The country has had .... government since it became independent.
7 She's very independent, she likes having .... place.
8 He seems to have left us .... again.
9 Exactly how long have they been running .... business?
10 You are expected to do a lot of work in .... time.
11 When the helicopter took off, he was left .... in the forest.
12 As a DJ, he plays a lot of different styles of music but .... taste is for good old rock n' roll.
13 "Is this .... car, sir?" "No, actually, I borrowed it."
14 What I've always wanted is to run a restaurant ....
15 Every person has a history ....

Each other means "one another". Compare the examples below.

*They laughed at **each other**.*

*They laughed at **themselves**.*

345 Fill in each other or an appropriate reflexive or emphatic pronoun.

1 Lucy and Frank do not like ...*each other*... at all. They're always arguing.
2 She told her guests to help .... to food and drink.
3 The police carried guns to protect .... in case they were shot at.
4 The boys told their mother that they'd clean up their room ....
5 He kept .... warm in the mountains by wearing lots of heavy clothing.
6 They talk to .... on the phone at least once a week.
7 They took a taxi to town to save .... some time.
8 They waved to .... as the train pulled out of the station.
9 Cats clean .... by licking their fur.
10 Bob and Terry are always arguing with ....
11 We haven't seen .... for days - not since the argument.
12 She taught .... basic French in six weeks.
13 To save money we decorated the house ....
14 The children were told off for being so rude to ....
15 You look dreadful! You should look after .... a little better.
16 The two children shared the bag of sweets with ....
17 I hope my parents enjoy .... at their surprise party tonight.
18 After her bad dream the child didn't want to sleep by ....

Is there **anything** I can do for you, sir?

You gave me a year's guarantee with my car and you said you'd mend **everything** that breaks.

That's right, sir. Has **something** broken?

Yes, I need **some** new gates for my neighbours!

Determiners

- **Determiners** are special words that are placed in front of nouns or noun phrases and they affect their meaning. Such words are: **indefinite article** (a/an), **definite article** (the), **demonstratives** (this/that /these/those), **possessive adjectives** (my/your/his etc), **quantifiers** (some/any/every/no/ both/each/either/neither/enough/several/all/most etc) and **numbers** (one/two etc).

	Adjectives	Pronouns	Adverbs	
		people	**things**	**places**
Positive	some any	someone/somebody anyone/anybody	something anything	somewhere anywhere
Interrogative	any	anyone/anybody	anything	anywhere
Negative	no/not any	no one/not anyone nobody/not anybody	nothing not anything	nowhere not anywhere
Positive/Negative/ Interrogative	every	everybody (all people) everyone	everything (all things)	everywhere (in all places)

- **Some** is used before countable or uncountable nouns. *Let's buy **some** biscuits. We've got **some** fruit.* **Some** and **its compounds** (somebody, something etc) are normally used in positive sentences. They are also used in questions when we want to make an offer, a request or when we expect a positive answer. *There is **someone** on the phone, he wants to talk to you. (= positive) Would you like **some** more wine? (= offer) Could I have **some** tea, please? (= request) Is there **someone** who can help me? (= I expect there will be.) but: Is there **anyone** who can help me? (= I'm asking in general.)*

- **Any** is used before countable or uncountable nouns. *Is there **any** instant coffee?* **Any** and **its** **compounds** (anyone, anything etc) are normally used in questions. *Is there **anything** wrong?* They are also used in positive sentences meaning "It doesn't matter how/what/which/when/who/where". *You can buy **anything** you want.* **Any** and **its compounds** can be used after **if** in a positive sentence. *If **anyone** asks for me, tell them I've left.*

- **No/not any** are used before countable or uncountable nouns. **No/not any** and **their compounds** (no one/not anyone, nothing/not anything etc) are used in negations. *There is **nothing** we can do. There **isn't anything** we can do.* **Any** and **its compounds** are used with negative words (hardly, never, without, seldom, rarely etc). *I **hardly** go **anywhere** these days. (not: I hardly go nowhere these days.)*

- **Every** is used before singular countable nouns. **Every** and **its compounds** take a verb in the singular. *Every citizen **has** to pay taxes. (= all citizens) We are doing **everything** in our power to help you. (= all things)*

346 ▸ Underline the correct item.

1 There is **no one/anyone** at home.
2 There are **some/any** books on my desk.
3 There is **any/no** ice-cream left.
4 Did she tell you **nothing/anything**?
5 There is hardly **no/any** milk left.
6 She won't lend you **no/any** money.
7 I need **any/some** time alone.
8 I get up at 8.00 **any/every** morning.
9 If **anybody/nobody** wants to leave, say so now.
10 **Nobody/Anybody** phoned this morning.
11 I haven't seen **nothing/anything** yet.
12 There is **anything/nothing** good on TV tonight.

13 **Some/Every** day he will be famous.
14 **No one/Anyone** was at home this morning.
15 **Somebody/Everybody** who went camping had a good time.
16 **Nobody/Anybody** told me that it was Ann's birthday.
17 Is there **everything/anything** I can do to help?
18 There is **something/everything** wrong with the drinks machine.
19 Are you going **nowhere/anywhere** this weekend?
20 This has **nothing/anything** to do with you.
21 I can't find my keys **anywhere/nowhere**.

347 ▸ Underline the correct item.

As soon as we arrived home we knew that **1) something/ anything** was wrong. We soon discovered that **2) someone/anyone** had broken into our home. Many things had been stolen, **3) everyone/each** had lost **4) something/anything**. **5) Every/Some** money had also been taken. Before we phoned the police, we went to ask our neighbour if she had seen **6) anyone/no one** or **7) anything/nothing** suspicious, but she hadn't. We went back home to phone the police. As we sat waiting for them to arrive, we surveyed the damage that was **8) everywhere/anywhere** around us. **9) No/Some** of our most personal possessions lay smashed and broken before us, **10) no one/someone** spoke. Eventually, the police arrived and asked us to make a list of **11) everything/something** that had been stolen, as they started to check for fingerprints. They warned us that it was unusual to find **12) any/some**, because most burglars wore gloves. When the police had finished checking for

prints, they took our list of **13) everything/something** that was missing, and they told us that **14) someone/anyone** would visit us over the next few days to advise us on new security measures.

348 ▸ Fill in: some, any or their compounds.

1 "Have we got ...*any*... milk?" "Oh no, I meant to get .... yesterday." "Shall I go and buy ....?"
2 "Does .... else want a lift?" "I'd like one if you've got .... space in the car."
3 "Shall we buy Jenny .... flowers?" "I don't know, ... practical might be better."
4 "Can .... give me a hand with these boxes?" "I can help if there are .... light ones."
5 "Does .... want to go to the cinema tonight? I've got .... free tickets." "Is there .... in particular on?" "Yes, a James Bond film."
6 "Do you want .... vegetables with your steak?" "Well, I wouldn't mind .... chips if you've got ...."
7 "Has Jasmine got .... exams this year?" "I think she's got .... in June." "Is there .... I can do to help her?"
8 "I've put .... blankets at the end of the bed but if you need more, or .... else, just ask." "Actually, there is .... Could I have .... towels, too?"
9 "Do you want to invite .... special to your birthday tea?" "Could I ask .... friends from the art college?" "Yes, of course."
10 "Shall I put .... music on?" "Yes, have you got .... relaxing?"
11 "I wish I had .... interesting to do." "I could give you .... ideas, but you never like .... I suggest."
12 "Did you go .... during the holidays?" "I wanted to go .... but unfortunately I didn't have .... money."

349 Fill in: anything, anywhere, everyone, hardly ever, no one or nothing.

Last year while I was in England, I went to a football match with an English friend. Manchester United were playing Ipswich and **1)** ...*no one*... thought Manchester could lose. I think **2)** .... will remember this game for the rest of their lives. Even my friend, who goes to every Manchester game, said he had never seen **3)** .... like it. Ipswich scored four goals in the first half and **4)** .... was sure they would win. Manchester was losing 0 - 4. Then, in the second half, the Manchester defender, Pallister, who **5)** .... scores, scored three times. That was surprising enough, but it was **6)** .... compared to him scoring for the fourth time with three minutes left. Not one person remained seated **7)** .... in the whole stadium. Then, with only one minute remaining, Pallister scored again and **8)** .... went crazy. Manchester United won 5 - 4. I am convinced there is **9)** .... better than seeing a football match in England.

350 Replace the highlighted words with some, any, every or one of their compounds.

1) A person once told me that it is possible to go **2) to all places** in Britain by train, so I decided to try. I took **3) a few days** off work. I had the timetable for **4) all the trains**, but **5) all the people** I spoke to told me there were always **6) several changes** to the published timetable and I should always ask before I took a train. In the end, **7) it all** went well and I didn't have **8) one difficulty** and, although there were **9) three or four places** I missed, I covered 2,000 miles in three days.

1 ...*Someone/Somebody*...	3	5	7	9 ....
2	4	6	8	

• The idea of **"any..."** can be expressed by adding the suffix **ever** to the following **wh-words**: whoever (anyone who), whatever (anything that), whichever (any of), whenever (any time that), wherever (any place that), however (in any way that). *Please call me* **whenever** *you want. (= any time that you want) He does* **whatever** *he thinks is best. (= anything that he thinks is best)*

351 Complete the following by using "ever" words.

1 We can go to the shops any time that suits you. We can go ...*whenever*... you want.
2 He's not sure what to do about the situation. I told him to do .... seems best.
3 There are five buses going to Oxford daily. We can take .... fits in with your plans.
4 It's not a formal party. You can dress .... you please.
5 I don't mind driving far. I can take you .... you want to go.
6 He's got tickets for everyone. .... wants to come is welcome.
7 She's such a spoilt child. She gets .... she wants.
8 There are three good films on at the cinema. We can go to .... you prefer.
9 You can begin your work .... you want, as long as it's finished on time.
10 It's true that .... she goes, she's always the centre of attention.

352 Fill in: hardly (ever) and anything, anywhere, anyone or any as in the example:

1 There ....*was hardly anyone*..................................... at the party. (not many people)
2 I .... in the shops. (not often see nice things)
3 He .... to the opera. (not go)
4 The old lady .... (not often go to places)

5 He did .... work. (very little)
6 We .... (not often visit people)
7 The museum had .... on show. (not much)
8 My parents .... free time. (not often have)
9 She knows .... about it. (not much)
10 There's .... to eat in this village. (not many places)

Else

- The adverb **else** means either "more" or "different". It can be used with the indefinite pronouns and adverbs **everyone, something, nobody, anywhere** etc. *I'm afraid I can't help you. Why don't you ask **someone else**? (= a different person) We must get one more assistant. Can you think of **anyone else**? (= one more person)*
- **Else** can be used with **who, what, where** and **how** to refer to people, things, places etc. *What else can I get you, sir? Who else have you invited? Where else can I look for help? How else should I do it?*
- **Else** is followed by a singular verb. *Everyone else is already here.*
- In the possessive case the **'s** goes after **else**. *Don't use my pen. Take **someone else's**.*
- **Anything (else)** and **nothing (else)** can be followed by **but**. *Nothing (else) but a warning would make him come to his senses.*
- **Or else** means "otherwise". *Hurry up **or else** you'll be late for your interview.*

353 Fill in with: else, or else, else's.

1 Behave yourself ...*or else*... you'll be expelled.
2 Nothing .... but stricter punishment will discourage criminals.
3 This can't be yours; I'm sure it is someone ....
4 I should really be going now .... I'll be late for my appointment.
5 My passport was checked by the officials and so was everyone ....
6 Let's try somewhere ....; this café is rather dull.
7 I'm desperate; I don't know what .... to do.
8 Place this file somewhere safe .... you might lose it.
9 Nowhere .... have I been treated with such kindness and understanding.
10 Do you know who .... has been asked to attend the meeting?
11 I can't think of anyone .... career that has been so brilliant as yours.
12 Screw the lid on tightly .... the jam will go off.
13 How .... should I do it?
14 Was anything .... said at the meeting?
15 This coat is definitely Mark's; it can't be anyone ....
16 We'd better ring them up .... they will be worried.
17 Is there anything .... that you need to know?
18 Apart from mine, nobody .... presence was required at the staff meeting.
19 No one .... but you can help us organise the sales team.
20 We must hurry .... we will never catch that train.

354 Complete the sentences using "else" as in the example:

1 (another place) I don't like it here. Let's go ....*somewhere else*........................ .
2 (all the other people) It's not fair that you won't let me go to the party. .... is going to be there.
3 (another person) I wasn't sitting at that desk. .... was working there.
4 (no other thing) I don't really want to do the ironing but, as there's .... to do, I might as well do it.
5 (a different thing) I'm bored playing cards. I want to do ....
6 (all the other things) We'll have to eat the chicken because we've used up ....

Demonstratives

This/These are used
- **for people or things near us.** *This vase here is a genuine antique.*
- **for present or future situations.** *I'm taking a test this week.*
- **when the speaker is in or near the place he/she is referring to.** *This church was built 900 years ago.*
  (The speaker is now in or near the church.)
- **to introduce people or when we introduce ourselves on the phone.** *"Mark, this is Elaine and this is Susie." "Hello. This is Melanie Brown speaking."*

That/Those are used
- **for people or things not near us.** *That man over there is a famous composer.*
- **for past situations.** *That week was the best of my life.*
- **to refer back to something mentioned before.** *"We're getting married." "That's great."*
- **when speaking on the phone to ask who the other person is.**
  "Hello? This is Jim Spike. Who's that, please?"
- **This/these - that/those are not always followed by nouns.**
  This is all I can say on the subject. That's how he was rescued.

355 **Fill in: this, that, these or those.**

1 ...*This*... shirt is too big.

2 .... flowers are for you.

3 ....'s a very funny hat.

4 Hey! .... are my suitcases.

356 **Fill in: this, that, these or those.**

1 "Hi Beryl. ...*This*... is my sister Sue." "Pleased to meet you, Sue."
2 " I won the competition!" "......................................'s great!"
3 "Can you see .... aeroplane in the sky? It's a Boeing."
4 "My friend is getting married .... year on Valentine's Day."
5 "...................................... are my new shoes. Do you like them?"
6 "Can you pass me .... book on the shelf behind you please?"
7 "Grandad, do you remember 1914?" "Yes, ... was the year I married your grandmother."
8 "...................................... people over there must be waiting for the train."
9 "Good evening. .... is the Prime Minister speaking to the nation."
10 "I bought .... socks today." "What a lovely shade of green!"
11 "Are you going away .... weekend?" "Yes, we're going camping."
12 "I hear she's getting married." "......................................'s right. She's getting married next month."
13 "...................................... jeans are so tight I can hardly move." "Why don't you buy some bigger ones?"
14 "I'm fed up. I've had enough of .... terrible weather." "So have I, but it'll soon be summer!"
15 "What's wrong, Sally?" "Well, you won't like ...., but I've got to tell you."
16 "Are .... children over there Mrs Brown's?" "Yes. They're very well-behaved, aren't they?"
17 "Their wedding is a fortnight today but I won't be able to go. I'm going away .... weekend."
18 "We are moving to a bigger house." "Really? ....'s fantastic!"
19 "............................... boots hurt my feet." "Maybe you should get another pair."
20 "I told him that no one trusts him." "There was no reason to say ....!"
21 "What do you think of this pair of sunglasses?" "I prefer .... ones over there."

None of the cars I've seen are painted that way. Why is yours painted a different colour on **each** side?

Well, if I have an accident, the witnesses will spend **all** their time contradicting each other.

- **All** refers to more than two people or things. It has a positive meaning and takes a verb in the plural. It is the opposite of none. *All the passengers went ashore. All of them felt seasick. They were all seasick. All three/four etc of them passed the exam.* **All + that-clause** means "the only thing" and takes a singular verb. *All that he did was complain about everything.*
- **Both** refers to two people or things. It has a positive meaning and takes a verb in the plural. It is the opposite of neither/not either. *Jo and Tonia are typists. Both Jo and Tonia are typists. They are both typists. Both of them are typists. Both girls are typists.*
- **Whole** (= complete) is used with countables. We always use a, the, this, my etc + whole + countable. *the whole month = all the month/all month but: all the coffee (not: the whole coffee)*
- **Either** (anyone of two) / **Neither** (not one and not the other) are used before singular countables. They refer to two people or things. *Neither man is rich. Neither of/Either of take a verb either in the singular or plural. Neither of us is/are rich. Jack or Dan have promised to help me. Either of them have/has promised to help me.*
- **None** refers to more than two people or things. It has a negative meaning and isn't followed by a noun. *"Are there any vacancies?" "No, none."* **None of** is also used before nouns or object pronouns followed by a verb either in the singular or plural. It is the opposite of all. *Paul, Keith and Rod haven't been to Paris. None of the boys/them has/have been to Paris.*
- **No** is followed by a noun. *There's no place like home.*
- **Every** is used with singular countables. It refers to a group of people or things and means "all", "everyone", "everything" etc. *Tenants have to pay the rent every month. He ate every apple.*
- **Each** is used with singular countables. It means "one by one", considered individually. *Each employee has to sign a contract. (all employees considered individually)*
- **Every one** and **each one** have of-constructions. *Each one of/Every one of the students had done their homework.* **Compare:** *There were two applicants for the job and I gave a form to each one. (not: every one). There were ten applicants for the job and I gave a form to each one/every one.*
- **One / Ones** are used to avoid repetition of a countable noun. *"Which shirt do you want?" "This one." (this shirt) "Which shoes did you buy?" "The black ones." (the black shoes)*

357 **Tick the appropriate boxes.**

	singular verb	plural verb
1 all		✔
2 both		
3 each/every		
4 either/neither		
5 either of/neither of		
6 none of		

358 Fill in: each, every, everyone, everything, all or whole.

1) ...*Everyone*... needs to relax and Mrs Emms was no different. She had worked 2) .... year without a break and she was ready for a holiday. 3) .... was planned, the 4) .... family were going to spend a week together in a cabin in the mountains. 5) .... year they had talked about getting away together but somehow they had never got round to it. This year it was actually going to happen. It had been seven years since 6) .... the family had gone away together and Mrs Emms was really looking forward to the holiday. They had rented the cabin and had planned a different outing for 7) .... day of the week. There would be something for 8) .... Mrs Emms just wanted a quiet relaxing holiday and to be able to spend 9) .... day in the fresh air. The rest of the family had different interests but they had planned the holiday well so that they would 10) .... enjoy themselves.

359 Fill in: all, every, none, both, either and neither.

Assistant:	Can I help you madam?
Customer:	Yes, I'd like to try 1) ...*both*... these skirts on please.
Assistant:	Of course. This way please. *[A few minutes later]* Is 2) .... of them any good?
Customer:	No. I'm afraid 3) .... of them are exactly what I'm looking for and they are 4) .... too big.
Assistant:	Would you like to try something else?
Customer:	Yes, please. I'd really like something colourful. 5) .... my clothes are dark and 6) .... of them are very nice. I'm fed up with them. 7) .... time I go shopping, I say I'll get something brighter and I never do.
Assistant:	Let's have a look. 8) .... our clothes are on offer at the moment and we have something for 9) .... age, size and taste. I'm sure we'll find something for you.

- **Both ... and** takes a plural verb. *Both* my father **and** my brother **are** here.
- **Neither ... nor / Either ... or, Not only ... but also** take either a singular or plural verb depending on the subject which follows nor, or, but also. *Neither* Fiona **nor** *Emma* **is** coming to my party. *Either John* **or** *his parents* **are** planning to call on her.

360 Use both ... and, either ... or, neither ... nor, or not only ... but also to rewrite the sentences.

1 Tracy and Stella watched the programme. ...*Both Tracy and Stella watched the programme.* ....
2 Christine wants to go to university; so does John. ....
3 Clare hasn't been to America and her sisters haven't either. ....
4 The teachers thought the exam results were unfair and so did the students. ....
5 James will pick up the parcel, or else Paul will. ....
6 James and David are not conservative. ....
7 Mother wasn't born in January, neither was Father. ....
8 Cathy is going to the meeting, or else Andrea is. ....

361 **Fill in: all, most, every, one, ones, whole.**

1 ...*Most*... students aren't here today. They've gone on an excursion.
2 Mary has three sisters, ... of whom look like her.
3 Choose a cake. Which .... would you like?
4 I can't decide whether to go to Italy, Greece or Spain. They're .... beautiful countries.
5 I've done a few of the exercises but I couldn't do the difficult ....
6 We've got the .... summer free to do whatever we want.
7 Tom goes to bed at eight .... night.

362 **Fill in: all, every, none, both, either, neither.**

Sue: Have you decided where to go on holiday?
Mary: Not yet. I have a brochure but 1) ...*all*... the hotels are so expensive. 2) .... of them provide full-board and I want 3) .... half-board or self-catering.
Sue: Why don't you rent a room? Two friends of mine did and they 4) .... said it was cheap and enjoyable. In fact, 5) .... of them spent much money.
Mary: Alright, let's have a look at some rooms in Spain and Greece. They 6) .... look nice and I see that 7) .... room has a sea-view. 8) .... of the hotel rooms available has any view at all.
Sue: Right - so it's 9) .... Spain or Greece.
Mary: Yes. 10) .... of them look perfect.

363 **Fill in: every or each.**

A: Four people live in our house. 1) ...*Each*... of us has his own room and we take turns doing the housework and cooking. 2) .... person has to cook an evening meal and keep the house clean and tidy for a week and 3) .... Monday we change over.
B: It sounds OK, but does this system really work?
A: Well, most of the time it does OK, except when it's Mike's turn. 4) .... time it's his turn to do the chores, he always finds an excuse. He gives a different one 5) .... time but they're never very good.
B: Can't you do anything about it?
A: We've tried, but 6) .... time we say something to him, he gets annoyed and thinks we're being unfair.

B: But he can't get away with it 7) .... time. It's not fair on the rest of you. If 8) .... of you made excuses like Mike, you would all be starving and living in a mess.

364 **Underline the correct item.**

1 It's not good for you to stay in bed **all/every** day. You should get up and do something.
2 **Neither/Either** Peter nor Tom came to the meeting.
3 I hope everyone **is/are** ready to leave.
4 She read the **all/whole** book in two hours.
5 **No/None** of my friends has phoned me this weekend.
6 You have to check **everyone/each one** of these contracts separately.
7 I don't like these biscuits. I prefer the **one/ones** Mum made.
8 **Either/Neither** Susan or Laura will tell you what to do.
9 We had a great weekend as the weather was perfect **both/all** days.
10 I've never been **anywhere/nowhere** I like more than Paris.

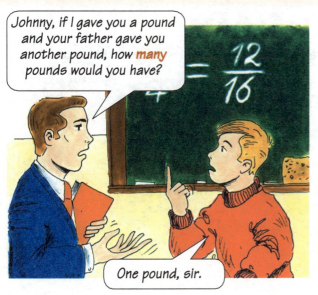

*Johnny, if I gave you a pound and your father gave you another pound, how **many** pounds would you have?*

One pound, sir.

*You don't study **much**, Johnny, do you?*

You haven't met my father sir, have you?

Much · Many · A lot of

	countables	uncountables	
Positive	a lot (of)/lots of/ many (formal)	a lot (of)/lots of/ much (formal)	*There are **a lot of** trees in the park. There is **a lot of** cheese in the fridge.*
Interrogative	many	much	*Are there **many** shops in York? Did you have **much** time to do any shopping?*
Negative	many	much	*There aren't **many** oranges. I haven't got **much** money, so I can't buy any.*
	a few (= some)/ (very) few (= not many, not enough)	a little (= some)/ (very) little (= not much, not enough)	*There were **a few** boys in the class. **Very few** students attended the lecture. **Very little** progress has been made.*

- **A lot (of)/Lots of** are used with countable or uncountable nouns and are normally used in positive sentences. *A lot of tourists visit this museum. He has got a lot of patience.* **A lot of** can be used in questions or negative sentences in informal English. *Was there **a lot of** opposition to your proposal? (informal)*
- **Many** is used with countables and **much** with uncountables. They are normally used in questions or negative sentences. *Has she got **many** records? We haven't got **much** time.* **Many** or **much** are often used in positive sentences after **too, so, how** or in formal English. *He wasted **too much** time. He's got **so many** worries. **Much** human labour was used in the building of the Pyramids. (formal)*
- **A few** is used with countables and **a little** with uncountables. They both have a positive meaning. **A few** means "some", "a small number". **A little** means "some", "a small amount of". *He needed a **little** peace so he went to a quiet island for **a few** days.*
- **Few/Little** both have a negative meaning. **Few** means "not many", "almost none". **Little** means "not much", "almost none". **Few** and **little** are rather formal English. **Very few/very little** are more usual in everyday speech. It is also common to use: **only a little, only a few**. *We're going on holiday for **a few** days. I'm exhausted because I've had **very few** days' holiday. She speaks German quite well but only **a little** French. Bob has **a little** knowledge of mechanics so he can check the car. Jane has **little** knowledge of mechanics so she can't check the car.*
- We use **most/all/some/any/many/a few/several/both/two/one/much/(a) little + of** when a noun follows, preceded by possessives or the words: this, that, these, those, the or a. ***Most of the guests** at the party were English. but: **Most** people prefer to go on holiday at least once a year.*

365 Tick the appropriate box.

Quantifiers	countable nouns	uncountable nouns
1 a lot of/lots of	✔	✔
2 a large/small amount/quantity of		
3 a large/great/good number of		
4 a great/good deal of		
5 (a) few		
6 (a) little		
7 much		
8 plenty of		
9 several		
10 many		
11 one		
12 each		
13 every		
14 both		
15 a couple of		
16 no/not any		
17 most		
18 all		

366 Add "of" where necessary.

1 Most .... people go on holiday in summer.
2 I've seen several .... Richard Gere's films.
3 A few .... friends came round last night.
4 Both .... these shirts are dirty.
5 Many .... his friends are from England.
6 Have you ever read any .... Erica's novels?
7 We bought a few .... antiques on our trip.
8 Please pass me a few .... those nails.
9 There are a few .... children playing outside.
10 Some .... Mike's friends bought him a present.
11 A few .... the boys were in the park.
12 Most .... the cars in the auction were sold.
13 They have hardly any .... money.
14 A lot .... people say he's brilliant.

367 Underline the expressions which can be used.

1 I have **several, many, a few, a little, too much** homework to do.
2 James did **a couple of, much, no** exercises in the morning.
3 They didn't have **much, several, a lot of, any, many** luck this season.
4 Let's plant **one, a little, a few, lots of, some** trees.
5 Read **one, both, each, a couple of, every** page.
6 She eats **a number of, a great deal of, most, no, each** meat.
7 You'll need **a few, a couple of, much, many, a little** tomatoes.
8 She has visited **whole, every, a number of, most, a great deal of** countries in Europe.
9 I have got **a few, several, plenty of, no, a little** time.
10 He wants to earn **some, each, a few, lots of, a great deal of** money.
11 They put **a great deal of, a few, many, a lot of** effort into the project.
12 This car uses **many, a large quantity of, much, a lot of** petrol.
13 **Much, Many, A large number of, Every** people disagree with his decision.

Other and its forms

- **another** = one more apart from those already mentioned. *Can I have **another** piece of cake?* "Another" can also be used with expressions of time, money and distance. *It should take **another** half an hour to reach Plymouth.*
- **others** = several more apart from those already mentioned. *Some articles are about science, **others** are about art.*
- **the other(s)** = the rest. *These are mine; **the others** are John's. This is yours; **the other** is mine.*
- **each other** = one another. *Let's help **each other**.*
- **every other** = alternate. *We visit our grandparents **every other** Sunday.*
- **the other day** = a few days ago. *I ran into Tim while shopping **the other day**.*
- **the other one/ones** refers to a specific alternative. *I don't like this blouse. Can I try **the other one**, please? I don't like these biscuits. Can I have **the other ones**?*

368 Fill in: another, (the) other(s), each other or every other.

1 My sister has ...*another*... two years to go before she finishes her university course.
2 Mr and Mrs White are arriving this evening but .... guests won't be here until tomorrow.
3 Now that John is working in Newcastle we don't get to see .... very often.
4 I don't have time to read a newspaper every day, so I buy one .... day.
5 Two new students started today. One is Jane Lloyd and .... is Ruth Howard.
6 I've got one of the five books I ordered but .... haven't arrived yet.
7 In .... five years I'll be running my own business.
8 Even though Clare and Frances see .... at school every day, they still spend half an hour talking to .... on the phone every evening.
9 One of the most environmentally-friendly means of transport is the bicycle; .... are the train and the tram.
10 Only two students passed the exam. All .... failed.
11 Some people liked the film while .... were shocked by it.

369 Fill in: several, a great deal of, all, a few, a lot of, many, a small amount of, a little, plenty of or a large number of.

Last winter's flood was so destructive that news reporters were calling it "the flood of the century". 1) ...*Several*... people were killed and 2) .... were left homeless. 3) .... damage occurred in one area because a local dam burst. The dam had cracked in 4) .... places and was being repaired. Engineers knew that if the dam burst, 5) .... the houses in the area would be flooded with water, so 6) .... the inhabitants were moved out beforehand. Still, there remained 7) .... people who refused to leave. 8) .... those people died. Those who survived had 9) .... help later, when hundreds of volunteers from neighbouring villages came to their rescue with boats and liferafts. The tragedy is that 10) .... more attention to maintenance rules would have prevented the dam from cracking in the first place.

370 Fill in: a lot, much or many.

Jim: You must be working 1) ...*a lot*... at the moment, I've hardly seen you.
Mary: There's 2) .... of work at the office and I've been doing too 3) ....
Jim: How 4) .... hours are you doing each day?
Mary: About ten, which is far too 5) ....
Jim: So you haven't been doing 6) .... except working?
Mary: Well, I've been going to the gym, but not as 7) .... times as I'd like.
Jim: How 8) .... longer will this go on?
Mary: Only two more weeks, I hope.
Jim: You must be under 9) .... of stress.
Mary: A bit, I'll be glad when it's over.
Jim: We should go out when you've finished.
Mary: Yes, there are so 10) .... other things I want to tell you.

371 **Complete the sentences with a few, (very) few, a little or (very) little.**

1 He has made ...*a few*... enemies already because he has ...*little*... praise for any of his colleagues.
2 I eat .... fatty foods these days as I'm trying to lose .... weight.
3 Desert areas receive .... rain. That's why .... animals can live there.
4 He feels .... depressed because he has had quite .... problems lately.
5 .... people realise what a nice person he is as he has .... to say to anyone. However, after spending .... time with him, I got to know him quite well.
6 Henry puts .... money aside each month so he can buy himself .... luxuries every now and then.
7 I met .... friends in town so we went to "Rozzie's" and had .... cups of coffee and .... chat.
8 We've experienced .... storms here over the winter but, fortunately, they caused .... damage.
9 Mary's had .... experience in this matter so she should be able to give you .... hints on what to do.
10 Would you like .... sugar in your coffee? And, please, have .... biscuits, too.

372 **Underline the correct item.**

The journey by train seemed to take for ever. 1) **All/Every** the passengers looked completely bored. The train had 2) **no/none** of the luxuries you'd usually expect on an inter-city train. Consequently there was 3) **nowhere/anywhere** to buy any food or drink. 4) **A few/Few** of the passengers had been sensible enough to bring their own packed lunches, and 5) **no one/everyone** watched enviously as they unwrapped them. At 6) **each/both** station we stopped, people looked out of the windows hoping to see 7) **some/any** vendors with 8) **something/nothing** in the way of refreshment. But, sadly, there were 9) **no/none** at all. It appeared that 10) **most/all** people would have to spend 11) **all the/the whole** time simply dreaming of a cup of coffee or a cheese sandwich! I had taken a couple of magazines with me but 12) **neither/either** of them held my attention for very long. I had 13) **little/a little** interest in 14) **something/anything** but ending the journey. 15) **Few/A few** had been as boring or uncomfortable as that one and I felt 16) **either/ neither** refreshed nor relaxed when I finally reached my destination.

373 **Underline the correct item.**

The Sydney Opera House

1 Two of the sights I would most like to see **is/are** the Pyramids and Sydney Opera House.
2 Half of the population in that country **are/is** starving.
3 The food in this restaurant **are/is** delicious.
4 Jane and her mother **has/have** blonde hair and blue eyes.
5 Every human being **has/have** a right to food and shelter.
6 Tonight's news **was/were** very interesting.
7 Each of the pupils **have/has** a desk.
8 One of the actors I most admire **are/is** Dustin Hoffman.
9 More news of the earthquake **is/are** coming in now.
10 Maths **is/are** my favourite school subject.
11 They say two weeks **is/are** a long time in politics.
12 The rich **is/are** complaining about high taxes.
13 The police in this city **is/are** very helpful.
14 The French language **is/are** not too difficult.
15 There **are/is** little information on that particular subject.

374 **Underline the correct item.**

How **1) many/much** centuries ago were people walking around on the earth? What would they think about modern life? There must be thousands of things they would find strange. **2) Much/A lot of** aspects of life have changed greatly. For example, there are **3) many/much** fewer green areas than in those days and the **4) numbers/number** of animals is **5) many/much** smaller too. Also, what about the thousands of modern appliances we use? What would they find most confusing, a television or a camera? A refrigerator or a washing machine? There are **6) plenty of/a large amount of** unusual things! What would people from the past have thought about various means of modern transport, such as cars, trains, ships and aeroplanes? There were **7) many/much** centuries between the invention of the wheel and the birth of the modern motor engine. Could people have imagined then that man would one day fly? What about space travel? Even within the first half of this century, rockets existed only in the realms of science fiction. Perhaps from the **8) numbers/number** of our modern inventions there is one which people from the past would have appreciated greatly and would have benefitted from - modern medicine. Of course, **9) a lot of/a lot** human inventions would probably horrify people from the past. What would they think about nuclear bombs and guns? We have created so **10) many/much** weapons! And with all the new technology we have, wouldn't they find it **11) a few/a bit** strange that we still wear animal skins like leather as clothes? If we look at our lives from their point of view, **12) the most/most** things seem odd. But how would we find life if we went back to the past and had to live without all our modern inventions and technology?

375 **Fill in the correct words from the list below to complete the sentences.**

a few, none of, any, half of, all of, each, much, most

1   ...*Most*... teachers have a lot of patience although there are ...*a few*... who are quite intolerant.
2   At the airport they weighed .... suitcase separately.
3   Can you lend me 10p? I haven't got .... money.
4   .... children like ice-cream and chocolate but, strangely enough, ... the children in our family ever eat either of them.
5   Only .... the food was eaten; the rest was thrown away.
6   The class was really pleased because .... them passed the exam; not one of them failed.
7   There isn't .... work to do today, so we can go home early.

376 **Fill in the blanks with one of the words from the list below:**

any, enough, few (of), hardly anything, many, no, plenty of, some, much, very little

Having been invited to a friend's wedding I decided to buy a new outfit. I had **1)** ...*plenty of*... dresses already, but **2)** .... them were suitable for such an occasion. I chose my favourite shop and looked at the selection, but there was **3)** .... to choose from. Fortunately, an assistant approached me and offered to give me **4)** .... help. I told her I had **5)** .... time because the wedding was the next day. She told me I'd come to the right place as very **6)** .... shops offered such a personal service. She showed me a cream suit but it wasn't long **7)** .... Another outfit had too **8)** .... frills for my taste. Finally, she picked out a dress that had **9)** .... frills at all and which had **10)** .... style. As I admired my reflection, the assistant told me that very **11)** .... people looked as good in pink as I did. Satisfied, I decided to buy the dress but realised I didn't have **12)** .... money with me. Fortunately, there was **13)** .... problem as they accepted credit cards. I left, only to return five minutes later, when I realised I had **14)** .... matching hat to wear.

377 ▶ **Fill in: one, either, others, other, another or some.**

The police asked me to help them identify **1)** ...*some*.. thieves they thought I had seen rob a bank. They asked me to look at **2)** .... photographs of known criminals and tell them which **3)** .... looked like the thieves. They told me that **4)** .... had been there earlier and so they now had **5)** .... idea as to what the thieves looked like. They began by showing me the photographs the **6)** .... had chosen. When I told them that none of these photos were familiar, they showed me **7)** .... photographs. We began to put together the thieves' faces from several pictures. We'd take **8)** .... the nose or eyes from **9)** .... photograph, then place it with the mouth of **10)** .... We finally had two clear pictures of what I thought the robbers looked like.

In Other Words

- Paul, Greg and David don't like horror films.
  None of them like/likes horror films.
- Jean is a teacher. Sue is a teacher, too.
  Both of them are teachers.
  Both Jean and Sue are teachers.
- John, Ted and Peter enjoy scuba-diving.
  All of them enjoy scuba-diving.

- There isn't anybody at the door.
  There's nobody at the door.
- Ann doesn't like meat. Lynn doesn't like meat either. Neither of them likes meat.
  Neither Ann nor Lynn like meat.
- Nothing will stop me going.
  There isn't anything that will stop me going.

378 ▶ **Rewrite the sentences without changing the meaning as in the example:**

1 Steve, Tom and Laura have bicycles. ...*All of them have bicycles.* ....
2 Tim works as a postman. Sam works as a postman too. ....
3 Anne, Mary and Helen don't like chocolate. ....
4 There wasn't anybody in the office. ....
5 Sarah hates smoking. Sue hates smoking too. ....
6 There wasn't anything I could do to make him stay. ....
7 Mary doesn't like frozen vegetables. Ted doesn't like frozen vegetables either. ....

Oral Activity 24

Look at the following notes and compare the three hotels using both-neither-all-none.

The Windsor Hotel	The Palm Court Hotel	The Richmond Hotel
no roof garden	no roof garden	no roof garden
4-star restaurant	3-star restaurant	4-star restaurant
swimming pool	no swimming pool	swimming pool
airport transfer service	airport transfer service	airport transfer service
pets not accepted	pets not accepted	pets not accepted
free newspapers available	no newspapers available	no newspapers available
close to town centre	close to town centre	close to town centre
exercise facilities	no exercise facilities	exercise facilities

eg. None of the hotels have roof gardens. ... etc

Writing Activity 10

Look at the notes about the three hotels then write a report to your boss using both, neither, all, none etc.

To: Mr E Jones, Managing Director   From: Alan Parr
Subject: Hotel accommodation

I have made enquiries about three hotels: The Windsor, The Palm Court and The Richmond. Both The Windsor and the Richmond have swimming pools. ...

379 Find the odd word out and write it in the boxes provided.

1	own
2	
3	
4	
5	
6	
7	
8	
9	
10	
11	
12	
13	
14	
15	
16	
17	
18	
19	
20	
21	
22	
23	
24	
25	
26	
27	
28	
29	
30	
31	
32	
33	

1 After we had been to Mary's house, we decided to go to Sophie's own.
2 I haven't got a car but I'm planning to buy one car.
3 The file it is on the desk.
4 This she is Emma speaking.
5 I can't help you as I've got another more job to do.
6 The tin-opener is easy to use it.
7 Neither of the chairman nor the secretary came to the meeting.
8 "I passed all my exams." " That it is great!"
9 This is it the least I can do for you.
10 There it seems to be something wrong with these figures.
11 The twins gave each one other a present on their birthday.
12 You can come any one day you want.
13 This is no any good.
14 Every one student has to have their own books.
15 Both of Elena and Susan are coming to my party.
16 Most of people agree that smoking in public areas should be banned.
17 A lots of people turned up at the airport to welcome the President.
18 He neither speaks Italian nor he understands it.
19 I was sleeping all the day.
20 Each of hotel room has its own private bathroom.
21 Can I have another one piece of cake?
22 The teacher he called to inform my parents of my absence.
23 My books are here; yours books are in your bag.
24 One should keep one's every promises at all costs.
25 We can't afford ourselves to buy a new car.
26 There is hardly any no peace in this house.
27 All of passengers must carry their I.D. cards.
28 Each one applicant was asked to send their C.V.
29 She has a very few friends so she feels lonely.
30 We've got a plenty of time, so let's not hurry.
31 I've been waiting for an opportunity like this my the whole life.
32 Everyone person knows that lying in court is punishable.
33 We need another one article on the subject of fashion.

380 Read the text and underline the correct item.

While I was baking **1) some/any** cakes on Saturday, the phone rang. It was a friend whom I hadn't seen for **2) most/several** years. She had **3) a large number/a great deal** to say to me so the phone call lasted **4) a couple of/plenty of** hours. Suddenly I noticed that **5) the whole/all** room had filled with smoke. I rushed into the kitchen. There was smoke **6) anywhere/everywhere**. I quickly opened the oven door and checked the cakes. Fortunately, the bigger **7) ones/few** could be saved but **8) either/all** of them were black on the outside. I was upset. **9) My/This** kind of accident happens to me quite often. In fact, it happens **10) each other/every other** day!

381 **Complete the sentences using the words in bold.**

1 The only person he didn't invite was Sarah.
   except   He ...*invited everyone except*...Sarah.

2 I have packed everything except my camera.
   only   The .... packed is my camera.

3 He sat alone waiting for his name to be called.
   by   He .... for his name to be called.

4 We haven't got any information about her travel arrangements.
   no   We .... her travel arrangements.

5 I invited Fiona to my party; I invited her husband too.
   both   I invited .... to my party.

6 Nothing can make up for the loss of so many human lives.
   not   There is .... make up for the loss of so many human lives.

7 You can go anywhere except the chairman's office.
   place   The .... go is the chairman's office.

8 They say we've got plenty of time to spare before the show begins.
   is   They say .... to spare before the show begins.

9 There were several filmstars at the premiere of "Dangerous Liaisons".
   few   There .... at the premiere of "Dangerous Liaisons".

10 I have got little time to spare.
   not   I .... to spare.

11 He said, "Emma is against my resigning and so is John."
   nor   He said that .... in favour of his resigning.

12 You'll have to walk a mile to get to the station from here.
   walk   It's ....to the station.

13 The class was so noisy that nobody could hear him at the back of the room.
   make   The class was so noisy that he .... at the back of the room.

14 He is going on holiday for a month at the end of the year.
   a   He is going .... at the end of the year.

15 He told me to leave whenever I felt like it.
   time   He told me .... felt like it.

16 He believes that reckless drivers should be heavily fined.
   who   He believes that .... should be heavily fined.

17 I don't mind being alone at weekends.
   on   I don't mind .... at weekends.

18 He used another person's car to go to work this morning.
   someone   He used .... to work this morning.

19 There wasn't much we could do to help them.
   little   There .... to help them.

20 He has given us so much encouragement.
   deal   He has given us .... encouragement.

21 Let's go to some other place to do our shopping.
   else   Let's go .... our shopping.

22 He said that I could do whatever I wanted as long as it was legal.
   anything   He said that I .... as long as it was legal.

23 It was proved that the three girls had nothing to do with the missing items.
   of   It was proved that .... had anything to do with the missing items.

24 It is true that John doesn't appreciate good music and nor does Judy.
   appreciates   It is true that .... good music.

25 He said that John was coming to his party and so was Lisa.
   only   He said that .... Lisa was coming to his party.

26 I can't make people understand me when I speak German.
   myself   I .... when I speak German.

27 I hope you have fun at the party.
   yourself   I hope .... at the party.

382 **Complete the sentences using the words in bold.**

1 Cynthia regretted sending the letter.
   wished   Cynthia ....*wished she hadn't sent*..the letter.
2 What do you think of my new shoes?
   opinion   What .... my new shoes?
3 The local bakery is making their wedding cake.
   are   They .... made by the local bakery.
4 Jane and her brother both hate cheese.
   and   Jane doesn't like cheese .... her brother.
5 It wasn't necessary to buy me such an expensive present.
   bought   You .... such an expensive present.
6 I don't feel like going to the cinema tonight.
   rather   I .... to the cinema tonight.
7 I had to wait more than an hour to see the hotel manager.
   kept   The hotel manager .... an hour before I saw him.
8 Strawberries should be washed before you eat them.
   washing   Strawberries .... you eat them.
9 Their car broke down, so they missed the concert.
   broken   If their car ...., they wouldn't have missed the concert.
10 I've never stayed in a luxury hotel before.
   first   It's the .... in a luxury hotel.

Do means to carry out a specific action. *Do your homework.* **Make** means to create, manufacture, prepare. *Can you make me a cup of coffee?* **Do** and **make** can also be used idiomatically as follows:

Expressions with "Do"	Expressions with "Make"
one's best/worst, business with sb, a crossword, damage to, one's duty, an exercise, an experiment, good, one's hair, harm, homework, housework, a job, lessons, sth for a living, miracles (for), research, right/wrong, a service, the shopping, a translation, the washing-up, work etc	an appointment, an arrangement, the beds, a cake, certain, changes, coffee, a deal with sb, a decision, a discovery, an effort, an excuse, a fortune, an impression, improvements, a joke, a mess, a mistake, money, a noise, an offer, peace, preparations, progress, a success of sth, sure, a translation, trouble, war etc

383 **Fill in do or make in an appropriate form.**

1 You must ...*make*...a decision now.
2 To .... a fortune you have to .... a lot of hard work.
3 I .... an appointment to see the optician.
4 After he .... his homework, he found he .... a mistake.
5 This drug can .... miracles for people with back problems.
6 They .... a lot of changes in the town centre recently.
7 You .... the right thing by telling the police.
8 He .... an archaeological discovery.
9 After being ill for two weeks, he is now .... an excellent recovery.
10 She .... a lot of research in the field of medicine.
11 I .... an arrangement to meet him at the cinema yesterday.
12 It is important that you .... exercise in order to keep fit.
13 All that smoking .... you harm.
14 He .... an excuse and left the office in a hurry.
15 I always tried .... my best, but she was never satisfied.
16 He .... some research into ancient religions at the moment.
17 If you don't .... an effort, you won't .... any progress.

384 **Look at Appendix 2, then fill in the correct particle(s).**

1 Don't worry. I will **stand** ...*by*... you if you get into trouble.
2 What does that red star you are wearing **stand** ....
3 I had to **stand** .... Steven when he was off sick.
4 You'll really **stand** .... in a crowd if you wear this yellow suit.
5 Timmy is too scared to **stand** .... to his boss.
6 Sheila has **taken** .... her mother in looks. They're very alike.
7 I was **taken** .... completely by all his lies.
8 When he retired, he **took** .... collecting postcards.
9 She **took** my mother .... the headmistress.
10 Please **take** .... your shoes before you come into the house.
11 He **took** .... the company when his father died.
12 We were all **taken** .... by his rude behaviour.

Phrasal Verbs

1 out, by, for, up
2 by, on, up for, for
3 about, in for, out, up
4 up to, for, up, out
5 up to, up, for, in for
6 away, for, after, off
7 on, in, down, out
8 out, to, back, up
9 off, for, aback, in
10 on, up, out, off
11 out, over, up, back
12 aback, to, away, down

385 **Fill in the correct prepositions of place or movement.**

between, down, on top of, over, in/inside, above, in front of, past, up, among, next to/by/beside, from...to, through, under, below, behind, along, opposite, at, round/around, near, outside, on, against, onto, out of, across, to/towards/in the direction of, into

1 .....*in/inside*....   2 ....   3 ....   4 ....   5 ....   6 ....

    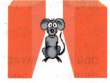

7 ....   8 ....   9 ....   10 ....   11 ....   12 ....

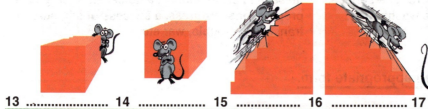 

13 ....   14 ....   15 ....   16 ....   17 ....   18 ....

   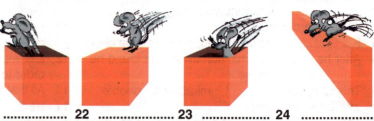

19 ....   20 ....   21 ....   22 ....   23 ....   24 ....

25 ....   26 ....   27 ....   28 ....   29 ....

386 **Choose the correct item.**

TWO WAYS TO IMPROVE YOUR MEMORY

The human memory is an incredibly powerful tool, but **(0)** ...*few*... (**less, few, little, most**) of us make the most of it. In these days of high performance, **(1)** .... (**too, even, always, that**) greater demands are made on our memories, so what can we do to **(2)** .... (**cause, have, induce, make**) them work more efficiently? The **(3)** .... (**earlier, former, old, ancient**) Greeks realised that, in order to remember anything, you have to **(4)** .... (**associate, divide, realise, mix**) it with something that is already fixed in your mind. They **(5)** .... (**found, discovered, invented, recovered**) memory aids or "mnemonics". Verbal mnemonics can be words or rhymes **(6)** .... (**placing, filling, holding, containing**), for example, the first letters of the items of a list to be **(7)** .... (**decided, remembered, settled, disputed**). These were popular in Victorian schools, where memorising lists was a major part of "education". Although modern educationalists tend to look **(8)** .... (**up, down on, over, in**) this method of learning, it is still sometimes necessary, as any medical student will tell you. Visual mnemonics have recently been found to be especially **(9)** .... (**powerful, colourful, casual, assisting**). So next **(10)** .... (**thing, occasion, time, date**) you have to remember how items are **(11)** .... (**relatives, married, related, jointed**), say for an exam, **(12)** .... (**build, show, reduce, create**) a "mind map". You can draw a plan with items radiating from a central point and use different coloured pens to make the relationship between items **(13)** .... (**clear, available, flexible, moving**). You learn as you draw and then the **(14)** .... (**seen, watched, visual, regarded**) image is easy to **(15)** .... (**reset, replace, recall, redo**).

387 **Read the text. Some of the lines are correct and some have a word which should not be there. If a line is correct, put a tick (✔) in the space provided. If a line has a word which should not be there, write it in the space provided.**

WHAT IS SMART?

0	The British are ever generally regarded as the most	*ever*
00	untidily dressed people in Europe, but I have often	✓
1	thought that to the opposite is true. Take, for example,	
2	the wearing of jeans. In many southern European	
3	countries, it seems more perfectly acceptable for	
4	both teachers and office staff to wear jeans, whereas	
5	in Britain jeans are been considered far too	
6	casual and are only acceptable if the work is so	
7	dirty or unskilled. One office workers in Britain must	
8	follow a very much strict dress code. Even in the hottest	
9	weather, male employees are most required to wear	
10	a suit and tie and female employees who must be	
11	dressed in a skirt and tights. In these schools, the	
12	dress code is not quite so formal, but staff still tend	
13	to wear out shirts and smartish trousers or skirts.	
14	The British may not be as stylish as like their European	
15	counterparts, but a dress code still does then exist.	

12 Questions / Short Answers

Do you want to come to my party?

Yes, I do! What's the address?

25, Broad St. Just press the bell with your elbow.

Why should I press the bell with my elbow?

Well, you'll be carrying my present, won't you?

Yes/No Questions

To form questions we put the auxiliary (can, be, will, have etc) before the subject. We use **do/does** to form questions in Present Simple and **did** to form questions in Past Simple. She is studying. ➡ **Is she** studying? He hates bowling. ➡ **Does he hate** bowling? (not: ~~Does he hates~~ bowling?) Kim left an hour ago. ➡ **Did Kim leave** an hour ago? (not: ~~Did Kim left~~ an hour ago?)

Wh- questions

Wh- questions begin with a question word (who, what, where, why, when, whose, which, how etc). *"What did you buy?" "A scarf." "How do you get to work?" "By bus."* When there is a preposition, it usually goes at the end of the question, though in formal English it can be put before the question word. *Who is this letter from? (more usual) From whom is this letter? (formal)*

We use questions to ask for information or permission. We also use questions to make suggestions, requests, offers or invitations.

Asking for information: *"How much does it cost?" "£10."*
Asking for permission: *"May I use your phone?" "Of course you may."*
Making suggestions: *"Shall we have a party?" "Yes, let's."*
Making requests: *"Could you carry this for me, please?" "Yes, of course."*
Making offers: *"Would you like some orange juice?" "Yes, please."*
Making invitations: *"Would you like to spend this weekend with us?" "Yes, I'd love to."*

388 First form questions, then write the speech situation for each question: asking for information/permission or making suggestions/requests/offers/invitations.

1 (we invite/David to dinner tonight?)   *Shall we invite David to dinner tonight? (suggestion)*
2 (you want a biscuit?) ....
3 (How far/it be from your house to the station?) ....
4 (you like/come sailing at the weekend?) ....
5 (you have/a good time last night?) ....
6 (you like/come to the cinema?) ....
7 (you help/me with my bags please?) ....
8 (we have/a party for your birthday?) ....
9 (Who/you see at the coffee shop yesterday?) ....
10 (you like/some coffee?) ....
11 (What time/your plane leave?) ....
12 (I have/a look at your newspaper?) ....

● We normally use the following question words to ask about:

people	things/animals/ actions	place	time	quantity	manner	reason
Who Whose Which What	What Which	Where	When How long What time How often	How much How many	How	Why

● **Who** is used without a noun to ask about people. *Who wrote "Gone With the Wind"?*
● **Whose** is used to express possession. *"Whose gloves are these?" "They're Tony's."*
● **Which** is used for people, animals or things alone or before nouns, one/ones or of. *Which is their office? Which coat is his? I've got two dictionaries. Which one would you like to use? Which of these applicants will be called for an interview?*
  Which is normally used when there is a limited choice. *Which are your favourite precious stones - diamonds or emeralds? (there are only two kinds of precious stones to choose from - limited choice)*
  Which can also be used with the comparative and superlative. *Which is cheaper, a saloon car or a convertible? Which is the easiest way to do it?*
● **What** is used alone or before a noun to ask about things. *What can I do for you? What size shoes do you wear?* **What** is also used for people, animals and things when there is an unlimited choice. *What kind of films do you enjoy watching? (there are many films to choose from - unlimited choice)*
● **What** can also be used in these patterns: What ... like?, What ... for?, What colour?, What size?, What kind/sort?, What time?, What is he like?, What is it used for? etc. *What are you waiting here for?*
● **What + be...like** asks for a description of character; what...look like asks for a description of physical appearance. *"What is Fiona like?" "She's kind and helpful." "What does Fiona look like?" "She's tall and slim."*
● **What** and **which** are sometimes both possible. *What/Which subjects do you teach?*

389 Fill in: what, when, which, who, whose, why, how, how many, how much, how often, what time, where or how long.

1 "...*Who*... has been wearing my coat?" "Sue has."
2 "..................... pencil case is this?" "It's John's."
3 "..................... one of you is the tallest?" "I am."
4 "........................ are you doing tomorrow?" "I'm going to the beach."
5 "........................ size are your shoes?" "Size 5."
6 "........................ star sign are you?" "I'm Libra."
7 "..................... did you go on holiday?" "I went to the Caribbean."
8 "............... did you start French lessons?" "Two years ago."
9 "............................ have you lived in America?" "Three years."
10 "............................. do you go to the cinema?" "About once a month."
11 "............................. shall we meet for dinner?" "About 8 o'clock."
12 "................................... cheese would you like?" "400 grams please."
13 "............................... cars has your family got?" "We've got two."
14 "..................... do you get to school?" "By bus."
15 "........................ did you call him?" "To confirm his travel arrangements."
16 "........................ motorbike is parked outside?" "It's Julie's."

390 Make questions from the following sentences. The words in bold should be the answer to your question.

1 It costs **ten pounds**. ....*How much does it cost?* ....
2 Janet lives **in the centre of London**. ....
3 I wash my hair **three times a week**. ....
4 **Her friend** rented a new apartment. ....
5 Ann is **friendly**. ....
6 **Mrs Brown** wants to see Sally. ....
7 The weather is **hot** today. ....

8 They are **Mr Brown's** children. ....

9 He has worked here **for twelve years**. ....

10 It takes **two hours** to get from here to London. ....

11 This record costs **£9**. ....

12 Megan has been **to Australia**. ....

13 He hasn't done his homework **because he didn't have time**. ....

14 ET was directed by **Steven Spielberg**. ....

15 **Rachel's** grandmother was a famous actress. ....

16 We're going to leave **at 6 pm**. ....

17 **The sad music** made Rosemary cry. ....

18 Sue's new neighbours are **Richard and Judy Day**. ....

19 They'll have finished painting the house **by Wednesday**. ....

20 The maths test was **difficult**. ....

21 I didn't buy it because **it cost too much**. ....

22 It took me **two hours** to finish the report. ....

23 He was travelling **by boat**. ....

391 **Fill in: which or what.**

Jim: **1)** ...*What*... shall we do this afternoon?

Tim: We could go to an art gallery.

Jim: That's a good idea. **2)** .... one?

Tim: We could go to the Barbican or the Tate.
3) .... one would you like to go to?

Jim: I don't know. **4)** .... exhibitions have they got on at the moment?

Tim: I'm not sure. I think the Barbican has got Van Gogh's early paintings and the Tate has got a special Picasso exhibition.

Jim: Oh, **5)** .... artist do you prefer?

Tim: I think probably Van Gogh. **6)** .... about you?

Jim: Yes, I agree. I particularly love his early work.

Tim: Great. Well, let's go to the Barbican then. **7)** .... time do you want to go?

Jim: I'm ready any time.

Tim: OK, let's go now. The only problem is, I don't know **8)** .... station to get off at.

Jim: Oh, I've got a guidebook in one of the drawers in my desk.

Tim: **9)** .... drawer, the one on the left or the right?

Jim: On the left, I think.

Tim: **10)** .... does it look like?

Jim: It's red and yellow.

392 **Use the prepositions in brackets to write questions to match the statements.**

1 Fred is very unhappy. What ....*is he unhappy about?* .... (about)

2 I went to the cinema last night. Who .... (with)

3 My grandfather comes from France. Where exactly .... (from)

4 Craig had an argument. Who .... (with)

5 My brother's going on holiday tomorrow. Where .... (to)

6 I bought a book yesterday. What .... (about)

7 I got a letter today. Who .... (from)

8 I fixed the shelf today. What .... (with)

9 I've got to buy a present. Who .... (for)

Subject/Object Questions

If **who**, **which** or **what** are the subject of the question, the word order is the same as in statements (subject questions). If they are the object of the question, the verb is in question form (object questions).

subject		object
Keith	*invited*	*Stella.*
Who *invited* Stella? (not: ~~Who did invite Stella?~~)		

subject		object
Stella	*invited*	**Fiona.**
Who **did** Stella **invite**?		

---

393 **Write questions for the sentences below. The words in bold should be the answers.**

1 **Josh** left the window open. ......*Who left the*..... *window open?* ....
2 Chris saved **a little girl**. ....
3 Claire likes **eating**. ....
4 **Jenny** likes Spain. ....
5 He shouted at **Jim**. ....
6 **Jane** saw the postman. ....
7 Shakespeare wrote **Hamlet**. ....
8 She hates **strawberries.** ....
9 **Steven** has no patience. ....
10 Sally loves **driving her car**. ....

11 Trevor hit **James**. ....
12 **Tom** went out with Tim. ....
13 Terry drove **a tractor**. ....
14 **Walter** stole a wallet. ....
15 Jane sent Paul **a letter**. ....
16 **The tiger** lives in the jungle. ....
17 **Jack** has read the newspaper. ....
18 The farmer chased **the fox**. ....
19 Maria opened **the window**. ....
20 **Ann** typed the letters. ....
21 **Kate** speaks five languages. ....

---

394 **Fill in: who, what, whose or which.**

1 "..............*Who*........... had the scissors last?" "John did."
2 "................................ kind of shoes do you want to buy?" "I want to buy boots."
3 "................................ did the thief look like?" "He was tall and thin."
4 "................................ trousers are these?" "They are John's."
5 "................................ would you like for Christmas?" "I would like a bicycle."
6 "................................ size shirt do you take?" "I take a size sixteen."
7 "................................ colour do you want?" "I would like the blue one."
8 "................................ won the race?" "I think Nigel Mansel did."
9 "................................ pop group do you like best?" "I like The Dooleys best."
10 "................................ is your favourite painting?" "Guernica".
11 "................................ house was broken into last week?" "Bill's was."
12 "................................ did you go to the cinema with last night?" "I went with Sam."
13 "................................ is your favourite book?" "Jane Eyre."

---

395 **Fill in: who, what or which.**

A: **1)** ...*What*... is the best way to get to France from London?
B: Well, it depends. **2)** .... type of journey do you want?
A: A cheap one! But I've got a friend who gets seasick.
B: Don't go on the ferry then! There's a train or a hovercraft - or you could fly of course.
A: **3)** .... is the cheapest?
B: The train and the hovercraft cost about the same but I'm not sure **4)** .... is the most comfortable. Of course, the train takes you straight to Paris.
A: Really? To **5)** .... station?
B: La Gare du Nord I think, but I don't know **6)** .... the arrival times are.
A: **7)** .... could give me that information?
B: Try ringing the tourist office.

12 Questions / Short Answers

396 Write questions to which the bold type words are the answers.

One of **Jim's** dogs ran away today. It happened **this morning**. It escaped **by running through the open gate**. **The postman** left it open. He was delivering **a parcel** to Jim's house. **The little white dog** ran out of the gate, but the black one stayed inside. Luckily, it was wearing a **dog-tag**. A young girl phoned Jim **an hour later**. She had found the dog **outside the butcher's**. It was eating **sausages**. **The butcher** was quite angry. The girl arranged to meet Jim **at 5 o'clock**.

1 ....*Whose dog ran away today*................?
2 ....?
3 ....?
4 ....?
5 ....?
6 ....?

7 ....?
8 ....?
9 ....?
10 ....?
11 ....?
12 ....?

Oral Activity 25

The students in teams, or in pairs, ask and answer questions based on the text.

A farmer, Isaac Jones, reported having seen a UFO. A scientist from the Centre for Extraterrestrial Activities interviewed him. It was around 11 pm and Isaac was out on the porch. All of a sudden he saw the sky light up. Then an object like a huge plate appeared out of nowhere. The horizon turned into a rainbow of colours. He was shocked. His wife came out. She started screaming because she thought they were being invaded by Martians. A strong wind started blowing. The lower part of the plate was surrounded by flames. It all lasted about five minutes. It was his wife's idea to contact the centre. They knew it was a UFO because it looked so strange.

Team A S1: *What time was it?*
Team B S1: *Around 11 pm.*

Team B S2: *Where was Isaac?*
Team A S2: *Out on the porch.*   etc

Indirect Questions

- **Indirect questions** are used when we ask for information politely. They are introduced with **Do you know...?, Can/Could you tell me ...?, Have you any idea...? + question word** or **if/whether**. *Do you know how* old Sam is? *Could you tell me how long* it takes to get there? *Have you any idea when* she is leaving? *Do you know if/whether* there are any vacancies here?
- The word order of indirect questions is the same as in statements (subject + verb).
  Can you tell me **where you saw him**? (not: Can you tell me where ~~did you see~~ him?)
  Do you know whether they are getting married? (not: Do you know whether ~~are they getting~~ married?)
  How far **did they travel**? ➡ *Do you know how far* **they travelled**?
  When **do you plan** to move? ➡ *Can you tell me when* **you plan** to move?

397 Turn the following into indirect questions.

1 What flavour is this drink? Can ....*you tell me what flavour this drink is?*............................
2 Why isn't Bob here yet? Do ....
3 What is the price of the car? Could ....

4   Where is the secretary? Could..

5   Has the film started yet? Could ....

6   What time does the last bus leave? Can ....

7   What does "laconic" mean? Have ....

8   Does this customer have credit facilities? Could ....

9   How much does Steve earn? Do ....

10 Did they appear in court? Have ....

11 What is the capital of Austria? Do ....

12 Where did I put my keys? Have ....

Negative Questions

- **Negative questions** are formed with not but there is a difference in word order between the short and full form.

  (Short form) **Didn't** they inform you? **Haven't** they returned yet? (auxiliary + n't + subject + verb)

  (Full form) **Did they not** inform you? **Have they not** returned yet? (auxiliary + subject + not + verb)

  We normally use the short form in everyday speech and the full form only for emphasis.

- **Negative questions are used to express:**

  a) **surprise** *Don't you* know who Pelé is?

  b) **annoyance/sarcasm** *Can't you* keep quiet for a second?

  c) **expectation of a "Yes"-answer** *Don't you* think she's rather mean?

  d) **wish to persuade sb** *Won't you* tell me who did it?

398 **In the following dialogues, make negative questions using the words given and decide if the expected response would be Yes or No, as in the example:**

1   A: You're late! ! ...*Didn't you set your alarm clock*...? (set your alarm clock)

    B: ...*Yes*..., but I missed the bus.

2   A: That was John on the other side of the road. ....? (notice him)

    B: .... I can't see a thing without my glasses.

3   A: You've been going to the gym for weeks now. ....? (lose any weight)

    B: .... I don't know what I'm doing wrong.

4   A: You're not wearing a coat! ....? (be cold)

    B: .... I'm used to weather like this.

5   A: Your mother is a maths teacher. ....? (help you)

    B: ...., but I still can't understand maths at all.

6   A: Why can't you come out tonight? ....? (do/homework)

    B: ...., but there's a TV programme I want to watch.

7   A: Why haven't you called Jane? ....? (have her number)

    B: ...., but I've been too busy to call.

8   A: Why didn't you go to Cornwall this year? ....? (want to go)

    B: .... I wanted to go somewhere different.

9   A: This cake is delicious. ....? (give me the recipe)

    B: ...., I'm sorry. It's a family secret.

399 **Fill in the right questions and verb forms.**

For a surprise, Donna decided to meet her friend Paul at the airport on his return from six months in Africa. She phoned his mother to ask about the flight. "**1)** ...*Which airport is he arriving at?*..." (which/airport/arrive at). "At Heathrow Airport I think," his mother said. "**2)** .... (what time/expect) him to land?" Donna asked. " About 8 tonight, if there are no delays," his mother replied. **3)** "........................... .... (who/meet) him?" Donna asked. "Nobody, dear," his mother said. "**4)** .... (what/think) about me meeting him?" Donna asked. "That's a great idea," his mother said. "**5)** .... (what/be) the best way to get there?" Donna inquired. "The M25, but **6)** .... (who/drive) you?" Paul's mother asked. "Oh, my dad will. Thanks for your help. See you later," said Donna.

Question Tags

- **Question tags** are short questions which we add at the end of a statement. We use them to ask for **confirmation** of, or **agreement** with, our statement. *They're leaving soon, **aren't they**?*
- Question tags are formed with an auxiliary verb and the appropriate personal pronoun. They take the same auxiliary verb as in the statement if there is one, otherwise they take **do/does** (Present Simple) or **did** (Past Simple). *He **has been** at home, **hasn't he**? She **arrived** early, **didn't she**?*
- A positive statement is followed by a negative question tag, and a negative statement is followed by a positive question tag. *She **is** going to apply for that job, **isn't she**? You **weren't** listening, **were you**? They **called** off the wedding, **didn't they**?*
- **Everyone/someone/anyone/no one** form their question tags with an **auxiliary verb + they**. ***Everyone** knows the way to the church, **don't they**?*
- **Question tags** can be said with a **rising intonation** when we are not sure and we expect an answer, or a **falling intonation** when we are sure and don't really expect an answer.
  *He has been to Paris, **hasn't he**?↗ (not sure)*   *She has got a pet dog, **hasn't she**?*↘
- **Question tags** can also be affirmative - affirmative. If said with a rising intonation, we mean "Tell me more". *She's getting married, **is she**?* If said with a falling intonation, we express negative feelings such as disappointment or disapproval. We don't expect an answer. *I'll get my money back, **will I**?*
- **Echo tags** are a response to an affirmative or negative sentence. They are used in everyday speech to ask for **more information,** to show **interest, concern, anger, surprise** etc.
  Affirmative: *He's leaving. - **He is, isn't he**? (confirmation)   He's leaving. - **He is**? (surprise)*
  Negative: *He isn't leaving. - **He isn't, is he**? (confirmation)   He isn't leaving. - **He isn't**? (surprise)*

Study the following question tags.

1	"I am"	"aren't I?"	*I am shorter than her, **aren't I**?*
2	"I used to"	"didn't I?"	*She used to like it here, **didn't she**?*
3	Imperative	"will you/won't you?" "can you/could you?"	*Please leave the door open, **will you/won't you/ can you/could you**?*
4	"Let's"	"shall we?"	*Let's consult a specialist, **shall we**?*
5	"Let me/him" etc	"will you/won't you?	*Let the children decide, **will you/won't you**?*
6	"Don't"	"will you?"	*Don't bother to call me again, **will you**?*
7	"I have" (= possess)	"haven't I?"	*He has got a yacht, **hasn't he**?*
8	"I have" (used idiomatically)	" don't I?"	*They had a party last night, **didn't they**?*
9	"There is/are"	"isn't/aren't there?"	*There is some coffee for me, **isn't there**?*
10	"This/That is"	'isn't it?"	*This coat is Peter's, **isn't it**?*

400 Add the question tags then read the sentences with a rising or falling intonation.

	sure	not sure
1		✔
2	✔	
3		✔
4		✔
5	✔	
6		✔
7	✔	
8	✔	
9		✔
10		✔

1 There's more food, ...*isn't there?*............?
2 No one knows me, ...?
3 Let me try it, ...?
4 They won't go without us, ...?
5 This is our stop, ...?
6 You used to smoke, ...?
7 You want a pizza, ...?
8 We shouldn't have done that, ...?
9 The tigers escaped, ...?
10 He had an accident, ...?

401 Fill in the blanks with the correct question tags.

Mark: Excuse me. You're Jack Trap the famous singer, **1)** ...*aren't you?*....
Jack: Why do you ask? You're not an autograph hunter, **2)** ....?
Mark: Yes, I am actually. There's nothing wrong with that, **3)** ....?
Jack: I don't suppose you can understand just how tired we stars get of signing autographs, **4)** ....?
Mark: No, I suppose not. But I bet you didn't complain about it when you weren't famous, **5)** ....?

Jack: Look. Let's get this straight, **6)** ....?I don't feel like signing autographs today, OK?
Mark: Oh, come on. One little signature isn't much to ask for, **7)** ....?
Jack: You don't give up easily, **8)** ....?
Mark: No.
Jack: OK. Here you are. Now leave me in peace, **9)** ....?
Mark: You're a pretty rude person, **10)** ....?

Oral Activity 26

The students in teams use the picture as a stimulus to make sentences with question tags. Each correct sentence gets 1 point. The team with the most points is the winner.

Team A S1: **There's been a car crash, hasn't there?**
Team B S1: **The ambulance has just arrived, hasn't it?**
Team A S2: **The bicycle is damaged, isn't it?**
Team B S2: **The policeman is asking questions, isn't he? etc**

Short Answers

Short answers are used to avoid repetition of the question asked before. **Positive short answers** are formed with **Yes + personal pronoun + auxiliary verb** (do, can, will, have, may etc). *"Will she be leaving soon?" "Yes, she will."* **Negative short answers** are formed with **No + personal pronoun + negative auxiliary verb.** *"Did he arrive on time?" "No, he didn't."*

402 **Complete the dialogue using short answers.**

A: Have you decided what you want to do when you leave school?
B: Yes, 1) ...*I have*... . I saw the careers advisor yesterday.
A: Did he give you any ideas?
B: Yes, 2) .... He was very helpful.
A: Are you going to look for a job?
B: No, 3) .... I want to go to college.
A: Did you pass all your exams?
B: Yes, 4) ....
A: Are your grades good enough?
B: Yes, 5) .... I worked really hard and
    got very good grades.
A: Were your parents pleased?
B: Yes, 6) ....
    They said they'd buy me a present.
A: Can you choose it yourself?
B: Yes, 7) ....
A: Will you have a party?

B: Yes, 8) ....
A: Do you know when?
B: Yes, 9) .... Next Saturday. I'd like you to come.
A: Can I bring a friend?
B: Yes, 10) .... See you on Saturday.

403 **Add question tags and short answers to the statements below.**

1 "You like Chinese food, ...*don't you*...?" "Yes, ...*I do*... ."
2 "You've seen Peter recently, ...?" "No, ..."
3 "He isn't leaving, ...?" "No, ..."
4 "She won't marry him, ...?" "Yes, ..."
5 "He wants to go out tomorrow, ...?" "Yes, ..."
6 "You've travelled around Australia, ...?" "No, ..."
7 "She thinks I was right, ...?" "Yes, ..."
8 "I am a bit taller than you, ...?" "Yes, ..."
9 "They set up their business last year, ...?" "No, ..."
10 "They'll probably be late, ...?" "Yes, ..."

So - Neither/Nor - But

● **So + auxiliary verb + personal pronoun/noun** (positive addition to a positive sentence). *She owns a car.* **So do we.** *(We own a car too.) Ted listened to the news.* **So did Mary.** *(Mary listened to the news too.)*

● **Neither/Nor + auxiliary verb + personal pronoun/noun** (negative addition to a negative sentence). *Jim can't come tonight.* **Neither/Nor can I.** *not:* ~~So can I.~~

● **But + personal pronoun/noun + affirmative auxiliary verb** (positive contrast to negative statement). *Katie has never flown in a plane before,* **but I have.** *Mike hasn't finished,* **but James has.**

● **But + personal pronoun/noun + negative auxiliary verb** (negative contrast to positive statement). *He looks like my father,* **but I don't.** *Mike has already finished,* **but John hasn't.**

● **When we wish to express surprise at what sb has said, we use so + subject + auxiliary verb.** *Clare: Look, that man's wearing a wig. Tina:* **So he is!**

404 Write sentences with so or neither as in the example:

	Tom	Beth	Ray	Pam
like dancing		✔	✔	
travel abroad	✔			✔
work in town	✔		✔	
keep a pet		✔	✔	

1 Beth likes dancing. *So does Ray, but Tom and Pam don't.*
2 Pam travels abroad. ....
3 Tom works in town. ....
4 Ray keeps a pet. ....
5 Pam doesn't work in town. ....
6 Ray doesn't travel abroad. ....
7 Pam doesn't keep a pet. ....
8 Tom doesn't like dancing. ....

405 Tick which statements are positive additions and which show confirmation or surprise.

		positive addition	surprise/confirmation
1	He's telling that awful joke again! - So he is!		✔
2	He's looking for another job. - So is she.		
3	They go abroad every year. - So do we.		
4	I've passed my exams! - So you have!		
5	I've bought a new house. - So has John.		
6	He's won first prize! - So he has!		
7	I've been promoted! - So you have!		
8	She's leaving her job. - So is he.		
9	He's moving to London. - So is Barbara.		
10	Shelley is acting the fool again! - So she is!		

Asking for permission / Making requests	**Giving/Refusing permission / Answering requests**
Can I/Could I make a phone call? **May I/Might I** use your car?	Yes, you can./Yes, of course (you can)./No, you can't. Yes, you may./Yes, of course (you may)./No, you may not./I'd rather you didn't./I'm afraid not.
Making suggestions/invitations	**Answering suggestions/invitations**
Will you/Would you/Would you like to have tea with me some day? **Shall we** have tea some day?	I'd like to./I'd love to./Yes, all right./I'm afraid I can't./ I'd love to but I can't./I'm sorry I can't.
Making offers	**Answering offers**
Shall I/we, Can I/we, Would you like me to help you move the sofa?	Yes, please./No, thank you./No, thanks.

406 Fill in short answers as in the example:

1 A: May I use your telephone?
   B: ...*Yes, you may*..., but don't talk for too long.
2 A: Will you have dinner with me tonight?
   B: .... What about 6.30?
3 A: Shall I take your library books back for you?
   B: .... I'm too busy to do it myself.
4 A: Would you like sugar in your coffee?
   B: .... I'm on a diet.

5 A: Can I have some time off work?
   B: .... I need you here at the moment.
6 A: Would you like to come to Paris?
   B: .... I don't have any other plans.
7 A: Shall we play golf today?
   B: .... I've arranged to play squash.
8 A: Shall I take your dog for a walk?
   B: .... He hasn't been out all day.

So - Not

So and not can be used in short answers after: **think, hope, expect, suppose, I'm afraid, guess, it seems, say, tell sb, it appears, believe** or **imagine.**

I think so - I don't think so/I think not	It seems so - It doesn't seem so/It seems not
I hope so - I hope not	He says so/He said so - He didn't say so
I expect so - I don't expect so/I expect not	He told me so - He didn't tell me so
I suppose so - I don't suppose so/I suppose not	I guess so - I guess not
I'm afraid so - I'm afraid not	I believe so - I don't believe so/I believe not
It appears so - It doesn't appear so/It appears not	I imagine so - I don't imagine so/I imagine not

"Will they buy it?" **"I hope so."** *"Is he planning to retire?"* **"He didn't say so."**

407 **Fill in the blanks with phrases using the verbs given and so or not.**

1 A: She isn't coming then? (guess)
   B: ...*I guess not*... . It's already 10 o'clock.

2 A: Is he a good singer? (imagine)
   B: .... Everybody shouts "Stop!" when he sings.

3 A: Is a cauliflower as beautiful as a rose? (think)
   B: .... A rose is far more beautiful.

4 A: Is it serious, doctor? (afraid)
   B: .... You'll need an operation.

5 A: Will he be better soon, doctor? (expect)
   B: .... The operation was successful.

6 A: Can you fix it? (think)
   B: .... It's not badly damaged.

7 A: Was it murder? (appear)
   B: .... Somebody has admitted doing it.

8 A: Is David coming? (hope)
   B: .... Julie will be terribly disappointed if he doesn't.

9 A: Does she like parties? (appear)
   B: .... She's been laughing all night.

10 A: Have they caught the murderer? (believe)
    B: .... They're still looking.

11 A: Is he going to London on Saturday? (tell me)
    B: I doubt it. ....

12 A: Is Joe going to the cinema with Sara? (expect)
    B: .... He hates horror films.

13 A: Are you going away for Easter? (suppose)
    B: .... I've only got two days off.

14 A: Will you see Jo later? (afraid)
    B: .... She's gone away for a few days.

15 A: So Tony isn't coming with us? (appear)
    B: .... He says he has to work.

16 A: Has John got a new job? (appear)
    B: .... He handed in his resignation today.

Oral Activity 27

Students in pairs look at the information below. One student asks the question and the other answers using the verb in brackets and a reason of his/her own as in the example:

		Mrs Brown	Mrs Green	Mrs Smith
1	earn a lot of money	(Yes/believe)	(No/think)	(No/suppose)
2	have many friends	(Yes/imagine)	(No/suppose)	(No/think)
3	going to decorate the house	(No/suppose)	(Yes/appear)	(Yes/think)
4	have children	(No/guess)	(Yes/think)	(Yes/say)
5	go away at weekends	(No/believe)	(Yes/think)	(No/guess)
6	stay up late at night	(Yes/seem)	(No/imagine)	(Yes/suppose)
7	go out a lot	(Yes/imagine)	(Yes/appear)	(No/think)
8	paid a lot for the house	(Yes/think)	(No/guess)	(No/believe)
9	have lots of pets	(No/suppose)	(Yes/afraid)	(Yes/appear)
10	buy a new car	(Yes/say)	(Yes/expect)	(No/suppose)

eg. S1: **Does Mrs Brown earn a lot of money?**
     S2: **I believe so. She seems to spend a lot.**

408 **Complete the sentences using the words in bold.**

1 My suitcase is lighter than yours.
   not My suitcase is ....*not as/so heavy as* .... yours.
2 They have been discussing the plans for over a year.
   under The plans .... for over a year.
3 The room where the baby sleeps is pink.
   in The room .... is pink.
4 I haven't seen Christine since Easter.
   last I .... Easter.
5 Mr Jones left and so did his wife.
   leave Not only .... also his wife.
6 You'll fall over if you don't look where you're going.
   unless You'll fall .... where you're going.
7 We'd prefer you to pay cash for the goods.
   paid We .... cash for the goods.
8 Is he the man you spoke to when you phoned?
   him Is .... when you phoned?
9 "Why don't we invite Sue for dinner?" he said.
   inviting He .... for dinner.
10 Do you think they will finish the project on time?
    finished Do you think .... on time?
11 He got married last year.
    that It .... got married.

409 **Look at Appendix 2, then fill in the correct particle.**

1 Can you **turn** ...*down*... the radio; it's too loud.
2 This factory's been **turning** .... TV sets for 25 years now.
3 In a crisis, I always **turn** .... my father for help.
4 We were surprised when John **turned** .... at Ann's wedding.
5 They **turned** the attic .... a playroom.
6 **Turn** .... the page and start reading silently.
7 I'm rather tired, I think I'll **turn** ....
8 The face of the statue had been **worn** .... by wind and rain.
9 All excitement about the trip **wore** .... when we realised how much money was needed.
10 Your shoes are **worn** .... You'd better buy a new pair.
11 It took me a long time to **work** .... the solution to my problems.
12 My father started as an office boy and **worked** his way .... to become a manager.

	Phrasal Verbs
1	on, off, in, down
2	up, into, out, over
3	away, on, in, to
4	up, in, off, down
5	on, to, into, out
6	over, up, out, on
7	on, in, down, off
8	up, in, away, over
9	off, down, away, out
10	in, out, on, off
11	on, out, up, down
12	up, down, on, out

410 **Look at Appendix 3 on page 246, then fill in the correct preposition.**

Why not take a break **1)** ...*from*... Wales this year! A relaxing holiday **2)** .... another place would be a nice change. Treat yourself to a long weekend **3)** .... one of Cornwall's top hotels or, alternatively, try a week **4)** .... one of the area's many campsites. The best way to discover Cornwall is either **5)** .... foot or **6)** .... boat or, for the really energetic, why not explore the countryside **7)** .... a bicycle? When you are ready for a bite to eat, treat yourself to lunch **8)** .... one of Cornwall's many charming pubs. And for an exciting and educational day out, drop in **9)** .... the British Marine Life Museum. Whatever you decide to do, there's something for everyone in Cornwall.

411 Look at Appendix 3 on page 253, then fill in the correct prepositions of time.

1) ...*In*... 1993 I spent Christmas with my family at the Royal Hotel in Chester. We arrived 2) .... 10 am 3) .... Christmas Eve and decided to spend the morning shopping. However, 4) .... less than an hour, we were so exhausted that we decided to go back to the hotel. 5) .... lunchtime, we ordered some sandwiches in the restaurant and then had a quick rest before beginning our tour of the city 6) .... the afternoon. 7) .... midnight, we went to a Christmas service at the Cathedral and then returned to the hotel for a well-earned night's sleep. 8) .... Christmas morning, I woke up to hear my sisters knocking on the door. 9) .... that time they still believed in Father Christmas and wanted to see if he had left any presents. Once all the excitement was over, we spent a relaxing morning in the hotel lounge and then, 10) .... noon, we all filed into the restaurant for the spectacular Christmas buffet. Everyone ate so much that we spent the afternoon recovering in front of the televison.

412 Think of the word which best fits each space. Write only one word in each space.

CORAL

Coral reefs are (0) ...*the*... largest structures formed by living creatures (1) .... earth; the Great Barrier Reef near Australia, (2) .... instance, is nearly 2000 kilometres long. They are composed (3) .... the remains of sea creatures, the skeletons of (4) .... become part of the reef when they die. Coral has (5) .... used to make jewellery for a long time because of (6) .... beautiful colours, but now it has a new use. Scientists have discovered that it is suitable (7) .... replacing bones in the human body. Bone can be taken from another part of the body for this (8) ...., but this causes the patient a (9) .... of distress because he must have two operations. Alternatively, metal can be used, but bone cannot naturally assimilate (10) .... a material. The use of coral is not completely free (11) .... problems, as it absorbs poisonous metals easily, which (12) .... harm the human body. On the other (13) ...., its structure is very like that of bone and is less likely to (14) .... rejected by a patient's body. Two researchers in France have already carried (15) .... a number of successful replacements and, with luck, the success stories will continue.

413 Read the text. Some of the lines are correct and some have a word which should not be there. If a line is correct, put a tick (✔) in the space provided. If a line has a word which should not be there, write it in the space provided.

CROSSWORDS

0	A crossword is a form of word puzzle which it is thought to	0 *It* ▭⁰■
00	have originated as a children's game in Britain in the	00 ✔ ▭⁰⁰■
1	19th century. "The New York World" began to publishing	1
2	crosswords in 1913. By the 1923, newspaper crosswords	2
3	had become a popular trend, spreading across the America	3
4	and later Britain. As like a feature in daily newspapers,	4
5	the crossword is now popular in many languages all over the	5
6	world. A crossword it consists of numbered white squares set	6
7	in a frame with some black squares that are most generally	7
8	been placed to form a symmetrical pattern. The black	8
9	squares are there to separate individual words. In addition	9
10	to being the frame, a set of numbered clues	10
11	is given. The object of the puzzle oneself is to use the given	11
12	clues to fill the white squares with letters for making complete	12
13	words which run across and down the frame. The clues they are	13
14	often difficult, to having many alternatives and a wide general	14
15	knowledge is required to complete the puzzle successfully.	15

414 **Find the odd word out and write it in the space provided.**

1	He was used to work hard when he was young.		1	*was*
2	He must be is calling her now.		2	
3	They seem to have been enjoyed their holiday.		3	
4	She should have had let us know about her plans.		4	
5	Tom enjoys to taking part in car races.		5	
6	My parents are to pick me up when I will arrive at the station.		6	
7	She came to Greece for to spend her summer holidays.		7	
8	He made her to give him the car keys.		8	
9	They went for hunting last weekend.		9	
10	Will you let me to borrow the car on Friday?		10	
11	Learning a foreign language it is a long-term process.		11	
12	She would rather to see him.		12	
13	Sarah prefers eating out than to cooking her own meals.		13	
14	The audience were being amazed by the conjurer's tricks.		14	
15	You needn't to go see Grandma this afternoon.		15	
16	They had better to spend the night with us.		16	
17	He is more happier here than at home.		17	
18	I could hardly not see anything in the dark.		18	
19	She is the most cleverest student of all.		19	
20	Your car is twice as more expensive as ours.		20	
21	I'll call them in case they will need to know what time we are coming.		21	
22	I spent two hours at the airport because of my flight was delayed.		22	
23	We had such a nice weather during our holiday!		23	
24	What an expensive furniture you have got here!		24	
25	She's got two brothers whose their names are Philip and Jonathan.		25	
26	He has been had his car repaired.		26	
27	The boss had his secretary for write down the minutes of the meeting.		27	
28	John told to me that he was going out with Sue.		28	
29	He immigrated into this country since 20 years ago.		29	
30	She wrote me a letter about the holiday she has had two weeks ago.		30	
31	He entered in the competition to gain some experience.		31	
32	That sports car is far too expensive for us to buy it.		32	
33	They do not allow to parking here.		33	
34	I suggest you to write them a letter explaining the situation.		34	
35	Although he was born in Spain, but he doesn't speak Spanish.		35	
36	Brilliant though the film as was, it wasn't nominated for an award.		36	
37	If had I known about the situation, I would have offered to help.		37	
38	She hasn't returned my calls and neither has returned John.		38	
39	He won't agree to come unless being officially invited.		39	
40	Mr Brown isn't at home. He's on his way to the work.		40	
41	We will go to Australia by a boat.		41	
42	He dislikes big parties and so do I dislike.		42	
43	Had it rained, so we would have had to call off the party.		43	

Practice test 6

PART 1

For questions 1 - 15, read the text below and decide which word A, B, C or D best fits each space. Mark your answer in the answer boxes provided.

MORE THAN YOU'D EXPECT

Florida has a lot more to **(0)** .... than Mickey Mouse. It may be the theme park capital of the world, but outside the man-made world of fantasy, it is also possible to see **(1)** .... animals you've never seen outside a zoo. A visit to Florida would not be **(2)** .... without seeing the alligators at **(3)** .... range. If you are lucky, you'll be able to touch a baby alligator, **(4)** .... you must be careful not to **(5)** .... your fingers anywhere near its teeth, as they are extremely **(6)** .... . While you are in the major towns, a car is not **(7)** ...., but if you want to travel round the state you will need one. However, driving in America can be a pleasurable **(8)** .... . American cars are **(9)** .... for comfort and are easy to drive. In **(10)** ...., the roads are **(11)** ...., the speed limit is low and petrol is cheap. The beaches are many and varied. The rich and famous **(12)** .... for Palm Beach, whereas those with **(13)** .... children than money go to the beaches on Florida's Western Gulf coast. Alternatively, there is Fort Myers for those who want to **(14)** .... watersports, or Sanibel for anyone **(15)** .... in shell collecting.

0	**A** present	**B** offer	**C** provide	**D** show
1	**A** savage	**B** natural	**C** wild	**D** mad
2	**A** complete	**B** whole	**C** entire	**D** all
3	**A** near	**B** next	**C** closed	**D** close
4	**A** despite	**B** although	**C** otherwise	**D** moreover
5	**A** form	**B** situate	**C** put	**D** direct
6	**A** sore	**B** hard	**C** painful	**D** sharp
7	**A** optional	**B** essential	**C** compulsory	**D** extreme
8	**A** extent	**B** way	**C** time	**D** experience
9	**A** built	**B** done	**C** planned	**D** formed
10	**A** addition	**B** order	**C** all	**D** fact
11	**A** extended	**B** large	**C** wide	**D** long
12	**A** prefer	**B** head	**C** leave	**D** meet
13	**A** much	**B** many	**C** most	**D** more
14	**A** perform	**B** do	**C** make	**D** have
15	**A** interested	**B** curious	**C** fascinated	**D** amazed

	A	B	C	D
0		■		
1				
2				
3				
4				
5				
6				
7				
8				
9				
10				
11				
12				
13				
14				
15				

PART 2

For questions 16 - 30, read the text below and think of the word which best fits each space. Use only one word in each space. Write your word in the answer boxes provided.

AIRSHIPS

Having been ignored for years because they were considered unreliable and unsafe, airships are now coming back **(0)** .... fashion. In the past, the gas used to keep the airship aloft was dangerous, as it could be **(16)** .... alight very easily; but modern airships are **(17)** .... safer. In **(18)** ...., the airship is now one of **(19)** .... safest **(20)** .... of transport. Combining the features of an aeroplane with those of a hot-air balloon, the airship is becoming an increasingly common **(21)** .... in our cities. More and more people are discovering just **(22)** .... useful it can be. As **(23)** .... as carrying cameras for major sports events **(24)** .... as the Cup Final, airships are being used to **(25)** .... an eye on day-to-day life. As they make virtually **(26)** .... noise, they can monitor special events without creating an unnecessary disturbance. The airship is also popular in the advertising business. Its size and slow speed mean that it can be seen by **(27)** .... numbers of people, making it an ideal advertising medium. At night, it can be lit up from inside, which creates an **(28)** .... more visible advertisement. The airship is most widely used, however, in traffic control, as it can not **(29)** .... remain in the air while travelling very slowly, but also move from one traffic jam to **(30)** .... at speeds of up to 60 mph.

0	*into*	0 ▭ ▬
16		16 ▭ ▭
17		17 ▭ ▭
18		18 ▭ ▭
19		19 ▭ ▭
20		20 ▭ ▭
21		21 ▭ ▭
22		22 ▭ ▭
23		23 ▭ ▭
24		24 ▭ ▭
25		25 ▭ ▭
26		26 ▭ ▭
27		27 ▭ ▭
28		28 ▭ ▭
29		29 ▭ ▭
30		30 ▭ ▭

PART 3

For questions 31 - 40, complete the second sentence so that it has a similar meaning to the first sentence. Use the word given and other words to complete each sentence. You must use between two and five words. Do not change the word given. Write your answers in the boxes provided.

0 I finished the book in two days.
took
It .... to finish the book.

| 0 | *took me two days* | 0 |

31 How long have you been learning to drive?
start
When .... to drive?

| 31 | | 31 |

32 Could you help me put these curtains up?
helping
Would .... these curtains up?

| 32 | | 32 |

33 Their telephone was disconnected because they hadn't paid the bill.
cut
Their telephone .... they hadn't paid the bill.

| 33 | | 33 |

34 The journey from Geneva to Milan was seven hours long.
travel
It .... from Geneva to Milan.

| 34 | | 34 |

35 It's pointless to keep these empty bottles.
worth
It .... these empty bottles.

| 35 | | 35 |

36 What's wrong with Jane?
idea
Do you .... wrong with Jane?

| 36 | | 36 |

37 We couldn't go to work because of a strike.
prevented
A .... to work.

| 37 | | 37 |

38 Greg finally managed to escape from his prison cell.
succeeded
Greg .... his prison cell.

| 38 | | 38 |

39 The only thing he forgot was his toothbrush.
except
He .... his toothbrush.

| 39 | | 39 |

40 It was wrong of you to speak to Julie like that.
have
You .... to Julie like that.

| 40 | | 40 |

PART 4

For questions 41 - 55, read the text below and look carefully at each line.

Some of the lines are correct and some have a word which should not be there.

If a line is correct, put a tick (✔) by the number in the answer boxes provided.

If a line has a word which should not be there, write the word in the answer boxes.

ALSACE

0	The region of Alsace in the north-eastern France is like	0	*the*
00	a country in itself. Situated in the Vosges mountains,	00	✔
41	Alsace is unique, with its breathtaking scenery,	41	
42	high standards of living and cuisine quite unlike of	42	
43	any other be found elsewhere. A major Alsatian city is	43	
44	Strasbourg, controversial in it itself due to its claim to be	44	
45	the European capital because the Council of Europe it is	45	
46	located there. This body, representing more 26 nations,	46	
47	deals mainly with issues of culture and human body rights.	47	
48	Many major multinational companies have chosen Alsace	48	
49	as the place to set up with their European offices. The main	49	
50	reason for they doing so is the ideal location of the	50	
51	region, which borders at both Germany and Switzerland.	51	
52	Alsace has had an eventful history, having often been	52	
53	seized by Germany in times of war. Despite of the	53	
54	German influence which still evident in dialect, buildings	54	
55	and customs, a strong local feeling of the independence persists.	55	

PART 5

For questions 56 - 65, read the text below. Use the word given in capitals at the end of each line to form a word that fits in the space in the same line. Write your word in the answer boxes provided.

TRAVELLER'S CHEQUES

If you're planning a holiday, remember the (0) .... way to carry money is to take traveller's cheques. If you lose them or they are stolen, (56) .... cheques are provided by the bank. Such cheques are (57) .... all over the world. Take traveller's cheques and you can be (58) .... you will not be left without funds. Sterling and dollar cheques are (59) .... at most banks. You should be prepared for the worst: take out (60) .... to cover any (61) .... of luggage, travel delays and medical (62) .... . Not all insurance policies cover injuries caused by sporting (63) ...., so check your policy. Some companies have a helpline to provide (64) .... and advice, which could be very (65) .... .

SAFE	0	*safest*	0
	56		56
REPLACE	57		57
VALIDITY	58		58
CERTAINTY	59		59
AVAILABILITY	60		60
INSURE			
LOSE	61		61
EXPENSIVE	62		62
ACTIVE	63		63
ASSIST	64		64
VALUE	65		65

Pre - test 3

A **Choose the correct item.**

1. I don't need .... sugar from the shops.
   A no
   B every
   C any
   D some

2. Next week I'm going .... a school trip to a museum.
   A on
   B by
   C at
   D in

3. Take your raincoat. .... looks as if it's going to rain.
   A Else
   B There
   C It
   D Here

4. I prefer travelling .... bus.
   A on
   B in
   C at
   D by

5. We go to the cinema .... Monday.
   A the other
   B every other
   C another
   D each other

6. .... of the two pictures do you prefer?
   A What
   B Who
   C Which
   D Whose

7. We donated our money from the fashion show to a charity that helps .... poor.
   A a
   B a large quantity
   C an
   D the

8. It was .... beautiful weather that we decided to go to the beach.
   A what
   B such
   C such a
   D so

9. If you don't study for your exams, you won't .... progress.
   A happen
   B have
   C make
   D do

10. He has a nap every day, ... ?
    A hasn't he
    B isn't he
    C didn't he
    D doesn't he

11. .... television programmes do you like?
    A What
    B Who
    C Why
    D How

12. He spent a month in .... hospital after his accident.
    A the
    B an
    C ---
    D any

13. She spent the .... week writing her report.
    A whole
    B every
    C all
    D each

14. Mum went to .... school to get my marks.
    A a
    B an
    C ---
    D the

15. Everyone knows what he did to her, ...?
    A doesn't he
    B do you
    C don't they
    D don't you

16. "Are there any buses today?" "No, ..."
    A neither
    B none
    C either
    D no

17. Do they sell .... clothes here?
    A childrens'
    B children's
    C childrens
    D childrens's

18. He can't come out tonight; he hasn't got .... money.
    A a little
    B few
    C much
    D many

19. We can meet .... Saturday morning.
    A on
    B in
    C of
    D at

20. Many actors were .... the invited guests at the award ceremony.
    A in
    B between
    C among
    D off

21. Smoking .... harm to your health.
    A happens
    B does
    C occurs
    D makes

22. Lynn doesn't like meat and Ann doesn't ....
    A either
    B nor
    C neither
    D too

23. Hardly .... students passed the test.
    A some
    B every
    C any
    D no

24. I rarely go out .... the weekends.
    A by
    B at
    C of
    D in

B **Using the word given complete the sentences so that the second sentence has a similar meaning to the first sentence.**

1 Uncle Bert gave Jane a dog for her birthday.
   given   Jane .... for her birthday.

2 I'm sure the decision was difficult to accept.
   been   The decision .... difficult to accept.

3 I would have gone to the concert, but I didn't have a ticket.
   wish   I .... a ticket for the concert; then I would have gone.

4 That man's daughter has an original Picasso painting.
   man   That .... has an original Picasso painting.

5 I don't think he caught measles from Sally.
   caught   He .... measles from Sally.

6 They are building a new shopping centre just outside the town.
   being   A new shopping centre .... just outside the town.

7 We called the train station. Otherwise we wouldn't have known the time of your train.
   not   If .... the train station, we wouldn't have known the time of your train.

8 He is a talented footballer and an excellent basketball player as well.
   only   Not .... footballer, but he's also an excellent basketball player.

9 No one in the club can beat him at tennis.
   player   He is .... in the club.

10 She would have come to the party but she had to work.
   not   If .... work, she would have come to the party.

11 The class was so noisy that nobody at the back of the room could hear him.
   make   The class was so noisy that he .... at the back of the room.

12 The decorators were painting the office while we were working.
   painted   The office .... while we were working.

13 "Yes, I drank all the Coke," she said.
   drinking She .... all the Coke.

14 I don't want to go to the gym today.
   rather   I .... the gym today.

15 It was only after she'd bought the milk, that she realised she already had some at home.
   realise   Only after she'd bought the milk .... she already had some at home.

16 Our boss insisted that we all wore a uniform.
   made   Our boss .... a uniform.

17 I wasn't feeling well and ate almost nothing yesterday.
   anything I .... yesterday because I wasn't feeling well.

18 Someone stole my camera while I was walking round the museum.
   had   I .... while I was walking round the museum.

19 "You must go to the supermarket," my mother said.
   on   My mother .... to the supermarket.

20 Is it true that Tracy doesn't eat chocolate and Julie doesn't either?
   eats   Is it true that .... chocolate?

21 As soon as she had finished her report, she left the office to meet her friends.
   had   No .... her report than she left the office to meet her friends.

22 We bought more food than we really needed.
   have   We .... much food.

23 Mrs Jones is 70 but she still goes for a run every day.
   her   In ...., Mrs Jones still goes for a run every day.

24 He reminded me to buy some milk.
   not   He .... to buy some milk.

25 "Honestly, I didn't steal the chocolate," the boy said.
   having   The boy .... the chocolate.

26 Fruit isn't as fattening as cheese.
   more   Cheese .... fruit.

27 They employed more staff. They wanted to increase production.
   view   They employed more staff .... production.

28 Someone should have already told him about his schedule.
been He .... about his schedule.

29 They arrived here an hour ago.
for They .... an hour.

30 A burglar broke into our office yesterday.
had We .... yesterday by a burglar.

31 "Let's go to Majorca this year," she said.
going She .... Majorca this year.

32 Cathy organised the party for my birthday.
that It .... party for my birthday.

33 She sunbathed every day, so she had a good tan.
due Her good tan .... every day.

34 Betty likes swimming. Jo likes swimming too.
and Both .... swimming.

35 It wasn't necessary for him to work late and he didn't.
work He .... late.

36 James travelled round Europe all winter.
spent James .... round Europe.

C **Fill in the correct particle(s).**

1 I've run .... sugar. Please get me some.
2 Jo always stands .... me when I need her.
3 Let's put .... our wedding until the summer.
4 She takes .... her mother; she's got her eyes.
5 When I left college, I set .... my own business.
6 Dave saw Mike .... at the coach station.
7 Who can work .... the answer to this question?
8 I turned .... late for the concert.

D **Fill in the correct preposition(s).**

1 Plans for the trip are still .... discussion.
2 We're .... schedule so hurry up!
3 We can't use the bridge because it's .... repair.
4 After his jog, he was .... breath.
5 .... my astonishment, I won £1,000.
6 Actors have to learn their lines ....heart.
7 Man is .... danger of ruining the planet.
8 Is Nurse Smith .... duty tonight?

E **Find the word which should not be in the sentence.**

1 Emma is one of the most nicest people I know.
2 I got a huge electric bill which I couldn't pay it.
3 The robber told everyone person to lie on the floor.
4 Both of Sue and Jenny love swimming.
5 I love going to shopping in Oxford Street.
6 The problem it is that the workers aren't happy.
7 This shop is the more expensive than any other.

8 They couldn't afford themselves a holiday.
9 All taxes not been paid on time will be subject to a penalty.
10 We worked hard all month so as that we could get the project finished.
11 The detective made him to tell the truth.
12 Jane's always tired after work. She's as a victim of today's stressful environment.

F **Fill in the correct word derived from the words in bold.**

1 It is ...., when going on a long trip, to plan well in advance. **NECESSITY**
2 She became a .... singer after many years of hard work. **SUCCESS**
3 I was under the .... that I needed qualifications for this job. **IMPRESS**
4 Reading a newspaper is an .... way of keeping informed. **EFFECT**
5 That shop has a .... of sweets to choose from. **VARIOUS**
6 You must take out .... before you can drive a car. **INSURE**
7 It's important to get a good .... in order to find a job. **EDUCATE**
8 The police are always happy to give you .... **ASSIST**
9 This boutique has a wide .... of clothes. **SELECT**
10 They were repairing the road, much to the .... of the nearby residents. **ANNOY**
11 Honesty is a very .... asset. **VALUE**
12 If you don't have your boarding pass, you'll be .... to board the plane. **ABLE**

Appendix 1

Present Forms

Present Simple	Present Continuous	Present Perfect	Present Perf. Continuous
Affirmative	**Affirmative**	**Affirmative**	**Affirmative**
I work You work He works etc	I **am** work**ing** You are working He is working etc	I **have** work**ed** You have worked He **has** work**ed** etc	I **have been** work**ing** You have been working He **has been** work**ing** etc
Negative	**Negative**	**Negative**	**Negative**
I **don't** work You don't work He **doesn't** work etc	I'm not working You aren't working He isn't working etc	I haven't worked You haven't worked He hasn't worked etc	I haven't been working You haven't been working He hasn't been working etc
Interrogative	**Interrogative**	**Interrogative**	**Interrogative**
Do I work? Do you work? **Does** he work? etc	Am I working? Are you working? Is he working? etc	Have I worked? Have you worked? Has he worked? etc	Have I been working? Have you been working? Has he been working? etc
permanent situations or states He *lives* in a caravan. **permanent truths or laws of nature** Water *boils* at 100˚C.	**temporary situations** She *is working* in Paris this week. **changing or developing situations** Mary *is putting* on weight.	**recently completed actions** He *has cut* the grass. (The action is complete. The grass is now cut. - evidence in the present)	**actions started in the past and continuing up to the present.** He *has been washing* his bike for an hour. (He started an hour ago and he's still washing it.)
repeated/habitual actions (especially with frequency adverbs: often, usually, always etc) He always *does* his homework. (Here "always" means every day.)	**frequently repeated actions with always, constantly, continually expressing annoyance or criticism** He*'s always asking* stupid questions. (Here "always" means constantly.)	**complete past actions connected to the present with stated or unstated time reference** He *has sold* his car. (Now he has no car.) He *has just bought* a bike. (stated time reference)	**past actions of certain duration having visible results or effects in the present** He *has been fighting*. That's why he's got a black eye.
reviews/sports commentaries/ dramatic narrative Pavarotti *sings* wonderfully in this opera.	**actions happening at or around the moment of speaking** The baby *is sleeping* at the moment.	**personal experiences/ changes which have happened** I *have learnt* a lot this year.	**to express anger, irritation, annoyance, explanation or criticism** Someone *has been lying* to me. (annoyance)
timetables/programmes (future meaning) The race *starts* at 3.00. **in exclamatory sentences** Here *comes* the bride!	**fixed arrangements in the near future** I*'m seeing* Rachel tonight.	**emphasis on number** He *has read three* novels this week. She *has interviewed seven* students this morning.	**Present Perfect Continuous is normally used with for, since or how long to put emphasis on duration** She *has been waiting* since 4 o'clock.

Time expressions usually used with Present Forms

Present Simple	Present Continuous	Present Perfect & Present Perfect Continuous
every day/week/month/ year, usually, sometimes, always, rarely, never, often, in the morning/ evening/afternoon, at night, on Mondays etc	now, at the moment, at present, nowadays, today, tonight, always, still etc	just, ever, never, already, yet (negations & questions), always, how long, so far, recently, since (= from a starting point in the past), for (= over a period of time), today, this week/month etc **For** and **since** are usually used with Present Perfect Continuous to emphasise the duration of an action

Past Forms

Past Simple	Past Continuous	Past Perfect	Past Perf. Continuous
Affirmative I work**ed** You worked He worked etc	**Affirmative** I **was** work**ing** You **were** work**ing** He was working etc	**Affirmative** I **had** work**ed** You had worked He had worked etc	**Affirmative** I **had been** work**ing** You had been working He had been working etc
Negative I **didn't** work You didn't work He didn't work etc	**Negative** I wasn't working You weren't working He wasn't working etc	**Negative** I hadn't worked You hadn't worked He hadn't worked etc	**Negative** I hadn't been working You hadn't been working He hadn't been working etc
Interrogative **Did** I work? Did you work? Did he work? etc	**Interrogative** Was I working? Were you working? Was he working? etc	**Interrogative** Had I worked? Had you worked? Had he worked? etc	**Interrogative** Had I been working? Had you been working? Had he been working? etc
past actions which happened one immediately after the other He **got in** the car, **started** the engine and **drove** off.	**action in the middle of happening at a stated past time** I **was living** in Spain this time last year.	**past action which occurred before another action or before a stated past time** He **had spent** all his money by the end of the month.	**action continuing over a period up to a specific time in the past** She **had been trying** to get a visa for months before she gave up.
past habit or state He **used to walk**/**walked** to work every day. **complete action or event which happened at a stated past time** She **passed** her exam **last week**. ("When?" "Last week" - stated past time)	**past action in progress interrupted by another past action. The longer action is in the Past Continuous, the shorter action is in the Past Simple.** I **was playing** football when I broke my ankle.	**complete past action which had visible results in the past** He was delighted because he **had found** a new job.	**past action of certain duration which had visible results in the past** Her fingers hurt because she **had been playing** the guitar all day.
complete past actions not connected to the present with a stated or implied time reference Elvis Presley **made** lots of records. (Elvis is dead; he won't record any more. - period of time now finished - implied time reference)	**two or more simultaneous past actions of certain duration** He **was cooking** while she **was sleeping.** **or background description to events in a story/ description** They **were travelling** to Swansea...	**the Past Perfect is the past equivalent of the Present Perfect** There was no pudding left; he **had eaten** it all. (Present Perfect: There's no pudding left; he has eaten it all.)	**the Past Perfect Cont. is the past equivalent of the Present Perfect** He stayed in bed that day because he **had been feeling** ill all week. (Present Perfect: He's staying in bed today because he's been feeling ill all week.)

Time Expressions usually used with Past Forms

Past Simple	Past Continuous	Past Perfect	Past Perf. Continuous
yesterday, last week etc, (how long) ago, then, just now, when, in 1992 etc	while, when, as, the moment that etc	for, since, already, after, just, never, yet, before, by, by the time etc	for, since

Future Forms

Future Simple (Will)	Be going to	Future Continuous	Future Perfect
Affirmative I **will** work You will work He will work etc	**Affirmative** I **am going to** work You are going to work He is going to work etc	**Affirmative** I **will be** work**ing** You will be working He will be working etc	**Affirmative** I **will have** work**ed** etc **Negative** I **won't** have worked etc **Interrogative** Will I have worked? etc
Negative I **won't** work You won't work He won't work etc	**Negative** I'm not going to work You're not going to work He's not going to work etc	**Negative** I **won't** be working You won't be working He won't be working etc	**Future Perfect Cont.**
Interrogative **Shall/Will** I work? Will you work? Will he work? etc	**Interrogative** Am I going to work? Are you going to work? Is he going to work? etc	**Interrogative** Will I be working? Will you be working? Will he be working? etc	**Affirmative** I **will have been** work**ing** etc **Negative** I won't have been working etc **Interrogative** Will I have been working? etc
decisions taken at the moment of speaking (on-the-spot decisions) *It's cold in here. I'll turn on the heating.*	**actions intended to be performed in the near future** *I'm going to buy some new clothes next week.*	**actions in progress at a stated future time** *I'll be skiing in the Alps this Christmas.*	**Future Perfect** **action finished before a stated future time** *They* ***will have finished*** *building their house* ***by*** *May.*
hopes, fears, threats, offers, promises, warnings, predictions, requests, comments etc, esp. with: expect, hope, believe, I'm sure, I'm afraid, probably etc *I hope he'll like his birthday present.*	**planned actions or intentions** *Now that she's rich, she's **going to travel** round the world.*	**actions which are the result of a routine (instead of Present Continuous)** *I'll be going to the bank tomorrow. (I go there every Friday - it's part of my routine)*	**Note: by or not ... until/till are used with Future Perf. Until/till are normally used with Future Perfect only in negative sentences.** *She **will have written** it **by** next week. (not: ~~till/until~~) She **won't** have finished **until** tomorrow.*
actions or predictions which may (not) happen in the future *She'll probably win.* **or actions which we cannot control and will inevitably happen** *The baby **will be born** after Christmas.*	**evidence that something will definitely happen in the near future** *It looks like the plane **is going to take** off now. I think I'm **going to be** sick!*	**when we ask politely about people's arrangements to see if they can do sth for us or because we want to offer to do sth for them. Will you be driving** *into town this afternoon? Can you give me a lift?*	**Future Perfect Cont.** **duration of an action up to a certain time in the future** *By this time next month he **will have been studying** the piano **for 2 years.***
things we are not yet sure about or we haven't decided to do yet *Maybe I'll buy a car.* **Note: Shall is used with I/we in questions, suggestions, offers or when asking for advice** *Shall we play tennis?*	**things we are sure about or we have already decided to do in the near future** *They are **going to offer** the job to Ann. (It has been decided.)*	**Present Simple with future meaning** **timetables/programmes** *The boat **leaves** at 8 o'clock in the morning.*	**Present Continuous with future meaning** **fixed arrangement in the near future** *I'm **having** dinner with Jane this evening. (It's a date.)*

Shall is used:	Will is used:
with I/we in questions, suggestions, offers or when asking for advice. *Shall* we go for a walk? Who *shall* I invite?	to express offers, threats, promises, predictions, warnings, requests, hopes, fears, on-the-spot decisions, comments (mainly with: think, expect, believe, I'm sure, hope, know, suppose and probably). *I'm sure* John *will pass* his driving test.

Time Expressions used with :

Future Simple & Be going to	Future Perfect	Future Perfect Cont.
tomorrow, tonight, next week/month, in two/three etc days, the day after tomorrow, soon, in a week/month etc	before, by, by then, by the time, (until is used only in negative sentences with this tense)	by ... for

Spelling Rules

1 **-(e)s ending**
   a. **words ending in -s, -ss, -ch, -x, -sh, -z, -o * add -es**

   lens - lenses, kiss - kisses, match - matches, fox - foxes, flash - flashes, buzz - buzzes, go - goes

   b. **nouns ending in vowel + o, double o, short forms/ musical instruments/proper nouns ending in -o add -s**

   patio - patios, kangaroo - kangaroos, stereo - stereos, cello - cellos, Navajo - Navajos

2 **-f/-fe ending**
   nouns ending in -f/-fe drop -f/-fe and add -ves

   handkerchief - handkerchieves, knife - knives

3 **-y ending**
   a. **words ending in consonant + y drop -y and add -ies, -ied, -ier, -iest, -ily**

   copy - copies - copied, happy - happier - happiest, happy - happily

   b. **words ending in consonant + y add -ing**

   copy - copying

   c. **words ending in vowel + y add -s, -ed, -ing, -er, -est**

   enjoy - enjoys - enjoyed - enjoying, grey - greyer - greyest

4 **-ie ending**
   words ending in -ie change -ie to -y before -ing

   lie - lying

5 **dropping -e**
   a. **words ending in -e drop -e and add -ing, -ed, -er, -est**

   crave - craving - craved (but: be - being) large - larger - largest

   b. **adjectives ending in -e add -ly to form their adverbs**

   sore - sorely, fine - finely (but: true - truly)

   c. **adjectives ending in -le change -le to -ly to form their adverbs**

   unbelievable - unbelievably (but: whole - wholly)

   d. **verbs ending in -ee add -ing**

   flee - fleeing

Pronunciation

Pronunciation of -(e)s ending (noun plurals and the 3rd person singular of verbs in the Present Simple)

/s/ after /f/, /t/, /p/, /k/	/ɪz/ after /z/, /dʒ/, /tʃ/, /s/, /ʃ/	/z/ after /b/, /g/, /m/, /d/, /l/, /n/, /v/ or any vowel sound
coughs, cuts leaps, picks	loses, lodges, matches, misses, pushes	rubs, hugs, dreams, demands, calls, contains, waves, stays

Pronunciation of -ed ending

/ɪd/ after /t/, /d/	/t/ after /k/, /tʃ/, /f/, /s/, /ʃ/, /p/	/d/ after /b/, /dʒ/, /m/, /v/, /g/, /l/, /n/, /z/, vowel + /r/
lasted, ended	joked, fetched, coughed, minced, rushed, skipped	dabbed, lodged, crammed, waved, mugged, billed, happened, sneezed, purred

Appendix 2

Phrasal Verbs

Be

be after = 1) (tr) to want, to try to gain,
2) (tr) to chase

be against = (tr) to oppose

be at = (tr) to scold

be away = 1) (int) to be absent, 2) (int) to leave

be back = 1) (int) to return, 2) (int) to become
fashionable again

be down with = (tr) to be ill with; **go down with**

be for = (tr) to be in favour of (opp: **be against**)

be in = 1) (int) to be at one's home, office (opp:
be out), 2) (int) to be fashionable (opp: **be out**)

be in for = (tr) to expect sth (usu bad)

be off = 1) (int) to leave, 2) (tr) to cease to want,
3) (tr) to be absent (from school/work)

be on = 1) (tr) to be shown (on TV, at the cinema,
theatre etc), 2) (int) to be on duty

be on at = (tr) to scold

be out = 1) (int) not to be at one's home, office,
(opp: **be in**), 2) (int) to be unfashionable (opp: **be in**),
3) (int) (of light/fire) to have stopped burning,
4) (int) to become known, 5) to have been removed

be out of = (tr) not to have sth; lack; **run out of**

be over = 1) (int) to come to an end

be through with = (int) to have finished (a
relationship, job etc)

be up = 1) (int) to be awake and out of bed, 2) (int)
to stay awake at night; **stay up**, 3) (int) to be wrong
or unusual

be up against = (tr) to be opposed by

be up to = 1) (tr) to do (usu sth wrong), 2) (tr) to be
equal to, 3) (tr) to depend on

be with = 1) (tr) to support, 2) (tr) to understand
(and like)

Break

break down = 1) (int) (of machinery) to stop
working, 2) (int) (of a person) to lose control of
feelings, 3) (tr) to destroy, 4) (tr) to separate under
headings or sections, 5) (int) to fail (talks,
negotiations)

break in = 1) (int) to enter by force or illegally,
2) (int) to interrupt, 3) (tr) to train (a horse) to obey

break into = 1) (tr) to enter by force,
2) (tr) to interrupt

break off = 1) to stop (temporarily), 2) (tr) to end
(a relationship, agreement), 3) (int) to become
separate (from sth)

break out = 1) (int) to begin suddenly (war etc),
2) (int) to escape from a place

break through = 1) (int) to advance in spite of
opposition, 2) (int) to make advances towards
discovery or any other aim, 3) (tr) to break a way
through (sth solid)

break to = to tell (usually bad news) to sb in
a kind way

break up = 1) (int) to stop for holidays (school etc),
2) (int) to separate; split up, 3) (int) to separate into
pieces, 4) (tr) to (cause to) be destroyed, 5) (tr) to
terminate or end, 6) (of a group) to cease to be
together

Bring

bring about = to cause to happen

bring along = to bring sb/sth with one

bring back = 1) (tr) to recall; bring to mind,
2) to reintroduce

bring down = 1) (tr) to cause to fall, 2) (tr) to
reduce prices/temperature, 3) to remove
from power

bring forward = 1) to suggest an idea (often
passive), 2) to arrange for sth to be done at an
earlier time than originally proposed

bring in = 1) (tr) to create profit, money, 2) (tr) to
introduce an idea, 3) (tr) to take sb to a police
station etc

bring off = to make sth succeed

bring on = 1) (tr) to cause usu sth unpleasant,
2) (tr) to cause sb/sth to appear

bring out = 1) (tr) to publish; put on the market,
2) (tr) to cause sth to be seen or known,
3) to introduce

bring over = to bring sb usu to one's home

bring round = 1) (tr) to cause to regain consciousness; **bring to**, 2) (tr) to persuade; **bring over (to)**,
3) (tr) to take sb or sth to a place (usu home)

bring to = 1) (tr) to make sb regain consciousness;
bring round, 2) (tr) to cause (sth/sb) to reach
(a total state or condition)

bring together = 1) (tr) to cause (things) to meet
or join, 2) (tr) to make (two people or groups) meet

bring up = 1) (tr) to raise a child, 2) to mention;
introduce a subject, 3) (tr) to vomit

Call

call back = 1) (int) to return a phone call, 2) (tr) to ask to return

call for = 1) (tr) to need; demand, 2) (tr) to go to collect sth/sb; pick up

call in = 1) to visit briefly; **look in**, 2) (tr) to order the return of (sth), 3) to ask sb to come to offer professional advice

call off = (tr) to cancel

call on sb = (tr) to visit (formally)

call out = 1) (int) to shout, 2) (tr) to order to come to one's help (eg fire brigade)

call over = (tr) to read aloud a list

call up = 1) (tr) to bring to mind, 2) to order to join the army

Carry

be carried away = to be very excited

carry off = 1) (tr) to do sth successfully, 2) (tr) to take sth/sb by force, 3) (tr) to take sb/sth away (from a place)

carry on (with) = 1) (tr) to continue with, 2) (tr) to have an affair with

carry out = 1) (tr) to fulfil (orders, tasks), 2) (tr) to conduct (an experiment)

carry over = (tr) to postpone; **put off**

carry through = 1) (tr) to complete (sth) in spite of difficulties, 2) (tr) to help sb survive during troubled times

Come

come across = 1) (tr) to find/meet by chance; **run across**, 2) (tr) to be well received (by an audience)

come along = 1) (int) to hurry up; **come on**, 2) (int) to arrive; appear

come at sth = (tr) to discover (truth etc); **get at**

come back = 1) (int) to return to memory (tr: **bring back**), 2) (int) to become fashionable again; **be back**

come between = (tr) to separate

come by = (tr) to obtain

come down = 1) (int) to move to a lower level, 2) (int) (of planes) to land (opp: **take off**), 3) (int) to fall

come down to = 1) to be passed on to sb by inheritance, 2) (tr) to reach a point

come down with = (tr) to become ill; **go down with**

come in = (int) to become fashionable (opp: **go out**)

come into = (tr) to inherit

come off = 1) (int) to succeed, 2) (int) to take place as planned, 3) to cease being joined to sth

come on = 1) (int) (of electrical machines) to begin working, 2) (int) to progress

come out = 1) to go on strike, 2) (of flowers) to begin to blossom, 3) (int) (news, truth) to be revealed (tr: **bring out**), 4) (int) to be published (tr: **bring out**), 5) to be able to be removed (stains), 6) to appear (sun)

come over = 1) (int) to visit, 2) (int) to travel (from a distance or crossing the sea)

come round = 1) to visit casually, 2) (int) to recover consciousness; **come to** (tr: **bring round**), 3) to change one's point of view

come through = (tr) to survive

come to = (tr) to amount to a total

come up = 1) (int) to rise to the surface, 2) (int) to be mentioned (tr: **bring up**), 3) to arise; occur

come up against = (tr) to encounter (difficulties); **run up against**

come up to = 1) (tr) to approach, 2) (tr) to equal; **be up to** (expectations)

come up with = (tr) to find (an answer, solution etc)

Cut

cut across = 1) (tr) take a shorter way

cut back (on) = (tr) to reduce (expenses, production)

cut down = 1) (tr) to cause to fall by cutting, 2) (tr) (of clothes, writing) to reduce the size, 3) (tr) to reduce sth in order to save money; **cut back**

cut down on = (tr) to reduce consumption; **cut back on**

cut in = 1) (int) to move suddenly in front of another car, 2) (int) to interrupt sb (speaking, dancing etc)

cut into = 1) (tr) to divide into parts, 2) (tr) to interrupt; **break in**

cut off = 1) to disconnect, 2) to isolate (usu pass)

cut out = 1) (tr) to cut pieces from paper, fabric etc, 2) (tr) to omit; leave out, 3) to stop sth or doing sth

be cut out for = to be suited for (a profession)

cut through = (tr) to cut

cut to = 1) (tr) to reduce, 2) (int) to reach sth by omitting part of it

cut up = to cut into small pieces

Do

do away with = 1) (tr) to abolish, 2) (tr) to murder

do down = (tr) to speak badly of sb

do in = (tr) to kill

do out = (tr) to clean

do out of = (tr) to deceive sb so as to gain; **cheat out of**

do up = 1) (tr) to fasten; tie, 2) (tr) to repair; redecorate, 3) (tr) to wrap, 4) (tr) to make oneself more attractive; **dress up**

do with = (tr) to need; want

do without = (tr) to live or continue without having sth/sb

Draw

draw back = 1) (int) to move away, 2) (tr) to be unwilling to fulfil a promise

draw in = 1) (int) (of a train/bus) to arrive at a station slowing down to stop, 2) (tr) to attract people

draw on = (tr) to make use of sth (eg money)

draw out = 1) (tr) to show the general idea of, 2) (tr) to encourage sb to be less shy, 3) (tr) to take money out of a bank account

draw up = 1) (of a vehicle) to stop, 2) (tr) to write sth (will, contract)

Fall

fall apart = 1) (int) to break into pieces, 2) (int) to end in failure

fall back = (int) to retreat

fall back on = to turn to sb/sth for help when other plans have failed; **turn to**

fall behind = 1) (int) to fail to keep up with, 2) (int) to be late (with payment)

fall for = 1) (tr) to be deceived, 2) (tr) to fall in love with sb

fall in = to collapse

fall in with = (tr) to agree with; **go along with**

fall into = 1) (tr) to begin sth; enter a state, 2) (tr) to be divided into (categories)

fall off = 1) (int) to become worse, 2) (int) to become fewer or less

fall on 1) (tr) to attack, 2) (tr) to eat (food) hungrily

fall out (with) = to quarrel

fall through = (int) to fail to be completed

Get

get about = 1) (int) to move around; travel, 2) to be mobile again after illness

get across = to communicate ideas; to become understood

get after = (int) to chase

get along (with) = to be on friendly terms; **get on**

get at = 1) (tr) to reach; find, 2) (tr) to imply

get away = 1) to leave, 2) to go on holiday, 3) to avoid capture

get away from = (int) to escape

get away with = 1) (tr) to escape punishment for a wrongful, illegal act, 2) (tr) to escape capture with stolen goods

get back = 1) (tr) to recover possession of, 2) (int) to reach home again, 3) to return to a former condition

get back to = 1) to return to, 2) (tr) to speak to sb again about sth

get behind = to fail to produce sth at the right time

get by = to have enough money for one's needs

get down = 1) (tr) to swallow with difficulty, 2) (tr) to depress, 3) (int) to descend

get down to = to start doing sth seriously

get into = 1) (tr) to enter, 2) (tr) to have an effect on behaviour, 3) (tr) to start (a habit), 4) to fit (clothes)

get off = 1) (int) to avoid punishment, 2) (tr) to leave; start a journey, 3) to descend from a bus, train

get on = 1) (int) to advance; make progress, 2) (tr) to enter (a bus, train); climb onto (a bike, horse), 3) (int) to have a friendly relationship with; **get along**, 4) to manage

get on with = 1) (tr) to be on good terms with, 2) (tr) to continue after an interruption, 3) to go on with sth; advance

get out (of) = 1) (tr) to come out of a space, building, 2) (int) to become known (news), 3) (int) to remove (a mark, dirt), 4) (tr) to escape

get out of = (tr) to avoid a responsibility

get over = 1) to recover, 2) to overcome, 3) to make (a point) understood

get round = 1) (tr) to persuade; **bring round**, 2) (int) to move around; **get about**, 3) (int) to spread (news)

get round to = (tr) to find the necessary time to do sth

get through = 1) (tr) to finish (a piece of work), 2) (tr) to succeed in (exams), 3) (int) to go on living through difficult times, 4) (tr) to use up all of sth (food, money, supplies)

get through to = 1) (tr) to reach by telephone, 2) to make oneself understood

get to = 1) (int) to arrive, 2) (int) to reach a point, stage, 3) (tr) to start doing sth after a delay, 4) (tr) to have an effect on the feelings of sb

get up = 1) to move to a higher level, 2) (int) to rise from bed

get up to = to do (usu sth bad)

Give

give away = 1) (tr) to reveal sth; betray sb, 2) (tr) to give sth free of charge, 3) (tr) to deliver a woman to her husband at their wedding

give back = (tr) to return

give in 1) (int) to surrender; yield, 2) (tr) to hand in

give off = (tr) to emit (smells, heat, fumes etc)

give out = 1) (int) to come to an end, 2) (tr) to distribute; hand out, 3) (tr) to announce

give to = 1) (tr) to present with, 2) (tr) to supply; provide

give up = 1) (tr) to stop/abandon an attempt/habit, 2) (tr) to surrender; offer oneself as a prisoner, 3) (tr) to stop doing or having sth

Go

go about = to get about

go ahead = 1) (int) to proceed, 2) (int) to be in front, 3) (int) to continue

go along = 1) (int) to proceed, 2) (int) to advance; make progress; **go on**

go along with = 1) (tr) to agree with sb/sth, 2) (tr) to advance with sth

go at = (tr) to attack

go away = 1) (int) to leave, 2) (int) to stop

go back = 1) (int) to date back, 2) (int) to return, 3) (int) (of clocks/watches) to be set to an earlier time

go back on = 1) (tr) to break a promise or agreement, 2) (tr) to let down; be disloyal

go by = 1) (int) (of time) to pass, 2) (int) (of a chance) to let it pass without taking it

go down = 1) (int) to be reduced, 2) (int) (of the sun/moon) to set, 3) (int) to sink or drown, 4) (int) to be swallowed

go down with = (tr) to become ill

go for = 1) (tr) to attack, 2) (tr) to apply for (usu a job), 3) (tr) to support, 4) (tr) to aim at sth

go in for = 1) (tr) to take part in (a competition), 2) (tr) to be interested in sth

go into = 1) (tr) to investigate thoroughly, 2) (tr) to join/enter sth (group, business etc), 3) (tr) to crash, 4) (tr) to start an activity

go off = 1) (int) to explode (bomb); ring (alarm), 2) (int) to be switched off, 2) (int) (of food) to go bad, 4) (int) to stop, 5) (int) to succeed

go on = 1) (int) to continue; **carry on**, 2) (int) to happen, 3) (int) to make progress, 4) to go ahead, 5) to be turned on

go out = 1) (int) to stop burning; be extinguished, 2) (int) to cease to be fashionable (opp: **come in**), 3) (int) to mix socially

go over 1) (tr) to examine details, 2) (tr) to repeat, 3) (int) to approach (sb to speak to)

go round = 1) (int) to be enough for everyone to have a share, 2) (int) to visit; **look round**, 3) (int) (news/disease) to spread; circulate; **go about**

go through = 1) (tr) to examine carefully; **go over**, 2) (tr) to discuss in detail, 3) (tr) (of money, food etc) to use up; spend, 4) (tr) (of a deal/agreement) to be completed (with success), 5) (tr) to pass through, 6) to experience; endure

go through with = to complete sth in spite of opposition; **carry out**

go up = 1) (int) to rise (in price); increase, 2) (int) to ascend

go with = 1) (tr) to match, 2) (tr) to be part of

go without = (tr) to endure the lack of sth; **do without**

Hold

hold back = 1) (tr) to control (tears, laughter), 2) (int) to hesitate, 3) (tr) to delay, 4) (tr) to keep secret; **keep back** 5) (int) to be reluctant to act

hold down = (tr) to keep sth at a lower level

hold in = (tr) to restrain; keep under control

hold off = 1) (int) to keep at a distance, 2) (int) to happen later

hold on = 1) (int) to wait (esp on the phone), 2) (int) to continue despite difficulties, 3) (int) to last, 4) to maintain in place

hold out = 1) (int) to persist; not to give way, 2) (int) to last

hold over = to postpone; **put off**

hold to = to follow exactly (rules, customs)

hold up = 1) (tr) to delay, 2) (tr) to use violence in order to rob, 3) (int) to last

hold with = (tr) to approve of

Keep

keep after = 1) (tr) to continue to pursue, 2) (tr) to scold

keep at = (tr) to continue working at sth

keep away (from) = (tr) to stay away

keep back = 1) (tr) to stay back, 2) (tr) to conceal, 3) (tr) to delay; **hold back**

keep behind = (tr) to make sb remain after others have left

keep down = 1) (tr) (of feelings) to control; **keep back**, 2) (tr) to repress, 3) (tr) to maintain at a lower level

keep (oneself) from = 1) (tr) to prevent from, 2) (tr) to avoid

keep in = (tr) to make sb stay indoors (esp as a punishment)

keep in with = (tr) to remain friendly with

keep off = 1) (tr) to stay away from, 2) (tr) to avoid (food, a habit etc); **keep away from**, 3) (tr) to avoid mentioning a subject

keep on = 1) (int) to continue in spite of difficulties, 2) (tr) to continue doing sth

keep out = to exclude sb/sth

keep out of = (tr) to stay away from (trouble)

keep to = 1) (tr) to limit to, 2) (tr) to follow

keep up = 1) (tr) to maintain sth at the same level, 2) (tr) to keep sb out of bed, 3) (tr) to keep sth in good condition

keep up with = 1) (tr) to proceed at an equal pace with, 2) (tr) to continue to be informed (news, events)

Let

let down = 1) (tr) to lower, 2) (tr) (of clothes) to lengthen (opp: **take up**), 3) (tr) to disappoint

let in = 1) to allow sth (water, air etc) to leak in

let in(to) = 1) to allow sb to enter (a place), 2) (tr) to allow sb to join (a group)

let off = 1) (tr) not to punish, 2) (tr) to make sth explode (fireworks)

let on = 1) (int) to reveal a secret, 2) (int) to pretend

let out = 1) (tr) to allow to go out (opp: **let in**), 2) (tr) to release, 3) (tr) (of clothes) to make wider, (opp: **take in**), 4) (tr) to say sth unintentionally

let up = (int) to become less strong

Look

look after = (tr) to take care of

look ahead = (int) to think of the future

look back (on) = (int) to consider the past; remember

look down on = (tr) to despise (opp: **look up to**)

look for = (tr) to search for

look forward to = (tr) to anticipate (with pleasure)

look into = (tr) to investigate

look in on sb = to pay a short visit to

look on = 1) (int) to observe, 2) (tr) to regard as

look onto/look out on to = (tr) to face; have a view of

Look out = (int) Watch out!

look out for = (tr) to be alert in order to see/find sb

look over = 1) to examine carefully; **go through**, 2) to revise briefly and quickly

look round = to survey; examine an area

look through = 1) (tr) to look at quickly, 2) (tr) to study sth carefully, 3) not to notice sb

look up = 1) (tr) to look for sth (such as an address, etc) in an appropriate book or list, 2) to visit sb after a lapse of time (specially sb living at some distance)

look up to = (tr) to respect (opp: **look down on**)

Make

be made for = to suit exactly

make for = (tr) to go towards; head for

make off = (int) to run away; escape; **make away**

make out = 1) (tr) to distinguish, 2) (tr) to understand; **work out**, 3) (tr) to write out; **fill in**

make over = (tr) to give the possession of sth to sb else

make sth up to sb = to compensate sb for sth

make up = 1) (tr) to invent; **think up**, 2) (tr) to put cosmetics on, 3) (int) to reconcile, 4) (tr) to compose; put together, 5) (tr) to keep sth burning, 6) (tr) to make an amount complete

make up for = to compensate

make up one's mind = to decide

Pass

pass away = 1) (int) to cease, 2) (int) to die

pass by = (tr) to overlook; **pass over**

pass off as = (tr) to pretend to be sth/sb else successfully

pass on = (tr) to give from person to person

pass out = 1) (int) to lose consciousness, 2) (tr) to give freely; **give out**

Pay

pay back = 1) (tr) to return money owed, 2) (tr) to get revenge on sb

pay down = (tr) to pay part of the price for sth and the rest over a period of time

pay for = (tr) to receive punishment

pay off = 1) (tr) to act in order to settle (an old quarrel etc), 2) (tr) to pay sb to leave employment

pay up = (tr) to pay in full (a debt); **pay off**

Pull

pull back = 1) (int) to move away, 2) (int) to be unwilling to fulfil a promise; **draw back**

pull down = (tr) to demolish

pull in = (int) (of trains etc) to arrive; **draw in** (opp: **pull out**)

pull oneself together = to bring one's feelings under control

pull out = 1) (tr) to stretch, 2) (int) (of trains/ships) to leave; **draw out**

pull through = (tr) to succeed despite difficulties

pull up = 1) to move forward, 2) to stop

Put

put aside = (tr) to save; **put by**

put across = (tr) to communicate successfully; **get across; get over**

put away = 1) (tr) to store, 2) (tr) to put sb into prison or mental hospital, 3) (tr) to save (usu money)

put back = 1) (tr) (of clocks/watches) to set to an earlier time; **go back** (opp: **put forward**), 2) (tr) to cause to be delayed, 3) (tr) to replace sth, 4) to delay till a later time

put down = 1) (tr) to make a note; **write down**, 2) (tr) to lay sth down (opp: **pick up**), 3) (tr) to suppress forcibly, 4) (tr) to stop (work)

put down to = (tr) to attribute to

put forward = 1) (tr) to propose, 2) (tr) (of clocks/watches) to set to a later time (opp: **put back**)

put in = 1) (tr) to include, 2) (tr) to arrive at a port (ships, boats), 3) (tr) to apply for, 4) (tr) to interrupt

put in for = 1) (tr) to make a formal request; **put in**, 2) (tr) to apply for

put off = 1) (tr) to postpone, 2) (tr) to discourage from liking

put on = 1) (tr) to dress oneself in, 2) (tr) to increase (in weight), 3) (tr) to switch on, 4) (tr) to pretend, 5) (tr) to cause to take place (show/performance)

put out = 1) (tr) to extinguish (fire etc), 2) (tr) to expel, 3) to cause inconvenience, 4) to make sth public

be put out = to be annoyed

put through = 1) (tr) to connect by telephone, 2) (tr) to make sb undergo or suffer sth

put up = 1) (tr) to erect; build, 2) (tr) (of prices) to increase, 3) (tr) to offer hospitality (put sb up), 4) (tr) to offer (resistance), 5) (tr) to show in a public place

put up to = (tr) to give sb the idea of (doing sth usu wrong)

put up with = to tolerate; bear

Run

run across = (tr) to meet/find by chance; **come across**

run after = (tr) to chase

run away = (int) to escape; flee (from home, duty etc); **run off**

run away with = to steal sth and leave with it

run down = 1) (tr) to knock down (with a vehicle), 2) (tr) to speak badly of sb, 3)(int) (of clock/batteries) to stop working, 4) (passive) to tire

run in = (tr) to bring a new car engine into full use (carefully by driving it slowly for a set period)

run into = 1) (tr) to meet unexpectedly, 2) (tr) to collide with, 3) (tr) to experience (difficulties)

run off = 1) (tr) to make prints/copies, 2) (int) to escape from home/duty

run on = 1) (int) to talk continuously, 2) (int) (of time) to pass, 3) (tr) (of thoughts, talk) to be concerned with

run over = 1) (tr) to knock down (with a vehicle); **run down**, 2) (tr) to read through quickly, 3) (int) to overflow, 4) to pass a limit

run out (of) = (tr) to no longer have a supply

run through = 1) (tr) to use up, 2) (tr) to rehearse, check or revise quickly

run up = 1) (tr) to accumulate; add up, 2) (int) to increase quickly

run up against = (tr) to face; **run into**

See

see about = 1) (tr) to make enquiries or arrangements about sth, 2) (tr) to deal with sth; **see to**

see for oneself = to form an opinion using one's own judgement

see into = (tr) to have knowledge of

see off = 1) (tr) to accompany a traveller to his/her plane, train etc, 2) (tr) to make sure that sb leaves one's property

see out = 1) (tr) to accompany sb to the door/exit of a house/building, 2) (tr) to last until the end of

see over = (tr) to inspect a place; **look around**

see through = 1) (tr) not to be deceived, 2) (tr) to support sb in difficulties

see to = (tr) to take care of; **see about**

Set

set about = 1) (tr) to begin to do, 2) (tr) to attack

set aside = 1) (tr) to save for a special purpose, 2) (tr) to stop sth (eg work) for some time; **set by**

set back = 1) (tr) to hinder, 2) (tr) to cost (slang), 3) to move the hands of a clock/watch to show an earlier time

set down = to make (rules etc)

set in = (int) (of weather) to start and seem likely to continue

set off = 1) (int) to start a journey, 2) (int) to intend (to do sth)

set on/be set on = 1) (tr) to cause to attack, 2) to be determined

set out = 1) (int) to begin a journey, 2) to intend (to do sth)

set sb up = (tr) to cause sb to receive blame

set to = 1) to begin working hard, 2) to start quarrelling

set up = 1) (tr) to start a business, 2) (tr) to erect; **put up**, 3) (tr) to establish

Stand

stand about = (int) to stand lazily/inactively; **stand around**

stand by = 1) (tr) to support sb esp in difficulties, 2) (int) to watch remaining inactive, 3) (int) to be ready for action, 4) (tr) to remain loyal

stand for = 1) (tr) to represent, 2) (int) to offer oneself for election, 3) (tr) to tolerate; **put up with**, 4) (tr) to believe (in principles)

stand in for = (tr) to replace sb temporarily

stand on = (tr) to act firmly according to what one believes

stand out = (int) to be noticeable, prominent

stand up = 1) (int) to rise to one's feet, 2) (tr) to fail to meet

stand up for = 1) (tr) to support; defend; **stick up for**, 2) (tr) to demand (one's rights)

stand up to = 1) (tr) to resist; defend oneself against without fear, 2) (tr) to match in quality

Take

take after = (tr) to look or act like a relative; resemble

take away = 1) (tr) to remove, 2) (tr) to lead sb to another place, 3) (tr) to seize from people

take back = 1) (tr) to apologise, 2) (tr) to remind of the past, 3) to withdraw

take down = 1) (tr) to write down, 2) (tr) to separate into pieces so as to repair or remove, 3) (tr) to lengthen a garment; **let down**

take for = 1) (tr) to identify wrongly, 2) (tr) to rob/cheat

take in = 1) (tr) to give accommodation, 2) (tr) to make clothes narrower (opp: **let out**), 3) (tr) to fully understand

take off = 1) (tr) to remove clothes (opp: **put on**), 2) (int) (of planes) to leave the ground (opp: **come down**), 3) (tr) to imitate, 4) (tr) to reduce (weight) (opp: **put on**), 5) (tr) (of time) to take time as a holiday, 6) (int) to start to improve

take on = 1) (tr) to undertake work or responsibility, 2) (tr) to employ, 3) (tr) to accept as an opponent

take out = 1) (tr) to remove; extract, 2) (tr) to clean (a mark, dirt)

take over = 1) (tr) to gain control of sth, 2) (tr) to spend time on

take sb out = (tr) to take sb to a restaurant etc

take to = 1) (tr) to like, 2) (tr) to begin a habit

take up = 1) (tr) to begin a hobby, sport, job, 2) (tr) to shorten a garment (opp: **take down**), 3) (tr) to fill (time, space), 4) (tr) to continue after an interruption

be taken aback = to be strongly surprised

be taken in = (tr) to be deceived

Turn

turn away = 1) (tr) to refuse admittance to, 2) (tr) to refuse to help

turn down = 1) (tr) to refuse an offer; reject, 2) (tr) to reduce loudness etc (opp: **turn up**)

turn in = 1) (int) to go to bed, 2) (tr) to give to the police

turn into = (tr) to convert into

turn off = (tr) to switch off (opp: **turn on**)

turn on = 1) to switch on, 2) (tr) to attack

turn out = 1) (tr) to produce, 2) (int) to prove to be in the end; result, 3) (tr) to evict, 4) (tr) to empty (one's pockets, handbag etc), 5) (tr) to clean a room thoroughly (putting the furniture outside), 6) (int) to assemble, 7) (tr) to get rid of

turn over = 1) (tr) (of a business) to trade a sum of money, 2) (tr) to give the control of sth to sb, 3) (tr) to deliver sb (to the police, authorities), 4) to turn to a new page; change TV channel

turn to = 1) (tr) to go to sb for help, advice, 2) (tr) to begin (a way of life or doing sth)

turn up = 1) (int) to arrive or appear (unexpectedly), 2) (int) (of opportunity) to arise, 3) (tr) to increase (volume, pressure)

Wear

wear away = 1) (tr) (of wood or stone) to reduce gradually, 2) (int) (of time) to pass slowly

wear down = (tr) to reduce opposition gradually

wear off = 1) (int) to stop gradually, 2) (of feelings) to disappear gradually

wear out = 1) (tr) to use until no longer serviceable, 2) (tr) to exhaust

Work

work on = (tr) to have an effect on

work out = 1) (tr) to find the solution to a problem by reasoning or calculation, 2) (int) to develop successfully

work up = 1) (tr) to develop, 2) (int) to make progress in business

Appendix 3

Verbs, Adjectives, Nouns with Prepositions

A

abide by (v)
absent from (adj)
abstain from (v)
accompanied by (adj)
according to (prep)
account for (v)
accuse sb of (v)
accustomed to (adj)
acquainted with (adj)
addicted to (adj)
adequate for (adj)
adjacent to (adj)
advantage of (n)
(but: there's an **advantage in** - (have) an **advantage over** sb)
advice on (n)

afraid of (adj)
agree to/on sth (v)
agree with sb (v)
ahead of (prep)
aim at (v)
allergic to (adj)
amazed at/by (adj)
amount to (v)
amused at/with (adj)
angry at what sb does (adj)
angry with sb about sth (adj)
angry with sb for doing sth (adj)
annoyed with sb about sth (adj)
(in) answer to (n)
anxious about sth (adj)
(be) anxious for sth to happen (adj)
apologise to sb for sth (v)
(make an) appeal to sb for sth (n)

appeal to/against (v)
apply to sb for sth (v)
approve of (v)
argue with sb about sth (v)
arrest sb for sth (v)
arrive at (a small place) (v)
arrive in (a town) (v)
ashamed of (adj)
ask for (v) (but: ask sb a question)
assure (sb) of (v)
astonished at/by (adj)
attached to (adj)
attack on (n)
attend to (v)
(un) aware of (adj)

B

bad at (adj) (but: He was very **bad to** me.)
base on (v)
basis for (n)
beg for (v)
begin with (v)
believe in (v)

benefit from (v)
bet on (v)
beware of (v)
(put the) blame on sb (n)
blame sb for sth (v)
blame sth on sb (v)

boast about/of (v)
bored with/of (adj)
borrow sth from sb (v)
brilliant at (adj)
bump into (v)
busy with (adj)

C

call at/on (phr v)
call for (= demand) (phr v)
campaign against/for (v)
capable of (adj)
care about (v)
care for sb (v) (= like)
(take) care of (n)
care for sth (v) (= like to do sth)
careful of (adj)
careless about (adj)
cause of (n)
certain of (adj)
change into (v)
characteristic of (n/adj)
charge for (v)
charge sb with (v)
cheque for (n)
choice between/of (n)
clever at (adj) (but: It was very **clever of** you to buy it.)
close to (adj)
coax sb into (v)
coincide with (v)

collaborate with (v)
collide with (v)
comment on (v)
communicate with (v)
compare with (v) (how people and things are alike and how they are different)
compare to (v) (show the likeness between sb/sth and sb/sth else)
comparison between (n)
complain of (v) (= suffer from)
complain to sb about sth (v) (= be annoyed at)
compliment sb on (v)
comply with (v)
conceal sth from sb (v)
concentrate on (v)
(have) confidence in sb (n)
confine to (v)
confusion over (n)
congratulate sb on sth (v)
connection between (n)
(but: **in connection with**)
conscious of (adj)
connect to/with (v)

consist of (v)
contact between (n) (but: in contact with)
content with (adj)
contrary to (prep)
contrast with (v)
contribute to (v)
convert to/into (v)
cope with (v)
correspond to/with (v)
count against (v)
count on sb (phr v)
cover in/with (v)
covered in/with (adj)
crash into (v)
(have) a craving for sth (n)
crazy about (adj)
crowded with (adj)
cruel to (adj)
cruelty towards/to (n)
cure for (n)
curious about (adj)
cut into (phr v) (= interrupt sb/a conversation)

Verbs, Adjectives, Nouns with Prepositions

D

damage to (n)
date back to (v)
date from (v)
deal with (v)
dear to (adj)
decide on/against (v)
decrease in (n)
dedicate to (v)
deficient in (adj)
definition of (n)
delay in (n)
delight in (v)
delighted with (adj)
demand for (n)
demand from (v)
depart from (v)
departure from (n)

depend on/upon (v)
dependent on (adj)
deputise for (v)
descended from (adj)
describe sb/sth to sb else (v)
description of (n)
die of/from (v)
die in an accident (v)
differ from (v)
(have) difference between/of (n)
different from (adj)
difficulty in/with (n)
disadvantage of (n) (but: there's a
disadvantage in doing sth)
disagree with (v)
disappointed with/about (adj)
disapprove of (v)

discharge sb from (v)
discouraged from (adj)
discussion about/on (n)
disgusted by/at (adj)
dismiss from (v)
dispose of (v)
disqualified from (adj)
dissatisfied with (adj)
distinguish between (v)
divide between/among (v)
divide into/by (v)
do sth about (v)
doubtful about (adj)
dream about (v)
dream of (v) (= imagine)
dressed in (adj)

E

eager for (adj)
economise on (v)
efficient at (adj)
(put) effort into sth (n)
emphasis on (n)
engaged to sb/in sth (adj)
engagement to sb (n)
enter into (= start) (v)
enthusiastic about (adj)
envious of (adj)

equal to (adj)
escape from/to (v)
example of (n)
excellent at (adj)
exception to (n)
exchange sth for sth else (v)
excited about (adj)
exclaim at (v)
excuse for (n)
excuse sb for (v)

exempt from (adj)
expel from (v)
experienced in (adj)
experiment on/with (v)
expert at/in (sth/doing sth) (n)
(= person good at)
expert at/in/on (sth/doing sth) (adj)
(= done with skill or involving great
knowledge)
expert with sth (n) (= good at using sth)
expert on (n) (= person knowledge-
able about a subject)

F

face up to (phr v)
fail in an attempt (v)
fail to do sth (v)
failure in (an exam) (n)
failure to (do sth) (n)
faithful to (adj)
fall in (n)
familiar to sb (= known to
sb) (adj)

familiar with (= have knowledge of)
(adj)
famous for (adj)
fed up with (adj)
fill sth with sth else (v)
finish with (v)
fire at (v)
flee from (v)
fond of (adj)

forget about (v)
forgive sb for (v)
fortunate in (adj)
friendly with/to (adj)
frightened of (adj)
full of (adj)
furious with sb about/at sth (adj)

G

generosity to/towards (n)
genius at (n)
glance at (v)
glare at (v)

good at (adj) (but: He was very
good to me.)
grateful to sb for sth (adj)
grudge against (n)

guess at (v)
guilty of (adj) (but: he felt **guilty
about** his crime)

H

happen to (v)
happy about/with (adj)
harmful to (adj)
hear about (v) (= be told)
hear from (v) (= receive a
letter)

hear of (v) (– learn that sth or sb
exists)
heir to (n)
hinder from (v)
hint to sb about sth (v) (but: **hint at**
sth)

hope for (v)
hope to do sth (v)
(no) hope of (n)
hopeless at (adj)

Verbs, Adjectives, Nouns with Prepositions

I		
idea of (n)	increase in (n)	intent on (adj)
identical to (adj)	independent of (adj)	(have no) intention of (n)
ignorant of/about (adj)	indifferent to (adj)	interest in (n)
ill with (adj)	indulge in (v)	interested in (adj)
impact on (n)	inferior to (adj)	interfere with/in (v)
impressed by/with (adj)	information about/on (n)	invasion of (n)
(make an) impression on	(be) informed about (adj)	invest in (v)
sb (n)	inoculate against (v)	invitation to (n)
improvement in/on (n)	insist on (v)	invite sb to (v)
incapable of (adj)	insure against (v)	involve in (v)
include in (v)	intelligent at (adj)	irritated by (adj)

J		
jealous of (adj)	join in (v)	joke about (v)

K		
knock at/on (v)	keen to do sth (adj)	key to (n)
know about/of (v)	kind to (adj)	knowledge of (n)
keen on sth (adj)		

L		
lack in (v)	leave for (v) (= head for)	long for (v)
lack of (n)	lend sth to sb (v)	look after (phr v) (= take care of)
laugh at (v)	listen to (v)	look at (v)
lean on/against (v)	live on (v)	look for (= search for) (v)

M		
married to (adj)	mean to (adj)	mistake sb for (v)
marvel at (v)	mention to (v)	mix with (v)

N		
name after (v)	nervous about (adj)	nominate sb (for/as sth) (v)
necessary for (adj)	new to (adj)	(take) (no) notice of (n)
need for (n)	nice to (adj)	notorious for doing sth (adj)
neglect of (n)		

O		
obedient to (adj)	obvious to (adj)	operate on (v)
object to (v)	occur to (v)	opinion of/on (n)
objection to (n)	offence against (n)	opposite of/to (n)
obliged to sb for sth (adj)		

P		
part with (v)	pleased with (adj)	(take) pride in (n)
patient with (adj)	(take) pleasure in (n)	pride oneself on sth/on doing (v)
pay by (cheque) (v)	(have the) pleasure of (n)	prohibit sb from doing sth (v)
pay for (v) (but: **pay a bill**)	point at/to (v)	prone to (adj)
pay in (cash) (v)	(im)polite to (adj)	protect against/from (v)
peculiar to (adj)	popular with (adj)	protection from (n)
persist in (v)	praise sb for (v)	protest about/at (v)
(but: **insist on**)	pray for sth/sb (v)	proud of (adj)
(take a) photograph of (n)	prefer sth to sth else (v)	provide sb with (v)
picture of (n)	(have a) preference for (n)	punish sb for (v)
pity for (n)	prepare for (v)	puzzled about/by (adj)
take pity on sb (exp)	present sb with (v)	
pleasant to (adj)	prevent sb from (v)	

Q		
quarrel about sth/with sb (v/n)	qualified for (adj)	quotation from (n)
	quick at (adj)	

Verbs, Adjectives, Nouns with Prepositions

R

rave about (v)	regardless of (prep)	respond to (v)
react to (v)	related to (adj)	responsiblity for (n)
reaction to (n)	relationship between (n) (but: a	responsible for (adj)
ready for (adj)	good **relationship with** sb)	result from (v) (= be the
reason for (n)	relevant to (adj)	consequence of)
reason with (v)	rely on (v)	result in (v) (= cause)
rebel against (v)	remind sb of/about (v)	result of (n)
receive from (v)	remove from (v)	resulting from (adj)
(keep) a record of (n)	replace sth with sth else (v)	rhyme with (v)
recover from (v)	reply to (n/v)	rich in (adj)
reduction in (n)	report on (n/v)	(get) rid of (phr)
refer to (v)	reputation for/of (n)	rise in (n)
(in/with) reference to (n)	research on/into (n)	(make) room for (n)
refrain from (v)	respect for (n)	rude to (adj)
regard as (v)	respected for (adj)	run into (phr v)

S

safe from (adj)	shy of (adj)	stand for (phr v)
same as (adj)	sick of (adj)	stare at (v)
satisfied with (adj)	silly to do sth (adj) (but: it was	strain on (n)
save sb from (v)	**silly of** him)	subject to (adj/v)
scared of (adj)	similar to (adj)	submit to (v) (but: **submit for**
search for (v/n)	skilful/skilled at (adj)	publication)
(be) in search of (n)	slow in/about doing sth/to sth (adj)	subscribe to (v)
sensible of sth (adj) (=	smell of (n/v)	succeed in (v)
aware of sth)	smile at (v)	suffer from (v)
sensitive to (adj)	solution to (n)	sufficient for sth/sb (adj)
sentence sb to (v)	sorry about (adj) (= feel sorry for	superior to (adj)
separate from (v)	sb) (but: I'm **sorry for** doing sth)	sure of/about (adj)
serious about (adj)	speak to/with sb about (v)	surprised at/by (adj)
share in/of sth (n)	specialise in (v)	surrender to (v)
shelter from (v)	specialist in (n)	surrounded by (adj)
shocked at/by (adj)	spend money on sth (v)	suspect sb of (v)
shoot at (v)	spend time in/doing sth (v)	suspicious of (adj)
short of (adj)	split into/in (v)	sympathetic to/towards (adj)
shout at (v)	spy on (v)	sympathise with (v)

T

take sth to sb/sth (v)	thank sb for (v)	tired from (adj)
talent for sth (n)	thankful for (adj)	tired of (adj) (= fed up with)
talk to sb about sth (v)	think about/of (v)	translate from ... into (v)
(have) taste in (n)	threat to sb/sth of sth (n)	tread on (v)
taste of (v)	threaten sb with sth (v)	trip over (v)
terrible at (adj)	throw at (v) (in order to hit)	trouble with (n)
terrified of (adj)	throw to (v) (in order to catch)	typical of (adj)

U

unaware of (adj)	uneasy about (adj)	(make) use of (n)
understanding of (n)	upset about/over sth (adj)	used to (adj)

V

valid for (length of time)	valid in (places) (adj)	vote against/for (v)
(adj)	value sth at (v)	vouch for (v)

W

wait for (v)	weak in/at (adj)	worthy of (adj)
warn sb against/about/of	wink at (v)	write to sb (v)
(v)	wonder about (v)	wrong about (adj)
waste (time/money) on (v)	worry about (v)	

Prepositional Phrases

At

at the age of
at the airport
at an auction
at the beginning of (when sth started) (but: **in the beginning** = originally)
at one's best
at breakfast/lunch etc
at the bottom of
at the bus stop
at church
at the corner/on the corner
at all costs
at the crossroads
at dawn
at one's desk
at the door
at ease
at the end (= when sth is finished) (but: **in the end** = finally at all events)
at fault
at first

at first hand
at first sight
at a glance
at a guess
at hand
at heart
at home
at/in a hotel
at ... km per hour
at large
at last
at the latest
at least
at length
at liberty
at a loss
at the match
at midnight
at the moment
at most
at night (but: **in the** night)
at noon
at once

at peace/war
at present
at a profit
at the prospect
at random
at any rate
at one's request
at the same time
at school
at sea
at the seaside
at short notice
at/in the station
at sunset
at the table
at the time
at times
at the top of (but: **on top of**)
at university
at the weekend
at work
at 23 Oxford St.

By

by accident
by all accounts
by appointment
by the arm/hand
by auction
by birth
by bus/train/plane/ helicopter/taxi/ coach/ ship/boat/sea/air/car etc (but: **on a/the** bus/plane/ train/coach/ship/boat **in a** taxi/car helicopter/ plane)
by chance
by cheque

by correspondence
by day/night
by degrees
by the dozen
by far
by force
by hand
by heart
by invitation
by land/sea/air
by law
by luck
by marriage
by means of
by mistake

by nature
by now
by oneself
by order of
by phone
by post/airmail
by profession
by request
by (the/one's) side
by sight
by surprise
by the time
by the way
by yourself
by one's watch

For

for ages
for breakfast/lunch/dinner
for certain
for a change
for ever
for fear (of)
for fun (= for amusement)
for good
for granted

for hire
for keeps
for instance
for luck
for life
for love
for nothing
for once
for the rest of

for safe keeping
for one's sake
for the sake of
for sale
for short
for the time being
for a visit/holiday
for a walk
for a while

Prepositional Phrases

In

in action	in future	in person
in addition to (+ -ing form)	in gear	in pieces
in advance (of)	in general	in place of
in agreement (with)	in good time	in politics
in aid of	in half	in pounds
in all (all in all)	in hand	in practice/theory
in answer to	in haste	in principle
in an armchair	in good/bad health	in prison
in a bad temper	in hiding	in private/public
in bed	in honour of	in all probability
in the beginning	in the hope of	in progress
(= originally)	in hospital	in a queue
in blossom	in a hotel	in reality
in a book	in a hurry	in return
in brief	in ink/pencil/pen	in the right/wrong
in any case	in sb's interest	in a row/rows
in cash	in length/width etc	in ruins
in the centre of	in all sb's life	in safety
in charge (of)	in the limelight	in season
in cities	in a line	in secret
in code	in the long run	in self-defence
in colour	in love (with)	in short
in comfort	in luxury	in sight (of)
in common	in the meantime	in the sky
in comparison with	in a mess	in some respects
in conclusion (to)	in the middle of	in stock
in (good/bad) condition	in a mirror	in the streets
in confidence	in moderation	in succession
in control (of)	in a moment	in the suburbs
in the country	in a good/bad mood	in the sun/shade
in danger	in the mood	in good/bad taste
in the dark	in the morning	in tears
in debt	in mourning	in theory
in demand	in name only (= not in reality)	in a tick
in detail	in need of	in time
(be) in difficulty	in the news	in no time
in the direction of	in a newspaper	in touch
in doubt	in the name of (= on behalf of)	in town
in a ... dress	in the nick of time	in tune (with)
in due course	in the north/south	in turn
in the end (= finally)	in a nutshell	in two/half
in exchange for	in oils	in uniform
in existence	in the open	in use
in fact	in one's opinion	in vain
in fashion	in orbit	in view of
in favour of/with	in order of/to	in a loud/low voice
in flames	in other words	in a way (= in a manner)
in the flesh	in pain	in the way
in focus	in pairs	in writing
in one's free time	in the park	in a word
in full swing	in particular	
in fun	in the past	

Prepositional Phrases

On

on account of
on a ... afternoon/evening
on the agenda
on the air
on approval
on arrival
on average
on bail
on balance
on the beach
on behalf of
on one's birthday
on board
on the border
on business
on call
on a campsite (at a campsite)
on the coast
on condition
on the contrary
on credit
on a cruise/excursion/trip/tour
on (a ...) day
on demand
on a diet
on the dole

on duty
on earth
on edge
on an expedition
on a farm (but: **in a field**)
on fire
on the (4th) floor (of)
on the floor
on foot
on the one hand
on the other hand
on holiday
on horseback
on impulse
on the increase
on an island (but: **in the mountains**)
on a journey
on one's knees
on leave
on the left
on loan
on the market (= available to the public)
on one's mind
on that morning
on the move
on New Year's Day
on the news

on order
on the outskirts
on one's own
on page ...
on parade
on the pavement
on the phone
on a platform
on principle
on purpose
on the radio/TV
on the right
on the River Seine
on sale
on schedule
on the screen
on second thoughts
on sight
on the sofa
on this street/on the street(s)
on strike
on good/bad terms
on time
on top of
on the trail of
on a trip
on the way (to) (= as I was going)
on the whole

Out of

out of breath
out of character
out of condition
out of control
out of danger
out of date
out of debt
out of doors
out of fashion

out of focus
out of hand
out of luck
out of order
out of the ordinary
out of place
out of practice
out of print
out of the question

out of reach
out of season
out of sight
out of step
out of stock
out of tune
out of turn
out of use
out of work

Off

off air
off colour
off duty
off limits

off the map
off the peg
off the point

off the record
off the road
off school/work

Under

under age
under arrest
under one's breath
under control

under discussion
under the impression
under orders

under pressure
under repair
under the weather

Prepositional Phrases

Against	against the law
Ahead	ahead of schedule
Before	before long
Behind	behind schedule, behind the times
From	from time to time, from now on, from experience, from memory, from scratch
Into	into pieces
To	to one's astonishment, to one's surprise, to this day, to some extent
With	with regard to, with a view to (+ -ing form)
Within	within minutes
Without	without delay, without fail, without success, without warning

Prepositions of Time

AT	IN	ON
at 10.30	in the morning/evening/afternoon/night	on Monday
at Christmas/Easter	in the Easter/Christmas holiday(s)	on Easter Sunday etc
at noon/night/midnight	in January (months)	on Christmas Day
at lunch/dinner/breakfast (time)	in (the) winter (seasons)	on Friday night
at that time	in 1992 (years)	on July 30th
at the moment	in the 19th century	on a summer afternoon
at the weekend (on the weekend: Am. English)	in two hours (two hours from now)	on that day

We never use **at**, **in** or **on** before **yesterday**, **tomorrow**, **next**, **this**, **last**, **every**. *She's leaving **next** Sunday.*

Concrete Noun	Abstract Noun	Verb	Adjective
	(in/dis)ability	enable	(un)able, disabled
	accommodation	accommodate	(un)accommodating
	accuracy		(in)accurate
	achievement	achieve	
actor, actress	act, action, activity	act	(in)active
admirer	admiration	admire	admirable
adventurer	adventure		adventurous
advertiser, advertisement	advertising	advertise	advertising
adviser	advice	advise	(in)advisable
	amusement	amuse	amusing, -ed
	anger	anger	angry
	annoyance	annoy	annoying, -ed
	anxiety		anxious
applicant, application		apply	applying, -ed
	(dis)appearance	(dis)appear	disappearing
	attraction	attract	(un)attractive
	bother	bother	bothersome

Appendix 4

Concrete Noun	Abstract Noun	Verb	Adjective
	breakage	break	(un)broken, (un)breakable
carer	care, carefulness, carelessness	care	careful, careless
centre		centre	central
	change	change	(un)changeable
child (children)	childhood		childish, childlike
	climate		climatic
	combination	combine	combined
communicator	communication	communicate	(un)communicative
	completion	complete	(in)complete
	(in)comprehension	comprehend	(in)comprehensible
	confidence	confide	confident, confidential
conversationalist	conversation	converse	conversational
correction	correction, correctness	correct	(in)correct
crowd		crowd	crowded
	danger	endanger	dangerous
	depression	depress	depressive, depressed, depressing
	determination	determine	determining, -ed
developer	development	develop	developing, -ed
	difficulty		difficult
dramatist, drama	drama	dramatise	dramatic
	east		east, eastern, easterly
economist	economy, economics	economise	(un)economic(al)
educator	education	educate	educative, educational
	effect	effect	(in)effective, (in)effectual
	elegance		(in)elegant
	emphasis	emphasise	emphatic
employer, employee	(un)employment	employ	(un)employed, (un)employable
	encouragement	encourage	encouraging
equipment	equipment	equip	equipped
examiner, examinee	exam(ination)	examine	
	exclusion	exclude	exclusive
	expectation, expentancy	expect	(un)expected
expenses	expense, expenditure		(in)expensive
explosive	explosion	explode	explosive
extremist	extremity, extreme, extremism		extreme
failure	fail, failure	fail	
	fame		(in)famous
	familiarity	familiarise	(un)familiar
foreigner			foreign
harm	harm	harm	harmful, -less
	height	heighten	high
immigrant	immigration	immigrate	
	importance		(un)important
	impression	impress	(un)impressive
industrialist	industry, industrialisation	industrialise	industrial
injury	injury	injure	injured, injurious
	intelligence		(un)intelligent
interviewer, interviewee	interview	interview	
invader	invasion	invade	invasive
	involvement	involve	involved
	knowledge	know	knowing, knowledgeable
	life, living	live	(a)live, lively, living
loner	loneliness		(a)lone, lonely, lonesome
	luck		(un)lucky
	majority		major

Concrete Noun	Abstract Noun	Verb	Adjective
mix, mixture, mixer	mix, mixture	mix	mixed
mountain, mountaineer	mountaineering		mountainous
	necessity	necessitate	(un)necessary
occupier, occupant	occupation	occupy	occupied
	patience		(im)patient
perfectionist	perfection	perfect	(im)perfect
photograph, -er	photography	photograph	photographic
politician	politics	politicise	political
pollutant	pollution	pollute	(un)polluted
	possibility		(im)possible
predictor	prediction, predictability	predict	(un)predictable
producer, product	produce, production	produce	(un)productive
	pronunciation	pronounce	(un)pronounceable, pronounced
pursuer	pursuit	pursue	
qualifier	qualification	qualify	(un)qualified
reactor	reaction	react	reactive
	refreshment	refresh	refreshing
	relaxation	relax	relaxing, -ed
	reluctance		reluctant
resident, residence	residence	reside	residential
	(dis)respect, respectability	respect	(dis)respectful, respectable
safe	safety	save	(un)safe
selector	selection, selectivity	select	select, selective
	shame	shame	ashamed, shameful, shameless
	shyness		shy
	similarity		(dis)similar
ski, skier	skiing	ski	
	society	socialise	social, (un)sociable
specialist	speciality, specialisation	specialise	(e)special, specialised
	success	succeed	(un)successful
	temptation	tempt	tempting
tourist	tour, tourism	tour	
tranquilliser	tranquillity	tranquillise	tranquil
	treatment	treat	treatable
	(mis)understanding	(mis)understand	understanding, understandable
valuer	value	value	valuable
	variation, variety	vary	various, variable, (un)varied
visitor	visit	visit	visiting
	warning	warn	warning
youth, youngster	youth, youthfulness		young, youthful

Irregular Verbs

Infinitive	Past	Past Participle	Infinitive	Past	Past Participle
be	was	been	lie	lay	lain
bear	bore	born(e)	light	lit	lit
beat	beat	beaten	lose	lost	lost
become	became	become	make	made	made
begin	began	begun	mean	meant	meant
bite	bit	bitten	meet	met	met
blow	blew	blown	pay	paid	paid
break	broke	broken	put	put	put
bring	brought	brought	read	read	read
build	built	built	ride	rode	ridden
burn	burnt	burnt	ring	rang	rung
burst	burst	burst	rise	rose	risen
buy	bought	bought	run	ran	run
can	could	(been able to)	say	said	said
catch	caught	caught	see	saw	seen
choose	chose	chosen	seek	sought	sought
come	came	come	sell	sold	sold
cost	cost	cost	send	sent	sent
cut	cut	cut	set	set	set
deal	dealt	dealt	sew	sewed	sewn
dig	dug	dug	shake	shook	shaken
do	did	done	shine	shone	shone
draw	drew	drawn	shoot	shot	shot
dream	dreamt	dreamt	show	showed	shown
drink	drank	drunk	shut	shut	shut
drive	drove	driven	sing	sang	sung
eat	ate	eaten	sit	sat	sat
fall	fell	fallen	sleep	slept	slept
feed	fed	fed	smell	smelt	smelt
feel	felt	felt	speak	spoke	spoken
fight	fought	fought	spell	spelt	spelt
find	found	found	spend	spent	spent
fly	flew	flown	spill	spilt	spilt
forbid	forbade	forbidden	split	split	split
forget	forgot	forgotten	spoil	spoilt	spoilt
forgive	forgave	forgiven	spread	spread	spread
freeze	froze	frozen	spring	sprang	sprung
get	got	got	stand	stood	stood
give	gave	given	steal	stole	stolen
go	went	gone	stick	stuck	stuck
grow	grew	grown	sting	stung	stung
hang	hung	hung	strike	struck	struck
have	had	had	swear	swore	sworn
hear	heard	heard	sweep	swept	swept
hide	hid	hidden	swim	swam	swum
hit	hit	hit	take	took	taken
hold	held	held	teach	taught	taught
hurt	hurt	hurt	tear	tore	torn
keep	kept	kept	tell	told	told
know	knew	known	think	thought	thought
lay	laid	laid	throw	threw	thrown
lead	led	led	understand	understood	understood
learn	learnt	learnt	wake	woke	woken
leave	left	left	wear	wore	worn
lend	lent	lent	win	won	won
let	let	let	write	wrote	written